THE

HANDBOOK

THE CALLA™ HANDBOOK

Implementing the Cognitive Academic Language Learning Approach

Anna Uhl Chamot

J. Michael O'Malley

Addison-Wesley Publishing Company

Reading, Massachusetts • Menlo Park, California • New York
Don Mills, Ontario • Wokingham, England • Amsterdam
Bonn • Sydney • Singapore • Tokyo • Madrid • San Juan
Paris • Seoul • Milan • Mexico City • Taipei

A Publication of the ESL Publishing Group

Product Development Director: Judith M. Bittinger
Editorial: Elinor Chamas, Clare Siska
Production/Manufacturing: James W. Gibbons
Cover, Text Design, and Production: Marshall Henrichs
Illustrations: Marcy Ramsey

Credits: Page 30: Elementary text from *Addison-Wesley Science,* by Charles Barman, et al. © 1989 Addison-Wesley Publishing Co. Reprinted with permission. Page 30: Middle School text and art from *Introduction to Physical Science,* by Michael B. Leydon, et al. © 1988 Addison-Wesley Publishing Co. Reprinted with permission. Page 30: High School text and art from *Conceptual Physics: The High School Physics Program—Second Edition,* by Paul G. Hewitt. © 1992 Addison-Wesley Publishing Co. Reprinted with permission. Page 69: Excerpt from a T-List. From *Language Development Through Content: America: The Early Years,* by Anna Uhl Chamot. © 1987 Addison-Wesley Publishing Company. Page 115: "Three religions and their holy books," from Europe, Africa, Asia and Australia, by Kenneth S. Cooper. © 1986 Silver Burdett Company. Used by permission of Silver Burdett Ginn. Pages 249-252: From *Mathematics Book A: Learning Strategies for Problem Solving,* by Anna Uhl Chamot and J. Michael O'Malley. © 1988 Addison-Wesley Publishing Company. Page 274: From *Teacher's Guide—America: The Early Years and America: After Independence,* by Anna Uhl Chamot. © 1987 Addison-Wesley Publishing Company. Pages 275-279: From *Language Development Through Content: America: The Early Years,* by Anna Uhl Chamot. © 1987 Addison-Wesley Publishing Company. Page 297: Think "Plan Sheet" from *Cognitive Strategy Instruction That Really Works,* by Michael Pressley and Associates. © 1990 Brookline Books. Used by permission of Brookline Books. Page 308 & 310: *Ooka and the Stolen Smell* from *Ooka the Wise: Tales of Old Japan,* by I.G. Edmonds. © 1961 I.G. Edmonds. Reprinted with the permission of Macmillan Publishing Company, a Division of Macmillan, Inc., and by permission of the author and the author's agents, Scott Meredith Literary Agency, Inc., 845 Third Avenue, New York, New York 10022.

Printed in the United States of America.
ISBN: 0-201-53963-2

10-CRS-99 98 97

Preface

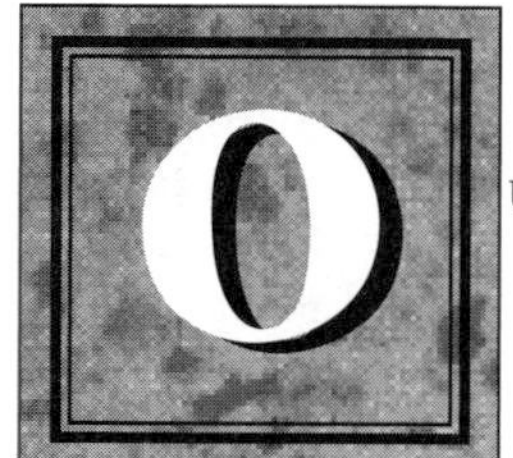

OUR GOALS IN WRITING THIS BOOK are to provide a foundation for using the Cognitive Academic Language Learning Approach (CALLA), practical guidelines for designing a CALLA program, and suggestions for implementing CALLA in major subject areas of the curriculum.

In developing CALLA, we have been guided by our conviction that a coherent theoretical framework based on research is necessary for guiding and implementing any instructional model. A framework is particularly important for a model like CALLA in which learning, rather than teaching, is the central focus. We believe that only by understanding how students learn can teachers learn how to teach. We have been guided in our efforts to understand the characteristics of the good learner by the ideas and insights of John Anderson and Michael Pressley and other researchers of cognition and cognitive instruction, and have attempted to translate their ideas into second language learning contexts.

We became aware of the academic needs of language minority students in large part through the work of Jim Cummins, and have tried to implement his theories and research in the CALLA model. In suggesting how a CALLA program can be designed to meet the needs of language minority students, we have also been aided by our own experiences with teachers and administrators in school districts which have been interested in planning a CALLA instructional program. These exchanges and working sessions with school district personnel have provided us with important practical insights on transforming theory into practice. This practical experience, combined with a conceptual understanding of learning and instruction, have led us to identify four major conditions for improving the education of language minority students. These conditions are: (1) an institutional environment that has high expectations for language minority students; (2) an instructional approach that integrates academic language development with content area instruction and learning strategies; (3) continuing staff development that provides teachers with the expertise and support needed to advance the academic development and success of language minority students; and (4) an assessment approach that is consistent with the instructional model and enables teachers to plan instruction effectively.

Our suggestions for implementing CALLA instruction in different content areas of the curriculum have developed from a combination of the theoretical framework we have adopted, the curricular reforms espoused by professional associations in the different content areas, national education goals for literacy and content expertise, and—most importantly—the experiences of content teachers in ESL, bilingual, elementary, and secondary subject area contexts.

We would like to express our appreciation, enthusiasm, and respect for the ideas and comments offered by teachers who are striving in many creative ways to contribute to the academic success of language minority students. Teachers understand better than anyone the many problems encountered by students who need to learn how to navigate the educational system with some success. Teachers know how to encourage and offer specific techniques and learning strategies to help students be more successful. Our research, theory-building, and implementation guidelines for CALLA have been constructed on the experiences, insights, and wisdom of teachers.

We have had the opportunity to be personally involved with implementing CALLA in the content subjects of Mathematics and Science in the Arlington

(Virginia) Public Schools. We are deeply appreciative of the interest, support, and enthusiasm expressed by Dr. Emma Violand-Sánchez, Supervisor of Arlington's English for Speakers of Other Languages and High Intensity Language Training (ESOL/HILT) Department. Other Arlington professionals who have made important contributions to the CALLA projects include: Barbara Fagan, ESOL/HILT secondary specialist; Etta Johnson, ESOL/HILT elementary specialist; George Spanos, curriculum and materials specialist for the CALLA Mathematics and the CALLA Science projects; Marsha Dale, evaluation specialist for the CALLA Mathematics project; Lee Gough, science resource specialist for the CALLA Science project; Carolyn Smith, Supervisor of Mathematics; Pat Robertson, Mathematics project specialist; Dorothy Knowlton, Supervisor of Science; Susan Steward, Science project specialist; Linda Smith, HILT resource specialist and teacher at Williamsburg Middle School and Yorktown High School; Stephen Oxenrider, HILT mathematics and science teacher at Swanson Middle School; Elsa Lenches, HILT mathematics teacher and resource specialist at Washington-Lee High School; Elizabeth Akers Varela, HILT mathematics and science teacher at Williamsburg Middle School; Danielle Guryansky, HILT mathematics and science teacher and resource specialist at Thomas Jefferson Middle School; and Marsha Mottesheard, CALLA projects secretary and invaluable contributor to the final form of this manuscript. Many other people in Arlington Public Schools have contributed to this book through their interest in CALLA, their willingness to try out CALLA techniques in their classrooms, and their support of content and learning strategy instruction for language minority students. We are enormously in their debt.

We would also like to recognize the expertise, interest, and hard work of the external evaluator of the CALLA Mathematics project in Arlington, Dr. Wayne P. Thomas of George Mason University. Dr. Thomas has guided the evaluation plan development and execution for the project, and has been extremely generous in providing analyses of student performance in more dimensions and for a greater number of students than we had originally anticipated in 1988. Dr. Thomas has now completed three years of evaluation of CALLA mathematics instruction in Arlington (Virginia) Public Schools. Students in the project have made significant yearly gains in mathematics achievement as measured by the mathematics subtests (Computation and Concepts and Application) of the California Achievement Test. These gains (an average of 7 NCEs for Computation and of 10 NCEs for math Concepts and Application) have been summarized by Dr. Thomas as follows:[1]

> The evaluations of the CALLA program for the past three years have demonstrated clearly that the CALLA instructional approach represents one of several possible powerful approaches to increasing the achievement of limited-English-proficient (LEP) students in the long term so that they may receive maximum benefit from their schooling . . . Arlington educators are encouraged to add it to their instructional program as a full-fledged part of the effort to improve the educational opportunities for language minority children. CALLA represents a set of now-proven instructional strategies from which all students can benefit and by means of which successful programs can be made even more successful.

We will always appreciate the support extended by the National Clearinghouse for Bilingual Education (NCBE) in producing our original 1986 CALLA monograph. At that time NCBE was operated by InterAmerica Research Associates, which produced and disseminated the first CALLA publication. However, at present, NCBE is operated by George Washington University/Center for Applied Linguistics, who have continued to make information about CALLA available to interested educators.

We have listened to and interacted with bilingual, ESL, and grade-level content teachers nationwide through many years of staff development workshops. These interactions have been crucial in developing the CALLA model from its original conception to the model described in this book. We expect to continue these interactions with teachers so that their classroom experiences and comments will play a major role in the continuing elaboration of the CALLA model.

Our development of the CALLA model led to the integration of CALLA ideas into instructional materials which we first developed with Addison-Wesley Publishing Company. These materials have included social studies textbooks on American History, and a mathematics textbook emphasizing learning strategies for solving word problems. Working on these books brought us into contact with the exceptional editorial team at Addison-Wesley. We are most appreciative of the inspirational vision and enthusiasm of Judith Bittinger, good friend and excellent advisor, who is now Product Development Director for the ESL Publishing Group. We also acknowledge the role of Evelyn Nelson, Marketing Manager, who has espoused CALLA in countless workshops across the country, and who continues to provide us with insights from teachers' reactions and suggestions for improving CALLA. Elinor Chamas, Executive Editor, has shepherded us through the writing and publication process with patience, good humor, and incisiveness. Our final editor in the process of producing this book has been Clare Siska, who, with the help of Claire L. Smith and Kathleen Sands-Boehmer, has managed the difficult task of converting our manuscript into a handbook which presents our ideas in a teacher-friendly format that we hope will prove to be practical and useful in improving the instruction of language minority students.

While it is traditional to mention the authors' families last in book acknowledgements, we would like to make it clear that our respective families are in fact first in our appreciation for continuing support. Families have to put up with missed weekend activities, bad temper when the writing is not going well, late solitary nights when deadlines have to be met, and glazed stares at breakfast when thoughts are focused on the book. Guy, Alain, Carol, and Shannon have put up with all of this with grace, understanding, and support. We could not have completed *The CALLA Handbook* without them.

Anna Uhl Chamot

J. Michael O'Malley

Contents

List of Tables

PART ONE

Introducing CALLA

CHAPTER 1

What is CALLA?

Overview

The Cognitive Academic Language Learning Approach (CALLA) is an instructional model that was developed to meet the academic needs of students learning English as a second language in American schools.

Who This Book is For
Definitions Used in This Book

Background and Rationale

Learning Strategies
Academic Language Skills
Academic Content
Influence of Cognitive Theory

Overview of CALLA

The CALLA Approach
The CALLA Model

Theoretical Framework

What is Learned?
How is New Information Learned?
Implications for Instruction

Related Instructional Concepts

Langugage Across the Curriculum
Language Experience Approach
Whole Language
Process Writing
Cooperative Learning
Cognitive Instruction

CHAPTER 1 What is CALLA?

THE COGNITIVE ACADEMIC LANGUAGE LEARNING APPROACH (CALLA) is an instructional model that we developed to meet the academic needs of students learning English as a second language in American schools.[1] Language minority students represent a dramatically increasing percentage of the school-age population in the United States and in some schools, cities, and entire geographic areas are the majority population rather than a minority. Language minority students in this and in other countries have historically encountered difficulties in learning the majority language and in academic achievement. Various reasons for these difficulties have been suggested, including a cultural mismatch with the majority culture, failure to provide for initial cognitive and linguistic success in the first language, and inadequate curriculum, instruction, and staff development. Our own view has focused on attempts to strengthen instruction, curriculum, and staff development during the critical period in which language minority students are initially gaining mastery over English, and particularly while they are encountering academic content in English in preparation for the transition to grade-level classrooms.

Since the initial conceptualization of CALLA, we have enlarged and refined the model so that it is both more specific and more encompassing in its components and applications. Not only have we devoted considerable effort to staff development—through workshops, presentations, and personal and sustained contacts with schools—but we have developed materials integrating CALLA that can be used by teachers and students in classrooms. Through our contacts with teachers, schools, and students, we have gained experience and suggestions on the most effective methods for implementing CALLA, the design of effective teacher and student materials, and the potential areas to which CALLA can be extended. This book represents a distillation of those experiences and suggestions and is intended in every sense to be a "handbook" for implementing CALLA in schools, that is, a reference book or manual that can be easily accessed and consulted.

WHO THIS BOOK IS FOR

This book is for all teachers, administrators, and staff development specialists who work with students learning English as a second language (ESL) and, more generally, for all those who work in second language settings. These may include ESL, bilingual, EFL, and foreign language classrooms both in the United States and elsewhere, as in English as a foreign language programs. The four chapters in Part One of the book provide a rationale for CALLA, beginning with this introductory chapter and continuing with a chapter describing each of CALLA's three components. The four chapters in the Part Two provide information about CALLA program design, including planning, assessment, and administration. Finally, Part Three focuses on implementation of CALLA, with a separate chapter devoted to applications of CALLA in each of the four major content subjects (science, mathematics, social studies, and language arts).

DEFINITIONS USED IN THIS BOOK

Before proceeding, we would like to clarify some of the terms and acronyms used throughout the book. We use the acronym **CALLA** throughout the book instead of the complete name, the Cognitive Academic Language Learning Approach. CALLA is pronounced /ka-la'/, stressing the last syllable. Pronounced this way, CALLA evokes a number of positive connotations from various languages, including Greek (*kala* = fine, good), Sanskrit (*kala* = art), Hawaiian (*kala* = money), and Hebrew (*kala* = bride). Unfortunately, when CALLA is pronounced in Spanish, it evokes a connotation that is contrary to the intent of the instructional approach, for it means "be quiet." In CALLA classrooms, students are not asked to be quiet—they are asked to be active and verbal participants in the learning process.

In continuing our emphasis on the positive, we refer to students who are learning English as "English as a second language" (ESL) students rather than "limited English proficient" (LEP) students. These students should not be construed as limited since they often possess advanced linguistic and academic skills in their native languages. We use the terms **first language** and **native language** interchangeably to refer to the language children first learned from their parents. When we refer to **language minority** students, we are not referring specifically to ethnic or racial minorities. We are referring to students who were reared in a home where a language other than English was often used or whose first language was not English and who therefore constitute a minority in the general population relative to native speakers of English.

We refer to **content area teachers** as teachers who specialize in a particular subject area of the curriculum, such as language arts, mathematics, science, and social studies. Although many content area teachers are found at the secondary level, there are also content specialists at the elementary level. Finally, we have borrowed Enright and McCloskey's[2] term **grade-level** classroom (rather than "mainstream" or "regular" classroom) to refer to classrooms designed for native English-speaking students. We use the term **mainstream** only in connection with special education students.

We use the terms **content area** and **content subject** interchangeably to refer to subjects of the curriculum such as science, mathematics, social studies, and language arts.

Background and Rationale

The idea for CALLA grew out of research we conducted in the early and mid 1980s and prior experiences with instructional programs and staff development in ESL and other second language programs, including bilingual education. Our research built on earlier research on learning strategies and cognition conducted with English- speaking students[3] and on the first studies of learning strategies in second language acquisition.[4] This research interested us because it identified some of the characteristics of effective learners, including second language learners, and because some of the studies in first language contexts were showing that strategies could be successfully taught to less effective learners. Research methodology and findings in these studies were helpful in guiding us as we developed a research design for our initial work. Each of us had very different experiences in instructional programs, one (Chamot) primarily as a language teacher, teacher educator, program designer, and materials developer, and the other (O'Malley) in assessment, evaluation, and research.

LEARNING STRATEGIES

Our own research started with an investigation of the learning strategies used by beginning and intermediate-level high school ESL students nominated by teachers as having high academic ability. In this study, we interviewed students and asked them to describe special methods or "tricks" they used for various language learning activities selected to represent their classroom instruction.[5] These effective language learners were very much aware of their own mental processes and could describe these processes in some detail. Although the students could describe their own thinking and learning strategies, most of their teachers were unable to describe *how* their students learned what was taught to them. We used information from the student interviews to describe, classify, and analyze strategies used by effective and less effective language learners for different types of language tasks, both within and beyond the classroom. One important finding was that students often used combinations of strategies in complex and interesting ways.

Having identified a number of learning strategies used by ESL students who were encountering success in their efforts to learn English, we next embarked on an experimental study to find out if some of the learning strategies used by effective ESL students could be successfully taught to other ESL students in a classroom setting.[6] This study revealed that students can learn to use learning strategies through instruction and that the use of learning strategies can improve performance on language learning tasks.

One indirect outcome of the experimental study was a reconsideration of the role of the student. In the experimental study, for example, we had taught a single set of strategies and found that they were not adopted by all students, particularly with less complex tasks such as vocabulary learning. On more complex language tasks, such as listening and speaking, fewer students had already developed their own strategies, and they were more amenable to new suggestions. We concluded that students should have an important role in selecting strategies from a menu and in adapting strategies to different types of tasks.

We also learned that learning strategy instruction requires a thoughtful reconsideration of the teacher's role. Once students begin to regulate their own learning through a strategic approach to learning tasks, they are no longer totally dependent on the teacher. Because of this, successful learning strategy teachers undergo an important shift in their instructional approach. Simply using ample amounts of language and conveying information and skills are insufficient methods to support learning. Instead, teachers should be aware of their students' approaches to learning and expand the students' repertoires of strategic approaches by involving them as collaborators in developing the knowledge and processes needed to attain common goals.

In our third study of ESL students, we focused on the differences in strategy use of more and less effective students on listening comprehension tasks.[7] Not only did effective learners use more strategies than less effective learners, but they used strategies that seemed particularly appropriate for listening comprehension. In other words, effective listeners were able to select and use strategies that were especially helpful in understanding an oral text. By asking students to "think aloud" as they performed listening tasks in English, we confirmed the complexity of strategy combinations discovered earlier and obtained a rich record of the ways in which students adapted strategies based on their own experiences and knowledge.

In subsequent research with foreign language students, we confirmed the finding that differences between more and less effective learners are not so much in the number of overall strategies used, but in how the strategies are used and whether they are appropriate for the student and the task. We began to see that the type of task is a major determiner of what strategy or strategies can be used most effectively for different types of students. For example, we found that some strategies used by beginning-level effective language learners are used less by the same learners when they reach intermediate-level classes and that new strategies are developed to meet the requirements of new tasks. We also explored (and are continuing to explore) how best to teach learning strategies to second language learners and how to help teachers incorporate learning strategy instruction in their classrooms.

Our research has convinced us that most students can profit from instruction in learning strategies. ESL students, in particular, often need learning strategies to help them cope with the dual demands of learning a new language and learning academic content through that new language. Since the early years of our own research program, our understanding of second language learning strategies has also grown through the work of other researchers who continue to identify the strategies used by successful language learners in both ESL and foreign language contexts.[8]

ACADEMIC LANGUAGE SKILLS

At the same time that we were becoming convinced of the positive role that learning strategy instruction could play in second language acquisition, we became increasingly aware that most ESL programs were not completely successful in preparing upper elementary and secondary students for grade-level content classrooms. Teachers and administrators were expressing concern that ESL students who apparently could speak and understand English fairly well were nevertheless encountering serious difficulties in content classrooms where they were expected to *use English as a tool for learning.* Cummins[9] had recently published his research on immigrant students in Canada, in which he found that while most students learned sufficient English to engage in social communication in about two years, they typically needed five to seven years to acquire the type of language skills needed for successful participation in content classrooms. He described these types of language skills as *cognitive academic language proficiency,* which is much slower to develop than social interactive language skills. The cognitive demands of the tasks for which academic language is used, and the fact that academic language is frequently not supported by the rich array of non-verbal and contextual clues that characterize the language of face-to-face interaction, make academic language more difficult to learn.[10]

ACADEMIC CONTENT

In reviewing Cummins's work, which has since been confirmed and extended in American settings by Collier,[11] we wondered if changes in ESL instructional programs could in any way shorten the amount of time students need to develop academic language skills in English. Meanwhile, we had also been studying Mohan's[12] work advocating the integration of language and content for ESL instruction. Another body of research which influenced our thinking was the work of DeAvila and Duncan[13] and Cohen, DeAvila, and Intili,[14] in which an innovative science and mathematics program was successful not only in teaching science and mathematics to language minority students not yet proficient in English, but was also extraordinarily effective in developing students' English language proficiency.

Considering the work of researchers such as Cummins, DeAvila, and Mohan, we began to examine the problems encountered by ESL students in attaining academic success from the dual perspectives of curriculum and instruction. We proposed adding academic content to the ESL curriculum to better prepare students for grade-level content classrooms, and at the same time we proposed using explicit instruction in learning strategies as the principal method for delivering content-ESL instruction. This is how the concept of CALLA was born.

While we were developing our ideas in written form (having borrowed part of Cummins's term *cognitive academic language proficiency* for the name of our approach), a number of other researchers and practitioners also began to advocate the inclusion of content in ESL instruction. In fact, just after we completed the manuscript for the original CALLA monograph published by the National Clearinghouse for Bilingual Education,[15] we were invited to attend a conference organized by the Center for Applied Linguistics on integrating language and content in ESL, where we shared some of the ideas we had developed in the course of writing the monograph. We were encouraged to see that other researchers and educators had also been reaching similar conclusions about the need for change in ESL curriculum. In ensuing years the Center for Applied Linguistics has sponsored a number of publications on integrating language and content,[16] as has the National Clearinghouse for Bilingual Education.[17] Mohan has continued to expand and refine his Integrated Language and Content (ILC) model, and he and his colleagues have added numerous practical teaching activities.[18] Cantoni-Harvey[19] has outlined a number of teacher-oriented suggestions for content-based ESL instruction, and Enright and McCloskey[20] have provided a rich source of ideas and techniques for introducing thematic units which include content into ESL teaching. More recently, Snow, Met, and Genesee[21] outlined a model of content-based language instruction which provides guidelines for systematically analyzing language which is essential or obligatory in a particular content area, and language which is compatible with a content area and can be easily taught through content activities. Spanos[22] recently reviewed current initiatives and programs for integrated language and content instruction programs.

INFLUENCE OF COGNITIVE THEORY

Another major influence in the development of CALLA has been research on cognition and instruction conducted with native English-speaking students. In the last ten years our understanding has been continually expanded by the insights of researchers such as Pressley[23] and his colleagues, who have identified the learning strategies in different areas of the curriculum that have significant research support. We also have benefited from studying and seeking ESL applications of the work of first language researchers in specific content areas such as reading, writing, and problem-solving in mathematics and science.[24]

There has been a continuing and substantial influence on our thinking from cognitive theory. This influence began just after our first descriptive and theoretical studies of learning strategies in ESL had been completed and after the first CALLA monograph had been published. We began our analysis of cognitive theory with the work of John Anderson[25] at the suggestion of a colleague, Carol Walker, with whom we published the first examination of how cognitive theory applies to second language acquisition.[26] We continue to rely heavily on Anderson's work in our theory formulations,[27] although we have expanded our views considerably based on writings of others such as Gagné,[28] Shuell,[29] Weinstein and Mayer,[30] and Zimmerman and Pons.[31]

Finally, we have been and continue to be guided in our development of the CALLA model by the experiences of teachers and students in school districts around the country. Their input and suggestions have been invaluable in identifying what works in CALLA classrooms.

Background and Rationale

- ❖ Most students can profit from instruction in learning strategies.
- ❖ Many students lack academic language skills that would enable them to use English as a tool for learning.
- ❖ Adding academic content to the ESL curriculum prepares students for grade-level content classrooms.
- ❖ CALLA has been influenced and supported by cognitive theory, research, and ongoing classroom use.

Overview of CALLA

THE CALLA APPROACH

The CALLA approach is targeted at language minority students at the advanced beginning and intermediate levels of English language proficiency. CALLA is designed to assist ESL students to succeed in school by providing transitional instruction from either standard ESL programs or bilingual programs to grade-level content classrooms. CALLA was originally developed[32] to meet the academic needs of three types of ESL students:

- Students who have developed social communicative skills through beginning level ESL classes or through exposure to an English-speaking environment, but have not yet developed academic language skills appropriate to their grade level;
- Students who have acquired academic language skills in their native language and initial proficiency in English, but who need assistance in transferring concepts and skills learned in the first language to English; and

- Bilingual English-dominant students who have not yet developed academic language skills in either language.

Since this initial formulation, we have gained considerable experience in seeing CALLA applied to other types of students and in other types of settings, as will be described in this book. CALLA integrates grade-appropriate content topics, academic language development, and explicit instruction and practice in using learning strategies to acquire both declarative and procedural knowledge in the content areas.

CALLA lessons are designed following a comprehensive lesson plan model that is based in part on cognitive theory and in part on efforts to integrate language, content, and learning strategies. In all CALLA lessons, the content always is selected first through curriculum alignment. The content determines the academic language objectives and the types of learning strategies that are appropriate. Because CALLA lessons are cognitively demanding, they rely heavily on *scaffolding:* the provision of extensive instructional supports when concepts and skills are being first introduced and the gradual removal of supports when students begin to develop greater proficiency, skills, or knowledge.

THE CALLA MODEL

The CALLA model includes three components and instructional objectives in its curricular and instructional design: topics from the major content subjects, the development of academic language skills, and explicit instruction in learning strategies for both content and language acquisition.

CONTENT TOPICS. The content topics are aligned with an all-English curriculum so that practice is provided with a selection of actual topics students will encounter in grade-level classrooms. We have recommended introducing the content areas gradually so that students do not become overwhelmed with both language and content. The first content subject introduced should either have extensive contextual supports for learning or reduced language demands. We have suggested beginning with science instruction[33] because a discovery and hands-on approach to science is compatible with providing ample contextual support for academic language development. We also believe that the intrinsic interest of science to many students is a built-in motivator for effective learning. The next content subject that can be introduced in a CALLA program is mathematics, which has its own unique language, especially in solving word problems, but which nevertheless has fewer language demands than some of the other content areas. Social studies is the third content subject introduced in a recommended CALLA program, although some teachers have suggested that geography in particular can be introduced much earlier because of the reduced language demands and the potential relationship to students' prior knowledge. Language arts might be introduced last in a CALLA program, although there are arguments that can be made for introducing some aspects of language arts much earlier, especially where stories have cultural relevance or where writing expresses personal experiences.

Throughout the introduction of content, CALLA teachers do not repeat what is taught in grade-level content area classrooms, but rather strive to enable students to experience success through teaching in depth rather than in breadth. CALLA teachers also encourage students to use higher-order thinking skills from the onset of instruction by a variety of means that reduce the language demands for conceptual activity in content areas.

ACADEMIC LANGUAGE SKILLS. The second component of CALLA, academic language development, includes all four language skills (listening, speaking, reading, and writing) in daily lessons on the content subject. Language is used as a functional tool for learning academic subject matter. Students learn not just the vocabulary and grammar of the content area but also learn important concepts and skills using academic language. Students learn the language functions that are important for performing effectively in the content area, such as *analyzing, evaluating, justifying,* and *persuading*. Students develop academic language skills in English through cognitively demanding activities in which comprehension is assisted by contextual supports and in which scaffolded instruction guides the acquisition of content.

LEARNING STRATEGY INSTRUCTION. The third and central component of CALLA is instruction in learning strategies. We emphasize repeatedly that students who are mentally active and who analyze and reflect on their learning activities will learn, retain, and be able to use new information more effectively. Furthermore, students will be able to learn and apply strategies more effectively with new tasks if they verbalize and describe their efforts to apply strategies with learning activities. Based on our own research and studies by others, we identify three major types of strategies: Metacognitive, Cognitive, and Social/Affective. (See Chapter 4 for a discussion about these strategies.)

Learning strategies are selected in CALLA lessons based on the specific type of strategy that seems most suited for the content materials and language task. For example, if the task entails reading a passage in science, strategies appropriate for analyzing text organization and deriving meaning from science texts would be appropriate. Other strategies are appropriate for solving word problems in mathematics, for conducting and reporting on experiments in science, for researching and reporting on social studies activities, and for reading and conveying the meaning in literature. Appropriate strategy combinations might be selected depending on their suitability for the task and the students. Strategies are taught explicitly by naming the strategy, telling students what the strategy does to assist learning, and then providing ample instructional supports while students practice and apply the strategy. The objective is to provide students with a menu from which they can select strategies they have found to be appropriate for specific types of learning activities and tasks. Because the research on strategy instruction with second language acquisition is still developing, we rely on research with first language tasks and the consistency of CALLA with cognitive theory in order to derive a more complete understanding of how to implement strategy instruction.

Overview of CALLA

CALLA integrates:

- ❖ language development;
- ❖ content area instruction;
- ❖ explicit instruction in learning strategies.

Theoretical Framework

Any instructional approach such as CALLA should be based on a theory that meets at least three criteria: (a) it is grounded in research, (b) it explains what is learned as well as how it is learned, and (c) it provides guidance for instruction. More specifically, for our purposes, the theory must say something about how academic content is learned as well as how language is learned and why the use of learning strategies results in improved learning. Furthermore, the theory should say something about learning in two languages. We have reviewed the research on learning extensively and found many answers in cognitive theory that we do not find elsewhere, including explanations for both basic as well as complex forms of learning.[36]

Part of the importance of cognitive theory concerns the model both students and teachers have of learning. That is, what is learned and how do teachers or students believe that second language learning occurs? The way that second language learning is believed to occur often determines how teachers teach and how students learn.

WHAT IS LEARNED?

Cognitive theory provides insights that enable us to examine these personal theories. Some students believe that the major task in second language acquisition is to learn the vocabulary. Other students who recognize that more complicated elements are involved nevertheless believe that what they know in their first language is irrelevant for second language acquisition.

An example will serve to illustrate the point. In one of the studies we conducted,[37] we asked high school students learning English as a second language to identify learning strategies ("special ways of learning") for specific tasks of the kind they experienced in their ESL classrooms. One high school student from a Spanish-speaking country was asked to think aloud while performing a science task. She indicated that she was uncertain how to proceed or what to do. As a result, she not only supplied little information about the correct solution but was uninformative concerning the use of learning strategies. However, in response to probe questions, she indicated that she had received instruction in this area in her native country, but that "that was in Spanish and this (the task which she was asked to perform) is in English." This student was expressing a view of learning based on an inaccurate but prevalent model of second language learning.

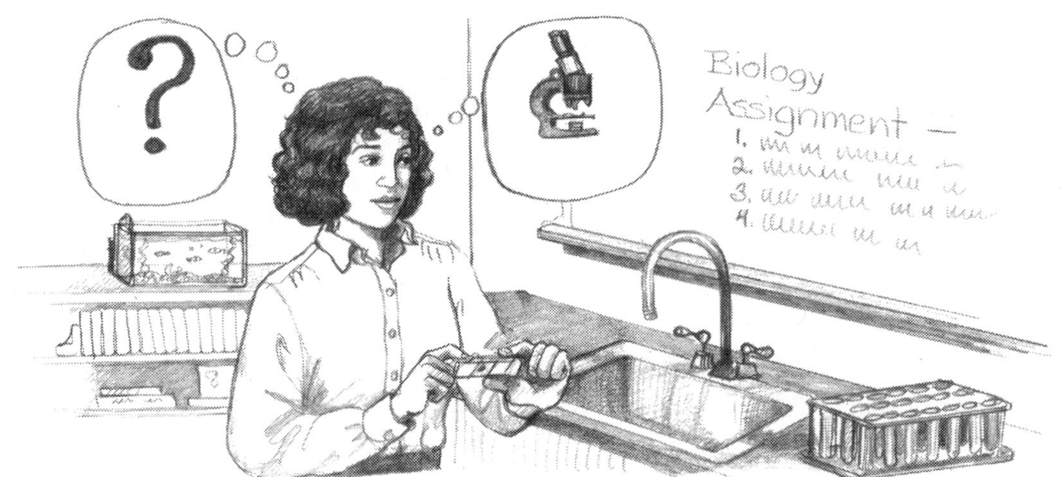

Some students fail to recognize their own knowledge when problems are presented in a new language.

COGNITIVE THEORY. What does a cognitive theory have to say about this example? How is the information to which the student did not believe she had access stored in memory? Can it be retrieved and used? Is there some device that would enable this and other students to capitalize on what they *do* know rather than be troubled by what they *do not* know?

The cognitive model of learning indicates that learning is an active, dynamic process in which learners select information from their environment, organize the information, relate it to what they already know, retain what they consider to be important, use the information in appropriate contexts, and reflect on the success of their learning efforts.[38] Cognitive theories of learning begin with a distinction between three types of functions in memory.[39] We use the term **functions** to indicate that we are discussing mental functions based on developmental, cognitive, and information processing theory, rather than mental structures based on neural or anatomical components of the brain. However, neural components which accompany or parallel observed mental functions may be occurring.

KIND OF MEMORY. There appears to be a *long-term memory* in which information of the kind the student remembered in Spanish is stored along with much other information derived from personal experience and education. A *short-term memory* is used to remember telephone numbers and other similar information that is unimportant to retain more than a few moments or is easily forgotten. There also seems to be a *working memory* in which we manipulate information, as in performing mathematical calculations, solving problems, reorganizing information, or comparing what we already know with new information just being presented. We modify and expand on information in long-term memory based on new information that is stored in short-term memory or manipulated while in working memory.

The student in our example was using her working memory to think about the problem at hand, but did not recognize that her long-term memory contained relevant information that would help in the solution. In a sense, the student's preconceived model of what was relevant for the problem solution (only information in the same language) led her to fail in matching the pattern of the "problem in English" to the "problem in Spanish." We would say that she did not use *elaboration* as a strategy to connect what she already knew with the problem she needed to solve.

DECLARATIVE KNOWLEDGE. Why do we believe that the information this student had learned in Spanish was accessible? Most information is stored in long-term memory as either *declarative knowledge* or *procedural knowledge*.[40] Declarative knowledge consists of "what" we know or can declare, and procedural knowledge consists of the things that we know "how" to do. Declarative knowledge is stored in memory frameworks or *schemata* that are interconnected concepts and ideas. The connections between these concepts are extremely complex and may result from formal education, such as the hierarchy of the animal kingdom, or other experiences in which we sometimes link objects, people, or concepts in idiosyncratic ways. Depending on prior learning experiences, the concepts are connected with varying strengths of association such that recall of one concept will evoke recall of others.

The information stored through schemata can be altered when we have new experiences that add to, expand upon, or challenge some of the previous information. There is an advantage to linking previous knowledge with new concepts because schemata can be modified or expanded rather than constructed anew. There is no reason to believe that the memory schemata in one language cannot be used to assist solving problems or understanding similar information in a second language, provided that the concepts in each language are similar. Often the memory of one item in a schemata will jog the recall of other items with which it is linked or connected down a memory pathway. Such connections occur when people free associate or engage in brainstorming, an approach apparently not considered by the student in the example.

PROCEDURAL KNOWLEDGE. The second way of storing information in memory, procedural knowledge, concerns what we know "how" to do. This includes both simple and complex physical or mental procedures. Procedural knowledge is stored in memory as production systems. Production systems consist of a series of steps in which there is a "condition" and an "action." The condition and action are connected by an IF—THEN sequence, usually with an intermediate "and" clause, which controls whether or not the action follows from the condition. Production systems can be used to explain a variety of language and other complex mental procedures, including learning strategies and problem solving.

Production systems may be the basis for storing information in memory that permits individuals to express communicative competence. Canale and Swain[41] define communicative competence as the ability to use grammatical, sociolinguistic, discourse, and strategic skills. An individual who is communicatively competent in a second language might engage in the following exchange.[42]

1 **IF** my goal is to engage in conversation with Sally,
and Sally is monolingual in English,
THEN the subgoal is to use my second language.

2 **IF** my goal is to use my second language,
THEN the subgoal is to initiate a conversation.
(sociolinguistic competence)

3 **IF** my goal is to initiate a conversation,
THEN my subgoal is to say a memorized greeting.
(discourse competence)

4 **IF** my goal is to say a memorized greeting,
and the context is an informal one,
THEN choose the appropriate language style.
(Sociolinguistic competence)

5 **IF** my goal is to choose an appropriate language style,
THEN the subgoal is to say, "How's it going, Sally?"
(grammatical and sociolinguistic competence)

This example illustrates some important features of production systems. First, they are oriented toward attaining specific goals, such as interpersonal goals in communication. Second, they are conditional and may proceed in a number of directions depending on the "and" portion of the production. The speaker checks on the identity of the person to be greeted, determines that she is monolingual in English, and then formulates a statement. If the condition specified in the "and" portion is not met, the production could go in an entirely different direction. Third, production systems are sequential. The last clause of each individual production cues the first clause of the next. A fourth feature is their flexibility. At each step, because of the conditionality of the "and" clause, a number of different types of conditions can be accommodated. The example could continue with a series of other exchanges depending on the way in which the person responds to the greeting.

Production systems can also be used to represent the way that learning strategies are stored in memory. Imagine a student using a learning strategy such as *inferring meaning* while reading. The student encounters an unfamiliar word, determines that the word is important to understand the sentence, pauses to reflect on the meaning of the overall paragraph and sentence in which the word occurs, and determines if the position of the word provides a clue to meaning. The following production system illustrates this:

1 **IF** I encounter a word I don't know,
and the word is needed to understand the sentence,
THEN guess the meaning of the word.

2 **IF** I want to guess the meaning of the word,
and the word is connected to the paragraph meaning,
THEN determine if the paragraph meaning cues the word.

3 **IF** the paragraph meaning does not cue the word meaning,
and I still believe the word is important,
THEN determine the word's part of speech.

4 **IF** I want to find the word's part of speech,
and the word conveys the action of the sentence,
THEN the word must be a verb.

5 **IF** the word is a verb,
and the sentence occurs in the past,
THEN the verb must be in the past tense.

As with the previous example, this illustration shows how production systems are goal-oriented, conditional, sequential, and flexible.

PRODUCTION SYSTEMS IN MATH PROBLEM SOLVING. Another example illustrates how production systems can be used to represent the complex mental procedures used in mathematics problem solving. In one of our studies,[43] we tape-recorded the responses of a group of elementary and secondary school language minority students with intermediate-level skills in English as they verbalized solutions to math word problems. Some of the students had received CALLA instruction in learning and problem-solving strategies for half a school year, while others were in regular high intensity English language training. Part of the CALLA instruction entailed familiarizing students with a five-point checklist for solving problems that, in one form or another, is represented in many middle grade math texts and is based on Polya's problem-solving procedure.[44] The five steps are as follows:

- Understand the question.
- Find the needed data.
- Develop a plan.
- Solve the problem.
- Check back.

The students with CALLA instruction responded by identifying more learning strategies and more often mentioned these problem-solving steps in the correct sequence than did students without CALLA instruction. They had mastered an involved procedural skill and were able to apply this skill or strategy on novel problems.

A highly complex set of cognitive processes is involved in this type of mental activity. The set of procedures associated with solving math word problems is stored in long-term memory, which the students learned through CALLA instruction. When the students see a new word problem, they analyze the similarity between this problem and other problems they have experienced. Recognizing a similarity, they know that the strategies which worked previously are likely to work on this new problem. They approach the problem by using these problem-solving steps, verbalizing the process as they seek to understand the problem. They then find the data needed for the solution, develop a plan, execute the plan, and check back to ensure that the procedure resulted in a correct solution.

METACOGNITIVE KNOWLEDGE. A considerable amount of *metacognitive knowledge* is required to recognize the similarity between new and previous problems. Awareness of this knowledge is a first step in the problem solution. Metacognitive knowledge entails matching the pattern of the new problem with the pattern of the problems experienced in the past, and applying strategies that worked in the past to the problem at hand. This type of matching requires the use of declarative knowledge since long-term memory contains experiences with problems that have similar features. Production systems can nevertheless be used to show how problem-solving steps of this kind are stored in memory:

1 **IF** I want to solve this problem, and the problem is like other problems where the problem-solving steps have worked (as determined from the pat tern match), **THEN** try to use the same problem-solving steps here.

2 **IF** the first problem-solving step is to understand the question, and the sentence with the question ends with a question mark, **THEN** look for the sentence with the question mark.

etc.

This particular set of problem-solving steps is highly domain dependent, that is, they are particularly suited to solving math word problems. However, other problem-solving steps would be stored in a similar manner, as in science problem solving.

HOW IS NEW INFORMATION LEARNED?

Apart from identifying the ways in which information is stored in memory, why is the distinction between declarative and procedural knowledge important? The major reason is that declarative and procedural knowledge appear to be learned in different ways. Furthermore, the information is retrieved from memory in different ways as well. This has implications for what teachers should do during instruction and what students should do while learning.

LEARNING DECLARATIVE KNOWLEDGE. Declarative knowledge is learned most effectively by capitalizing on existing memory structures or schemata and building on previous knowledge. In learning new information in a content area, students should identify what they already know about the material, even if what they know consists of a few words or some preliminary concepts in their native language. They can expand on this knowledge by checking what they know against new information being presented, by looking for the organization of the new knowledge to determine if it matches their familiar organization, and by looking for new concepts that expand on previous concepts.

The more ways in which new information is linked to existing information, the stronger the associations become and the easier it should be to remember. Contrast two types of learning processes—learning by repetition and learning by elaboration. In learning by repetition, students "go over and over" a list of vocabulary or other items, forming minimal linkages with existing schemata. In learning by elaboration, students develop images of new words, organize new words into groups, think of what they know about the concept the word represents, try to use words in sentences, act out sentences, and otherwise build strong associations in multiple ways with existing memory. Cognitive theory indicates that the greater linkages and pathways to existing memory frameworks will lead to enhanced learning and recall, which is, in fact, what typically occurs.

LEARNING PROCEDURAL KNOWLEDGE. In contrast to declarative knowledge, procedural knowledge is learned most effectively through practicing a complex procedure that has meaning and achieves an important goal. This can be contrasted with rule-based memorization of which condition-action sequences go together or which production systems occur in the correct sequence. For example, in language learning, one can learn numerous rules, such as the following:[45]

> **IF** the goal is to generate a plural of a noun,
> and the noun ends in a voiceless consonant,
> **THEN** generate the noun +/s/.

However, when there are many such rules, as there are in language, individuals often have difficulty recalling which rule applies in a particular instance, and find that they need to refer to the rule whenever performing a skill. Requiring individuals to remember the rules for execution of each step in the sequence is tedious and prolongs learning of the complete action sequence.[46]

A preferred method of learning procedural knowledge is to identify manageable but meaningful and integrated components of the complete process, gain partial mastery over the components by practicing them with feedback, and piece them together to make a complete action sequence that achieves a communication goal. The feedback can be either from the teacher or from more skilled peers. This avoids the tedious learning and compilation of minuscule pieces of knowledge based on rules that are difficult to combine and never seem to achieve a meaningful end. Individuals can improve execution of a complete process through practice until it looks like "expert" performance by modeling an ideal performance *or* by referring back to the rules only as needed for refinements in performance. When students have mastered a complex cognitive process, they can perform it rapidly and with a minimum of errors. At this point, a complex cognitive process may be performed without awareness of the many steps and decisions made while it is being executed.

WHAT SUCCESSFUL LANGUAGE LEARNERS DO. We have encountered a number of examples of accomplished language learners who avoid rule-based learning by practicing complete and meaningful components of complex language procedures. In these cases, the students' model of learning coincided with cognitive theory. One second language student approached reading in the second language by looking through authentic passages for words that she recognized in order to piece together some impression of the meaning of the passage. She reflected on what she knew about the topic, building on her declarative knowledge, even though it was in an unfamiliar language. She then returned to reread the passage, inferring the meaning of unfamiliar words only as necessary to understand the message. She gained a better understanding of the intent and message being communicated as well as the use of the language in authentic contexts. As she developed more competence, she would develop an advanced organizer of the topic, the elements discussed, and how they were linked together to communicate the message, just as she would in English. This is in contrast to reading from the first word in the passage, looking up all unfamiliar words, trying to remember the rules for word and sentence formation, etc., as far too many students actually do.

Individuals can have declarative knowledge about a complex mental procedure such as a learning strategy but not be able to apply the strategy effectively without conscious effort and deliberation. Verbalizing the strategy application with various materials early in the learning process aids in establishing control over the strategy use. Through repeated applications of the strategy with various learning materials, the individual can gradually "proceduralize" or learn to use the strategy automatically so that it functions rapidly and without errors with specific tasks. This eases the burden on short-term memory, which can then focus on the passage meaning. Individuals can ease proceduralization of learning strategies and other production systems by taking the "high road" to learning or by recognizing parallels between new tasks and more familiar tasks on which the strategy has been applied in the past, thereby transferring the strategy.[47] In contrast, using the "low road" to learning, individuals treat the strategy as if it must be relearned because they do not recognize the way in which it has been used previously. Verbalizing strategy use helps learners link potential strategy uses.

IMPLICATIONS FOR INSTRUCTION

One direct implication for instruction is that teachers should be able to identify declarative and procedural knowledge in their instructional materials and in the content areas. By capitalizing on ways in which each of these types of information are learned most effectively, teachers will take a major step toward facilitating learning by their students. Another implication is that both students and teachers should be aware of the strategies that students use while learning. By gaining greater awareness of initial strategy use by students, teachers and students can expand the repertoire of strategies the students are capable of using with new materials. A third implication is that teachers can play an active role in influencing strategy use and in assisting students in using strategies more effectively. At least one more implication is that students can take command over their own learning activities and initiate strategic applications that will lead them toward more autonomous learning. When students take control over their own learning, they see themselves as more effective and thereby gain in confidence with future learning activities.

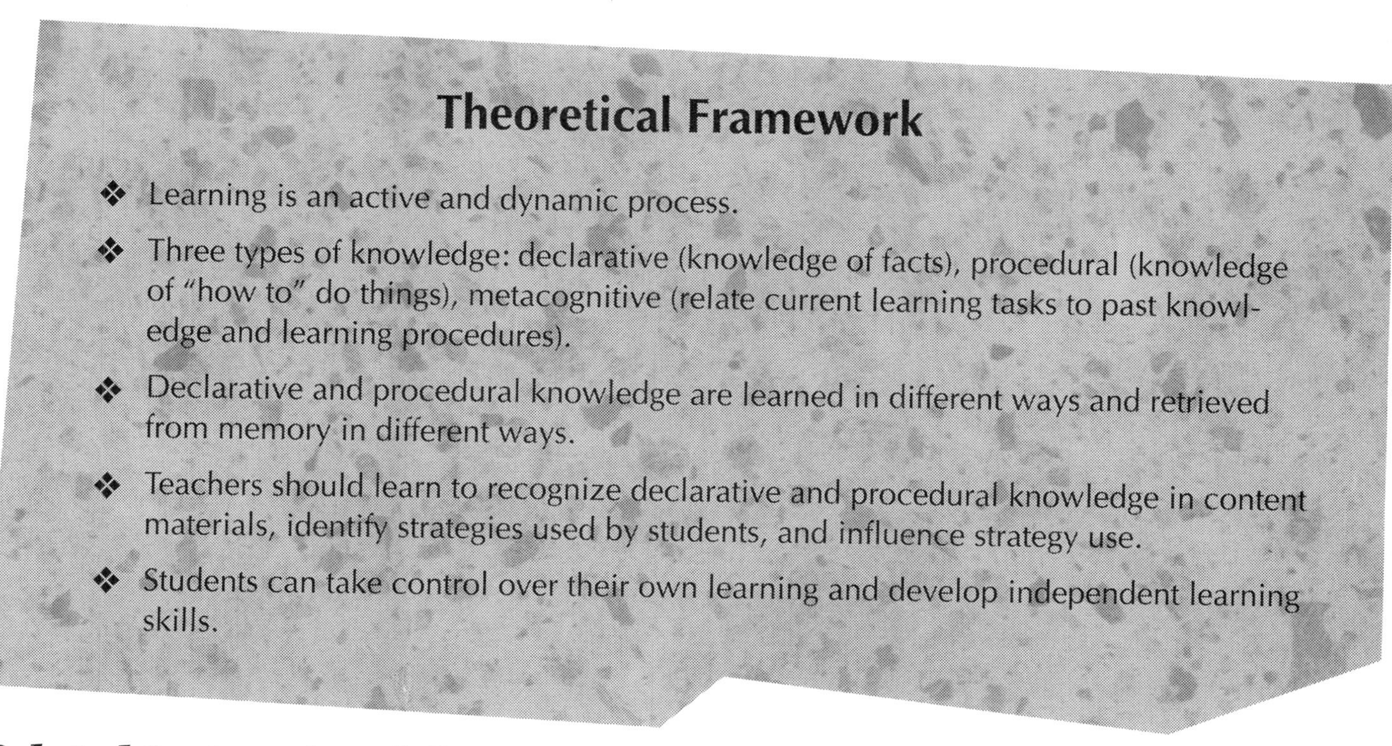

Theoretical Framework

- ❖ Learning is an active and dynamic process.
- ❖ Three types of knowledge: declarative (knowledge of facts), procedural (knowledge of "how to" do things), metacognitive (relate current learning tasks to past knowledge and learning procedures).
- ❖ Declarative and procedural knowledge are learned in different ways and retrieved from memory in different ways.
- ❖ Teachers should learn to recognize declarative and procedural knowledge in content materials, identify strategies used by students, and influence strategy use.
- ❖ Students can take control over their own learning and develop independent learning skills.

Related Instructional Concepts

CALLA has many roots and parallel branches. Many educational reforms proposed within the last fifteen or more years can be traced to the thinking of psychologists such as Anderson, Ausubel, Bruner, Piaget, and Vygotsky. Each of these thinkers has advanced our understanding of human learning. Though each has chosen a somewhat different lens to investigate learning processes, each has operated from the basic belief that human beings think, seek knowledge, enjoy learning, and make intellectual leaps when the right conditions (developmental, experiential, social, individual) are present. In this section we trace some of the influences and parallel thinking that have guided our development of the CALLA model.

First, and most important, CALLA is based on a cognitive model of learning. As explained earlier in this chapter, this means that we are more interested in what is going on in students' minds than in their overt responses to stimuli. We believe that instruction should be guided by how students think and learn. Allied with this principle is the idea that language facilitates and illustrates thinking. Listening and reading give us access to the ideas of others, and speaking and writing provide us with the means of transforming ideas through our own individual experiences and outlooks.

Instructional innovations that are in harmony with the CALLA philosophy are many and varied. We discuss only some examples here, limiting our discussion to Language Across the Curriculum, the Language Experience Approach, Whole Language, Process Writing, Cooperative Learning, and Cognitive Instruction.

LANGUAGE ACROSS THE CURRICULUM

This model seeks to infuse language teaching and learning into all areas of the curriculum.[48] In a Language Across the Curriculum model, all teachers, including science, mathematics, and social studies teachers, carry out language development activities associated with their individual content areas. This model was originally

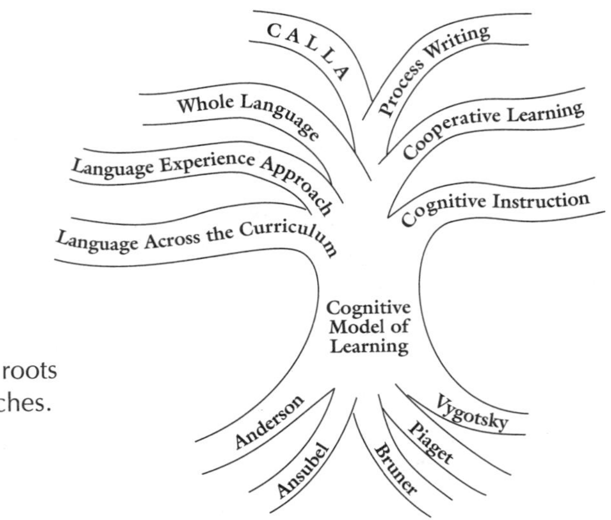

CALLA has many roots and parallel branches.

developed for native English-speaking students, but it has enormous potential in addressing the needs of language minority students. Parallels of the Language Across the Curriculum philosophy with CALLA are that language skills are practiced in all subjects, including mathematics and science.

LANGUAGE EXPERIENCE APPROACH

The Language Experience Approach (LEA) was developed for native English-speaking students as a way of providing support for initial reading experiences. In this approach students learn that what is said can be written down and that what has been written down can be read.[49] The Language Experience Approach is based philosophically on the notion that students' prior experience needs to be used as a bridge to new ideas and concepts. In this approach students talk about personal experiences, and this recounting is written down by the teacher, an aide, or another student. Later, the student and perhaps other classmates use the written-down account as a reading text. An important aspect of the Language Experience Approach is that vocabulary and grammatical structures are experienced first within the language knowledge base known by students. The Language Experience Approach thus encompasses many of the same principles that underlie CALLA's approach to literacy development and is particularly advantageous with beginning-level ESL students. (See Chapter 8 for a discussion of how to adapt CALLA for beginning-level and preliterate students.)

WHOLE LANGUAGE

This approach to literacy development is based on the belief that language should not be separated into component skills, but rather experienced as a whole system of communication.[50] To this end, students are given many opportunities to interact with authentic texts, especially literature, and to use language for personal communicative purposes. Activities in a Whole Language classroom include reading aloud by the teacher, journal writing, story writing, sustained silent reading, higher-order thinking skills discussions about what is read, student choice in reading materials, and frequent conferences with the teacher and other students about what is being read and written. We agree that this philosophy and instructional approach is valuable for all students, including students learning English.

While Whole Language approaches provide many suggestions on *what* should be read and experienced and how reading should *not* be taught (through decontextualized skill-based exercises), they are less specific on *how* reading development takes place and what instructional procedures can help students become better readers. In CALLA we have incorporated findings from current research on reading comprehension, and have focused on the benefits of reading strategy instruction.[51] We do not believe that reading authentic texts needs to be in opposition with strategy instruction for reading comprehension. (See Chapter 12 for a discussion of literature in the CALLA class.)

PROCESS WRITING

In Process Writing approaches students learn that writing involves thinking, reflection, and multiple revisions. Teachers model the writing process by thinking aloud about their own ideas, jotting them down, organizing them, developing a draft, reading it aloud, making revisions, asking students for their comments, and continuing to make more revisions. The classroom becomes a writing workshop in which students learn the craft of writing through discussion, sharing, and conferencing.

Process Writing is recommended in CALLA classrooms for all types of writing and in all content areas. In addition, we believe that ESL students can profit from instruction in writing strategies just as instruction in using strategies and in self-regulation has proven beneficial for native English-speaking students.[52] By teaching students effective strategies for planning, accessing prior knowledge, composing, and revising, and also teaching them how to select and manage writing strategies, teachers can help students develop both confidence and increased skill in their writing. (See Chapter 12 for a discussion of our recommendations for composition.)

COOPERATIVE LEARNING

In Cooperative Learning students work in heterogeneous groups on learning tasks that are structured so that all students share in the responsibility for completing the task. While there are a number of models of Cooperative Learning, all provide multiple opportunities for students to engage in active practice of language and content.[53] In Cooperative Learning, students of varying degrees of linguistic proficiency and content knowledge work in a group setting that fosters mutual learning rather than competitiveness.[54] For language minority students, the benefits of Cooperative Learning include additional practice with academic English, the use of the native language to draw on prior knowledge, the incorporation of content into ESL classes, and the opportunity for students to become more independent learners.[55] Teachers who set up cooperative activities in which group members have differing levels of English proficiency make it possible for students to help each other understand and complete the task.

Cooperative Learning is an integral part of CALLA lessons. Cooperative Learning activities are featured in the *Practice* phase of the CALLA instructional sequence, and can also be used successfully during the *Preparation* phase when students are identifying their prior knowledge of a topic, during the *Evaluation* phase when students assess their own level of learning and strategy use, and during the *Expansion* phase in which students make applications of the new information to their own lives. In CALLA, *cooperation* is identified as a particular learning strategy which is taught overtly so that students understand the value of working collaboratively on academic tasks.

COGNITIVE INSTRUCTION

Cognitive Instruction is used to describe a number of approaches to teaching thinking and to infuse thinking into all areas of the curriculum.[56] New instructional approaches in science, mathematics, social studies, reading comprehension, and writing all share a common cognitive orientation. Students are seen as active co-constructors of knowledge. The role of students' prior knowledge is seen as a critical influence on the acquisition of new information.[57] The curriculum calls for fewer topics and greater depth.[58] Teachers foster the development of higher-order thinking skills through challenging questions, modeling the learning process, and engaging in interactive dialogue with students.[59] Another common feature of cognitive instructional approaches is that learning strategies are taught explicitly. Students are told the names of particular strategies, they are given reasons for using the strategy, they observe the teacher modeling the strategy, and they are given opportunities to practice the strategy with ordinary classroom tasks. Later, the teacher leads a debriefing discussion in which students describe how they used the strategy and the degree to which it was effective for completing the learning task. Finally, the teacher suggests ways in which the student can apply the same strategy to different learning situations.

CALLA is based on the same theory and research as the Cognitive Instruction models described for different subject areas. We have tried to identify general aspects of the Cognitive Instruction model which need to be adapted for ESL students, and specific adaptations which seem called for by the needs of students learning a new language.

Related Instructional Concepts

- ❖ Language Across the Curriculum: practiced in all subjects.
- ❖ The Language Experience Approach: particularly advantageous with beginning level ESL students.
- ❖ Whole Language: valuable for all students.
- ❖ Process Writing: recommended for all types of writing in all content areas.
- ❖ Cooperative Learning: a learning strategy taught overtly in CALLA.
- ❖ Cognitive Instruction: CALLA is based on cognitive theory and research.

Application Activities

The purpose of these activities is for teachers and program administrators to develop an understanding of the development and main features of CALLA, the theoretical framework on which the approach is based, and the relationship of CALLA to other models of instruction.

1. In this handbook we have used the term **grade-level classroom** (borrowed from Enright and McCloskey[60]) to refer to classrooms designed exclusively for native English-speaking students. Work with a group of colleagues to discuss these questions:

    a. What term is used to describe grade-level classrooms in your school district?

    b. What advantages and disadvantages are there to the term used in your school district?

    c. What other terms can you think of to describe classrooms designed for English-speaking students? What are their advantages and disadvantages?

2. Work in a group to brainstorm differences and similarities that have been observed between effective and less effective second language learners. Identify the characteristics that could be changed through instruction. Make a chart of your information and present it to the whole group.

3. Cummins[61] has postulated two dimensions which regulate the level of difficulty of language input. These dimensions are the degree of context in which language is embedded and the level of cognitive complexity demanded by the language task. To explain how these two dimensions interact with each other, he has proposed a model in which they intersect, forming four quadrants which can be used to describe language activities encountered in first and second language learning contexts. Refer to Table 1.1 on the following page, which presents a modified version of Cummins's model. Working with a colleague, describe a recent language experience in your own lives for each of the four quadrants.

4. Ask your ESL students to answer the following questions, orally or in writing:

    a. What's the most important thing about English to learn?

    b. What's the best way to learn English?

    c. Did anything that you learned in school in your country help you with what you are learning in your school here?

    d. What advice would you give to a new student from your country? Why?

    Use this information to construct profiles of student beliefs about second language learning. Share your results with colleagues. Which student beliefs are accurate? Which are inaccurate? What can the teacher do to help students change inaccurate beliefs?

5. Declarative knowledge consists of facts and information that we know. Procedural knowledge consists of things that we know how to do.
   a. Free-write for five minutes describing how you teach declarative knowledge.
   b. Free-write for five minutes describing how you teach procedural knowledge.
   c. Work with a group of colleagues to compare your approaches to teaching declarative and procedural knowledge.
6. Six instructional approaches related to CALLA were described: Language Across the Curriculum, the Language Experience Approach, Whole Language, Process Writing, Cooperative Learning, and Cognitive Instruction. Working with a group of colleagues, choose one of these six instructional approaches to discuss. Then make a graphic organizer which displays the similarities and differences between the approach selected and CALLA. Present your graphic organizer to the class.

Table 1.1
USING CUMMINS'S FRAMEWORK TO CLASSIFY LANGUAGE ACTIVITIES

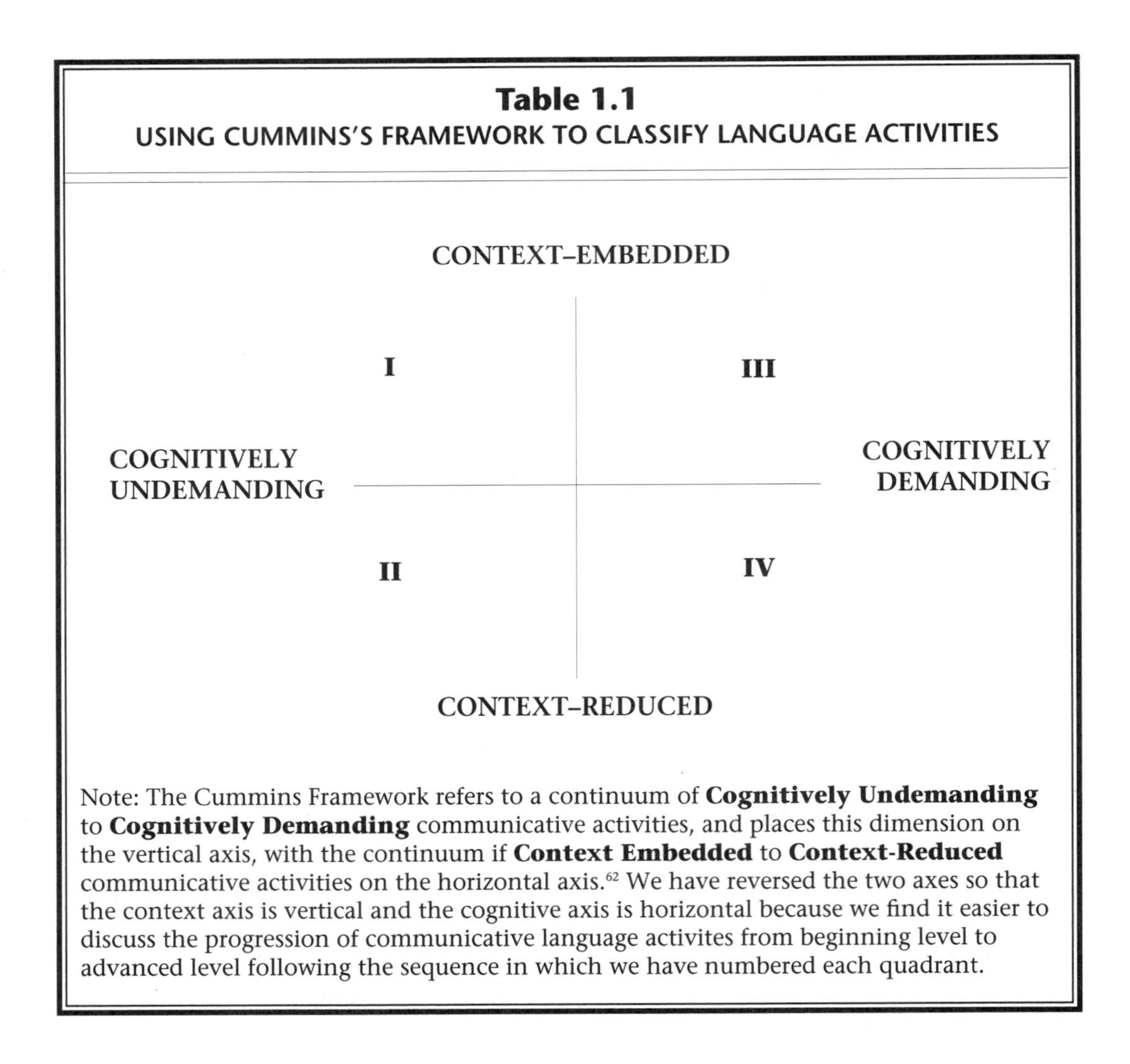

Note: The Cummins Framework refers to a continuum of **Cognitively Undemanding** to **Cognitively Demanding** communicative activities, and places this dimension on the vertical axis, with the continuum if **Context Embedded** to **Context-Reduced** communicative activities on the horizontal axis.[62] We have reversed the two axes so that the context axis is vertical and the cognitive axis is horizontal because we find it easier to discuss the progression of communicative language activites from beginning level to advanced level following the sequence in which we have numbered each quadrant.

CHAPTER 2
The Content-based Curriculum in CALLA

Overview

The first component of the CALLA model: the primary focus is on academic tasks within a communicative context.

Why Teach Content?

- Knowledge Base
- Procedures
- Motivation
- Learning Strategies

How to Select Content

- Content Teachers
- Curriculum
- Textbooks
- Curriculum Analysis
- Student Interests

How to Teach Content

- Activities
- Prior Knowledge
- Technical Vocabulary
- Learning Styles
- Overviews
- Questioning
- Teacher Monitoring
- Student Monitoring
- Graphic Organizers
- Resources
- Learning Strategies

CHAPTER 2 THE CONTENT-BASED CURRICULUM IN CALLA

TWO BASIC PREMISES IN CALLA are that content should be the primary focus of instruction and that academic language skills can be developed as the need for them emerges from the content. Content, rather than language, drives the curriculum. Language modalities (e.g., listening, speaking, reading, writing) are developed for content area activities as they are needed, rather than being taught sequentially. Language skills will be most meaningful when students perceive that they are needed in order to accomplish a communicative or academic task. CALLA's focus is on academic tasks within a communicative context. Students learn how to use academic language to communicate subject matter concepts and processes.

Why Teach Content?

There are at least four reasons for incorporating content into the ESL class. First, content provides students with an opportunity to develop important knowledge in different subject areas. This knowledge provides the foundation for learning grade-level information and processes in science, mathematics, social studies, and other academic areas of the curriculum. Second, students are able to practice the language functions and skills needed to understand, discuss, read about, and write about the concepts developed. A third reason for introducing content into the ESL class is that many students exhibit greater motivation when they are learning content than when they are learning language only. Finally, content provides a context for teaching students learning strategies that can be applied in the grade-level classroom. These four reasons for incorporating content into ESL are discussed in this section.

KNOWLEDGE BASE

Subject-area concepts and relationships are a foundation. Students making the transition from a special language program such as bilingual education or beginning-level ESL need to be prepared for the type of instruction they will encounter in the grade-level classroom. They need experiences in learning concepts, relationships, and processes in different subject areas. An occasional ESL lesson on a topic in social studies or science will not adequately prepare students for the type of language-related activities that they will encounter in the grade-level classroom. This is especially true in the middle and upper grade levels, where the curriculum in the content areas becomes progressively more demanding, both in terms of cognitive complexity and of language demands.

The content area topics incorporated into the curriculum should be authentic and important for the grade level of the student, and should provide for the development of new knowledge and skills. A curriculum that contains no new knowledge can rapidly become a series of exercises in translation of vocabulary and skills from the first language to the second, and may not stimulate students to begin to use English as a tool for learning. Instead, students who already have a background in a content area and who have already developed English proficiency through ESL instruction need a content-based curriculum in which they use English to solve problems and develop higher-order concepts that are appropriate for their grade and achievement level.

The content-based ESL curriculum should be aligned with the school district's curriculum for native English-speaking students. Curriculum alignment means that both the topics selected and the sequence in which they are taught parallel the curricular scope and sequence of the school district or state adopted curriculum for each content area. The curriculum should not be watered-down or simplified to the point where it is no longer appropriate for the cognitive level of students. To be most effective, a content-based ESL curriculum should encompass the sequence and major scope areas of the standard grade-level curriculum. Specific topics can be adjusted for students whose previous schooling has been interrupted and who are therefore not at grade level in their native language. (See Chapter 11 for a discussion of adapting CALLA for educationally delayed and pre-literate students.) As with any instructional program, teachers should discover what students already know about a subject and then build on this previous knowledge by providing them with experiences that develop new concepts, expand previous ones, and trace relationships between concepts.

PROCEDURES

Students need to learn procedures in the content areas. Students need to acquire the skills and processes (procedural knowledge) that will help them actively apply the concepts or information base (declarative knowledge) in these subjects. ESL students need to not only learn important information in different content areas, but also how to use this information procedurally. This means using information in a variety of ways, including oral and written observation, description, classification, interpretation, and evaluation. This use of procedural knowledge leads to active use and application of declarative knowledge in different content areas and diminishes the importance of mere recitation of facts. We believe that CALLA teachers can provide a balance between declarative and procedural knowledge by including extensive hands-on and interactive experiences for students that go far beyond the acquisition of subject-specific vocabulary and factual knowledge.

MOTIVATION

Content is motivating. Content-based ESL is not only important for developing academic language skills, but is also inherently more interesting to many students than classes which focus on language only. Content areas such as science, mathematics, social studies, and literature present numerous topics related to a variety of personal interests. ESL students can be motivated not only by the topics presented but also by knowing that they are developing the concepts and skills associated with these subjects, in other words, that they are actually doing "real" schoolwork instead of merely learning English. ESL teachers have also reported increased personal motivation as they rediscover areas of knowledge outside their own field of specialization.

LEARNING STRATEGIES

Content learning requires learning strategies. Students in a content-ESL program like CALLA are faced with a formidable task: learning academic content *and* learning academic language at the same time. Both aspects of learning can be facilitated by the application of appropriate learning strategies. For learning content, students should use learning strategies such as elaboration, or associating their prior knowledge with new information to be learned. They should also learn how to take notes and organize content information to be learned. Students need to learn how to recognize and capitalize on their own approaches to learning and how to evaluate the degree of success of their learning strategies. (Chapter 4 describes different categories of learning strategies and provides guidelines for learning strategy instruction.)

Why Teach Content?

- Subject-area concepts and relationships provide a foundation for learning grade-level information in important subjects.
- Students can practice skills and processes needed in the content areas.
- Content is more motivating than language alone.
- Content provides a context for learning and applying learning strategies.

How to Select Content

ESL teachers cannot and should not attempt to teach all of the academic curriculum for native English-speaking students. To do so would merely replicate the grade-level curriculum. Without special language support, a content-ESL curriculum would be quite similar to a submersion model in which ESL students are expected to "sink or swim" in a classroom designed for native English speakers. In a content-ESL program the CALLA ESL teacher carefully selects the high priority topics and skills from the curriculum for native English speakers and integrates them into lessons that develop both academic language proficiency and learning strategies. Selection is the key, and depth—rather than breadth—is the objective.

The selection process requires an understanding of the curriculum for different content areas at grade levels prior to and after the current grade-level placements of particular ESL students. For example, ten and eleven-year-old ESL students in intermediate-level ESL classes need to learn about the major concepts and skills explored in the first four to five years of elementary school instruction in content areas such as science, mathematics, social studies, and literature. Students need to understand the most important concepts, practice the major skills and processes, and learn to use the language associated with these concepts and processes to prepare them for the content of the all-English curriculum.

CONTENT TEACHERS

Content teachers are important resources for content selection. Content specialist teachers have extensive knowledge about their subject areas and are also experienced in effective ways of presenting content-specific material. In addition, the content teacher knows what prior knowledge and skills are needed before introducing particular topics. ESL teachers should meet with grade-level content teachers to discuss aspects of the local curriculum students should know upon entering the grade-level classroom. Content teachers should be asked how they select content. Are they guided by a curriculum framework? Do they rely mainly on textbooks for content selection, and if so, do they try to cover an entire textbook or select certain topics from it? Do they choose content based on their own experience in assessing the needs and interests of students? Content teachers may use a combination of approaches to content selection. In any case, ESL teachers can benefit from the advice of content experts.

CURRICULUM

State and local curriculum frameworks are another source of assistance. These frameworks or guides provide a description of both the scope and sequence for a particular subject and the major topics studied at different grade levels. Study of curriculum frameworks will reveal which topics and skills are reviewed and elaborated in succeeding grade levels. A topic studied over various grade levels is clearly a high priority topic that should be included in the content-ESL curriculum.

TEXTBOOKS

Grade-level textbooks provide information about the scope of content topics and a sequence in which to present them. It is important to study content textbooks over several grade levels in order to understand how the same topic is repeated and presented in greater depth at higher grade levels to accommodate students' cognitive development. The sequencing of content in textbooks is also worth studying because of the insight it provides into the structure of the discipline. While many textbooks are still based on traditional sequences and emphasize the learning of factual knowledge, some newer textbooks take a thematic approach to knowledge organization and suggest process-oriented activities to help students understand new concepts and relationships. Textbooks that make explicit the linkages between different topics within a content area and even between content areas are valuable resources for content-ESL teachers in selecting content topics with wide applications. Similarly, suggestions in textbooks for hands-on experiences can help ESL teachers plan activities for students to practice procedures designed to develop their understanding of the content presented.

CURRICULUM ANALYSIS

An analysis of the curriculum can help the CALLA teacher select and organize content. Table 2.1, a Curriculum Analysis Form, is a sample that can be used to record information derived from the content specialist teacher, the curriculum framework, and the grade-level textbooks. For *Content Area,* indicate the subject (e.g. science, mathematics, social studies, literature). *Unit Topics* are the high priority topics selected in consultation with the content teacher and through examination of curriculum frameworks and textbooks. Use a separate form to record each Unit Topic. For each unit topic indicate the *Grade Level(s)* at which the topic is presented.

In the seventeenth century, Isaac Newton (1642–1727) suggested a different explanation. He believed that as long as the forces on an object are balanced, the object does not change its motion. This tendency of an object to resist changes in its motion is called the **inertia** (ih-NER′-shuh) of the object. Because of inertia, an object at rest tends to stay at rest. Because of inertia, a moving object tends to move in a straight line at constant speed. Changes in motion can take place only if the forces on an object are unbalanced. This is Newton's first law of motion. An unbalanced force is needed to change the motion of an object.

Figure 3-14. How did the early Greek philosophers explain why a rolling cart soon stops? How did Newton explain it?

from *Introduction to Physical Science.* © Addison-Wesley Publishing Co.[2] (Middle School)

Objects Resist Change in Motion

You have learned that a force is needed to make an object move. You have also learned that a force is needed to slow down or stop a moving object. These forces are needed because of a certain property that all matter has. The property is called inertia (in UR shuh). **Inertia** causes all matter that is moving to stay in motion. It also causes all matter that is not moving to stay at rest.

If you have ridden in a car, you have probably experienced inertia. When a car quickly starts to move, you may have had the feeling of being pushed back in the seat. Your body had the tendency to stay at rest while the car started to move forward. The motion of the car caused the car seat to push forward against your motionless body.

from *Addison-Wesley Science.* © Addison-Wesley Publishing Co.[1] (Elementary)

Important content topics are studied more than once. For example, *inertia* is a topic in elementary, middle school, and high school textbooks.

Important Terms

law of inertia
Newton's first law

Fig. 3-4 Objects at rest tend to remain at rest.

Within a year of Galileo's death, Isaac Newton was born. In 1665, at the age of 23, Newton developed his famous laws of motion. They replaced the Aristotelian ideas that had dominated the thinking of the best minds for nearly 2000 years. This chapter covers the first of Newton's three laws of motion. The other two are covered in the next two chapters.

Newton's first law, usually called the **law of inertia**, is a restatement of Galileo's idea.

> Every object continues in its state of rest, or of motion in a straight line at constant speed, unless it is compelled to change that state by forces exerted upon it.

from *Conceptual Physics.* © Addison-Wesley Publishing Co.[3] (High School)

Table 2.1

CURRICULUM ANALYSIS FORM

Content Area ______________________ Unit Topic ______________________

Grade Level(s) ____

Major Concepts and Relationships:

1. ____
2. ____
3. ____
4. ____

Skills and Processes:

1. ____
2. ____
3. ____

Prerequisite Knowledge (Concepts and Skills):

1. ____
2. ____
3. ____
4. ____
5. ____

Curriculum Source(s):

1. ____
2. ____
3. ____

English Proficiency Level ____

Next, identify the *Major Concepts/Relationships* that will be addressed in the unit. An example of a concept is: Rocks are classified as igneous, sedimentary, or metamorphic, depending on how they were formed. An example of a chain of relationships is: Rocks are broken into small pieces by water, wind, and glaciers. The small pieces of rock mix with dead plants and animals to form soil. Soil provides mineral and water for plants. Animals need plants for food.

In the next part of the Curriculum Analysis Form, identify the *Skills and Processes* that students will need to understand the Unit Topic. For example, students might need to observe, describe, and identify different types of rocks. Or they might need to conduct an experiment in which they record what happens when plants are grown in different types of soil.

Identifying *Prerequisite Concepts* and Skills for a specific topic is important because some necessary prior knowledge may have to be taught before students can work successfully on the Unit Topic.

Finally, indicate the *Source* of curriculum information (content teacher, curriculum framework, and/or textbooks) and the English Proficiency Level needed for students to participate in the Unit Topic.

STUDENT INTERESTS

Students should be offered some options in what they study. Having prepared an outline of high priority content topics, the CALLA teacher should next consider students' personal interests and motivation. As mentioned earlier, depth is preferable to breadth in providing content learning experiences for students. Not every topic has to be covered, and not every student has to study exactly the same topics. Rather than attempt to cover a great deal of content, the teacher should provide opportunities for students to discover content which they find personally interesting and rewarding. For example, in a unit on the American Revolution, individual students could choose one particular revolutionary hero or heroine for in-depth study. Students choosing the same person could then work together on a group project to find out about the life and contributions of their hero, then develop a group oral or written report to share with the rest of the class. When students are allowed options in choosing what to study, they experience a higher level of motivation and a greater degree of personal involvement in learning.

How to Select Content

- ❖ Ask content teachers to help select high priority topics and skills for the grade level.
- ❖ Study curriculum frameworks to see how topics selected are sequenced and reentered over several grades.
- ❖ Read my school's adopted textbooks for different subjects—for this grade level plus lower and higher grades.
- ❖ Identify major components for each content topic.
- ❖ Allow students to select some content topics for in-depth study.

How to Teach Content

The way in which content is taught in grade level classrooms varies widely and often depends as much on the individual style of the teacher as the nature of the discipline. For example, in a history classroom students might be participating rather noisily in a class discussion, while a mathematics classroom across the hall may be totally silent as students work quietly on solving problems. In this section we suggest a variety of ways in which CALLA teachers can make content more relevant and accessible to students learning English.

ACTIVITIES

Content should be taught as experiences rather than merely as facts. Instead of being drilled on content vocabulary and facts, students should be provided with opportunities to understand new information and practice new skills within meaningful contexts, and then to apply the information and skills to their own experiences. Cooperative learning and other types of hands-on group activities are particularly effective in providing experiential learning opportunities.

PRIOR KNOWLEDGE

All new information needs to be linked to students' relevant prior knowledge. The link between what students already know and what they are to learn should be made explicit so that students understand that they are building on knowledge frameworks acquired through prior schooling and life experiences, even if these were acquired through another language and a different cultural context. Teachers can help students activate their prior knowledge through brainstorming discussions about the lesson topic, semantic mapping or other graphic organizers, or a cooperative activity in which they have to draw on their prior knowledge. Deliberately activating students' prior knowledge is important because teachers often *think* they know what the linkages are between students' prior knowledge and the new topic, and provide what they believe is the prior knowledge students need. This approach misses the point, which is that students need to make their own linkages between their prior knowledge and the topic being studied.

TECHNICAL VOCABULARY

Teach the major vocabulary for each content area. Technical vocabulary is important because in many cases a word represents an important concept or relationship. For example, *democracy* represents a number of important concepts in the study of history and government. Similarly, understanding a term like *branches of government* requires not only the identification of the functions of each branch, but also the relationships between them. When presenting and explaining new information teachers should use appropriate technical vocabulary, providing paraphrases, definitions, and examples to clarify meanings.

LEARNING STYLES

Students learn in different ways. Some students learn best by seeing information visually, whether as a written text, pictures, or diagrams. Other students learn best by listening to the teacher or to other students. Many students learn best through concrete experiences, such as manipulating objects or equipment, building models, or representing information through art or drama. In order to address these different student learning styles, the teacher should make use of visual, auditory, and kinesthetic means of presenting new content. Whenever possible, these different types of input should be combined so that students have multisensory experiences with the new content. It is particularly important that students not be asked to rely only on reading for new content presentation. Reading about the new information is most effective with students acquiring English after the information has been previewed orally and experientially. When presenting content information orally, teachers should make certain that their language is comprehensible to students. Comprehensibility of language input is enhanced when teachers use simple and unambiguous language, define and provide examples of new technical vocabulary, provide visual cues that illustrate the concepts presented, and relate the new concepts to experiences familiar to the students.

OVERVIEWS

Provide students with an overview of the content topic to be studied. Overviews provide students with a general understanding of major points that they will be studying and how these points are interrelated. However, do not present large chunks of information at a time. Intersperse practice activities with the presentation of information so that students have an opportunity to use and think about the new information. For example, students can work in groups to answer questions, write

Students need to make their own linkages between their prior knowledge and the topic being studied.

summaries, or make diagrams about the new information after each presentation of new content. This allows them to select and organize major concepts to be remembered.

QUESTIONING

Model higher-order thinking skills. Teachers can show students how to ask and answer higher-level questions about the content being studied. Higher-level questions ask students to speculate, predict, synthesize, and make judgments about the content material they are learning, rather than merely recall facts. For example, when studying a unit on animal species that are extinct and today's endangered species, the teacher could show students drawings of several imaginary animals, each with different characteristics. The teacher could ask students to study these characteristics (such as habitat, food, locomotion, reproduction, enemies, defenses) and answer these higher-level questions:

> "Given each of these animal's characteristics, which animal will probably become extinct first? Why? Which animal is most likely to survive? Why?"

These types of questions require students to use their prior knowledge and understanding of what is being studied in the unit to express their thoughts and insights about important issues and problems. Teachers not only ask higher-level questions, but also model higher-order thinking, thus making their own thinking visible. This helps students develop their own ability to think about the content they are studying at higher levels than recall or information, and provides a context that is conducive to making the CALLA classroom a learning community.[4]

TEACHER MONITORING

Constantly monitor students' comprehension of the content. The teacher can monitor comprehension with oral and written questions, exercises, checklists, observation scales, and performance measures. (See Chapter 5 for guidelines on monitoring student progress.)

STUDENT MONITORING

Teach students to monitor their own comprehension. When students monitor their comprehension, they know when they are not understanding and can ask questions to resolve their comprehension difficulties. In monitoring their own learning, students should compare new information with their prior knowledge and correct any misconceptions they may have had at the beginning of the lesson or unit. Students should set learning goals and monitor whether or not their efforts at learning are successful. Various techniques can be used to help students restructure their knowledge in this way. An example of a knowledge-restructuring technique is K-W-L.[5] In this technique, students first list what they already *know* and what they *want* to find out about a topic. After completing their study of the topic, students document what they have *learned*, which provides them with an opportunity to compare their new knowledge with their prior understanding.

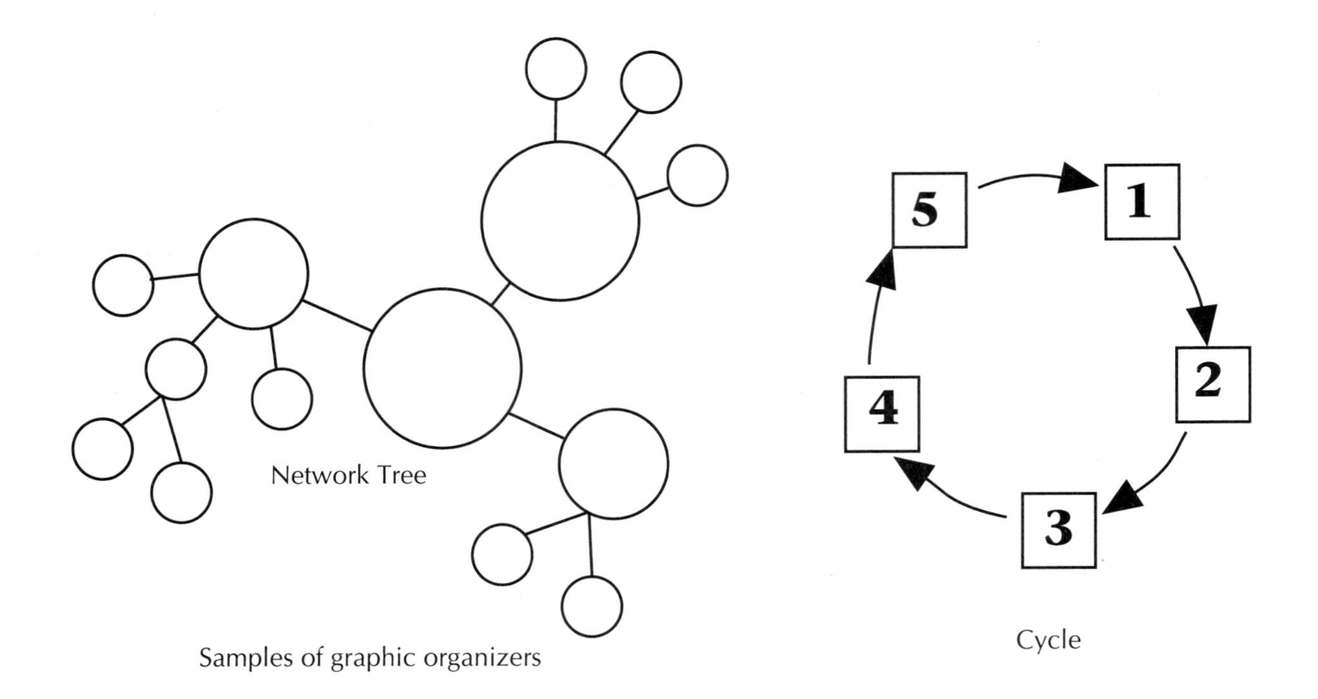

Samples of graphic organizers

GRAPHIC ORGANIZERS

Teach students to use graphic organizers. Graphic organizers, or schematic representations of information, can help students understand and remember content information.[6] Types of graphic organizers are semantic webs, spider maps, Venn diagrams, timelines, T-Lists, flow charts, story maps, and charts of various kinds. Graphic organizers can be used by students to record their prior knowledge about a topic and later add to or revise that knowledge as they encounter new information. When students are listening or reading for information, they can write down the main ideas on a graphic organizer. When completed, the graphic organizer becomes an integrated summary of the content presented in the lesson or unit, and can then be used as a study guide. Graphic organizers can also be used by students to reflect on and evaluate what they have learned. Similarly, graphic organizers can be used to organize ideas and information that are to be written about or presented orally.

RESOURCES

Give students access to a variety of content resources in your classroom. Grade-level textbooks, library books, articles, pictures, software, and realia can be used as reference tools by students as they work on projects and reports. Students should be shown how to locate specific information in such resource materials even if their ability to comprehend the entire text is limited. Using resource materials helps students develop and extend their knowledge.

LEARNING STRATEGIES

Teach learning strategies overtly. Students studying content-ESL need strategies to help them learn both content and academic language. In Chapter 4 we describe how strategy instruction can help students learn content and language more effectively.

Guidelines for Teaching Content

- Provide hands-on and cooperative experiences.
- Start by linking the lesson topic to students' prior knowledge.
- Teach and have students use technical vocabulary appropriate to the content subject.
- Address different student learning styles: use visual, auditory, and kinesthetic means.
- Follow a general overview of the lesson or unit with new information in chunks; include active practice.
- Show students how to ask and answer higher-level questions about content.
- Monitor students' comprehension on an on-going basis.
- Teach students how to "know when they don't know"—and what action to take.
- Show students how to use graphic organizers to identify prior knowledge, prepare study guides, and restructure prior knowledge.
- Provide books, articles, and other resources on content topics; teach students how to use them.
- Provide explicit instruction in learning strategies for understanding, remembering, and using content.

Application Activities

The purpose of these activities is for teachers to develop an understanding of school content subjects and to demonstrate this understanding by identifying curriculum objectives, observing grade-level classes, analyzing the subject matter concepts in sample textbooks, and developing activities that focus on authentic academic content.

1. Refer to Table 2.2, Declarative and Procedural Knowledge in Content Subjects. Work with a colleague on this activity. Discuss each content objective and decide whether each objective calls for mainly declarative knowledge, procedural knowledge, or both. Write your reason(s) in the WHY? column. Then discuss your answers with another pair of teachers.

2. Find a school district or state curriculum framework in your school or university library. Select a topic in one content area and use the Curriculum Analysis Form (Table 2.1) to identify the topic's major concepts and skills, the prerequisite prior knowledge, and the appropriate grade and English proficiency level.

Table 2.2

DECLARATIVE AND PROCEDURAL KNOWLEDGE IN CONTENT SUBJECTS

Directions: Select one person to be the recorder. Discuss each instructional objective for different content areas. Decide if the objective calls for predominantly declarative knowledge, predominantly procedural knowledge, or for an integration of both. The recorder writes the group's decisions and reasons in the appropriate columns.

INSTRUCTIONAL OBJECTIVE: WHAT THE STUDENT CAN DO	DECLARATIVE?	PROCEDURAL?	BOTH?	WHY?
Science				
Name parts of body.				
Classify living things.				
State differences between physical and chemical changes.				
Conduct an experiment.				
Mathematics				
Regroup in subtraction.				
Recite multiplication tables to 10.				
Solve word problem by making a table.				
Find area of a triangle.				
Social Studies				
Read a map.				
Identify events in Civil Rights Movement.				
Identify three branches of U.S. government.				
Write a report about Native Americans.				
Literature and Composition				
Name author of *"The Raven."*				
Read and retell a folk tale.				
Write autobiography.				
Copy words from board.				

CHAPTER 3

Academic Language Development in CALLA

Overview

The second component of the CALLA model: academic language skills (listening, speaking, reading, writing) can be developed as the need for them emerges from the content.

What is Academic Language?

Language Functions
Thinking Skills

Why Teach Academic Language?

Used in Content Subjects
Learned in School
Teacher Expectations
Develops Thinking
Learning Strategies

How to Select Academic Language

Content Classrooms
Content Textbooks
Activities
Student Interest

How to Teach Academic Language

Teacher Modeling
Student Input
Listening
Oral Language
Speaking
Reading and Writing
Thinking Skills
Learning Strategies

CHAPTER 3 ACADEMIC LANGUAGE DEVELOPMENT IN CALLA

WHILE CONTENT FORMS THE BASIS FOR THE CURRICULUM OF A CALLA CLASSROOM, language skills also need to be developed in every lesson. In grade-level content classes, students need to be able to understand the teacher's explanations, discuss what is being learned, read for different purposes, and write about their learning. We call this type of language **academic language**, the language that is used by teachers and students for the purpose of acquiring new knowledge and skills. Academic language differs in many ways from **social language**, the language that is used for the purpose of interaction in social settings. While both aspects of language are present in grade-level classrooms, the emphasis on academic language increases each year as students progress to higher grades.

What is Academic Language?

Academic language is more difficult and takes longer to learn than social language. According to Cummins,[1] two factors affect language comprehension: context and cognitive complexity. Language that takes place in a here-and-now context that has many non-verbal cues to meaning and that provides opportunities for interacting with others is easier to understand than language that is decontextualized, or without such non-verbal and interactive supports. The cognitive complexity of the information and the task for which language is used also affects comprehension. Language used for simple, familiar information on a task is much easier to understand than language used to impart new and complicated information. Because of its interactive nature, most social language involves contexts which facilitate comprehension. Social language also typically deals with fairly uncomplicated topics that are familiar to the speakers. Academic language, on the other hand, may be less interactive and may provide limited context clues to assist comprehension. Academic language has very specific purposes, including imparting new information, describing abstract ideas, and developing students' conceptual understanding. These purposes are cognitively demanding, thus increasing the comprehension difficulties students experience.

The identification of academic language is an inexact science, most probably because it is closely intertwined with academic content. In our view, academic language consists primarily of the language *functions* needed for authentic academic content. Academic language functions are the tasks that language users must be able to perform in the different content areas. These differ from social interactive language functions. For example, a social language function is greeting or addressing another person. Sub-categories of *greeting* are greeting a peer, a superior, or a subordinate, and making the greeting either formal or informal. On the other hand, academic language involves using language functions such as identifying and describing content information, explaining a process, analyzing and synthesizing concepts, justifying opinions, or evaluating knowledge. In many classrooms academic language tends to be unidirectional: the teacher and textbook impart information and students demonstrate their comprehension by answering oral and written questions. But academic language can also be interactive. Teachers and students can discuss new concepts, share analyses, and argue about values in both teacher-student and student-student interactions. In CALLA classrooms academic language is developed interactively.

LANGUAGE FUNCTIONS

Language functions needed in the grade-level academic classroom include explaining, informing, justifying, comparing, describing, classifying, proving, debating, persuading, and evaluating. Most of these functions are necessary in all content areas. For example, in order to *explain* how a word problem in mathematics was solved, a student needs to organize the explanation so that it communicates the desired message in a mathematically appropriate way. On the other hand, in order to *justify* a conclusion about the values of democracy as a form of government, a student might need to analyze the important features of democracy and compare them to other types of government. In this instance, academic language is used to justify values in one culture and to analyze different values in another. In science, students might have to *justify* a conclusion from an experiment that requires them to analyze and reject alternative hypotheses.

THINKING SKILLS

To accomplish these functions successfully with academic content requires the use of both lower-order and higher-order thinking skills. Examples of lower-order thinking skills for content include recalling facts, identifying vocabulary, and making definitions. Higher-order thinking skills involve using language to analyze, synthesize, and evaluate. The overlap in terminology used for thinking skills and for language functions (e.g., informing, explaining, analyzing, drawing conclusions, evaluating) suggest a close relationship between language functions and levels of thinking skills. The language functions needed for content activities requiring lower-order thinking skills can usually be expressed with simple grammatical structures. For example, if students are learning factual information about the geography of the United States, they will probably use the language function of *describing,* which can be expressed with simple sentences such as: *California is on the Pacific Ocean. Colorado is a mountainous state. Washington, D.C. is the capital of the United States.* On the other hand, content activities requiring higher-order thinking skills often involve both more complex language and larger chunks of language. For example, if a teacher asks students to discuss or write about how geography affected the lives of Native Americans in the Southwest compared with Native Americans in the Northeast, more complex and more extensive language is called for. The language function needed is *analyzing* and (perhaps) *comparing.* To express their ideas students need not only appropriate vocabulary, but must also take command of a variety of grammatical structures and discourse features to organize and explain their ideas.

In our view, academic language can be best identified by describing the language functions and the level of the thinking skills needed to engage in specific content activities. Thus discrete language elements such as vocabulary, grammatical structures, spelling, and pronunciation are integrated into the language functions used in the content activity, not taught as separate components. Integrative language skills are needed to carry out the linguistic functions of content subjects.

Table 3.1
Academic Language Functions

Academic Language Function	Student Uses Language to:	Examples
1. Seek Information	observe and explore the environment; acquire information; inquire	Use *who, what, when, where,* and *how* to gather information
2. Inform	identify, report, or describe information	Recount information presented by teacher or text, retell a story or personal experience
3. Compare	describe similarities and differences in objects or ideas	Make/explain a graphic organizer to show similarities and contrasts
4. Order	sequence objects, ideas, or events	Describe/make a timeline, continuum, cycle, or narrative sequence
5. Classify	group objects or ideas according to their characteristics	Describe organizing principle(s), explain why A is an example and B is not
6. Analyze	separate whole into parts; identify relationships and patterns	Describe parts, features, or main idea of information presented by teacher or text
7. Infer	make inferences; predict implications; hypothesize	Describe reasoning process (inductive or deductive) or generate hypothesis to suggest causes or outcomes
8. Justify and Persuade	give reasons for an action, decision, point of view; convince others	Tell why A is important and give evidence in support of a position
9. Solve Problems	define and represent a problem; determine solution	Describe problem-solving procedures; apply to real life problems and describe
10. Synthesize	combine or integrate ideas to form a new whole	Summarize information cohesively; incorporate new information into prior knowledge
11. Evaluate	assess and verify the worth of an object, idea, or decision	Identify criteria, explain priorities, indicate reasons for judgement, confirm truth

What is Academic Language?

- More difficult and takes longer to learn than social language.
- Consists primarily of the language functions needed for authentic academic content.
- Requires the use of both lower-order and higher-order thinking skills.

Why Teach Academic Language?

There are at least five reasons for focusing on academic language skills in the content-ESL classroom. First, for ESL students the ability to use academic language effectively is a key to success in the grade-level classroom. Second, academic language is not usually learned outside of the classroom setting. Third, grade-level teachers may assume that all of their students already know appropriate academic language, when, in fact, former ESL students in their classes have often only acquired social language skills. Fourth, academic language provides students with practice in using English as a medium of thought. Fifth, students may need assistance in using learning strategies with academic language, just as they do with content knowledge and skills. Reasons for teaching academic language skills in the ESL class are discussed in this section.

USED IN CONTENT SUBJECTS

Students need to know how to use academic language. An important difference between the language classroom and classrooms where other academic subjects are taught is that language itself is the focus of study in the language classroom, whereas language is used functionally as a means of learning about the subject in other academic subjects. In content classrooms academic language is used by the teacher and in instructional materials to present and explain new information. Students then use academic language for both lower and higher-order thinking skills as they listen, read, discuss, and write. In speaking, for example, they answer questions, explain problem solutions, describe observations, and discuss causes. In writing they use academic language to write about the content they are learning. In listening and reading as well, academic language is used to identify and comprehend new concepts. In the academic classroom, language is used as a means of communicating, analyzing, synthesizing, and evaluating information gained from listening, reading, and engaging in learning experiences of many kinds.

LEARNED IN SCHOOL

Academic language is best acquired in the classroom. Native English speakers learn how to understand and use academic language gradually as they progress through the grades, so that most have developed age-appropriate academic language fluency by upper elementary and secondary grade levels. Non-native English speakers, on the other hand, have often had far fewer years in which to develop academic language skills, so that they may lag behind their native English-speaking classmates in this aspect of language development. Students learning English as a new language can develop substantial fluency in social and survival language through exposure to

Academic language differs from social language.

and interaction with an English-speaking community. But while their exposure to social language in their communities may account for a considerable part of each day, their exposure to academic language is limited to academic subjects at school. In fact, their exposure to academic language may be quite limited if their ESL classes do not include academic language development. Furthermore, academic language requires different functional uses of language, which involve both lower and higher-order thinking skills. This is why CALLA classrooms include a strong academic language component.

TEACHER EXPECTATIONS

Grade-level teachers expect their students to be able to use academic language appropriately. When ESL and former ESL students are fluent in social language and appear to have no difficulty in conversing with teachers and other students, the non-language specialist may find it difficult to understand why the same students are encountering serious problems in functioning successfully in content classrooms. Grade-level teachers may have unrealistic assumptions and expectations about former ESL students in their classrooms. This problem can be alleviated at least partially by including substantial practice in academic language skills while students are still in the ESL program so that they are better prepared for transition into grade-level classrooms.

DEVELOPS THINKING

Academic language fosters thinking. When students listen and read to acquire new information and understanding, and when they speak and write to express their thoughts, interpretations, and judgements about what they are learning, they are using language as a medium for thinking. Academic language skills are an integral part of higher-level thinking. For example, in Bloom's Taxonomy, the higher levels of thinking involve analysis, synthesis, and evaluation of information;[2] academic language is needed to explore these higher levels, that is, to analyze, synthesize, and evaluate what is being learned in different content areas. Other analyses of thinking skills also imply the use of academic language. The Dimensions of Thinking framework includes the core thinking skills of focusing, information-gathering, remembering, organizing, analyzing, generating, integrating, and evaluating information.[3] While these thinking skills are not presented hierarchically, as in Bloom, they do include both lower-order and higher-order thinking skills and require not only content-related vocabulary but also academic language functions.

LEARNING STRATEGIES

Academic language provides a focus for learning strategies instruction. The acquisition of academic language, like the acquisition of content knowledge, can be greatly facilitated by the use of learning strategies. Students trying to master the complexities of academic language are generally more than willing to learn strategies for tasks such as reading and remembering information in a social studies text or learning science terminology. A number of effective strategies for vocabulary development, listening and reading comprehension, and oral and written production have been identified. For example, students can *group* or classify content vocabulary to facilitate recall, or they can *elaborate* their prior knowledge in order to help them understand a text or write a paragraph. Students can also use learning strategies for language functions involving higher-order thinking skills, such as *monitoring* their comprehension, *summarizing* the major ideas in a text, or using *self-evaluation* to assess their level of performance on an academic task. These learning strategies, which are discussed in the next chapter, provide students with assistance in developing academic language competence.

Why Teach Academic Language?

- ❖ Command of academic language is a key to success in the grade-level classroom.
- ❖ Academic language is not usually learned outside the classroom setting.
- ❖ Content classroom teachers may assume that students already have appropriate academic language skills.
- ❖ Academic language promotes higher-level thinking and provides practice in using English as a medium of thought.

How to Select Academic Language

The selection of academic language to include in the CALLA classroom involves identifying both authentic language functions and the language skills needed to carry out these functions or tasks.

How does the CALLA teacher select specific academic language functions to teach? As with selecting content, the selection process for academic language involves learning about the functions of language in grade-level classrooms. Only by understanding the language demands faced by ESL students when they become part of the content classroom can the ESL teacher design instruction that will prepare students for academic study in non-ESL classrooms.

Table 3.2

CLASSROOM OBSERVATION FORM FOR ACADEMIC LANGUAGE

Teacher ______________________ Subject ______________________ Date ________

Grade Level __________Topic ____

Vocabulary

Vocabulary explicitly taught:

____

____

How taught:

____

____

Vocabulary assumed but not taught:____

____

Oral Language

Academic language functions used by teacher (e.g., presenting information, classifying information, demonstrating a process, giving directions):

____

____

Academic language functions used by students (e.g., explaining an answer, justifying viewpoint, describing, discussing):

____

____

Written Language

Used by teacher (e.g., board, overheads, handouts, tests):

____

____

Used by students (e.g., sentences, paragraphs, extended text, fill-in-the-blank, lab reports, research reports):

____

____

Classroom Context

Types of academic print available to students in the classroom:

____

____

Academic audio material available to students in the classroom:

____

____

Software and other sources of academic language in the classroom:

____

____

Instructional Approach

Percentage of teacher talk: ______________________________

Percentage of student talk: ______________________________

Percentage of silent work: ______________________________

Circle instructional techniques observed:

Cooperative Learning	Group/Team Work
Demonstration by teacher	Hands-on Activities
Demonstration by student(s)	Lecture
Individual worksheets	Class discussion

Other:______________________________

____

Additional Comments

____

____

____

CONTENT CLASSROOMS

The ESL teacher can see academic language in action by visiting content classrooms. Classroom observation can be particularly valuable in identifying oral language demands and written assignments. Taking notes on language observed in content classrooms will help guide CALLA lesson plan development. Table 3.2 is an observation form which can aid ESL teachers in selecting important academic language skills to teach in a CALLA classroom. Information recorded on the classroom observation form should be descriptive rather than interpretive. In other words, the ESL teacher should record examples of the type of academic language that occurs in the classroom and describe the instructional techniques observed without making value judgements. The content teacher's permission should be secured before using this or any classroom observation form.

CONTENT TEXTBOOKS

Grade-level textbooks for different content areas can provide information about academic language. Textbooks are a good source of information about technical vocabulary, complex grammatical structures, and discourse organization for different content areas. The academic language in textbooks can be difficult for students in a number of ways. For example, many textbooks carry a heavy load of unfamiliar vocabulary or of familiar vocabulary used in a special way. Unfamiliar grammatical structures such as passive constructions may also increase the difficulty of textbook language. The discourse organization of a textbook may impede comprehension if the text is poorly organized or if it is organized in an unfamiliar way. Other difficulties students may encounter in a content textbook may be related to the content or to lack of learning strategies. If the content presupposes prior knowledge that the student does not have, or makes unwarranted cultural assumptions, the text will be difficult to understand. If students are not proficient in using learning strategies for reading and note-taking, they will find the content text difficult to understand and remember.

The Textbook Analysis Form in Table 3.3 can be used to identify the academic language demands of textbooks that ESL students will be expected to read in the grade-level classroom. ESL teachers can use the form to analyze content textbooks, and this information can guide the selection of language development activities in the CALLA classroom.

ACTIVITIES

The CALLA teacher should select authentic academic language tasks. In a CALLA classroom authentic language tasks are those in which language is used to further the learning of the topics selected for the content-ESL curriculum. As described earlier in this chapter, these are high priority topics selected from the mainstream curriculum in the school. When students work on an authentic language task based on content, they can use language in a variety of integrative ways, as illustrated by the following objectives for a unit on slavery in the United States:

- Discuss prior knowledge about slavery with a group of classmates and write a list of facts known.
- Read information about slavery in the United States.
- Find new vocabulary words in the reading selection and use context clues to guess at meanings.
- Discuss what you have learned about slavery that you did not know before.
- Watch and listen to a videotape about causes of the Civil War.

Table 3.3
TEXTBOOK LANGUAGE ANALYSIS FORM

Content Area______________Textbook Title______________________________

Grade Level ______ Publication Date ________ Chapter/Unit/Pages ______________________

Vocabulary

Essential new vocabulary ______________________________

____

Known vocabulary used in a new way ______________________________

____

Grammatical Structures

New word forms and verb tenses ______________________________

____

New sentence structures ______________________________

____

Other grammatical difficulties ______________________________

____

Discourse Organization

Paragraph organization ______________________________

____

Section organization ______________________________

____

Chapter/unit organization ______________________________

____

Prior Knowledge

Concepts requiring pre-teaching ______________________________

____

Unfamiliar cultural assumptions ______________________________

____

Learning Strategies

Reading strategies ______________________________

____

Note-taking ______________________________

____

Reference skills ______________________________

Map/chart/graph skills ______________________________

Other______________________________

- Use library resources to read for more information about slavery before the Civil War in the United States and about slavery in other countries during the same period.
- Work with a group of classmates to write a report comparing slavery in the United States with slavery in other parts of the world.
- Present an oral report of your research to the class.

These types of language activities utilize an important content topic to develop a variety of language skills embedded in an academic objective: Learning about slavery. Academic language elements addressed include speaking (discussion activities), reading for information, vocabulary (identifying and discussing new words), listening (videotape and oral reports), and writing (report on slavery). Vocabulary development and practice with grammatical structures is embedded in the language task rather than pulled out as a separate decontextualized exercise.

STUDENT INTEREST

Allow students some options in selecting academic language elements and tasks to work on. Instead of deciding which vocabulary students need to learn for a content topic, have students themselves select useful and interesting new words they want to learn. Options for language activities might include choices such as either individual or group book reports, which could be presented either orally or in written form, depending on student preferences. Not every student needs to learn and practice academic language in exactly the same way.

How to Select Academic Language

- ❖ Observe and record language used in content classrooms.
- ❖ Analyze language used in content textbooks.
- ❖ Select authentic language tasks; have students use a variety of language skills and functions to learn, read, talk, write, and think about content topics.
- ❖ Allow students options in selecting academic language to learn and practice.

How to Teach Academic Language

Academic language, as with other types of procedural knowledge, should be taught as a whole rather than segmented into discrete skills. Authentic topics from the content curriculum provide many opportunities for using academic language functionally rather than artificially. In this section we suggest a number of ways in which CALLA teachers can develop academic language through content.

TEACHER MODELING

The teacher should model academic language. Teachers are experts in using academic language, while students learning English as a new language are novices. Experts can help novices by providing them with a model of polished language performance, by showing them how to practice the performance, and by providing feedback on their performance as it gradually becomes more expert. When presenting and explaining new information, teachers should use appropriate technical vocabulary and grammatical structures, if necessary providing paraphrases, definitions, and examples to clarify meanings. Teacher modeling is a powerful incentive for students: when they observe how their teacher uses academic language they will be encouraged to use the same kind of language.

STUDENT INPUT

Give students opportunities to identify the academic language they need to learn. For example, before presenting new information ask students to listen for important *science* (or *mathematics, history, literature*, etc.) words and write down the words as they hear them. Spelling is not important at this point; the purpose in writing down the words is to help students identify content-specific vocabulary by using the learning strategy *selective attention*, which is described more fully in the next chapter. In a similar way, ask students to identify new or confusing grammatical structures as they read content materials. Have them work in groups to discuss and explain their understanding of unfamiliar structures, providing explanations on a "need to know" basis.

The teacher should model academic language.

LISTENING

Provide frequent practice in listening to content information. In grade-level classrooms teachers provide a great deal of basic information orally and expect their students to understand and learn by listening attentively. CALLA teachers can help their students become better listeners by giving them frequent opportunities to practice listening to information in different content areas. These mini-lectures should be modeled on the presentations of grade-level teachers with the addition of features designed to facilitate comprehension. Such comprehension-enhancing features can include pre-listening discussions of the topic, the use of visuals and demonstrations, practice in note-taking and other appropriate learning strategies, and post-listening discussions in which students describe what they understood and what comprehension difficulties they experienced. In addition to teacher presentations, students can also practice academic listening skills by watching videotapes of content teachers presenting information to students in a grade-level classroom. Other useful content topic videotapes can be found in the school's media center or even taped directly from television programs on science, social studies, or other content topics related to the school's curriculum.

ORAL LANGUAGE

Students also need to practice using academic language interactively. Many opportunities should be provided for students to talk about what they are learning with each other. Cooperative learning activities, group projects, and hands-on activities give students a reason to use academic language for functional purposes. For example, when students work together to conduct and then report on a science experiment they need to refer to their materials, observations, procedures, and findings in scientific terms. Similarly, mathematical language will be used when a group of students work together to chart a bar graph of the hours per week that each student spends on homework (or television watching) or when they work jointly on solving a word problem. In social studies groups, of students might work together on making maps, building models, or developing timelines. In literature, a group of students might be responsible for presenting their interpretation of a chapter in a novel to the rest of the class. In writing, students can work cooperatively to read their compositions to each other, make comments, and suggest revisions. All of these types of activities promote the use of oral academic language in authentic contexts.

SPEAKING

Students also need to develop academic speaking skills for responding to the content teacher. In the grade-level classroom students will need to answer teachers' questions, explain a procedure or problem solution, and make oral presentations to a group. CALLA teachers should provide practice opportunities in all content areas for students to explain their answers, ask clarification questions when they do not understand, explain and justify their conclusions, express their own ideas about the information, and present new information to their classmates. Learning these oral academic language functions will help students achieve success in grade-level classrooms.

READING AND WRITING

Reading and writing across the curriculum is another important CALLA goal for academic language development. Many ESL classrooms focus exclusively on reading narratives and writing about personal reactions and experiences. These are impor-

Give students opportunities to explain and justify their conclusions.

tant language arts goals. However, ESL students also need to learn how to read and write in content areas. CALLA encourages reading and writing in every content area. Academic reading and writing are facilitated by a number of learning strategies. For example, *selective attention* to main ideas in a reading passage can increase a student's comprehension. Similarly, *planning* before writing can help a student determine major ideas and sequence in a writing assignment. CALLA students should practice reading science information, mathematics explanations and word problems, maps in geography and narratives in history, and stories, poems, and novels in literature. They should also engage concurrently in writing about what they are learning. In science they may write a lab report, in mathematics they may write word problems for their classmates to solve, in geography they may write descriptions of different areas of the world, in history they may write a research report, and in language arts they may write about their personal reactions to a piece of literature. All of these reading and writing activities are important in developing students' written academic language.

THINKING SKILLS

CALLA teachers should ask students higher-level questions. Higher-level questions are those which ask students to consider reasons, compare alternatives, find similarities and differences, form opinions, and analyze evidence. These kinds of questions ask students to really think, not just regurgitate facts. When students' command of English is limited, teachers may be inclined to pose easily answered questions, such as, "Who was the discoverer of ... ," "What is the capital of ... ," or "When did ... ." These kinds of questions can usually be answered in one or two words, which makes it possible for ESL students to answer correctly by rote. However, rote answers do not require students to engage in the kind of higher-order thinking skills which will enable them to think objectively and creatively. Students should be asked questions which require explanation on a daily basis. For example, in response to the math problem illustrated here, the teacher might ask, "Do you think that Mimi found a good solution to her problem? How else could she have solved the problem? What would have happened?" At first students' answers may be hesitant and their language inaccurate, but with sufficient practice they will be able to express complex thoughts in English.

LEARNING STRATEGIES

Teach students learning strategies to assist their academic language acquisition. Every aspect of academic language learning can be facilitated by using appropriate learning strategies. Students can learn useful strategies for carrying out academic language functions such as informing, explaining, summarizing, synthesizing, and evaluating. Learning strategies can also assist acquisition of discrete language such as academic vocabulary, and integrative language such as listening and reading comprehension, and speaking and writing. In the next chapter we describe specific strategies to use with a variety of language functions and content tasks.

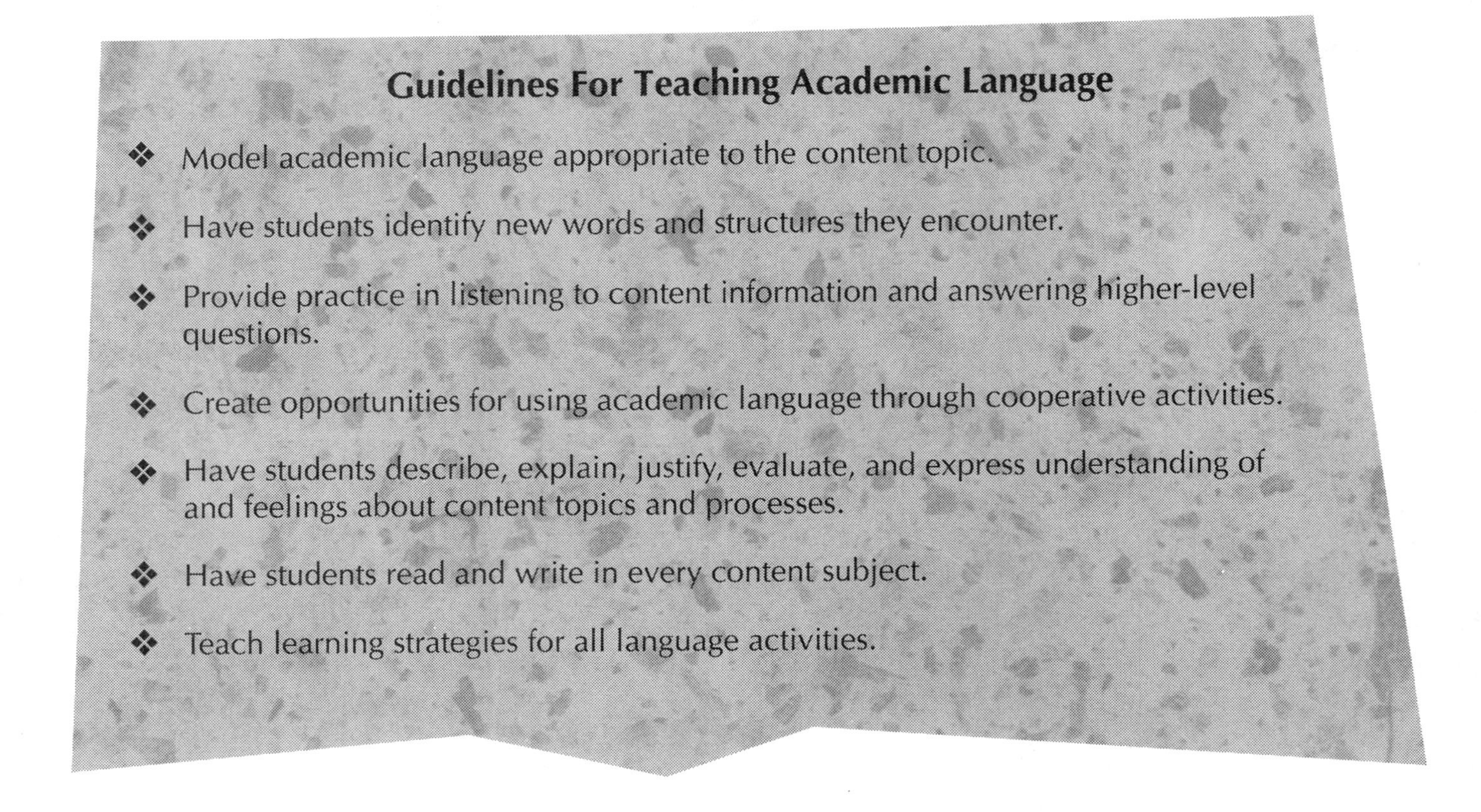

Guidelines For Teaching Academic Language

- Model academic language appropriate to the content topic.
- Have students identify new words and structures they encounter.
- Provide practice in listening to content information and answering higher-level questions.
- Create opportunities for using academic language through cooperative activities.
- Have students describe, explain, justify, evaluate, and express understanding of and feelings about content topics and processes.
- Have students read and write in every content subject.
- Teach learning strategies for all language activities.

Application Activities

The purpose of these activities is for teachers to develop an understanding of the relationship of academic language to curriculum content and higher-level thinking skills. Activities to develop this understanding include observing grade-level classes, analyzing the academic language of sample textbooks, and creating a graphic organizer of the information in this chapter.

1. Arrange to visit a grade-level classroom to observe academic language in use. Use the Classroom Observation Form for Academic Language (Table 3.2) to record your observations. Discuss your observations with grade-level teachers.

2. Borrow a grade-level textbook for a content subject. Work with another teacher to analyze the academic language of two or three pages in the textbook, using the Textbook Academic Language Analysis Form (Table 3.2).
3. Refer to Table 3.1, Academic Language Functions. Work with one or more colleagues to design a content-based activity for science that provides practice with one of the academic language functions identified in the table. Present your activity to the rest of the group.
4. Continue by designing activities for mathematics, social studies, and literature, focusing on a different academic language function for each. If possible, try the activities with students and report on the results.
5. Work with a group of teachers to prepare a graphic organizer that summarizes the major ideas presented in this chapter.

CHAPTER 4
Learning Strategy Instruction in CALLA

Overview

The third and a central component of CALLA is the integration of learning strategies with instruction in academic language and content.

Why Learning Strategies are Important

Theoretical Background
Research on Learning Strategy Effectiveness

Types of Learning Strategies

Metacognitive Strategies
Cognitive Strategies
Social/Affective Strategies

How to Select Learning Strategies

The Curriculum Determines the Strategy
Start With a Small Number of Strategies
Use Tasks of Moderate Difficulty
Choose Strategies With Strong Empirical Support
Use Strategies That Apply to Different Content Domains

How to Teach Learning Strategies

Preparation
Presentation
Practice
Evaluation
Expansion

Using Learning Strategies for Motivation

Expectations of Success
Value of Task
Attribution of Responsibility

CHAPTER 4 LEARNING STRATEGY INSTRUCTION IN CALLA

CENTRAL COMPONENT OF CALLA is the integration of learning strategies with instruction in academic language and content. The basic premise is that students will learn academic language and content more effectively by using learning strategies. That is, students who use strategic approaches to learning will comprehend spoken and written language more effectively, learn new information with greater facility, and be able to retain and use their second language better than students who do not use learning strategies. Accompanying the use of learning strategies, students gain an important perspective on their own learning, see the relationship between the strategies they use and their own learning effectiveness, plan for and reflect on their learning, and gain greater autonomy as a learner. Because learning strategies can be taught, the teacher has an important role in conveying to students the importance of using strategies, defining various strategies and their use with academic tasks, and supporting the students in their efforts to become more strategic, independent, and self-regulated.

Why Learning Strategies are Important

There are two major reasons why we integrate learning strategies into the instruction of academic language and content. The first is the theoretical consistency of learning strategies with the cognitive view of learning which underlies CALLA. The second is the impressive amount of research that supports using learning strategies with academic language and content information.

THEORETICAL BACKGROUND

The cognitive model of learning indicates that learning is an active, dynamic process in which learners select information from their environment, organize the information, relate it to what they already know, retain what they consider to be important, use the information in appropriate contexts, and reflect on the success of their learning efforts.[1]

This type of learning is often conscious and deliberate, although individuals who are highly accustomed to learning in this manner may do so rapidly and without a great deal of immediate awareness of their thoughts. As we noted in Chapter 1, the cognitive model specifies how information is stored in memory and how new information is learned. What is most significant is that the model is able to describe the selection, organization, and other mechanisms that constitute active and dynamic learning processes as well as to indicate why learning sometimes occurs without awareness. Furthermore, the model is able to handle many of the mechanisms involved in second language acquisition and in content learning.

The description of learning strategies hinges on the distinction between declarative and procedural knowledge. Once learned, learning strategies operate just like procedural knowledge. Individuals can have declarative knowledge about a strategy but not be able to apply it effectively without considerable deliberation. Through repeated efforts to apply the strategy with various learning materials, however, the individual can gradually "proceduralize" or learn to use the strategy automatically so that it functions rapidly and without errors with specific tasks. Strategy applications are particularly aided by taking the "high road" to learning by recognizing parallels between new tasks and more familiar tasks on which the strategy has been applied successfully, thereby facilitating transfer. Thus, in the cognitive view of learning, strategies have a prominent role because they represent the dynamic mechanisms underlying learning. Furthermore, learning strategies are totally consistent with the cognitive view and can be described within the cognitive model.

RESEARCH ON LEARNING STRATEGY EFFECTIVENESS

To better understand the mental processes involved in learning, cognitive researchers analyze and describe the performance of expert learners on specific types of tasks and contrast it with how novices approach the same learning activities. We obtain information about strategies by asking individuals to report on the "things they do that help them learn" both retrospectively and concurrently while working on specific tasks.[2] For example, in a content area, individuals might be presented with a math problem and be asked to describe their thoughts as they anticipate and solve the problem. Similarly, they might be presented with a reading passage on which, presumably, they will receive some comprehension questions and be asked to indicate what they do before, during, and after they read to better understand and remember the information.

An identical approach to collecting information on strategy awareness and applications is used with individuals learning a second language. However, in second language acquisition, the questions focus on listening, speaking, reading, and writing in the second language. Students operating at the beginning level of proficiency in the second language may be asked these questions in their native language. Findings from these studies indicate that individuals nominated by their teachers as effective second language learners tend to be more aware of their thought processes, use a richer variety of strategies, and use more appropriate strategies with learning tasks.[3]

Another approach taken in cognitive research on learning strategies is to instruct individuals on the importance and use of specific strategies with various tasks, provide them with opportunities to practice the strategies, and determine whether or not their learning is improved. This research approach has been tried with a number of different kinds of first language tasks, including vocabulary, reading, math, science, and problem solving[4] and with certain second language tasks, including listening and speaking.[5] Results indicate that instruction in learning strategies is effective in producing increased use of strategies and in enhancing learning, and that transfer of strategies can be developed provided that there is ample training for metacognitive awareness of task characteristics and demands.[6] However, there is far less supportive research for learning strategy instruction in second language acquisition than with native language skills in English. Nevertheless, there is little reason to suspect that strategy training would not be as broadly effective with second language tasks as it has been with native language skills. We have accumulated evidence supporting learning strategy instruction with CALLA for mathematics word problems,[7] and will have future studies of CALLA and strategy instruction in science.

Based on the theory and research related to learning strategies, there are four basic propositions that underlie the use of learning strategies in CALLA.

- **Active learners are better learners.** Students who organize and synthesize new information and actively relate it to existing knowledge should have more cognitive linkages to assist comprehension and recall than students who approach each new task by simple rote repetition.

- **Strategies can be learned.** Students who are taught to use strategies and who are given positive experiences where they are applied will learn more effectively than students who have had no experience with learning strategies.
- **Academic language learning is more effective with learning strategies.** Learning academic language in content areas among ESL students should follow the same principles that govern reading and problem solving among native speakers of English.
- **Learning strategies transfer to new tasks.** Learning strategies will be used by students on new tasks that are similar to the learning activities on which they were initially instructed to use learning strategies. Transfer will be facilitated with metacognitive training.

While extensive research evidence supports the first two propositions, and evidence is accumulating for the third,[8] studies are only recently beginning to evolve supporting the fourth proposition. The fourth proposition is based in part on our own and others' observation that strategies for language and content learning are not distinct[9] and in part on our positive experiences in training ESL students to use learning strategies on integrative language tasks.[10] We have made learning strategies instruction a pervasive part of CALLA both to encourage strategy use while the students are still in CALLA, and to encourage strategy use when the students exit to grade-level classes.

Why Learning Strategies are Important

- Strategies represent the dynamic processes underlying learning.
- Active learners are better learners.
- Strategies can be learned.
- Academic language learning is more effective with learning strategies.
- Learning strategies transfer to new tasks.

Types of Learning Strategies

Learning strategies are defined as thoughts or activities that assist in enhancing learning outcomes.[11] Strategies by definition are probably performed with awareness, or else they would not be strategic, although the same mental operations can be performed without awareness once they are proceduralized and have the same beneficial results with learning.

Three broad categories of learning strategies have been proposed in the cognitive literature[12] and in our own research.[13] These types of learning strategies are based in part on theory and in part on the observation that students report using what seem to be executive skills with learning tasks while also using strategies that apply directly to the learning activities. The three types of strategies are as follows:

- **Metacognitive Strategies**—planning for learning, monitoring one's own comprehension and production, and evaluating how well one has achieved a learning objective;

- **Cognitive Strategies**—manipulating the material to be learned mentally (as in making images or elaborating) or physically (as in grouping items to be learned or taking notes); and
- **Social/Affective Strategies**—either interacting with another person in order to assist learning, as in cooperative learning and asking questions for clarification, or using affective control to assist learning tasks.

The application of strategies to learning activities is assisted by what is referred to as metacognitive knowledge,[14] or knowledge of the task characteristics, of one's experiences with similar tasks, and of the strategies one can deploy in learning new information on the task. Metacognitive knowledge involves awareness and understanding of one's own mental processes and approach to learning. This is the basic process that enables using the "high road" to transfer described above.

METACOGNITIVE STRATEGIES

Metacognitive strategies are similar to executive processes that enable one to anticipate or plan for a task, determine how successfully the plan is being executed, and then evaluate the success of the learning and the plan after learning activities have been completed. Specific examples of metacognitive strategies are shown in Table 4.1 along with various types of cognitive and social/affective strategies. The metacognitive strategies include planning, monitoring, and evaluating learning activities. Individuals can plan for a learning activity by using the strategy *directed attention*, or encouraging themselves to attend to the learning task while ignoring distractions, and *selective attention*, or focusing on specific key words, phrases, or types of information in the learning activity. In a writing or speaking activity, a learner can use *organizational planning* by creating an outline or structure that will be followed in a communication. While the learning activity transpires, individuals can use *self-monitoring* to determine whether or not the learning is fulfilling the original learning goals or if they are attending satisfactorily to the task at hand. The usual procedure for doing this is with self-questions asked intermittently about learning progress. At the conclusion of the learning activity, individuals can use *self-evaluation* by checking on their success in accomplishing targets for learning. Metacognitive strategies tend to be independent of specific learning tasks and to have broad applications.

COGNITIVE STRATEGIES

The numerous cognitive strategies shown in Table 4.1 fall into three broad categories: rehearsal, organization, and elaboration strategies.[15] The latter category, elaboration, sometimes refers to a specific strategy, linking new information to prior knowledge, and sometimes is used as a generic category for other strategies, such as *imagery, summarization, inferencing, transfer,* and *deduction*. Unlike metacognitive strategies, which tend to have broad applications, cognitive strategies are often linked to individual tasks. For example, *classification* or *grouping* is often used in learning vocabulary or for organizing concepts (as in science), while *note-taking* and *summarizing* are more often used in listening or reading comprehension. *Inferencing* may be used in learning vocabulary or in reading, since the learner can use intrinsic cues for meaning (e.g., word endings) or extrinsic cues such as the context of meaning in which a word occurs. *Elaboration* of prior knowledge is a cognitive strategy which has applications to all types of content learning, and to listening, speaking, reading, and writing.

Table 4.1
LEARNING STRATEGIES IN THE CLASSROOM

Metacognitive Strategies

STRATEGY NAME	STRATEGY DESCRIPTION	STRATEGY DEFINITION
Planning		
Advance Organization	Preview Skim Gist	Previewing the main ideas and concepts of a text; identifying the organizing principle.
Organizational Planning	Plan what to do	Planning how to accomplish the learning task; planning the parts and sequence of ideas to express.
Selective Attention	Listen or read selectively Scan Find specific information	Attending to key words, phrases, ideas, linguistic markers, types of information.
Self-management	Plan when, where, and how to study	Seeking or arranging the conditions that help one learn.
Monitoring		
Monitoring Comprehension	Think while listening Think while reading	Checking one's comprehension during listening or reading.
Monitoring Production	Think while speaking Think while writing	Checking one's oral or written production while it is taking place.
Evaluating		
Self-assessment	Check back Keep a learning log Reflect on what you learned	Judging how well one has accomplished a learning task.

Cognitive Strategies

STRATEGY NAME	STRATEGY DESCRIPTION	STRATEGY DEFINITION
Resourcing	Use reference materials	Using reference materials such as dictionaries, encyclopedias, or textbooks.
Grouping	Classify Construct graphic organizers	Classifying words, terminology, quantities, or concepts according to their attributes.
Note-taking	Take notes on idea maps, T-lists, etc.	Writing down key words and concepts in abbreviated verbal, graphic, or numerical form.
Elaboration of Prior Knowledge	Use what you know Use background knowledge Make analogies	Relating new to known information and making personal associations.

Table 4.1 (continued)

Cognitive Strategies (continued)

STRATEGY NAME	STRATEGY DESCRIPTION	STRATEGY DEFINITION
Summarizing	Say or write the main idea	Making a mental, oral, or written summary of information gained from listening or reading.
Deduction/Induction	Use a rule/Make a rule	Applying or figuring out rules to understand a concept or complete a learning task.
Imagery	Visualize Make a picture	Using mental or real pictures to learn new information or solve a problem.
Auditory Representation	Use your mental tape recorder Hear it again	Replaying mentally a word, phrase, or piece of information.
Making Inferences	Use context clues Guess from context Predict	Using information in the text to guess meanings of new items or predict upcoming information.

Social / Affective Strategies

STRATEGY NAME	STRATEGY DESCRIPTION	STRATEGY DEFINITION
Questioning for Clarification	Ask questions	Getting additional explanation or verification from a teacher or other expert.
Cooperation	Cooperate Work with classmates Coach each other	Working with peers to complete a task, pool information, solve a problem, get feedback.
Self-Talk	Think positive!	Reducing anxiety by improving one's sense of competence.

SOCIAL/AFFECTIVE STRATEGIES

Social/affective strategies are particularly important in second language acquisition because language is so heavily involved in cooperation and asking questions for clarification. Students learning specific language functions or structures can practice these in cooperative learning settings and obtain feedback from other students on the effectiveness and coherence of efforts to communicate orally or in writing. *Asking questions for clarification* is particularly critical for ESL students because they will so often need to exercise this skill in their grade-level classrooms. Another social/affective strategy, *self-talk*, is useful for students who have any degree of anxiety about learning activities. In second language acquisition, as suggested by the well-known affective filter,[16] many individuals find that anxiety detracts from the attainment of learning objectives. In using self-talk, students reassure themselves through inner speech that they will be able to perform successfully on the task at hand. Their self-talk will be more convincing if they have prior successful experiences with tasks which are similar to the ones they are now encountering and for which they have developed effective learning strategies. *Cooperative learning* and *asking questions for clarification* tend to be useful regardless of the specific learning task, while *self-talk* may work best with tasks on which the student has had some prior experience.

In sum, the three types of learning strategies in combination with metacognitive knowledge can provide learners with a powerful array of techniques that can be used to assist learning. Now we address what teachers can do, first to select strategies and then to teach strategies to students.

Types of Learning Strategies

- ❖ Metacognitive Strategies: used in planning for learning, self-monitoring, and evaluating achievement.
- ❖ Metacognitive Knowledge: understanding one's own learning processes, the nature of the learning task, and the strategies that should be effective.
- ❖ Cognitive Strategies: manipulating the material to be learned through rehearsal, organization, or elaboration.
- ❖ Social/Affective Strategies: interacting with others for learning or using affective control for learning.

How to Select Learning Strategies

Having defined three broad classes of strategies, we now go on to indicate how teachers select one or more strategies to include in instruction. The selection process requires familiarity with the curriculum because strategies that are included in instruction must be valid for the types of activities students work on in classrooms. This will give the students a sense that the strategies are current and are directly linked to important classroom tasks and experiences. The steps in strategy selection are intended to produce a small set of strategies that are highly appealing to students, are teachable, and will readily assist learning.

THE CURRICULUM DETERMINES THE STRATEGY

The first general rule that governs strategy selection is that the strategies are determined by the nature of the instructional task. That is, teachers begin with the language and content goals, objectives, and tasks and then decide on the types of strategies that are appropriate and would be most effective. Basically, the language, content, and task drive the strategy selection. The language and content are often determined by local curriculum guides or frameworks which describe, depending on their specificity, the goals, objectives, and even representative lesson activities. The strategies selected should be compatible with these goals and objectives and with the types of activities and instructional procedures that are recommended in these documents. Not only should the teacher see the strategies as being useful for the local curriculum, but the students should see the strategies as being useful for important classroom activities. The strategies should therefore be seen as part of and essential to the local curriculum.

START WITH A SMALL NUMBER OF STRATEGIES

A second general rule is that teachers should start with a small number of strategies (one or two) for students to learn rather than attempt to introduce a lot of strategies all at once. Some researchers recommend starting with a single strategy, only expanding to others when the one strategy has been thoroughly learned.[17] In our experience there are some strategies that are so supportive of each other that they can be introduced simultaneously, e.g., *activating prior knowledge* and *inferencing*. However, even strategies that are reasonably easy to use or intuitively obvious to teachers will not be so obvious to all students, nor will the ways in which the strategy can be applied to important classroom tasks. Teachers should permit students to feel success with a small number of strategies and then move on to other strategies one at a time. Students will look forward to the next strategy when the one used previously has been so useful. At some point the students can be asked to use strategy combinations or to select a strategy from their repertoire which they find to be most useful with a particular learning activity. To begin with a highly complex strategy or too many strategies for students to learn easily could make students feel that strategies are too difficult to be worth the effort required to learn them.

USE TASKS OF MODERATE DIFFICULTY

A related rule is that the task with which the strategy is used should not be too difficult. If the task is exceedingly difficult, students will not have an opportunity to experience success early and will believe that the strategy is not useful. For example, a reading activity should be manageable and contain at least some material students are already familiar with rather than contain a large amount of new vocabulary with difficult syntax. In our experience, when materials are exceedingly difficult, even the best of strategies cannot overcome the density of the materials and students can too easily become frustrated.[18]

CHOOSE STRATEGIES WITH STRONG EMPIRICAL SUPPORT

Another important guideline in strategy selection is to choose strategies for which there is strong empirical support.[19] We do not believe that it is appropriate to begin otherwise because the teacher would take risks that might not pay off in student motivation and interest. Ideally, the research support for the strategies the teacher selects should be with the type of students to whom the strategy instruction will be applied. This is not always possible with language minority students, since the research has been limited. Nevertheless, we believe that teachers can select strategies for which there has been strong empirical support with native English-speaking students and tailor the strategy to students who are learning English.

USE STRATEGIES THAT APPLY TO DIFFERENT CONTENT DOMAINS

A fifth recommendation is to select a strategy that will prove useful across different content domains.[20] If the strategy is useful for reading comprehension in literature, social studies, and science, students will be more likely to adopt the strategy as a regular part of their repertoire. The reading comprehension strategies mentioned above —*inferring meaning from context, elaboration,* and *summarizing*—exemplify strategies that will be useful across content domains. Students may need fairly extensive instructional support to recognize the usefulness of a strategy across different content areas. *Scaffolding* or providing strong support early when the strategy is introduced and withdrawing support over time is an essential component of a teacher's repertoire for strategy instruction.

In sum, strategy selection requires teachers to use their familiarity with the local curriculum in selecting strategies that can be closely interwoven with the curriculum. The strategies should not be seen by students as something apart from the curriculum but as a natural part of learning in school. They should see the use of strategies as the primary way one participates in learning activities in the classroom and while studying at home. They should also see strategies as something one talks about in the classroom when discussing learning tasks with other students, teachers, and others such as their parents.

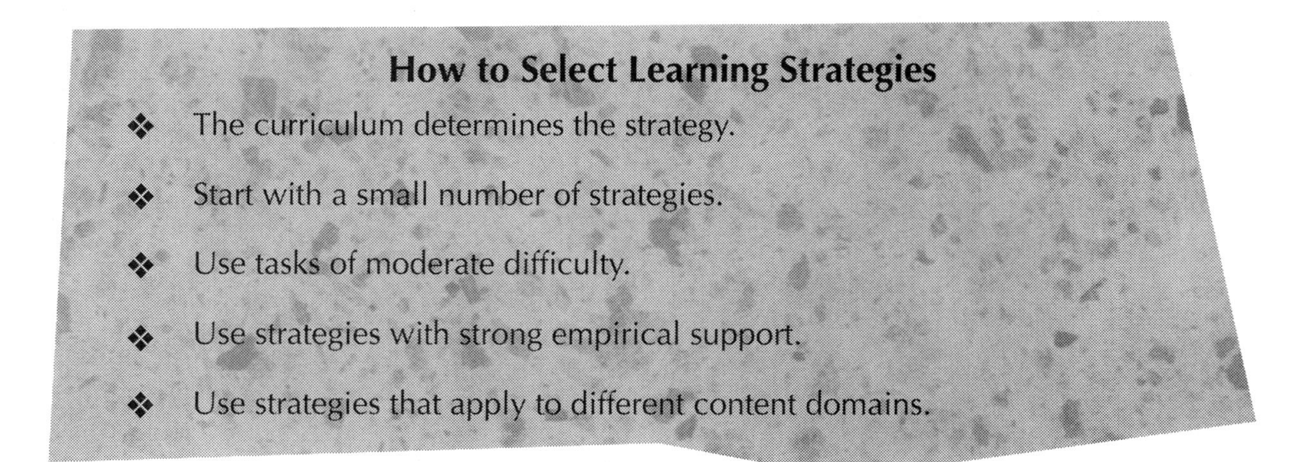

How to Teach Learning Strategies

The most important point to remember about teaching learning strategies is to use proven methods for strategy instruction.[21] The techniques we will describe have been researched extensively with students and have been successful in introducing students to strategies, encouraging their use, and sustaining use and transfer of the strategies over time. There is no reason to use less than the most effective strategy teaching procedures when highly effective ways to introduce strategies are known. We recommend a five-step procedure for strategy instruction that is organized consistent with the five phases of the CALLA instructional sequence: Preparation, Presentation, Practice, Evaluation, and Expansion.

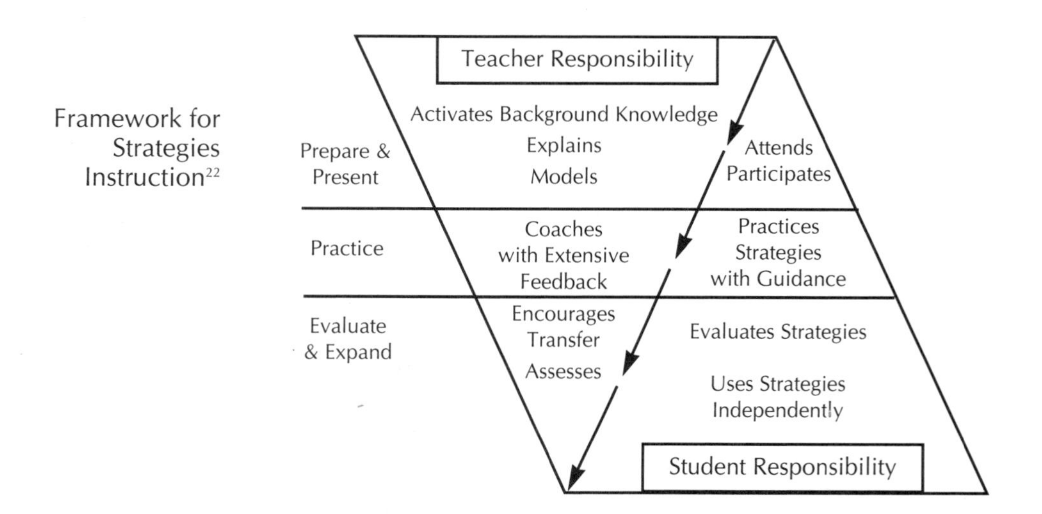

Framework for Strategies Instruction[22]

PREPARATION

The purpose of the Preparation phase is to develop students' awareness that their prior knowledge can be applied to the topic of the unit. Because the focus of these lessons is on learning strategies, that means developing students' awareness of their current strategies, the special techniques that help them learn, and their belief in whether the strategies they currently use are important. It means determining students' beliefs about learning and whether they believe that learning occurs as a result of effort, native intelligence, luck, or the systematic application of strategic techniques. It is during the Preparation phase that teachers encourage metacognitive knowledge, or the awareness of activities which assist in learning a language, the kinds of tasks that are involved, and the importance of having a strategic repertoire to assist in learning. Students may also understand that there is more than one way to learn, and that part of their task as a learner is to determine the learning approach that best suits them individually. They may understand and appreciate strategies by knowing that effective learning results from selection and application of effective strategies, the things that more able students do to help them learn.

There are a number of things teachers can do during the Preparation phase. One activity that will assist students to understand their own strategies and the importance of a strategic approach to learning is to organize students into small groups and ask them how they studied for or learned information in their native language. If the students have had at least some experience in American schools, they can be asked to identify how they learn information in English. Students can compare their strategic approaches in the two languages, determining if there are similarities in the techniques or strategies they use in their native language and in learning English. Each group should prepare a brief oral report to discuss their strategies with the class. Teachers can vary the assignment for each group, suggesting that one group think about the strategies for vocabulary learning, a second group think about strategies that help with following directions, reading a story, reading for content information, writing a description of a personal experience, etc. The tasks should be based on typical activities students have experienced in the classroom. Other possible classroom tasks might include understanding and recalling the main idea and supporting details of a story read aloud to them, asking questions, answering questions, and explaining information. Teachers may wish to include non-classroom tasks as well, depending on the age of the students, such as answering the telephone, initiating a social conversation, and applying for a job. This procedure is very similar to the approach we have used in prior research and which we found very successful in eliciting a variety of different kinds of strategies.[23]

Following the small group discussions, the teacher can direct a full-class discussion of the different strategies students in the various groups report. Teachers should write the strategies students report on the chalkboard, using the exact terms they use to describe the strategies. The discussion should focus on differences in strategies depending on the task and the variation in strategies preferred by different students for the each task. Students can try to evaluate whether some strategies seem preferable to others. If a particular strategy will be introduced during the Presentation phase, the teacher can highlight that strategy in the discussion or probe for whether or not anyone uses that strategy.

A second approach is for the teacher to model "thinking aloud" to identify one's own strategies. The purpose of modeling at this point is to increase student awareness of the strategies they currently use by giving them a tool to identify additional strategies. The teacher can assign small groups a specific language learning task and give them 10-15 minutes to work on the task as a group. The task could entail following directions, reading and understanding a passage, solving a problem, etc. After the students have tried to work on the task for a while, the teacher can model "thinking aloud" while working on the task. In modeling thinking aloud, teachers describe their own metacognitive knowledge of the task, i.e., what the task calls on them to do, of similar tasks they have experienced in the past, and of the strategies that should be useful in learning. Teachers then describe aloud what they are doing as they work on this task themselves, what step-by-step procedure they are following in learning, and how they are determining their success as a learner. The teacher then encourages students in small groups to take turns "thinking aloud" as they work on the task. This type of think aloud activity is particularly useful when students have difficulty in understanding what strategies are and in recalling strategies they have used in the past. As with the first approach, if a particular strategy will be introduced during the Presentation phase, the teacher can highlight that strategy during the discussion, or prompt for that strategy during the discussion.

The effectiveness of small group discussions and teacher modeling as ways to introduce strategies may vary depending on the classroom characteristics. For example, in an ESL classroom that is exclusively language oriented, teachers might model thinking aloud with language-learning tasks independent of content information. In a content ESL or CALLA classroom, teachers might ask students to think aloud while solving a math word problem, while setting up and reporting on a science problem, or while describing the best approach for performing a social studies project. The outcome of these activities should be a heightened awareness by the students of the strategies they currently use and in the connection between strategic effort and learning.

With students who are at the beginning level of English proficiency, teachers may need to teach students special vocabulary that will assist them in discussing their strategies. For example, words like "think," "strategy," and "learn" may require native language translation or the assistance of a peer who is relatively proficient in both languages. The effort to give priority to these vocabulary words in instruction will be well compensated as students begin to discuss more effective approaches to learning.

PRESENTATION

In the Presentation phase, the teacher uses explicit instruction to teach a particular learning strategy and in providing guidance on the use of the strategy. In teaching, the teacher explicitly names the strategy to be learned, indicates how the strategy is used with a specific task, and tells why the strategy is important for learning. This type of instruction increases the students' metacognitive awareness of the task requirements and of the connection between strategy use and learning.

The teacher can begin by refreshing the students' memories about the discussions of strategies which took place during the Preparation phase. The teacher then suggests a name for the strategy. Having a name for the strategy enables the teacher and students to communicate about learning processes for activities in the classroom. The teacher can use the technical name for the strategy that is provided in Table 4.1 if possible, or use a name the students have devised and feel comfortable with.

After having agreed on a name for the strategy, the teacher describes how the strategy is used with specific classroom learning activities. The description should be as complete as possible, identifying each step required to use the strategy, including recognizing why the strategy is appropriate for the task or materials being used. Teacher modeling of the strategy during the Presentation phase is an effective way to demonstrate to students how the strategy can be used. Teachers should describe use of the strategy with more than one example or activity so students see that the strategy is not limited to one specific task. Teachers might caution students that they may need to practice the strategy for a while before it begins to feel comfortable to them.

PRACTICE

The teacher's role in the Practice phase differs depending on the amount of experience students have had with the strategy. Early on in learning a strategy, teachers provide more guidance in strategy use than they do as students become more adept at using a strategy. Scaffolding is a process in which more extensive instructional supports are provided early in learning and gradually withdrawn as the students gain more skill and independence.[24] The teacher initially provides sufficient instructional supports to ensure that the students are learning to use the strategy effectively. For example, in learning to use a *T-List* for note-taking, students often require extensive information about how to identify a main idea, where to place these on the T-List, and how to identify or link supporting details to main ideas. Teachers can provide students with a nearly-completed T-List that has occasional key words missing, such as a specific main idea or a particular detail. Later, as students have gained more skill in using a T-List, teachers can begin to eliminate the word cues for the main ideas or details, until eventually students are presented with a blank sheet of paper on which they will draw their own T-List.

Teachers can provide students with a partially completed T-List

The Eskimos

LISTENING AND TAKING NOTES

Look at the *T-List* below. A *T-List* helps you take notes on information you hear or read.

On a T-List, the main ideas are on the left;	*the details or examples are on the right.*

This *T-List* is about the Eskimos. The main ideas on the left are already complete. You are going to listen to some information about the Eskimos.

- Listen carefully and complete the details on the right.
- When you have finished, read all the information silently.

MAIN IDEAS	DETAILS AND EXAMPLES
A. Early Eskimos crossed land bridge from Asia to America thousands of years ago.	1. Early Eskimos were last group of Asian ______ to cross land bridge. 2. Eskimos did not ______ south. 3. Today Eskimos live in North American polar regions of ______ and ______.
B. Eskimos learned to find food in cold Arctic region.	1. Eskimos hunted sea animals such as ______ and ______. 2. Hunted large ______ animals such as caribou and polar bears.

from: *Language Development Through Content: America: The Early years.* [25]

In the Practice phase, students are given either individual or group assignments in which they have opportunities to use and apply a strategy. The assignments should resemble the type of task on which the strategy was modeled by the teacher or with which the strategy was described in the Presentation phase. If students work independently in applying a strategy, they should be given an opportunity afterwards to discuss their use of the strategy in small groups. If they have worked from the onset in small groups, they should be encouraged to report their thinking and reasoning processes aloud for others in the group to hear. One of the keys to gaining skill in strategy use and in transferring strategies to a wide variety of materials is verbalization and discussion of the strategy and its applications with peers.

EVALUATION

In the Evaluation phase, students reflect on their strategy use and appraise their success in using it as well as the contribution the strategy makes to their learning. Essentially, students are being asked to plan for, monitor, and evaluate their strategy applications. Teachers can ask students to write down the strategies they used during an activity or classroom assignment, indicate how the strategy worked, and note any changes in the strategies from the way in which they were originally described in class. The teacher then guides a full class discussion of the strategies that seemed most useful for the assignment. Students can keep dialogue journals about strategy use and share these with the teacher. Students comment on their success in using the strategy, what difficulties they encountered, and how they overcame them. The dialogue journals can be maintained throughout the school year. Students might compare their own performance on a task completed without using learning strategies and a similar task in which they applied strategies. Students can also use a checklist to indicate strategies they have used with different materials.

One of the realities of strategy instruction is that not all strategies will be equally useful for all students. Students differ markedly in their approaches to learning and can be expected to have strong preferences in the types of strategies they like to use. Teachers should encourage students to collect a repertoire of strategies they can use with different types of materials or classroom activities and select from the repertoire in order to increase their own learning. Teachers should not force students to use one strategy or another, but encourage them to build their repertoire so they will increase their tools for learning. On the other hand, teachers should explore how fully students have examined strategy applications when they decline to use any of the strategy approaches.

EXPANSION

In the Expansion phase, teachers apply the strategies to materials that were not part of the original classroom examples or instruction. Teachers can give students reminders to use a strategy that was part of an earlier Presentation phase, providing scaffolding prompts as needed, and encourage students to try the strategies with materials they are using in other classes. Teachers can encourage students to try different strategies and compare them for effectiveness. For example, to assist reading comprehension, students can be encouraged to use an *Idea Map* with some materials and then try using a T-List to see which they prefer. Thus students not only evaluate the effectiveness of strategy use but can do so by comparing one strategy with another. Students can also bring examples for discussion of some of their strategy applications in other classes. The most useful instructional outcome of these discussions can be guidelines for students concerning where and when to use individual strategies. Perhaps the most important individual outcome for students will be automatic and skilled use of strategies with a wide variety of academic tasks and the knowledge base to use them effectively.

Table 4.2

HOW TO TEACH LEARNING STRATEGIES

Preparation

Develop students' metacognitive awareness and self-knowledge through activities such as:

- Discussions about strategies students already use for specific tasks;
- Small group interviews in which students describe and share their special techniques for completing a task successfully;
- Learning strategy questionnaires in which students indicate the frequency with which they use particular strategies for particular tasks; and
- Individual think-aloud interviews in which the student works on a task and describes his/her thoughts.

Presentation

Teach the strategy explicitly by:

- Modeling how you use the strategy with a specific academic task by thinking aloud as you work through a task (e.g., reading a text or writing a paragraph);
- Giving the strategy a name and referring to it consistently by that name;
- Explaining to students how the strategy will help them learn the material; and
- Describing when, how, and for what kinds of tasks they can use the strategy.

Practice

Provide many opportunities for strategy practice through activities such as:

- Cooperative Learning
- Reciprocal Teaching
- Hands-on science experiments
- Mathematics word problems
- Research projects
- Developing oral and written reports
- Analyzing literature
- Process writing

Evaluation

Develop students' metacognitive awareness of which strategies work for them—and why—through self-evaluation activities such as:

- Debriefing discussions after using strategies;
- Learning logs or journals in which students describe and evaluate their strategy use;
- Comparing their own performance on a task completed without using learning strategies and a similar task in which they applied strategies;
- Checklists of their degree of confidence in using specific strategies;
- Self-efficacy questionnaires about their degree of confidence in completing specific academic tasks; and
- Self-reports telling when they use or do not use a strategy, and why.

Expansion

Provide for transfer of strategies to new tasks through activities such as:

- Scaffolding, in which reminders to use a strategy are gradually diminished;
- Praise for independent use of a strategy;
- Self-report in which students bring tasks to class on which they have successfully transferred a strategy;
- Thinking skills discussions in which students brainstorm possible uses for strategies they are learning;
- Follow-up activities in which students apply the strategies to new tasks and contexts;
- Analysis and discussion of strategies individual students find effective for particular tasks.

Table 4.2 is an outline of suggestions for teaching learning strategies. The purpose of these suggestions is to illustrate how teachers can help their students identify their current learning strategies, gain information about additional learning strategies with which they may be unfamiliar, practice new strategies, and decide which strategies work best for them and how they can use these strategies in additional contexts.

How to Teach Learning Strategies

- ❖ Preparation: Develop students' awareness through a variety of activities.
- ❖ Presentation: Teach the strategy explicitly.
- ❖ Practice: Provide opportunities for practicing the strategy in varied contexts.
- ❖ Evaluation: Teach students to evaluate their own strategy use.
- ❖ Expansion: Encourage students to apply the strategies in other learning areas.

Using Learning Strategies for Motivation

Student motivation for school learning is the result of their *expectations* for success on academic tasks, the *value* they assign to learning, and their attribution of responsibility for successful performance.[26] These factors determine the amount of effort students are willing to expend on learning activities, and how long they will persist in attempting to learn new information. Each of these factors is linked to personal experiences which act to influence a student's overall motivation for school learning. Generally, students who have more "skill" in performing academic tasks can be expected to have more "will" that will lead them to expand their involvement in learning.[27]

EXPECTATIONS OF SUCCESS

Student expectations for success or failure in school develop over years of daily exposure to various types of instruction, teachers, learning conditions, environments, and materials. Students' experiences in either succeeding or failing in school often generalize to specific types of materials and content areas. For example, students often note that they have "an ear" for languages, "can't do math" or "can't remember history." Other students comment that they like areas "that they are good at." These expectations are deeply grounded in experience and influence every future encounter with instructional content. They are one of the major factors determining motivation and the effort students are willing to devote to learning. Teachers can support students' expectations for success gradually by presenting assignments that build on familiar knowledge, are scoffolded through manageable levels of conceptual or linguistic difficulty, and are accompanied by strategy instruction to facilitate success.

VALUE OF TASK

The value students give to specific content information is another major influence on motivation. Two possible sources of value are intrinsic interest and applicability. Educators always strive to ensure that new learning has intrinsic interest to students, sometimes by using authentic literature, by highlighting science or social studies activities that might have interest to students, and by selecting content that is believed to have intrinsic interest or cultural relevance. Educators also strive to ensure that goals and instructional activities in schools are authentic in recognition of the relationship between value and motivation. Authentic materials include content that has value in students' lives, that has parallels with previous experience, that can be immediately applied to new experiences, and that is related to other information they are learning. Material whose sole justification is to prepare for next year's courses or to satisfy a requirement in the curriculum almost by definition would have less value to students. As a result, one of the major issues faced by educators is to ensure that instructional content is valued by students.

Many ESL students view the curriculum in grade-level classes as the "real" curriculum in school and devalue learning language while they must wait to learn important content. This is one reason why we believe in the importance of combining content area instruction with instructional methods for English as a second language, in that it appeals to students' values for school learning.

ATTRIBUTION OF RESPONSIBILITY

Students attribute success or failure in school to a variety of factors including natural ability, effort, luck, personal influences, and—perhaps—skill as a learner. For the most part, however, students seem to think that learning results from natural ability and luck, with a touch of personal influence such as an exceptionally good (or not so good) teacher. Far less frequently do students indicate that success at school tasks results from skill as a learner. Good students succeed, they believe, because of their natural ability. As with expectations for their own success or failure, students' beliefs in this area have evolved over a long time period, are highly durable, and are resistant to change.

One of the goals of strategy instruction is to alter students' beliefs about themselves by teaching them that failures can be attributed to lack of effective strategies rather than lack of ability. Strategy instruction is also designed to provide students with a continuing string of successes so that they come to expect success on school tasks rather than anticipate failure with every new effort. Because expectation and motivation are so closely related, student performance should be monitored closely, and students should be given the means to monitor and evaluate their own learning activities. By linking academic content with English language development, as in CALLA, student value for learning should be high.

In sum, learning strategy instruction is designed to enable students to be independent and autonomous learners whose motivation for school learning comes from an awareness of their own skills as a learner, experience in using these skills with materials of the kind they expect to encounter, and value in being able to link new information either to personal experience or to new applications. Furthermore, if students believe that they are learning important tools for learning through strategy instruction, self-esteem and self-confidence should increase accordingly.

Using Learning Strategies for Motivation

- Expectations—support students' expectations of success by building on previous knowledge, scaffolding, and strategy instruction.
- Value—increase students' value of academic material by linking language to content.
- Attribution—encourage students to monitor their own learning activities and to identify strategies that effectively support their learning efforts.

Application Activities

1. Conduct a learning strategy interview to enable students to report on the strategies they use in second language learning tasks, to find out about approaches to learning other than the ones they are using, and to discuss with other students the best ways for learning in a second language classroom.

   a. Refer to Table 4.3, Learning Strategies in the Academic Curriculum: Interview Guide provided at the end of this chapter. This table describes both language tasks and content subject tasks requiring language.

   b. Select one of the tasks identified in Table 4.3 that is representative of work performed by your students. Interview students in small groups of three or four, and ask them to indicate the techniques or "special tricks" they use to understand, learn, or produce the language for that task. Use the specific questions indicated for each task.

   c. As students describe their techniques or learning strategies, comment on the use of the strategy. Ask questions to ensure that all students understand the way in which the student reporting uses the strategy. Ask additional questions if students do not understand what to do. If necessary, give an example of a strategy to prompt the discussion.

   d. Make brief notes of the strategies students describe for the task. You may want to assign labels to the strategies when you review your notes so that you can later refer to the strategies by name. Use the strategy names in Table 4.1, or invent other descriptive labels. Keep these notes for potential use in the Presentation phase of CALLA instruction, as some of the strategies students describe may be highly effective approaches that should be shared with all students.

   e. Continue with discussions of learning strategies for other tasks in the same manner as described in Steps b-d.

2. Make learning strategy posters. Learning strategy posters can be useful in the classroom as reminders of strategy names and the mental processes associated with each strategy. Review the samples of learning strategy posters provided on page 76. Adapt the strategy names if desired, and make a poster for each strategy category (metacognitive, cognitive, social/affective). You may also develop posters for specific content areas (see Table 9.3, Table 10.3, Table 11.2, and Table 12.1 for learning strategies for different subjects).

   a. Color-code the paper for learning strategy posters as follows: Metacognitive Strategies = blue (blue represents calmness and control); Cognitive Strategies = green (green represents growth); Social/Affective Strategies = orange or other warm color (warm color represents social and affective dimensions). Laminate the posters and display them in your classroom.
   b. Use the posters as a reminder to students about the strategies taught and practiced.
   c. Refer to the posters when modeling strategies.
   d. Have students refer to the posters when discussing strategies.

3. Design a learning strategies lesson in which students become aware of and learn how to use learning strategies. Use Table 4.4 to help you design the lesson.
   a. Select a content area appropriate for the curriculum you are teaching (e.g., science, math, language arts). Then select a content lesson from available materials in this area using the CALLA Instructional Sequence. (See Chapter 5.) As you design the lesson, identify one or more learning strategies appropriate for the content and learning tasks. Select one task and one learning strategy objective to teach with this content.
   b. Complete the information at the head of Table 4.4 (ESL and grade levels of students, task, strategy to be taught, materials needed). Complete the learning strategy lesson plan by answering the questions asked for each phase of the lesson (e.g., Preparation, Presentation, Practice, Evaluation, and Extension).
   c. Try the learning strategies lesson with your students, evaluate the results, and revise as needed.

4. Use the following learning strategy activities. They are useful for both teachers and students because they increase understanding of learning strategies and help in monitoring the acquisition and use of learning strategies.
   a. Keep a learning log on the strategies you have used/are using on tasks related to student tasks (e.g., acquiring information through listening, reading, conversing, writing). As you work on a task, describe aloud on tape or write how you are approaching the task. Identify the learning strategies *you* use and reflect on ways in which you can model these strategies for your students during the Presentation phase of CALLA instruction.
   b. Have students complete a learning log for learning strategies. Students should list the strategies on which they are working and indicate tasks with which the strategies are used. Ask students to describe the experiences they are encountering in working with these strategies, identifying successes and ways of overcoming difficulties. These learning logs can be shared with the teacher and with classmates in cooperative learning groups. Refer to the sample Student Learning Log on page 79.
   c. Ask students to identify a learning strategy with which they have experienced success and to share it with a classmate. Have students describe the task, the strategy, how to use it, and how they know it worked with the task.
   d. Have students identify new materials or a new task on which to apply a learning strategy they have used successfully in the past. This new application could be in another classroom, with a different teacher, in another content area, or with a different task. Ask students to report these new strategy applications to the class.

SAMPLE LEARNING STRATEGY POSTERS

METACOGNITIVE STRATEGIES

THINK:

How do I learn?

How can I learn better?

WHAT I CAN DO:

PLAN what I will do.

Use SELECTIVE ATTENTION.

MONITOR what I am doing.

EVALUATE what I have done.

COGNITIVE STRATEGIES

THINK:

How can I understand?

How can I remember?

WHAT I CAN DO:

ELABORATE prior knowledge.

CLASSIFY or GROUP ideas.

Make INFERENCES and PREDICT.

SUMMARIZE important ideas.

Use IMAGES and PICTURES.

SOCIAL/AFFECTIVE STRATEGIES

THINK:

How can I help others learn?

How can others help me learn?

WHAT I CAN DO:

ASK QUESTIONS for clarification.

COOPERATE with classmates to learn.

Use positive SELF-TALK.

PROBLEM-SOLVING STRATEGIES

THINK:

How can I solve math problems?

WHAT I CAN DO:

- **UNDERSTAND the question.**
  Rewrite the question as a statement.
  Leave a blank for the correct answer.
- **Find the DATA.**
  Look for the numbers needed to solve the problem.
- **Make a PLAN.**
  Choose the OPERATION.
  Make NUMBER SENTENCES.
  Make a LIST or TABLE.
  Draw a PICTURE.
  Solve a SIMPLER problem.
  GUESS and CHECK.
  Find PATTERNS in the numbers.
  Work BACKWARDS.
- **Find the ANSWER.**
- **CHECK BACK.**
  ESTIMATE the answer.
  Work BACKWARDS.
  READ the question again.

Table 4.3
LEARNING STRATEGIES IN THE ACADEMIC CURRICULUM

INTERVIEW GUIDE

Directions: Interview students individually or in small groups of 3-4. Ask about activities that students have actually done. If possible, interview students in their native language or seek the assistance of a bilingual student.

1. Vocabulary Learning - All Subjects

You have to learn the meanings of 20 new words in English.

Do you have any special tricks to help you learn and remember the new words and what they mean?

2. Following Directions - All Subjects

Your teacher gives you directions for a worksheet or a math problem or a science experiment. You have to understand what to do, and then do it.

Do you have any special tricks to help you understand what to do? What do you do if you forget what to do?

3. Listening to a Story - Language Arts

Your teacher is reading a story to the class. You don't understand all of the words. Then your teacher asks you to predict an ending for the story.

What do you do about the words you don't understand?

How do you make up a good ending for the story?

4. Listening for Information - All Subjects

Your teacher explains some important ideas in science, social studies, or literature. You have to understand and remember the information.

What do you do that helps you understand the teacher?

What do you do to remember the information later?

5. Reading Aloud - All Subjects

You have to read something aloud. You need to say the right words and pronounce the words correctly.

What do you do to figure out each word?

What do you do to help your pronunciation?

6. Reading Comprehension - Language Arts

You have to read a story or novel chapter silently. You need to understand the plot and characters, then retell the story.

What do you do to understand the plot and characters?

What do you do about new words? How can you remember and retell the story?

7. Solving Word Problems - Mathematics

You have to read and solve a word problem in math.

What special ways do you have to understand the problem?

How do you know which operation(s) to use?

How do you know if your answer is correct?

8. Reading for Information - All Subjects

You have to read several pages in your science or social studies book. You need to understand and remember the important information.

What do you do to understand the information as you read?

What do you do to remember the infoirmation later on?

9. Presenting an Oral Report - All Subjects

You have to give an oral report about a project that your group worked on in science or social studies.

What do you do to get ready for the report?

What helps you do a good job when you present the report?

10. Writing a Story, Composition, or Report - All Subjects

You have to write a story or a composition or a report.

What do you do first? What do you do while you are writing?

What do you do after you have written the story or report?

Table 4.4
DESIGN A LEARNING STRATEGY LESSON

TASK ______________________________ ESL LEVEL ________

STRATEGY ______________________________ GRADE(S) ______

MATERIALS ______________________________

1. Preparation Activity: How will you find out what strategies your students are already using for this type of task?

2. Presentation Activity: How will you model and describe the strategy? What name will you give the strategy?

3. Practice Activity: How will students practice the strategy?

4. Self-Evaluation Activity: How will students assess their success with the strategy?

5. Expansion Activity: How will you make sure that students transfer the strategy to other tasks and situations?

LEARNING STRATEGY LOG

NAME Domingo DATE 2/12

CLASS/GRADE ESL - Science / Gr. 7

1. Strategy elaboration - using prior knowledge

Task list differences between plants + animals

Use made two columns and described ways to take in food, movement, and other things

2. Strategy imagery

Task use scientific method to test hypothesis

Use imagined myself doing observations, collecting information, recording it in a table, testing hypothesis.

3. Strategy ______

Task ______

Use ______

4. Strategy ______

Task ______

Use ______

PART TWO

Establishing a CALLA Program

CHAPTER 5

Planning, Teaching, and Monitoring CALLA

Overview

CALLA instruction integrates key curriculum concepts, development of academic language functions and vocabulary, and explicit instruction in learning strategies.

How to Plan for CALLA Instruction

Assessing Students' Prior Knowledge
Setting Instructional Objectives
Assembling Materials for CALLA Instruction
Planning an Instructional Sequence

Teaching CALLA

Preparation
Presentation
Practice
Evaluation
Expansion

How to Monitor CALLA Instruction

Analyzing Current Teaching Strategies
Setting Realistic Goals
Coaching CALLA

CHAPTER 5 PLANNING, TEACHING, AND MONITORING CALLA

CALLA INSTRUCTION OFTEN INVOLVES TEACHERS in reorganizing effective techniques already in use, reflecting metacognitively on their successful teaching techniques, and developing an understanding of the learning processes of their students.

CALLA teaching requires thoughtful planning. The CALLA teacher not only thinks about the ways in which he or she will deliver instruction, but also thinks through how individual students will receive and act upon that instruction. Because CALLA instruction integrates key curriculum concepts, development of academic language functions and vocabulary, and explicit instruction in the learning strategies that facilitate both language and content development, CALLA teachers need to include all of these components in their lesson planning and delivery.

HOW TO PLAN FOR CALLA INSTRUCTION

Several steps are needed in planning for CALLA instruction. The first step is to select the content topic for a unit or lesson. In Chapter 2 we suggested a number of approaches for selecting content from the grade-level curriculum. In this section we describe the next planning steps. Following content selection, teachers need to assess their students' prior knowledge of the concepts and processes selected. This information can guide the teacher in the next planning step, setting objectives for student achievement in content, academic language, and learning strategies. The third step is to assemble the materials that will assist the teacher in making the unit or lesson meaningful to students. Finally, the teacher outlines the sequence of instruction that will enable students to understand, remember, and recall the concepts and processes taught.

ASSESSING STUDENTS' PRIOR KNOWLEDGE

The principle of starting where students are and then building on their conceptual framework by adding information is not new. In a second language context, however, it can be difficult for a teacher to know the exact composition of a student's background knowledge base. Teachers can employ a number of creative techniques to assist in discovering their students' prior knowledge. This prior knowledge can seem at first glance to be peripheral to the topic of instruction, but the CALLA teacher discusses and probes to find a relationship between students' prior knowledge and the new concepts to be taught.

STUDENTS' BACKGROUND. Rather than wait for fortuitous prompts from the textbook or class discussion, the CALLA teacher deliberately plans how to activate students' prior knowledge. First, it is necessary to have some information about and understanding of the cultural and experiential background of their students. This is

Assess student's prior knowledge of the concepts to be taught.

gleaned not only from school records, but also through interaction with parents (through an interpreter, if necessary), discussion with any colleagues who have knowledge about and insights into the students' background, but most importantly, through a genuine interest in the students which encourages sharing of previous experiences. This information can be organized in a chart like the one shown here. In keeping a chart like this, the teacher seeks constantly to verify the information and add new information as it is discovered.

MY STUDENTS' PRIOR KNOWLEDGE

Student Name and Age	Language and Country	Rural or City	Grades Completed	Additional Information
Miguel, 14	Spanish; El Salvador	rural	1+2	does not read or write Spanish
Thi Cuc, 13	Vietnamese	city	1-7	bilingual, biliterate Vietnamese, French
Irina, 14	Russian	city	Pre-K-8	strong math + science background
Isabel, 13	Spanish; Columbia	city	1-8	literate in Spanish limited Eng. reading

SELF-ASSESSMENT. A second way to identify students' background knowledge is by asking them to assess their own prior knowledge. Having students reflect on how their prior experience relates to what they are learning in an American school is valuable in two ways. It helps students activate their prior knowledge and it demonstrates to them the importance of *elaboration* as a learning strategy. This information can be elicited by the teacher through class brainstorming, or students can write down what they already know either individually or in small groups. The teacher can also have students make a class graphic organizer of their prior knowledge on chart paper. The chart can be displayed and, as the topic is studied, new information can be added and initial misconceptions can be rectified.

This type of activity not only helps students begin to relate what they already know to the new lesson, but also provides the teacher with diagnostic information about gaps and misconceptions in students' prior knowledge.

CONCRETE EXPERIENCE. A third way in which teachers can activate elaboration as a strategy to utilize prior knowledge is by planning for an actual experience designed to build prior knowledge that students may lack. In planning for this type of a concrete experience, CALLA teachers are seeking to replicate a life experience that their students have not had. For example, a field trip to observe and collect specimens of fallen autumn leaves can help students whose prior life experiences have been in tropical regions understand some of the characteristics of deciduous trees. Videos and films can also be used to simulate experiences that build prior knowledge.

CALLA teachers invent many ways to discover their students' prior knowledge because they know that what they teach has to be connected with what students already know.

SETTING INSTRUCTIONAL OBJECTIVES

Because CALLA integrates content, language, and learning strategies instruction, lesson plans specify objectives for each of these components. The statement of these objectives helps teachers plan lessons that incorporate all three types.

CONTENT OBJECTIVES. To identify content objectives, teachers should consult the grade-level curriculum and instructional materials and ask for the assistance of content specialist teachers in selecting high priority content topics. (See Chapter 2 for selection guidelines.) These topics should include important concepts that students need to prepare them for entry into grade-level classes. Concepts about content do not consist merely of factual or declarative knowledge, but also include processes, or the procedural knowledge inherent in each discipline. Concepts also include another aspect of declarative knowledge, the attitudes and beliefs considered valuable in each discipline.

LANGUAGE OBJECTIVES. In planning CALLA lessons, objectives also need to be established for academic language development. Academic language objectives include the academic language functions used in listening, reading, speaking, and writing in different content areas, and the development of discipline-specific vocabulary. CALLA does not emphasize the teaching of grammar as a separate strand because we see grammar as a means to an end, rather than as a discrete language component to be learned separately. As students become more proficient in using academic language functions, CALLA teachers may wish to call their attention to various grammatical points that appear within the context of language use.

MATERIALS FOR CONTEXTUALIZING INSTRUCTION

HEALTH SCIENCE: TOPIC—NUTRITION

- Poster showing example of food pyramid groups.
- Food sample from different food groups brought in by students, including foods from native countries.
- Graph showing relationship of calories of sample foods to type and amount of exercise needed to consume.
- Graphic organizer on which students are to record prior knowledge about nutritious and non-nutritious foods.
- Game in which student teams compete with other teams to plan nutritious menus.

MATHEMATICS: TOPIC—EQUIVALENT FRACTIONS

- Set of fractional parts in different colors for each student (e.g., yellow circle = 1; 2 green half circles = 1/2; 3 blue thirds of circles = 1/3; 4 orange quarter circles = 1/4; 6 red sixth circle segments = 1/6; 8 purple eighth circle segments = 1/8).
- A similar set of fractional parts to use on the overhead projector. These can be cut from colored transparency film or colored plastic fraction shapes can be purchased from educational supply stores or catalogs.
- Strips of paper in different colors for students to cut out different fractional parts.
- Photographs and drawings of real objects which can be divided into fractional parts.

SOCIAL STUDIES: TOPIC—EXPLORATION OF NORTH AMERICA

- Timeline showing dates and major events of Spanish, Portuguese, Dutch, French, and English exploration in North America.
- Reproductions of maps and drawings of North America from the period.
- Map of North America today.
- Scale model (or drawing) of 17th century sailing ship.
- Graphic organizer for taking notes on material presented orally.
- Film or video of European explorers in North America.
- Cause and effect graphic organizer to record results of early exploration in North America.

LITERATURE AND COMPOSITION: TOPIC—FOLK TALES

- Graphic organizer for students to record information about folk tales they know.
- Recordings, videos, and films of storytellers and folk tales.
- Pictures and posters illustrating folk tales from different countries.
- Library books of folk tales from different countries.
- Graphic organizer for students to map story grammar of folk tales read.
- Guidelines for family interviews.
- Computer and word processing program for production of a class book on folk tales from students' native countries.
- Paper, colors, paints, and other art materials for students to illustrate the folk tales they write.

LEARNING STRATEGY OBJECTIVES. Identifying learning strategy objectives is the cornerstone of the CALLA teacher's planning. Teachers plan for the specific learning strategies that will be introduced, modeled, practiced, and/or discussed in each CALLA lesson. Because students need extensive practice with new strategies, teachers need to provide many opportunities for practice and discussion of the strategies. As described in Chapter 3, learning strategies should be taught overtly through an instructional sequence in which the teacher first helps students discover the strategies they already use, then goes on to name and describe the strategy to be taught, explains its usefulness, and models the strategy (usually through a think-aloud demonstration). The teacher then provides students with multiple opportunities to practice the strategy and to reflect on and evaluate their strategy use. Finally, the teacher reminds students to apply the strategy to new tasks and asks them to describe their strategy applications.

ASSEMBLING MATERIALS FOR CALLA INSTRUCTION

In order to provide contextual clues to help students comprehend the content and language of CALLA lessons, teachers need to plan carefully for the materials needed. These materials include visuals, realia, content-specific equipment, manipulatives, instruments, directions for role-playing and dramatization, art materials, audio and video recordings, worksheets, and graphic organizers. Materials assembled for a CALLA lesson will vary depending on the content area and objectives of the lesson, but should always include a variety of materials that students can perceive through different learning modes—visual, aural, and kinesthetic/tactile.

Refer to the Materials for Contextualizing Instruction chart on the previous page, which provides examples of the types of materials a CALLA teacher might collect for different content lessons.

PLANNING AN INSTRUCTIONAL SEQUENCE

CALLA instruction consists of five phases: Preparation, Presentation, Practice, Evaluation, and Expansion. Each sequence should start with the Preparation phase in which students activate their prior knowledge and are made aware of the objectives of the lesson or unit, and end with an Expansion phase in which students reflect on what they have learned and restructure their prior knowledge to include the new information. The phases of CALLA instruction are often recursive. That is, within a single unit there may be several opportunities for preparation, presentation of new information, and practice activities. The Evaluation and Expansion phases may then encompass a number of sets of presentation and practice activities. The model units at the end of Chapters 9, 10, 11, and 12 illustrate how the five instructional phases can be sequenced. A CALLA instructional sequence can be as short as a single class period or as long as a unit spanning one or more weeks. In the next section of this chapter we suggest approaches to teaching each of the five phases of the CALLA instructional sequence.

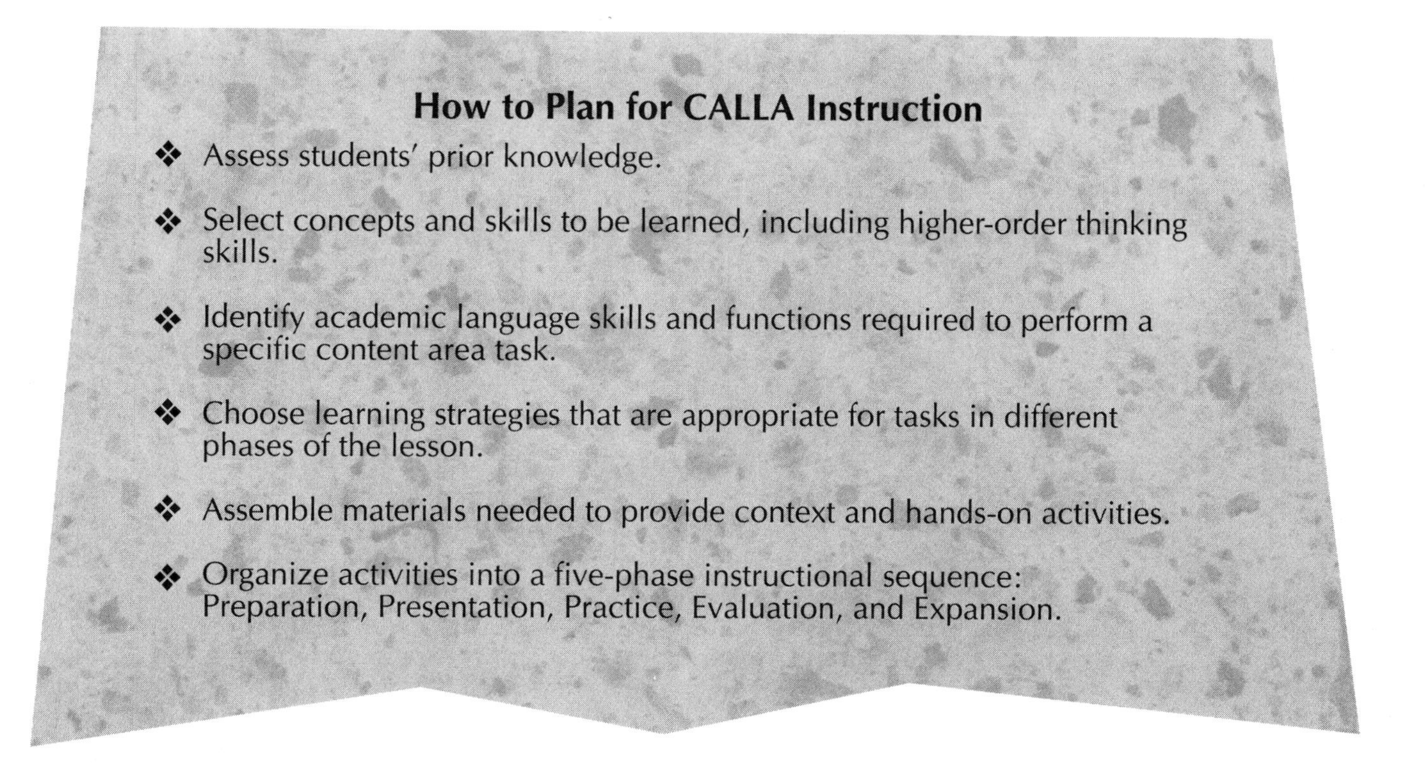

How to Plan for CALLA Instruction

- Assess students' prior knowledge.
- Select concepts and skills to be learned, including higher-order thinking skills.
- Identify academic language skills and functions required to perform a specific content area task.
- Choose learning strategies that are appropriate for tasks in different phases of the lesson.
- Assemble materials needed to provide context and hands-on activities.
- Organize activities into a five-phase instructional sequence: Preparation, Presentation, Practice, Evaluation, and Expansion.

Teaching CALLA

A CALLA classroom is a learner-centered classroom in which the teacher shows students how to recognize and use their prior knowledge, guides them in expanding and refining their knowledge frameworks, and provides meaningful practice opportunities for developing language skills and learning strategies. Higher-order thinking and development of the CALLA classroom as a learning community for both students and teacher are facilitated through frequent and extensive dialogue and discussion of important issues and ideas.[1]

In this section we describe typical activities for the five phases of a CALLA instructional sequence which can integrate the content, language, and learning strategy objectives identified during planning. Teachers may select types of activities in each of the five phases that best suit the instructional needs of their students.

PREPARATION

In this phase, the teacher finds out what students already know about the concepts to be presented and practiced, what gaps in prior knowledge need to be addressed, and how students have been taught to approach a particular math skill, science process, social studies concept, literary genre, or discourse organization. At the same time, students have the opportunity to recall and value their prior knowledge, to begin to link what they already know to the lesson topic, to develop labels in English for concepts that they already know, and to share different approaches to discussing and solving problems. Teachers should also provide an overview and objectives of the new topic in the Preparation phase so that students have a road map of where they are going in the lesson and what they are expected to accomplish. In this phase anticipated new vocabulary can be identified by students or teacher, or vocabulary introduction may be postponed until after students have information in the next phase of the CALLA instructional sequence. Activities in the Preparation phase that help students activate their prior knowledge include brainstorming, making class or group graphic organizers, concrete activities, working with manipulatives, teacher demonstrations, role play, use of videos and films, and field trips. Students may use learning strategies such as elaboration to identify their prior knowledge, advance organization to gain an overview of the topic, and prediction of key information.

PRESENTATION

In the Presentation phase of the lesson, new information is presented and explained to students. New content is generally presented first by the teacher and supported with sufficient contextual clues to assist comprehension. The textbook, library book, or teacher-prepared text is usually introduced after students have developed an initial understanding of the new content. Teachers need to monitor and perhaps modify their own language so that students can more easily comprehend the new information. New information can be presented to the whole class or to homogeneous small groups geared to students' prior knowledge and/or language proficiency level. Because students understand information in different ways, the CALLA teacher varies the mode of presentation so that students with differing learning styles can perceive the new information aurally, visually, and kinesthetically. The teacher should maintain a positive affective climate in the CALLA classroom, showing students that they are valued members of the classroom community. Finally, teachers need to make questioning an integral part of the Presentation phase. Students need to be encouraged and shown how to *ask* questions for clarification, and how to *answer* higher-level comprehension questions. Additional learning strategies useful to students in this phase are selective attention to key ideas presented and using elaboration and inferencing to assist comprehension.

PRACTICE

In this phase of a CALLA lesson, students are provided with numerous opportunities to engage in hands-on and exploratory discussions of the concepts presented during the previous teacher-directed phase of the lesson. Students can also identify new vocabulary that they determine is important to understand. Because students can learn from each other and expand their language and content knowledge through interaction with each other, cooperation is the major learning strategy recommended during the Practice phase of the CALLA lesson. Cooperative learning activities provide opportunities for students to use academic language functions as they work together to solve a problem or complete a project. In cooperative learning, students with varying degrees of English proficiency and content knowledge work in a group setting that fosters mutual learning rather than competitiveness.[2] Suggestions for organizing cooperative learning activities are provided here, in Chapter 3, and in suggested additional readings.[3]

Guidelines for Organizing Cooperative Learning

- Explain to students why cooperation as a learning strategy is effective in developing a better understanding of new concepts and skills, and in providing opportunities to practice academic English.

- Teach the social skills students need to work effectively together through team-building cooperative activities in which students learn how to work cooperatively and how to value the talents of their heterogeneously-chosen team members.
- Organize heterogeneous teams consisting of students with a high and low amount of relevant background knowledge, and students with greater and lesser proficiency in English.
- Structure cooperative learning activities so that the task can only be accomplished through group interaction. For example, students might have to pool individual information to develop a project or report, or students could have different responsibilities for completing a science experiment.
- Assign a role to each group member. Give students role cards that describe their responsibilities, or make a poster of this information.
- Allow cooperative groups the freedom to develop their ideas and solve the problem(s) assigned. Act as a facilitator rather than as a teacher.
- For cooperative learning activities, give group recognition (or grades, depending on task) as well as individual recognition.
- Conduct debriefing discussions in which students evaluate how successful they were in working together.

A variety of strategic activities should be provided during the Practice phase of the CALLA instructional sequence so that students can assimilate the new information and use it in different ways. For example, students can use manipulatives, draw pictures, conduct an experiment, and make a map, graph, timeline, or chart. Students can also discuss problem solutions, think aloud while solving a problem, share strategies used for a problem, and develop problems for others to solve.

In practicing reading, students can engage in Reciprocal Teaching.[4] In this strategic approach to reading, students sit in small groups and take turns "teaching" the text. The group first reads a section of the text, then one student makes a brief summary, asks the other students questions about the text read, identifies any difficult parts, and predicts what the next section will be about. Then the group continues reading and a different student goes through the same teaching process.

In developing writing skills, students can engage in strategic prewriting activities such as brainstorming, memory searches, organizational planning, note-taking, and concept-mapping. During the composing process students may use traditional pencil and paper, or they can work on a word processor or dictate their ideas to the teacher, aide, or another student. In revising, students can read their work to a classmate, ask for suggestions, consult with the teacher, and continue to refine their story, essay, or report.

EVALUATION

While most teachers are highly skilled in evaluating their students' progress, students are typically inexperienced in evaluating their own progress towards a learning goal. Because the metacognitive strategy of self-evaluation is so critical to developing self-regulated learners and is so important in increasing motivation, the CALLA instructional sequence contains a specific phase in which students are led to determine the effectiveness of their own learning efforts. Cognitive and affective strategies which help students evaluate themselves are summarizing, verifying predictions made in the Preparation phase, and using positive self-talk to reassure themselves of their capabilities. In the Evaluation phase, students check the level of their performance so that they can gain an understanding of what they have learned and identify any areas that need review. Evaluation activities can be cooperative or individual, and can take place in class or as a home assignment.

Cooperative Learning Roles

Coordinator/Team Leader:

Organizes the work and makes sure that everybody does their part. Introduces group report.

Recorder/Reporter:

Takes notes and makes group report to class.

Resource Manager:

Takes charge of materials, including distribution and cleanup.

Monitor:

Keeps track of group processing, including level of teamwork and use of learning strategies. Reports to class.

Cheerleader:

Encourages group members by making positive statements about their contributions.

A class poster defines each group member's role.

In cooperative self-evaluation, students can check and correct each others' answers in small groups, identify steps used by group members to solve a problem, and discuss effectiveness of different learning strategies used. In independent self-evaluation, students can check answers independently, keep a learning log recording progress, reactions, and difficulties, keep a cumulative check list on personal achievement, and discuss progress with the teacher. Both independent and cooperative self-evaluation can be important additions to student portfolios. (See Chapter 6 for additional ideas on student self-assessment and portfolio assessment.)

EXPANSION

The purpose of the Expansion phase of the CALLA instructional sequence is to help students integrate new information and skills into their existing conceptual frameworks. First, the teacher leads a discussion of the lesson's topic which concentrates on eliciting higher-order thinking skills. Students are asked to use learning strategies that cause them to reflect on the importance of the lesson's topic and skills, its relation to their prior knowledge, and the applications of the lesson to the world outside school and to their own lives in particular. As students reflect on what they have learned, they may find that aspects of their prior knowledge need to be revised or restructured as a result of the acquisition of new knowledge and skills. This knowledge restructuring is an important outcome of CALLA instruction.

Class and home activities are designed for students to apply the new information and skills on activities that have personal meaning. To this end, family involvement is encouraged and students are frequently asked to apply their new knowledge at home or to find relationships between the new knowledge and their own cultural background. Teachers may also assign reading for additional information on the topic studied, and then have individual students or groups work cooperatively to make oral or written reports on their extended reading.

In sum, CALLA instruction is designed to provide students with varied experiences in acquiring content, academic language, and learning strategies that will prepare them for greater success in grade-level classrooms.

In independent self-evaluation, students track their own progress and discuss it with the teacher.

Teaching CALLA

- Preparation: Students identify and reflect on prior knowledge related to the lesson topic; teacher provides overview of learning objectives, introduces essential new vocabulary, and may provide concrete experience to develop students' prior knowledge.
- Presentation: Teacher presents/explains new information, skills, and/or learning strategies; information is presented through a variety of modes to accommodate different students' learning styles.
- Practice: Students actively practice new concepts, skills, and/or learning strategies; cooperative learning activities are featured.
- Evaluation: Students practice individual and cooperative self-evaluation.
- Expansion: Students integrate what was learned in the lesson into their existing knowledge frameworks; restructure and refine prior knowledge as needed; apply new knowledge, skills, and/or learning situations in real-life contexts.

How to Monitor CALLA Instruction

Just as CALLA teachers seek to develop in their students an awareness of their learning strategies, so should they develop their awareness of their own teaching strategies. Just as students identify and reflect on their current learning strategies, then begin introducing and practicing new strategies to add to their repertoires, so can teachers analyze their present instructional approach and then begin adding new teaching strategies to their toolkits. Just as students need extensive practice before new learning strategies become automatic, so teachers need many trials to integrate new teaching strategies into their instructional approach.

In this section we suggest three ways in which teachers can develop and refine CALLA instruction. First, we describe a technique for analyzing current teaching strategies. Then we suggest an approach to planning for implementing CALLA instruction. Finally, we describe how peer coaching can provide both support and insight into the development and refining of CALLA teaching strategies.

ANALYZING CURRENT TEACHING STRATEGIES

To see ourselves as our students see us requires a minimum of technology and a maximum of self-analysis. The technology needed is either a videotape or an audiotape of a recently taught lesson. Position the video or tape recorder so that it will capture your speech and presentation style, and record two or three lessons over several days. Then use the checklist in Table 5.1 (or adapt it) to analyze your teaching strategies.

This checklist can help teachers identify areas of strength and weakness. Items marked "usually" show teaching strategies already in use that are important in CALLA instruction. Items marked "sometimes" or "rarely" indicate areas where teachers may wish to increase the frequency of or add to their repertoire of teaching strategies.

SETTING REALISTIC GOALS

To implement CALLA instruction, teachers may find it useful to make a long range plan, rather than try to change their whole approach to teaching overnight. In planning for change, it is helpful to set realistic goals that can be achieved successfully, rather than overly ambitious goals which have little likelihood of being met. For example, some CALLA teachers have started by introducing just two or three learning strategies at first in order to build a strategic approach to learning gradually. Others have started by teaching learning strategies in only one content area at a time. Still others have decided to spend the first few months of school in developing cooperative learning groups in their classroom. These teachers started implementing CALLA gradually, and then were able to add more components as they gained practice in integrating content, academic language, and learning strategy instruction.

Our experience in working with teachers indicates that four phases generally mark a teacher's journey from novice to expert CALLA teacher. These can be described as the Intellectual phase, the Trial-and-error phase, the Polishing phase, and the Sharing phase.

In the first (Intellectual) phase, teachers become convinced that CALLA will help their students become more academically successful and that non-strategic students can learn to become strategic. This is an important conviction, and not all teachers may adopt it. If they do, they then enter into the next phase of becoming a CALLA teacher.

In the Trial-and-error phase, the teacher experiments with CALLA instruction in the classroom. Some ideas work, but others are not successful. Sometimes students are resistant to change. As one teacher put it, "My students don't *like* to think. They want me to do all the work for them." During this difficult phase teachers need support and encouragement. The Trial-and-error phase often lasts as long as a year.

In the Polishing phase, teachers are ready to fine-tune the details of CALLA instruction. They have had an opportunity to reflect on the reasons for their successes and failures in teaching CALLA, and they know how much time it takes for students to learn certain types of content or particular learning strategies. The process of polishing CALLA instruction may take a year or longer, and teachers continue to need support and encouragement.

Finally, in the fourth (Sharing) phase, teachers are ready to share their approach to CALLA instruction with others. At this point they are eager to describe how they have implemented CALLA instruction to other teachers.

Table 5.1
TEACHING STRATEGIES CHECKLIST

How Comprehensible Is My Speech?

Usually	Sometimes	Rarely		
❑	❑	❑	1.	My enunciation is clear, with little slurring.
❑	❑	❑	2.	My pace of speaking is neither too fast nor too slow.
❑	❑	❑	3.	My speaking voice is neither too loud nor too soft.
❑	❑	❑	4.	My tone of voice is warm and engaged.
❑	❑	❑	5.	I explain new words and terms through definition or paraphrasing.
❑	❑	❑	6.	I provide natural redundancy in my speech by providing more than one presentation or explanation of an idea.
❑	❑	❑	7.	When necessary, I pause at phrase and sentence boundaries (not between words).
❑	❑	❑	8.	I carefully avoid the use of culturally-bound cliches and metaphors.

How Effectively Do I Present New Information and Provide Feedback?

❑	❑	❑	9.	I am knowledgeable about the topic.
❑	❑	❑	10.	I am interested in the topic.
❑	❑	❑	11.	I organize my presentation of the topic in a clear and logical way.
❑	❑	❑	12.	I explain the new information as many times and in as many different ways as my students need.
❑	❑	❑	13.	I provide visual and auditory context during my lesson presentation.
❑	❑	❑	14.	When the focus is communication, I respond to the meaning my students are trying to express rather than correctness of form.
❑	❑	❑	15.	I maintain a positive affective climate when providing corrective feedback.

How Adept Are My Classroom Organization Skills?

❑	❑	❑	16.	During a whole group presentation or discussion, I hold the attention of almost all of the class.
❑	❑	❑	17.	I give students meaningful tasks on which they have to work as pairs.
❑	❑	❑	18.	I organize and monitor small groups for cooperative learning.
❑	❑	❑	19.	I allow students to engage in self-directed learning.
❑	❑	❑	20.	I keep students on task, and can redirect their attention to the task when necessary.

Table 5.2

CALLA TEACHER LOG OF LEARNING STRATEGY INSTRUCTION

Teacher ______________________ Week of ______________

Grade(s)__________ ESL Level: ________Beginning ________Intermediate ________Advanced

Content Objectives______________________________

Language Objectives______________________________

____

Student Activity (check):

- ❑ Observing demonstration
- ❑ Doing hands-on activity
- ❑ Reading story/textbook, etc.
- ❑ Learning/remembering new information
- ❑ Giving oral report/demonstration
- ❑ Listening to explanation
- ❑ Practicing skills
- ❑ Explaining an answer
- ❑ Writing story/report, etc.
- ❑ Other (describe):

Strategies (list): ______________________________

____

Type of Instruction (check):

- ❑ Presentation of strategy (first time)
- ❑ Modeling of strategy
- ❑ Brief explanation of strategy (strategy named)
- ❑ Reminder to use strategy
- ❑ Questions answered about strategy

Opportunity to Apply Strategy(ies): None 1 2-3 4+

Notes/Problems/Suggestions:______________________________

____

____

____

____

COACHING CALLA

Working with another teacher in a coaching partnership is an excellent way to develop new teaching strategies in a collegial and supportive atmosphere.[5] Coaching partners work together to plan how they will carry out a new technique and then observe each other as they try out the technique in the classroom. After the observations, they meet again to compare notes and make suggestions. One teacher may ask the other to focus the observation on one particular aspect of an activity or presentation, or may ask the other teacher to monitor student reactions to the instruction. Teachers can also keep a teaching log of class activities that can be shared and discussed when meeting with coaching partners. Teachers that we have worked with have found that keeping a teaching log is particularly helpful for monitoring learning strategy instruction. Refer to the sample CALLA Teacher Log in Table 5.2.

Coaching is different from other types of classroom observation because both coaching partners operate on a basis of equality and because they determine what facets of instruction are to be observed and discussed. A coaching partnership should be ongoing, preferably throughout an entire school year. (For guidelines on coaching, see Chapter 6.)

How to Monitor CALLA Instruction

- ❖ Analyze current teaching strategies and identify those compatible with CALLA.
- ❖ Develop a realistic plan for change.
- ❖ Work with a coaching partner to plan CALLA lessons, observe each other, and discuss the observations.

Application Activities

The purpose of these activities is for teachers to gain practice in planning CALLA lessons, evaluating their current teaching strategies, monitoring their implementation of CALLA instruction, and setting up a coaching plan with another teacher.

1. Plan a CALLA Lesson.

a. First, activate your prior knowledge about instructional planning by writing down the major components of the lesson or unit plan you are currently using. Compare it to the CALLA Instructional Sequence on pages 89–94. Identify similarities and differences in objectives and procedures. Start a **K-W-L** chart (What I Know Now - What I Want to Know - What I Have Learned)[6] by: (1) **K** - Listing the parts of the CALLA Instructional Sequence that you are already using in your teaching; and (2) **W** - Listing CALLA activities that you would like to try with your students. After trying out the activities selected in your classroom, complete the K-W-L chart by: (3) **L** - Writing an evaluation of how the CALLA activities selected worked with your students.

b. Use the prompts in Table 5.3 to plan a CALLA lesson or unit.

2. Teach CALLA.

a. Work with one or more colleagues to share cooperative learning techniques. Using the Guidelines for Organizing Cooperative Learning on pages 90–91, conduct a cooperative learning activity in your classroom.
b. Review the directions for Reciprocal Teaching on page 91. Try this technique with your students.
c. Try out the CALLA lesson or unit that you planned with your students.

3. Monitor CALLA Instruction.

a. Assess your current teaching strategies. First, record a class you teach by videotaping it or making an audio tape recording. Then complete the Teaching Strategies Checklist (Table 5.1). Identify one to three areas in which you would like to strengthen your teaching strategies. Practice these teaching strategies for a month, then record your class again and complete the checklist again. Repeat this process periodically so that your self-assessment is ongoing.
b. Work with a colleague to make a coaching plan for developing learning strategy instruction in your respective classrooms. Use the CALLA Teacher Log of Learning Strategy Instruction (Table 5.2) as either a self-assessment form to discuss with your coaching partner, or as an observation checklist that you both use when you observe each other.
c. Refer to Table 5.4, Checklist for Evaluating CALLA Instruction. Use this checklist to evaluate the CALLA lesson or unit that you planned and implemented. Share your evaluation with your coaching partner and discuss areas of strength as well as areas which can be improved.

Table 5.3

CALLA INSTRUCTIONAL PLAN

SUBJECT ______________________ ESL LEVEL ______________________

TOPIC ______________________ GRADE(S) ______________________

CONTENT OBJECTIVES ______________________

____

LANGUAGE OBJECTIVES ______________________

____

LEARNING STRATEGIES ______________________

____

MATERIALS ______________________

____

PROCEDURES

1. Preparation: How will you find out what your students already know about the topic?

2. Presentation: How will you present and explain the topic?

3. Practice: What cooperative learning activities will provide meaningful practice?

4. Evaluation: How will students assess their own learning?

5. Expansion: What thinking skills discussion questions are appropriate? How will students apply what they have learned in the unit to new situations?

Table 5.4

CHECKLIST FOR EVALUATING CALLA INSTRUCTION

1. __________ Objectives stated for content, language, and learning strategies.
2. __________ Content selected is essential for grade level(s) and is aligned with state framework/local curriculum.
3. __________ Activities develop vocabulary, listening, reading, speaking, and writing.
4. __________ One or two learning strategies directly taught and/or practiced.
5. __________ Teacher's language somewhat simplified, but not tightly controlled for grammatical structures or vocabulary.
6. __________ Students' prior knowledge elicited in Preparation phase.
7. __________ Context provided through visuals, graphic organizers, manipulatives, realia, hands-on, etc.
8. __________ Instruction includes cooperative learning activity and active practice with new information.
9. __________ Student self-evaluation activity included.
10. __________ Higher-level questions posed and discussed.
11. __________ Activity and/or discussion addresses real-life applications of content.
12. __________ Contributions of students' own culture(s) related to topic are identified and discussed.
13. __________ Student self-efficacy and motivation developed through learning strategy instruction and opportunities for success.

CHAPTER 6

Assessing Student Progress in CALLA

Overview

Teachers can choose from a number of different types of alternative assessment. They can select appropriate forms of assessment to match the knowledge and skills being measured. Teachers are then more able to adapt instruction to students' needs.

Alternative Assessment

- Purposes of Assessment
- Why Use Alternative Assessment?
- Design of Alternative Assessment

Examples of Alternative Assessment

- Performance Measures
- Text Retelling
- Cloze Testing
- Holistic and Analytic Scoring of Writing Samples
- Teacher Rating Scales
- Student Self-Rating Scales
- Assessment of Higher-order Thinking Skills

Portfolio Assessment

- Reasons for Using Portfolios
- Guidelines for Portfolio Assessment

CHAPTER 6 ASSESSING STUDENT PROGRESS

ASSESSMENT OF STUDENT PROGRESS is essential in CALLA in order to maintain continuous information on student accomplishments in relationship to instructional goals. Teachers assess the student's initial performance upon entering a CALLA program and monitor performance periodically in order to adapt instruction to the student's needs. Teachers in a CALLA program are aware of where students stand with respect to goals in content areas, academic language, and learning strategies. CALLA teachers have a sense of what the student can do independently with respect to these goals and what the student can do with assistance from either the teacher or another student.

Alternative Assessment

The purposes of assessment should drive the way in which assessment is conducted, the type of information collected, and the interpretation of the information. As will be seen, the purposes of assessment in a CALLA program suggest that alternatives to standardized tests are necessary.

PURPOSES OF ASSESSMENT

Assessment of language minority students in schools is conducted for a number of reasons. These reasons include the following: to identify students in need of special language services, to place students into appropriate programs, to identify specific instructional needs, to monitor student progress in attaining English language and content objectives, and to exit students from special language programs.[1] More general reasons for assessment include: to conduct formative program evaluation (deciding the components of a program that need modification) or to conduct summative program evaluation (determining if a program will be adopted, expanded, or discontinued).

Standardized tests are often used in evaluating overall student progress for classrooms, schools, and the district. They also provide the most objective source of information about student achievement and are used for school or district accountability. However, because the tests are usually administered only once annually, they are not useful for monitoring interim student progress in instructional programs. Furthermore, standardized tests only assess one of the three areas in which objectives are formulated in a CALLA program, content knowledge. Standardized tests do not assess the language functions that are integral to academic language or the use of learning strategies, and many standardized tests are not designed to assess integrative language or higher-order thinking skills.[2]

In CALLA classrooms, students are encouraged to use important language functions in communicating meaningful academic content and to use higher-order thinking skills such as synthesis, analysis, and evaluation. The students are supported in their efforts to become independent and strategic learners. Students are asked to identify and convey meaningful information, generate products and results, and act responsibly with regard to their own learning and to other students. Thus, if the purpose of the assessment is to monitor student progress in a CALLA program, alternative measures will have to be used.

WHY USE ALTERNATIVE ASSESSMENT?

There are six basic reasons why alternative assessment is of interest to most educators and why it is valuable in CALLA instruction.

- **Authentic**—reflects actual classroom tasks in content areas and reveals information about academic language.
- **Varied**—looks at student performance from multiple perspectives instead of relying on only one assessment approach so that all aspects of content and academic knowledge are assessed.
- **Process as well as product oriented**—shows progress with respect to both work products and the processes and learning strategies used to complete the work.
- **Continuous**—provides information about student performance that shows growth throughout the entire school year.
- **Interacts with instruction**—can be used to adapt instruction to student needs and provide feedback on instructionally valued tasks.
- **Collaborative**—is planned and conducted by teachers interactively in order to share and gain independent views of student performance.

Alternative assessments should be more intrinsically interesting to students because they are authentic and varied. When assessments are interactive with instruction and are authentic, teaching to the test is less of a relevant concern than with multiple-choice items on a standardized test. Teaching important language functions and higher-order thinking skills should be part of both instruction and assessment.

DESIGN OF ALTERNATIVE ASSESSMENT

In planning the design of alternative assessment instruments, it is important to focus on four basic procedures in instrument development:

- Construction
- Administration
- Scoring
- Interpretation

CONSTRUCTION. The **construction** of alternative assessment entails at least three steps. First, teachers must determine the *purpose* of the assessment. The purpose could be to identify LEP students in need of special language services, place students into appropriate programs, monitor student progress, and exit students from programs designed to meet their needs. The purpose may well influence the form of the assessment. For example, assessment that is designed for entry or exit from an ESL or bilingual program is more likely to be conducted individually, be administered no more than once or twice annually, be somewhat demanding of teacher and student time, and have high inter-rater reliability. Assessment that is designed to monitor student progress once students are already in a special program will require less time demands on teachers and students, could be administered in group or individual sessions, and could include a greater variety of alternative measures.

A second step in the construction of alternative assessments is to determine the instructional **outcomes** the instruments will be designed to assess. Consider the following outcomes or goals of education:

- Students will be able to communicate effectively through oral and written expression;
- Students will be able to solve problems effectively in academic areas and in daily living;
- Students will be able to use an experimental approach to collect, interpret, and describe information about their world.

An instrument to assess effective communication skills might look quite different from an instrument to assess problem solving in mathematics or analysis skills in a science laboratory. An instrument to assess communication might be a holistically scored writing or speech sample, while a science test could involve a collaborative project involving three or four students working toward a common objective.

The third step in instrument construction is to identify the **standards** for student performance at any grade level and in any content area in which the outcomes will be taught. The standards indicate what students are expected to do to demonstrate mastery related to each outcome, given the purpose of the assessment. The standards for advancing from the beginning to intermediate level in English proficiency will be different from the standards for advancing from the intermediate to advanced levels, but the outcome might still be the same. For example, to advance to a particular ESL level, an outcome such as "communicates effectively through oral and written expression" might be represented as follows:

Intermediate:	communicates orally and in writing about personal daily experiences;
Advanced:	communicates orally and in writing brief summaries of written texts in grade-level content areas.

These standards might entail any of the three areas in which objectives are stated in CALLA, including content knowledge, language, and learning strategies. In this sense, standards are no different from CALLA objectives. Content knowledge requirements can specify the number of independent concepts students must be able to explain or relate to other known concepts. The standards for language could include vocabulary, grammatical structures, and language functions such as explaining, describing, or justifying. Strategic requirements in content areas could entail problem-solving procedures in mathematics or social skills necessary to attain an objective through cooperation with other students.

ADMINISTRATION. The instrument may require individual or group administration, extensive or limited time demands, or may entail paper and pencil assessment, specific types of materials, and specific procedures for observing and recording student responses. These procedures might include naturalistic observation, or use of rating scales or checklists. Students should always be given clear directions for performing a task and may require practice in performing similar activities, especially since some ESL students may have had little prior experience with the type of activities or test items used in U.S. classrooms. Unless the students are adequately prepared, activities that require performance, cooperation, and higher-order thinking skills may be as unfamiliar as items requiring the student to fill in a bubble and select the best choice among competing alternatives.

SCORING. Criteria for scoring alternative assessment procedures should always be determined in advance through the development of a scoring *rubric*. Approaches to the holistic scoring of writing samples and performance items in selected content domains will be discussed in a subsequent section. One approach sometimes used to score writing samples holistically is to assign scores based on observation of better students in a class. For example, students who are knowledgeable about a particular historical era might include more principles and concepts and fewer historical errors in their writing than students who are less knowledgeable about the era. These differences between more and less effective students can be used in scoring subsequent writing samples.[3] A scoring rubric based on this approach would have scores on a scale of 1-3, with 3 representing the higher scores. Papers scored at the 3 level might have mentioned at least two principles or concepts and included no factual errors. Scores of 2 might have one principle and no more than 1 factual error. A score of 1 can be assigned in a similar manner.

Differences between more and less effective students can also be useful in setting performance standards for scoring in other content areas. Effective students might give more evidence of higher-order thinking skills, provide an explanation as well as a correct solution for a problem-solving process, provide more structure and internal consistency to their written report, show more evidence of cooperation with other students, or respond more directly to a hypothesis or question they were asked to address.

INTERPRETATION. Interpretations are based on the standards for student performance expressed in the scoring rubric. The scoring rubric should be designed to have meaning for instruction. In the example above, the teacher would know that students with a score of 2 need assistance in formulating principles and concepts. In solving a math word problem, a score of 3 could mean that the student can both solve the problem and explain it, while a score of 2 might mean that the student can explain the answer but made a minor mistake in calculations, and a score of 1 means that the student can solve the problem but not explain it. Sometimes labels can be used to designate responses in the scoring rubric that reflect Advanced (= 3), Intermediate (= 2), or Beginning (= 1) levels of performance, or no response (= 0).

When alternative assessments are used to make decisions about advancing students to the next level of instruction, it may be important to use a criterion score (or a minimum score) a student must obtain in order to be considered for advancement. The criterion is the total score for a number of alternative measures on which information has been collected to make this decision. A number of alternative measures should be used in order for the scores to be reliable and the decisions to be accurate. Ten such alternative measures, each with a score range of 0-3, might produce a total possible score range of 0-30.

In decisions to advance students from the beginning to intermediate level of content-ESL instruction, the criterion score might be the mid-point of the distributions of scores for beginning and intermediate students. The mid-point is the average or mean score of the two distributions (or a weighted average if the number of students in each distribution differs). The criterion level should be refined based on experience in making placement decisions with other students, successes in using the criterion, or the sense that more effective placements can be made by adjusting the criterion level up or downward. Criterion scores for moving students to more advanced levels of instruction can be set in the same way, i.e., by finding the point of overlap between scores for students at higher vs. lower levels of content knowledge and English proficiency (as determined by other independent criteria). Students who score at or above a criterion and who meet criteria on other indicators can be assigned to more advanced levels of instruction or provided with more challenging curricula. Other indicators—such as grades, attention, study skills and learning strategies, persistence, etc.—are important and should be used whenever important decisions are made about students in order to complement the information obtained from alternative assessment.

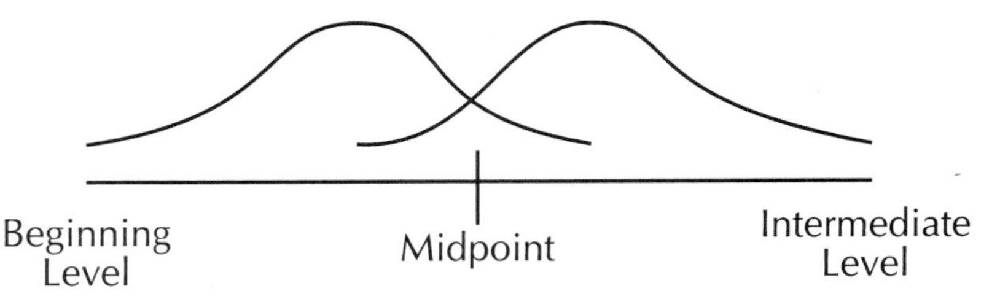

Base decisions to advance students from one level of instruction to the next on the mid-point of the distribution of scores for students in those levels.

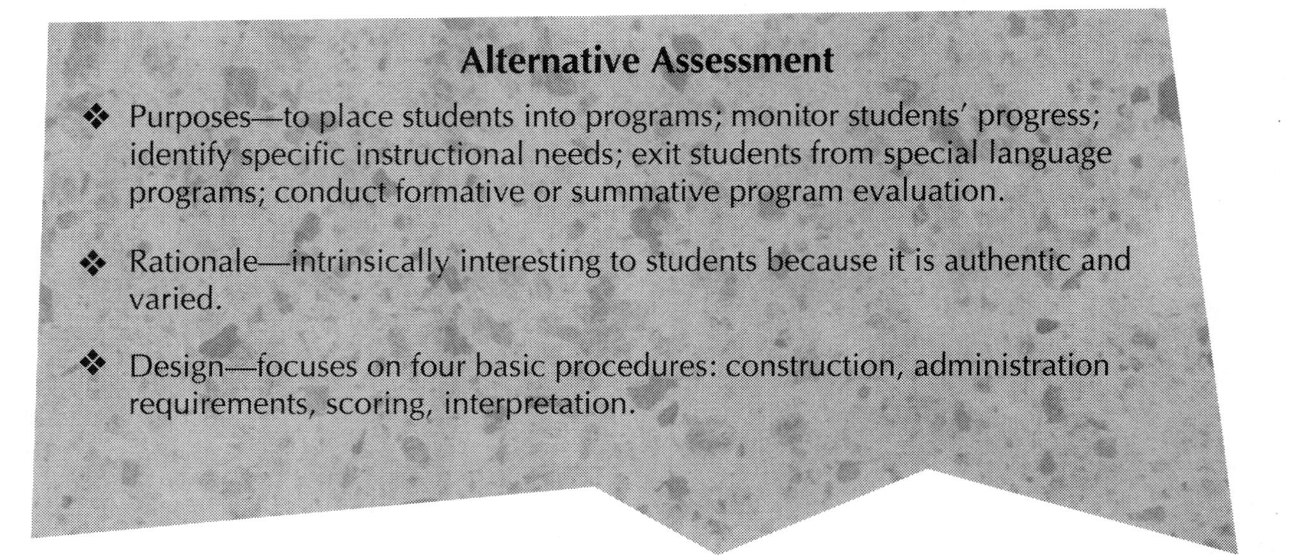

Examples of Alternative Assessment

Numerous forms of alternative assessment have been used in education generally[4] and in the instruction of language minority students.[5] The six forms of assessment that we believe will be most valuable to teachers and to students in CALLA are performance measures, text retelling, cloze testing, holistic scoring of writing samples, teacher rating scales, and student self-rating scales. In this section, we introduce these briefly and discuss how each can be used. Many of these forms of assessment can be used in the assessment of language arts or content areas such as science and social studies. Each of these approaches has its own purposes and its own strengths and limitations.

PERFORMANCE MEASURES

Performance assessment is a special type of alternative assessment that entails direct assessment of desired student behaviors such as speaking, writing, or problem solving.[6] In performance assessment, students are asked to use knowledge and skills to produce a product, working individually, in pairs, or in small groups. The product can be a response to an open-ended question, a drawing, an oral presentation or written document, a model or constructed figure, an exhibition or demonstration, or the results of an experiment or project. Teachers can assess the product using anecdotal records, a checklist, rating scale, or observation procedure. As in other alternative assessments, performance assessment requires teacher observation and judgment and integration of knowledge and skills by the student. The more generic term, "alternative assessment," can include any of these but may also include teacher ratings, observations, cloze tests, and student self-assessment.

Performance assessment calls upon students to demonstrate specific skills and competencies, and to apply the skills and knowledge they have mastered.[7] In CALLA, these skills and knowledge are in content areas, academic language, and learning strategies. Some specific examples of performance assessment in science and in math are given in the following sections. Other examples in specific content areas and for learning strategies are described in the model units in Chapter 9 (CALLA Science), Chapter 10 (CALLA Mathematics), Chapter 11 (CALLA Social Studies), and Chapter 12 (CALLA Literature and Composition). The examples which follow call on different kinds of skills and knowledge for students at different grade levels. There is an emphasis in each item on the **process** by which the solution is obtained rather than exclusively on the **product** or the correct answer, and the scoring should reflect this emphasis.

Performance Assessment—Science

1. Observe two animal specimens (which can be live, pictures, or plastic models) and list three ways they are alike and three ways they are different.[8]
2. Create a classification system for a collection of leaves and explain the adjustments necessary when a "mystery leaf" is introduced to the group.[9]
3. Perform a number of tests on a collection of rocks, record the results, and classify them based on the information provided.[10]
4. A small tree is planted in a meadow. After 20 years it has grown into a big tree, weighing 250 kg more than when it was planted. Where do the extra 250 kg come from? Explain your answer as fully as you can.[11]

Performance Assessment—Mathematics

1. Write a word problem that requires multiplying 59 x 12 for a solution.[12]
2. Draw as many diagrams as you can that represent the multiplication fact 12 x 59 = 708 and explain what each means.[13]
3. James knows that half of the students in his school are accepted at the public university nearby. Also, half are accepted at the local private college. Based on this information, he thinks he has a 100% chance of being accepted at one institution or the other. Explain why James may be wrong.[14]
4. You have a bag of 30 identical wooden cubes.
    a. If you spread the cubes out on a table, how many cubes would you need to completely cover the largest possible square surface on the table? Draw a diagram.
    b. What is the largest possible cube that you can make from the 30 cubes? Explain why this is the largest possible cube.[15]
5. You and a friend, Sheila, were shopping in a grocery store for food and beverages for a picnic. When you were buying soda, you noticed that you could

buy it in quart (32 oz.) bottles or in six-packs of 12 oz. bottles. The six-pack costs $1.49 and the quart bottle costs $0.73. Sheila suggested buying two quart bottles because it would be cheaper. Being thrifty, you took out your pocket calculator and concluded that the six-pack would get you more soda per dollar. Sheila asked how you knew that.

Write an explanation of how you knew the six-pack of soda was a better value than the two quart bottles. Give enough detail so that Sheila will be able to understand the approach and use it whenever she is in a similar situation.[16]

6. María wants to tie string around a box that is 12 inches long, 2 inches high, and 5 inches wide. If she needs an extra 6 inches to tie the knot, how much string will she need? Draw a picture of the box and explain how you got the answer and how you can check your answer.

Note that these items were developed for native English-speaking students. To use them or similar items for ESL students, language assistance will likely be necessary. For example, the items could be rewritten in simpler language, illustrated, and shortened where possible (e.g., Science 4 and Math 3 and 5 above). The simplified items could be read aloud to students or recorded on tape, and students should be allowed to ask for clarification of unknown words. Another possibility is for performance assessment directions to be written in students' native language and to accept responses in that language.

As is evident from these examples, the design of alternative assessment items will vary depending on the nature of the content and the objectives being assessed. Nevertheless, some general principles can be formulated, consistent with the specifications for design of alternative assessment instruments that we identified earlier.

HOW TO USE PERFORMANCE ASSESSMENT

Construction

- Establish whether the purpose of the assessment is to determine student placement, monitor student progress, or exit students from a program.
- Determine the outcomes and the specific standards or objectives the items will be designed to assess. Specify the requirements for performing this type of task during instruction. If appropriate, design the item so that separate scores can be assigned to the process for attaining the solution as well as to the correct answer.

Administration

- Select any materials needed to perform the task and make packets of these materials available for students.
- Determine if the items will be administered individually or as a small group assignment and specify any time limitations.
- Determine how to collect student responses, through written responses, ratings, observations, anecdotal records, or tapes.
- Provide students who are unfamiliar with this type of item with an opportunity to practice items of this type and inform the students about the criteria for scoring (both the process score and the product score).

Scoring

- Develop a scoring rubric which assigns scores on a 0-3, 0-6, or some similar range and that differentiates successful from unsuccessful student performance. One approach to scoring is to sort papers first into three stacks based on responses to each item and assign point values to each paper.[17]

Interpretation

- Identify the level or standard at which students must perform in order to meet the purposes of the assessment. That is, should the student have all "Advanced" responses in order to progress to the next instructional level or to exit from the program?

The exercises used in performance assessment should be varied so that students do not become bored with the type of item used. Some possibilities are: written items or group projects, debates, treasure hunts, oral history projects, role playing famous contemporary or historical figures, mock job interviews, games, design competitions, historical re-enactments, science fairs, merit badges, student-run banks and stores, designing newspaper ads, and making a class newspaper within set time and cost limits.[18]

One of the keys to successful performance assessment is the use of objective and reliable scoring criteria. All types of alternative assessment involve subjective judgments and are therefore liable to be inaccurate. This liability can be addressed directly by exerting caution in the item design such that the purposes of the assessment, the conditions under which the assessment is performed, the materials used, the instructions to students, and the scoring criteria are clearly specified in advance. If the products are written or recorded on tape, teachers can use sample "anchor" products representing Advanced, Intermediate, and Beginning performance to establish inter-rater agreement with other teachers.

TEXT RETELLING

Text retelling is based on the assessment procedures used in story retelling. Because expository and narrative texts are involved rather than only narrative texts, we have relabeled this approach "text retelling." Text retelling, as with story retelling, assesses listening and speaking skills and may be used with texts drawn from literature or with content materials, as in history or science. The technique is especially useful with students who are unable to read well in English. Reading aloud to students provides access to content they are not yet able to read independently.

Students who are acquiring English may not be familiar with the procedures of text retelling and may need support while they are learning. The text retelling process described here is intended to give students that support while at the same time engaging them in the assessment. The process described below is also intended to reduce the immediate influence of differences in memory for the text sequence. By following the procedures described here, students can be expected to have reasonable familiarity with the text by the time they are asked to retell it.

HOW TO USE TEXT RETELLING

Construction

- Select an appropriate text passage to read to the students. The text should contain content and language that are challenging to the student but not be so difficult that they will fail to understand the information. Students should have some familiarity with the topic.

Administration

- Read the text aloud using a natural pace and intonation, pausing at commas and periods. You may ask students to try to listen selectively for the main points, sequence of events, names, characters, or other important items appropriate to the text.
- Discuss the text with students in any convenient grouping, whether it is between the teacher and student, a peer-led group discussion, or a teacher-led group discussion. Ask students to review the main points, sequence, ideas, characters, etc. and to identify any vocabulary, concepts, or information they did not understand.
- Read the text again at the same pace as before, enabling students to answer any questions they had raised about the text or to fill in any missing information. At this point, students may take notes if they have sufficient writing and note-taking skills.
- Students can retell the text orally or in writing. Students should be allowed to use notes in their text retelling presentation. If the retelling is done orally, the students may retell the text to the entire class or in the same small group with which they discussed the story earlier.

Scoring

- The rating criteria for text retelling must be determined by the teacher in advance. The teacher can rate the same points as were emphasized previously: the main points, sequence, etc. The teacher can also rate aspects such as coherence and content knowledge. If students write the text, we do not encourage marking story retelling papers on more traditional language points such as vocabulary use and mechanics. If the retelling is done in a small group, other students can rate their peers and provide them with feedback provided that the teacher communicates the criteria clearly to the raters and that the student who makes the presentation can ask the raters questions.

Reliability

- The inter-rater reliability of the scoring needs to be checked. One way to do this is to have a second rater assign a rating and determine the level of agreement. Call in a third rater, if needed, to arbitrate disagreements. The arbitration rate on a 4-6 point scale (+ or −1 point) should be no more than 10 percent.

The text retelling technique is useful in providing students with skills in either oral presentations or in writing. We believe it is particularly useful in giving students experience in making oral presentations because it enables them to organize their thoughts around the main points and content information that are most important.

If individual students have difficulty with text retelling, the teacher can reduce the difficulty of the text or the material on which the text is based. The teacher can also ensure that the students have the vocabulary to handle the material and have the underlying concepts required to comprehend essential points in the text. Another approach is to reduce the task demands or the difficulty of what the student is expected to do with the material. That is, the teacher can call on thinking skills at the knowledge and comprehension levels rather than analysis and evaluation. Higher-order thinking skills can be introduced when the student has gained greater command over the material, but should not be postponed too long.

When the text retelling is a written rather than an oral product, teachers can provide feedback on more traditional language points such as grammar and language mechanics (capitalization, punctuation, and spelling) in a number of different ways other than covering each paper with red marks. While reading through the papers, teachers can make separate notes on the types of errors that students make. The teacher can then lead a group discussion of the correct language points related to these errors, using specific examples from student story retelling without identifying individual students. Students are then asked to edit their own papers and submit a revised and rewritten version with appropriate corrections. Students can work to improve the papers in cooperative learning groups based on general points the teacher has made after analyzing the papers. The teacher can also provide students with the scoring rubric and with papers that define the different scoring levels (perhaps with the teacher's annotated comments). These papers are often referred to as "anchor" papers, accurate illustrations of each point on the scoring continuum (e.g., one each for Advanced, Intermediate, High Beginning, and Low Beginning). Ask students to rewrite their paper individually or in small groups based on the anchor papers. Students can be grouped heterogeneously for these activities and, in order to avoid labeling, need not be given a score at this point.

CLOZE TESTING

A cloze test is based on a reading passage from which selected words have been deleted. The task for the student is to identify the missing words. The cloze test assesses reading comprehension.[19] Two advantages of this technique over other procedures for assessing reading comprehension is that the cloze technique calls on integrative language skills and is easy for the teacher to construct. The teacher need only identify a passage from a text and retype the passage, having deleted selected words. Cloze tests are excellent ways to assess content knowledge, because the teacher can select grade appropriate (or near grade appropriate) content passages for the reading text. Cloze testing eliminates the necessity of developing multiple-choice items, particularly the rather difficult chore of developing effective multiple-choice distractors.

In language arts, cloze tests are usually designed with a *random deletion* approach in which every seventh or ninth word is deleted following the first two complete sentences. However, cloze tests can be used to assess reading comprehension in content areas as well as to assess reading comprehension in language arts. In content areas, a *purposive deletion* cloze may be more appropriate than a random deletion cloze. In a purposive deletion cloze, the words deleted are selected intentionally to represent important content words in the subject area that occur approximately every seventh or ninth word.

HOW TO USE CLOZE TESTING

Construction

- Select a grade or near grade appropriate reading passage of approximately 150 words from a text. The text can be drawn from literature, social studies, or science, and students should have had some prior familiarity with the topic.
- Delete every seventh or ninth word from the reading text, but leave the first two sentences and the last sentence intact. Make all blanks the same size. In a *random deletion cloze,* the same interval is used throughout, whichever interval is selected. The deleted word may be any word that appears in the text. In a *purposive deletion cloze,* the interval may vary and the deleted word can be one type of word only, such as content area words. Another option is

to delete words for linguistic reasons, such as past tense words or plurals to determine if the student's command over structure or mechanics is maintained in a subject area context.

Administration

- Practice using a cloze test for students who may not be familiar with this type of assessment. If a student gets more than 57% of the answers correct, continue to give increasingly difficult passages.
- Give clear directions. Encourage students to (a) read the passage through completely to understand the topic and some of the main ideas before filling in any blanks, (b) skip over difficult items and return to them later, and (c) not worry about spelling.
- Use flexible time limits.

Scoring

- Decide on a rating procedure. Three forms of rating cloze items are (a) *exact* word scoring, in which students must supply the exact word used in the original; (b) *appropriate correct* word scoring, in which students supply an appropriate word that is grammatically correct; and (c) *appropriate* word scoring, in which students can supply any appropriate word regardless of its grammatical accuracy. Do not count off for spelling. The advantage of the exact word approach is in simplicity of scoring. However, accepting synonyms, especially with students learning English, can be advantageous because students may not know the exact word that appeared in the original text. Another option is to accept words written in the student's native language when *content*, rather than language, is being assessed.
- Score the papers.

  (a) To obtain the number of correct items, subtract the number incorrect from the total number of blanks in the cloze.

  (b) To get the proportion correct, divide the number correct by the total number of blanks.

  (c) To convert the proportion to a percent, multiply the proportion correct by 100.

  The papers can be scored by the teacher, or the students can score their own papers. If students score their own papers, they can assemble in small groups, discuss their answers, and decide on the most reasonable answer for the missing entry. This is a useful exercise because students are using academic language in the discussion. The teacher can provide feedback with the original deleted word after the students' discussion is completed.

Interpretation

- The following criteria are based on the exact word scoring method in a random deletion cloze. These criteria were developed for native English speakers. There are no similar criteria that have been established for other scoring methods.

  57% or more correct = student should be able to read a passage at this grade level with limited instruction.

  44-56% correct = student should be able to comprehend the material after some instruction.

  Less than 44% correct = material is too difficult even with instruction. Use easier material.

- To find normative performance, administer the cloze test to native English speaking students at the appropriate grade level. Then find the average score, and determine the quartile scores defining the bottom 25%, 50%, and 75% of the students. The average score for native English speakers is the target average performance for students acquiring English, and the percentages of students acquiring English in each quartile should be approximately 25%.

Three religions and their holy books.

The Middle East has long been a meeting place for people and ideas as well as a crossroads for trade. Three of the world's great religions began in the Middle East. These religions are Judaism, Christianity, and Islam. People who believe in these religions are called Jews, Christians, and Moslems. Judaism, Christianity, and Islam spread from the Middle East to all parts of the world. Today there are millions of Jews, Christians, and Moslems living all over the world.

Each of these religions has its own holy book. The Hebrew name for the Jewish holy book is *Tenach*. In English it is called the Bible. The word *bible* comes from a Greek word meaning books. Christians also call their holy book the Bible, but it is not exactly the same as the Jewish Bible. Moslems call their holy book the Koran.

The holy books of Judaism, Christianity, and Islam are very old. The most recent one, the Koran, was written over 1,300 years ago.

Directions: First read all three paragraphs. Then write in the missing words. If you do not know a word, skip it and come back to it later. Spelling does not count.

The Middle East has long been a meeting place for people and ideas as well as a crossroads for trade. Three of the world's great religions began in the Middle East. These religions are Judaism, Christianity, and x Jews. People who believe in these religions are called Jews, Christians, and Moslems. Judaism, Christianity, and Islam spread from the Middle East to all parts of the world. x On there are millions of Jews, Christians, x Judaism Moslems living all over the world.

all of these religions has its own holy book. The Hebrew name for the x this holy book is *Tenach*. In English it is called the Bible. The word *bible* came from a Greek word meaning books. x Hebrews also call their holy book the Bible, but it is not exactly the x name as the Jewish Bible. Moslems call x this holy book the Koran.

The holy book of Judaism, Christianity, and Islam are very old. The most recent one, the Koran, was written over 1,300 years ago.

9 correct answers
9 ÷ 16 = 0.56
0.56 × 100 = 56% correct
(average score for class = 61%)

from *Europe, Asia, Africa and Australia.*

Cloze procedures are important in CALLA classrooms because students are expected to learn both content and academic language. By assessing academic language in the context of the appropriate content area—whether the passage is in science, history, or another area—teachers are providing students an opportunity to use their inferencing and comprehension skills to their best advantage. If students have difficulty with cloze passages, the teacher should first ensure that the students understand the nature of the task and what is expected. The teacher can provide the students with background information related to the passage by introducing antecedent concepts using graphic organizers or visuals. The teacher can also reduce the complexity of the language in the passage or the concepts on which the passage is based.

HOLISTIC AND ANALYTIC SCORING OF WRITING SAMPLES

Teachers in CALLA score student writing samples for the overall conceptual information and for clarity of writing. The purpose of the assessment is to evaluate the student's ability to communicate in writing in a coherent way.[21] This is consistent with the process writing approach used in CALLA, in which students plan, write drafts, obtain feedback, edit, revise, and produce a final version of a paper that is scored on the student's success in communicating ideas. A writing sample is an example of a performance assessment since the direct purpose is to determine how well students write.

The purpose of the assessment and the criteria for successful performance should be identified clearly for students before they begin to write. These purposes will influence the *genre* or the topic and style students are asked to address in the writing prompt. The following guidelines will be useful in eliciting the writing sample and are appropriate for beginning-level students being asked to write about a familiar topic.[22]

GUIDELINES FOR OBTAINING A WRITING SAMPLE

- ***Planning***. Have lined, blank sheets of paper and a pencil ready for each student. Encourage students to use a pencil without an eraser and to scratch out first drafts since edited passages may reveal information about the student's writing processes.
- ***Administration.*** In the first writing sample collected, encourage students to select one of the following topics for writing one or two paragraphs: (a) My first day in school this year; (b) The most interesting person I have ever met; or (c) Something fun that happened to me. Give students five minutes to plan and between 15 and 30 minutes to write, depending on the proficiency or age of the students. Then have students review the paragraphs they wrote and correct any mistakes they may have made. Later writing samples can focus on topics introduced in CALLA classes, such as specific themes in literature or composition or a description of a science experiment.
- ***Scoring***. Student writing samples are rated as "Advanced," "Intermediate,""High Beginning," or "Low Beginning" in each of the following categories: organization, vocabulary, language use, and mechanics. (See scoring criteria below.) We recommend avoiding pejorative labels such as "inadequate" or "poor."
- ***Interpretation.*** Students whose writing samples receive the two lowest ratings in any of the four dimensions may be limited in their ability to write in English.

  Specific scoring criteria for evaluating the writing sample are shown in the following chart.

CRITERIA FOR SCORING A WRITING SAMPLE

ORGANIZATION: Relative to the writing of a native speaker of English of the same age, how smoothly do the thoughts in the written passage flow? This characteristic may be applied with more validity to the writing of students above the sixth grade. This criterion can be eliminated from the evaluation of samples from younger students.

Advanced: fluent expression, ideas clearly stated/supported, succinct, well-organized, logical sequencing, cohesive.

Intermediate: somewhat choppy, loosely organized but main ideas stand out, limited support, logical but incomplete sequencing.

High Beginning: non-fluent, ideas confused or disconnected, lacks logical sequencing and development.

Low Beginning: does not communicate, no organization, OR not enough to evaluate.

VOCABULARY AND WORD FORMS: Relative to the writing of a native speaker of English of the same age, how ade quate is the range of words used in the passage?

Advanced: sophisticated range, effective word/idiom choice and usage, word form mastery.

Intermediate: adequate range, occasional errors of word/idiom form, choice, usage *but meaning not obscured.*

Beginning: essentially translation, little knowledge of English vocabulary, idioms, word form OR not enough to evaluate.

LANGUAGE USE: Relative to the writing of a native speaker of English of the same age, how adequate are the grammatical structures used by the student?

Advanced: effective complex constructions, appropriate register, and few errors of agreement, tense, number, word order/function, articles, pronouns, prepositions.

Intermediate: effective but simple constructions, minor problems in complex constructions, several errors of agreement, tense, number, word order/function, articles, pronouns, prepositions *but meaning seldom obscured.*

Beginning: virtually no mastery of sentence construction rules, dominated by errors, does not communicate, OR not enough to evaluate.

MECHANICS: Relative to the writing of a native speaker of English of the same age, how well has the student mastered paragraphing, spelling, punctuation, and capitalization?

Advanced: demonstrates mastery of conventions, few errors of spelling, punctuation, capitalization, paragraphing.

Intermediate: occasional errors of spelling, punctuation, capitalization, paragraphing *but meaning not obscured.*

High Beginning: frequent errors of spelling, punctuation, capitalization, paragraphing, *meaning confused or obscured.*

Low Beginning: no mastery of conventions, dominated by errors of spelling, punctuation, capitalization, paragraphing OR not enough to evaluate.

In scoring *holistically*, the criteria are used to obtain a single overall score. In scoring *analytically*, the scores are assigned in each area (organization, etc.) and holistically as well.

In a CALLA program, students at the intermediate level of English proficiency should be asked to write in a number of different genres, such as narrative, expository, persuasive, and creative writing. For each genre, the criteria for scoring the writing samples will vary. For example, the papers submitted by students asked to write about a historical topic can be scored based on the number of principles or concepts and the chronological sequence identified and the absence of errors, as mentioned previously. Papers submitted by students asked to write about a science topic or to describe the outcomes of a science project can be scored based on their understanding of a scientific principle, ability to describe the steps of the scientific method in the project context, or on language structures and mechanics. If the purpose is to assess substantive knowledge, structures and mechanics should be given less weight in scoring.

Use writing samples to assess a student's ability to communicate in writing in a coherent way.

School will be over on June 16th. If I could travel back in time to the beginning of the school year, the one thing that I would change would be my study habits.

I really need to change my study habits because whenever my teachers were writing on the board, I would never take notes. When the test finally came up, I had nothing to study from.

I never wrote down the assignments that the teachers had given. When I got home, I always turned on the T.V. I watched it until 10 o'clock. Then, I tried to call my friend to ask about the homework, but it was too bad that nobody would pick up the phone because they had all gone to bed.

I would have had a better year in school if I took notes, wrote down the assignments, and tried to stop watching T.V. until 10 pm.

organization: advanced
vocabulary + word forms: advanced
language use: advanced
mechanics: advanced

TEACHER RATING SCALES

Teacher rating scales provide CALLA teachers with an effective means of developing continuous assessments of student progress. Teachers can collect data at varying intervals, whether the interval is monthly or quarterly. The frequency depends on the nature of the knowledge and skills the teacher wants to include in the rating, and how much these can be expected to change over time. Teacher ratings can be developed in any or all of the four language skills and in content areas and can reflect learning processes as well as learning outcomes. The rating scales can be based on direct observation of student language or on products and interim products.

We encourage teachers to make regular anecdotal records on student progress to supplement and expand on the information recorded on rating scales. These anecdotal records can be a rich source of information that will be useful for instructional planning. The anecdotal records can be noted on stick-on labels with the student's name, and can be transferred to a formal record book at a later time or to a portfolio. These anecdotal records can focus on the student's progress relative to instructional goals (content, language, or learning strategies), the student's responsiveness to various instructional materials or methods, evidence of the student's attitudes or motivation, responsiveness to various instructional materials or methods, or the processes the student employs in schoolwork or in problem solving.

Teacher rating scales are most useful for assessing language development and content knowledge in CALLA lessons. A sample rating scale for literacy skills that includes both affective and strategic processes is shown in Table 6.1.

Interpretation of the terms "effective," "sometimes effective," and "needs work" is of the greatest importance in order for this rating scale to be useful. We suggest that "effective" be used synonymously with "does this without assistance." Similarly, "sometimes effective" can be equated with "does this sometimes without assistance," and "needs work" is similar to "usually needs assistance."

Use of teacher rating scales in the content areas can be conducted by identifying lesson objectives in content, academic language, and learning strategies. The objectives appearing on a rating scale should be sufficiently general as to reflect the broader understandings and skills that are typical of CALLA lessons. The objectives should be linked directly to instructional activities in the classroom. One possibility for a geography lesson, as shown in Table 6.2, is to identify in columns the objectives for content, academic language, and learning strategies. These objectives will have appeared in the CALLA lesson plan. Student names can be listed down the left column. Attainment of the objectives indicated can be conducted using 3 = Meets Objective, 2 = Needs Improvement, or 1 = Does Not Meet Objective.

Similar rating scales in other content areas can be constructed by referring to the objectives of each CALLA lesson and setting up the columns to reflect content, language, and strategies. In this way, teachers can monitor student progress.

STUDENT SELF-RATING SCALES

Student self-rating scales are an important part of CALLA. Self-rating requires the student to exercise a variety of learning strategies and higher-order thinking skills that not only provide feedback to the student but also provide direction for future learning. Students performing self-ratings understand their goals for learning, monitor their success in achieving the goals, monitor their comprehension of reading or listening materials while they are learning, review the processes they used to learn the materials, and evaluate the success of their learning upon completion of an activity. All of this mental processing is useful for learning academic content and language. In addition, and perhaps of most importance, students are empowered by self-evaluation through analysis and planning for their own educational development.

Table 6.1

SAMPLE LITERACY DEVELOPMENT CHECKLIST

Mark: ☒ = Effective ⧄ = Sometimes Effective ⊟ = Needs Work

Reading Processes	**School Quarter: 1**	**2**	**3**	**4**
I. READING SKILLS				
Comprehends oral stories	☐	☐	☐	☐
Understands vocabulary	☐	☐	☐	☐
Fluently decodes	☐	☐	☐	☐
Comprehends literally	☐	☐	☐	☐
Comprehends inferentially	☐	☐	☐	☐
II. INTEREST				
Initiates own reading	☐	☐	☐	☐
Shows pleasure in reading	☐	☐	☐	☐
Selects books independently	☐	☐	☐	☐
Chooses books of appropriate difficulty	☐	☐	☐	☐
Samples a variety of materials	☐	☐	☐	☐
III. APPLICATIONS				
Participates in reading discussion groups	☐	☐	☐	☐
Writes appropriate dialogue journal entries	☐	☐	☐	☐
Uses reading in written communication	☐	☐	☐	☐
IV. STRATEGIES				
Monitors attention	☐	☐	☐	☐
Notices miscues that interfere with meaning	☐	☐	☐	☐
Infers word meaning	☐	☐	☐	☐
Summarizes main ideas or key events	☐	☐	☐	☐
Links details to main ideas	☐	☐	☐	☐
Remembers sequence of events	☐	☐	☐	☐
Predicts conclusions	☐	☐	☐	☐
Requests help if needed	☐	☐	☐	☐

Adapted from materials developed by the National Council of Teachers of English and by the Writing Laboratory of the University of New Hampshire.[23]

One of the important features of student self-ratings is that students can rate their progress in all three areas of a CALLA lesson: content, academic language, and learning strategies. Student self-ratings in these three areas can be placed on a single-page "Learning Log" summarizing content, language, and strategy objectives for a single lesson, or can be placed on separate pages to emphasize the different objectives or strategies. Although teachers can develop ratings in growth of student content knowledge and language, students are in the best position to analyze their own progress in strategy awareness and use because so many strategies are covert mental processes. Students can perform self-ratings on generic learning activities, answering questions such as "What is the most important thing I learned this week?" and "What was hard, and what was easy?" They can also conduct self-ratings on more specific learning processes and products such as "Which strategy worked best for me with these materials?" or "Can I write the main points and details for that chapter?"

A generic Learner Diary discussed by Nunan[23] that can be included as part of a portfolio of student work is shown in Table 6.3. In this self-rating, students reflect

Table 6.2

CALLA STUDENT ASSESSMENT FORM

Topic: World Geographical Regions

Evaluation of student progress in meeting content, language, and learning strategy objectives.
Scale: 3 = Meets Objective; 2 = Needs Improvement; 1 = Does Not Meet Objective.

Date	**Unit Objectives**		
	Content	**Language**	**Learning Strategies**
Student Name	**Identify/describe world geographical regions**	**Write paragraphs comparing features of two regions.**	**Listen selectively; Take notes on a T-List and compare/contrast**

on learning activities and focus on the way in which they used English and interacted with others using their English skills. They also analyze their learning difficulties and identify a plan for overcoming them.

A self-rating like the one shown in Table 6.3 can be entered into a student's portfolio and used as a reflection of student attitudes at one point in time. Later self-evaluations may change and can be used to analyze growth in self-perceptions of content and language learning. Teachers should review student self-evaluations from time to time and discuss improvements shown or comment on techniques students can use to overcome difficulties they are encountering.

Students can rate their progress in specific content areas using a form such as the one shown in Table 6.4. In this rating, students indicate their attitudes about what they have learned in math and identify easy and difficult topics in addition to topics on which they need assistance. Students can reflect on their learning and their accomplishments while developing an individual action plan for working on areas where they need assistance. In the rating scale shown in Table 6.4, the term "Math" could be replaced with the name of any other content area, such as science or social studies. As with all student self-assessments, the information can be entered into a portfolio and used for joint teacher-student discussions and planning.

Students can rate their use of learning strategies using a form such as the one shown in Table 6.5, which focuses on learning strategy applications in science. In designing any learning strategies questionnaire, identify a specific learning activity that is highly important to the content area, as in making observations in science. Then select a number of strategies that might be appropriate for this task, and formulate a number of questions that will detect whether or not any of these strategies are in fact being used. The learning strategies questionnaire in Table 6.5 will deter-

Table 6.3

LEARNER DIARY

Complete one diary sheet each week.

NAME: ______________________ DATE: ____________

This week I studied...	
This week I learned...	
This week I used English in these places...	
This week I spoke English with these people...	
This week I made these mistakes...	
This is difficult for me...	
I would like to know...	
My plan for learning and practicing next week is...	

mine the types of strategies students use in keeping a science notebook while conducting observations of a caterpillar turning into a butterfly. The questionnaire can be administered to classroom-size groups and used in a variety of ways. Teachers may want to make an overhead of the questionnaire and discuss each item with the class so that students understand the strategy descriptions in the questionnaire. Students might discuss their answers in small groups, describing the way in which they use a strategy to accomplish the goal indicated by the activity. There are no right or wrong answers, since individual students might combine or emphasize different strategies. However, students who fail to indicate any strategic approach whatsoever can be encouraged to select one or more strategies, try them out, and report on their success.

Table 6.4

MATH SELF-EVALUATION

NAME: ______________________________ Date: ____________

These are two important things I learned in math this week:

1. ____

____

2. ____

____

This is an *easy* problem for me:

This is a *difficult* problem for me:

I need more help with:

____

____

This is how I feel about math this week: (Circle the words that are true).

successful	confused	relaxed
interested	bored	excited
happy	worried	upset

This is where I got help this week: (Circle the words that are true.)

my teacher   my friend   my classmate   my parents

Table 6.5

CALLA LEARNING STRATEGIES QUESTIONNAIRE

Name ____ Date____________________

SCIENCE

You have a caterpillar in a jar, and you are going to observe how it changes. You have to write down what you learn in your science notebook.

Caterpillar

HOW DO YOU MAKE OBSERVATIONS AND WRITE A SCIENCE NOTEBOOK? CIRCLE THE WORDS THAT TELL WHAT YOU DO. THERE ARE NO RIGHT OR WRONG ANSWERS!

1. I look carefully at the caterpillar every day and I notice if there are any changes. (Selective Attention)

   Never Rarely Sometimes Usually Always

2. I work with a friend to make observations and to talk about what we see. (Cooperation)

   Never Rarely Sometimes Usually Always

3. I plan how I'm going to write or record my observations. (Organizational Planning)

   Never Rarely Sometimes Usually Always

4. I write down my observations every day. (Note-taking; Self-management)

   Never Rarely Sometimes Usually Always

5. I look in science books to find out more information about the life cycle of the butterfly. (Resourcing)

   Never Rarely Sometimes Usually Always

6. I ask my teacher to explain why the caterpillar changes. (Questioning for clarification)

   Never Rarely Sometimes Usually Always

7. I draw pictures or diagrams to show my observations. (Imagery)

   Never Rarely Sometimes Usually Always

8. I check my science notebook before I hand it in to my teacher. (Self-evaluation)

   Never Rarely Sometimes Usually Always

9. What other things do you do to learn about science?

Note: Strategy names in parenthesis would not appear on student page.

Table 6.6
QUESTIONS FOR QUALITY THINKING

Knowledge—Identification and recall of information

Who, what, when, where, how ______________________________?

Describe ______________________________

Comprehension—Organization and selection of facts and ideas

Retell ______________________________in your own words.

What is the main idea of______________________________?

Application—Use of facts, rules, principles

How is ____________________ an example of ____________________?

How is ____________________ related to ____________________?

Why is ______________________________ significant?

Analysis—Separation of a whole into component parts

What are the parts or features of ______________________________?

Classify ____________________according to ____________________?

Outline/diagram/web ______________________________.

How does ____________________ compare/contrast with ____________________?

What evidence can you present for ______________________________?

Synthesis—Combination of ideas to form a new whole

What would you predict/infer from ______________________________?

What ideas can you add to______________________________?

How would you create/design a new ______________________________?

What might happen if you combined____________________with ____________________?

What solutions would you suggest for ______________________________?

Evaluation—Development of opinions, judgments, or decisions

Do you agree with ______________________________?

What do you think about ______________________________?

What is the most important ______________________________?

Prioritize ____________________ according to ____________________.

How would you decide about ______________________________?

Adapted from *Questions for Quality Thinking,* Maryland State Department of Education.[24]

ASSESSMENT OF HIGHER-ORDER THINKING SKILLS

The introduction of higher-order thinking skills in CALLA pervades the entire instructional approach. There is no justification for waiting to introduce higher-order thinking until students have attained some minimal level of English proficiency. CALLA teachers introduce higher-order thinking skills in all aspects of their instruction, including presentations on new topics, question-answer sessions, small group work, and student presentations and essays, and in self-evaluation of students.

The items in Table 6.6 give teachers an idea of the variety of ways that information about all levels of the cognitive domain can be elicited from students. Questions at the Knowledge level are commonly asked of students with beginning skills in English proficiency, such as "Who was the main character in this story?" and "Where did the story happen?" What these examples illustrate is that questions at higher levels in the cognitive domain need not be reserved for students with advanced proficiency in English. Even beginning students can be asked questions at the Evaluation level, such as "Do you agree that (an evaluative statement)? Why or why not?" and "Here are three ways to evaluate (an assertion or ideas). Choose one way. Tell why it's a good way to evaluate (the assertion or idea)."

Before assessing higher-order thinking skills, students need practice with both the activities and the language associated with thinking. Teachers can facilitate student understanding by modeling both thinking skills and academic language through thinking aloud while analyzing, synthesizing, or evaluating concepts or actions.

Examples of Alternative Measures

- Performance Measures: The student is asked to perform a comprehensive task requiring integration of knowledge and skills in order to generate a written or subject-related product.
- Text Retelling: Similar to story retelling as a measure of oral proficiency but adapted to be used with academic content.
- Cloze Testing: Assessment of reading comprehension in which every seventh or ninth word is deleted from a narrative and the student is asked to supply the missing word.
- Holistic Scoring of Writing Samples: A passage written by the student that is given one global score or rating based on criteria such as organization, vocabulary and word forms, language use, and mechanics.
- Teacher Rating Scales: Teacher ratings of student performance related to instructional objectives based on observation.
- Student Self-Rating Scales: Self-ratings by the student on performance related to instructional objectives or other areas in which performance can be understood.

Portfolio Assessment

REASONS FOR USING PORTFOLIOS

A portfolio is a collection of student work and information about the student that shows progress in learning. Portfolios are useful for monitoring student progress and for adapting instruction to student needs.[25] The application of portfolios in education is based on its use in the arts where individuals maintain a sample of their paintings, photographs, or other representations of their work. "Portfolio assessment," as the term is used here, is a systematic collection of student work and other information about the student that is combined with a procedure for determining whether or not the student has maintained progress in accomplishing important instructional goals. Thus, portfolio assessment is more than merely a collection of the student's work—it is part of an integrative plan that enables teachers to monitor student progress in important curriculum areas. The portfolio enables teachers to judge student achievement, growth, and thinking processes. Portfolios enable the teacher to communicate with students, other teachers, parents, and administrators about the progress being made by students and enable the teacher to point to specific representations of the student's work that illustrate this progress. Portfolios arm the teacher with evidence in support of instructional decisions that affect the student, and are particularly useful to CALLA teachers who need to communicate with grade-level teachers. There are five basic reasons for using portfolio assessment in CALLA instruction.

PORTFOLIO ASSESSMENT IS SYSTEMATIC. Teachers who are monitoring student progress need a system for assembling all of the information they are collecting about student participation in the class. They need a mechanism for keeping track of this information and the way it is being used in instructional decisions. Although there are other systems for doing this, such as maintaining a computerized data base, the portfolio approach has the advantage of maintaining specific representations of the student's work that can illustrate progress both to the student and to others.

THE PORTFOLIO PROVIDES VISIBLE EVIDENCE OF STUDENT PROGRESS. Teachers will have more than simple test scores or grades to communicate student progress to interested individuals including the student, other teachers, parents, and administrators. Evidence of student progress is particularly important when periodic decisions about students must be communicated to others, such as advancement to a higher level of ESL instruction or exit from a program.

PORTFOLIOS ARE USEFUL FOR MAKING INSTRUCTIONAL DECISIONS. Teachers can use the portfolio information to modify instructional methods or materials for individual students or for groups of students. Because evidence of student progress is available on a continual basis, teachers can assess the effectiveness of various instructional approaches they have tested out with individual students.

THE PORTFOLIO IS ACCESSIBLE. It can be placed in a location where both the teacher and the student have access to it, and where entries to the portfolio can be made by either individual. Entries can also be made by other teachers who have contact with the student, such as teachers with whom the student is taking grade-level classes. One particularly useful approach is to give students the option to enter representations of their "best work" or work that shows continuous progress.

PORTFOLIO ASSESSMENT IS FOCUSED AND EFFICIENT. It is focused in that the information in the portfolio can be related directly to the goals of instruction, and it is efficient because the approach forces choices about the type of information that should be maintained in the portfolio. Portfolio assessment is particularly conducive to analysis of the many types of information that a teacher will have access to in using alternative assessment measures.

The purpose of portfolio assessment in CALLA is to monitor student progress relative to the content, language, and learning strategies identified at the beginning of each unit. Assessment information available from various forms of alternative assessment in addition to unit tests and standardized tests must be integrated in a systematic way and prepared for communication with other individuals. We recommend that teachers follow the general guidelines below in developing and using portfolio assessment.[26]

GUIDELINES FOR PORTFOLIO ASSESSMENT

- ***Determine the purpose.*** Reach agreement on what the portfolio's purpose(s) will be.
- ***Select information for the portfolio.*** Information for the portfolio must be selected relative to the purpose of the assessment and to the objectives that the portfolio will assist in evaluating.
- ***Decide how to organize the portfolio.*** Establish a plan for where to keep the portfolio and how to organize the contents.
- ***Establish a data collection plan.*** Determine how often to collect information for the portfolio, who will collect the information, how agreement among different individuals will be determined, when to update the contents, and how to decide which information is no longer needed.
- ***Review the student's progress.*** Both teachers and students review alternative sources of evidence to determine whether the student has met unit objectives or other goals established for instruction. The sources of evidence can include performance measures, text retelling, cloze tests, writing samples, ratings, and self-assessment. The portfolio can also include projects and various products such as audio or video tapes of student presentations.
- ***Portfolio use.*** Determine how to make instructional decisions based on the portfolio contents (e.g., grouping decisions, placement, and instructional planning), decide when and how to review the contents, and determine with whom to communicate the contents (students, other teachers, administrators, or parents).

There are a variety of means by which teachers can facilitate the use of portfolios. One is to develop a checklist of the portfolio contents that is used as a cover sheet for the portfolio. The checklist should contain a list of the contents and a time schedule for reviewing and updating the portfolio. A second is to minimize the size of the portfolio by ensuring that only materials that are current or useful to reflect student progress are maintained. A third is to involve aides or other teachers in collecting and maintaining portfolio data in order to reduce the burden on any single person. And a fourth is to involve the student in deciding which portfolio contents should be entered and maintained. The student can be asked to review the time schedule on the checklist to determine when it is appropriate to add new items, eliminate items that are no longer current, and review his or her own academic progress.

In a portfolio, the same information that is used in discussions with the student and in student grading can be used in discussions with aides, other teachers, parents, and administrators. By sharing this information with teachers in content areas, the

CHECKLIST OF PORTFOLIO CONTENTS

Name ______________________________ Year __________

Contents	**Collection Schedule** (by Quarter)*			
Autobiography				
CALLA Learning Strategies Questionaire				
Learner Diary				
Science Self-Evaluation				
Science Lab Report				
Problem Solving Worksheet				
Making a Graph				
Social Studies Oral Report (Tape)				
Social Studies Graphic Organizer				
Notes on My Favorite Book				
My Best Stories				
Writing Sample				
If I Could Go Back to the Beginning of the Year (Topic for final writing sample)				

*Shading indicates work will not be collected in the quarter indicated.

CALLA teacher will have a better idea of how content area teachers view the student's progress and will thereby improve the student's chances of success. Teachers may wish to vary the portfolio contents somewhat depending on the student's needs, while maintaining a core of assessment information that all students will have in common. Teachers may also want to include information from standardized achievement tests and language proficiency tests in the portfolio, using the information from alternative assessment to expand upon and assist in the interpretation of these results.

A worksheet for portfolio information can be prepared with the student's name at the top, three broad columns which will contain the objectives on the left, measures used to assess the objectives (in the center), and the degree to which the objective has been achieved (in the right column), and space at the bottom of the page for a summary statement about the student's progress and changes needed in the instructional program to meet student needs.[27]

In adapting this worksheet format for CALLA, the left column should include objectives for content, academic language, and learning strategies assessed in the portfolio. The second column lists the specific pieces of data or information that bear on these objectives, including both formal and alternative assessment measures. Identify the specific location, page, or even paragraph where information bearing on the objective is located in the portfolio. In the third column, indicate whether or not, in your judgment, the information provides sufficient evidence that the student

WORKSHEET FOR PORTFOLIO INFORMATION

Student Name Motoko Date 2/9

Objectives (Content, Academic Language, Learning Strategies)	Assessment Measures	Performance
Describe characteristics of simple organisms	Writing sample	Content good. Needs help with use of articles
Classify living things	Drawing	Effective and clear
Write lab report	Writing sample	Needs work stating hypothesis

Recommendations: Instruction should focus on scientific method, writing, and speaking to group.

has attained the objective in question. At the bottom of the page, write a brief summary about the student's progress in learning content, academic language, and learning strategies. Also indicate any adaptations that are needed in the CALLA program to best meet this student's needs.

Finally, teachers will often need to translate the information chart of student performance illustrated in the portfolio into report card grades. We recommend that this issue be addressed by a team of administrators and teachers so that mutual agreement on the weighting of different components of student portfolios can be reached. For example, the team might decide that the content, academic language, and learning strategies objective will carry equal weight, or that they will be weighted differently. The team would also decide on the relative weight of any formal assessments or unit tests that may be included in the portfolio. We recommend that these decisions be made prior to collecting student work for the portfolio.

Portfolio Assessment

- ❖ Rationale—systematic, accessible, focused, and efficient method for providing visible evidence of student progress; useful for making instructional decisions.
- ❖ Guidelines for use—determine the purpose; select information for the portfolio; decide how to organize it; establish a data collection plan; review the student's progress; decide on portfolio use.

Application Activities

The purpose of these activities is for teachers to gain familiarity with performance measures and other forms of alternative assessment in determining student progress. In these activities, we draw selectively from the alternative assessment measures discussed in the chapter.

1. Design and use performance assessment.
   a. Review the sample performance assessments identified on pp. 111–126. Select a content area for performance assessment, identify one or more assessment activities to try out, or design activities of your own. Consider using projects such as those suggested on pp. 109–110 in addition to or instead of paper and pencil tests. For example, have students solve a problem as a small group project and write a report.
   b. Devise an appropriate scoring rubric for the performance assessment that includes an analysis of the process of solving the problem as well as the accuracy of the response. Tell students what the scoring rubric will be before administering the items. Example: 3 = accurate response and able to describe problem-solving process; 2 = able to describe problem-solving process but inaccurate response; 1 = accurate response but unable to describe problem-solving process.
   c. Administer the items (or have students perform the project) and ensure that students write a verbal description of how they solved the problems in addition to providing the correct response. Use the scoring system you have designed.
   d. Adapt instruction to student responses by emphasizing problem-solving processes or by providing instruction in the content area, as needed.

2. Score writing samples holistically and analytically.
   a. Select a genre and a prompt for student writing. Ensure that the prompt is interesting and appropriate for the students' grade level and English proficiency.
   b. Select or devise an analytic or holistic scoring rubric for the writing samples. Discuss the rubric with language arts teachers at the same grade level and indicate how it will be used.
   c. Collect writing samples from students. Provide ample opportunity for students to complete the assignment.
   d. Gain the cooperation of at least one other teacher and collaboratively select anchor papers that are accurate illustrations of each point on the scoring continuum. Score the remainder of the papers using the rubric and anchor papers.
   e. Determine the number and percent of students obtaining a score at each point on the continuum. Next decide the percent of students who should meet a selected standard for the grade level, level of English proficiency, and extent of instruction of the students in your class. What percent of the students do teachers want to attain Intermediate-level skills by the end of the year?

f. Review the percentages and discuss them with teachers who have previously provided instruction to these students. Discuss what you as an instructional team have done to support students who obtain higher scores, and what you have done to support students who obtain lower scores. Decide what instructional adaptations should be implemented to improve the instruction.

g. At the end of the school year, ask students to review and evaluate or comment on samples of their work collected throughout the school year.

3. Develop a scoring criteria or a student rating scale.

a. Working with a team of teachers, use or design a student rating scale such as the Literacy Development Checklist (Table 6.1). Select or design the rating scale based on the match between components of the rating scale and an analysis of instructional outcomes or objectives that are important in your classroom.

b. Select one of the sections to work on, such as Interest (or a section of your own design). Decide with the team what criteria to use in scoring ratings in that section. Use the items under Interest to devise a scoring system like the following:

Score	Scoring Criteria
3	Consistently initiates own reading, selects books independently, chooses books of appropriate difficulty, and samples variety of materials.
2	Initiates reading, selects books, and varies reading materials with assistance.
1	Rarely initiates own reading.

c. Rate a group of students using the scoring criteria you have selected. Other members of the team rate students in their own classrooms. Discuss instructional approaches for students with the team that will address specific student needs. These might include determining student reading interests, matching book selections to student abilities, etc.

d. Revise the scoring procedure if needed and adapt the procedure for other sections of the Literacy Development Checklist, or develop another section for the student rating scale you have designed. Again discuss instructional approaches and ensure that students receive appropriate reading support.

4. Design and use a student portfolio.

a. Working with a team of teachers, design a portfolio for use with language minority students. The team might include language arts or other content area teachers in addition to ESL or bilingual teachers. Determine the purposes of the portfolio and the instructional objectives (content, language, or strategies) for which the portfolio information will be collected.

b. With the team, identify information and student work samples to be included in the portfolio. Differentiate a Core Section in the portfolio (essential contents that show progress over the year and that will be forwarded to future teachers) and a Supplementary Section (occasional pieces that reflect work in progress at a particular period of time). Design a checklist of portfolio contents to be placed on the cover page.

c. Work with the team to determine a data collection plan that includes how frequently the information will be collected, who will collect it, when to update the contents, and when and how to eliminate information.

d. Design a student progress record to assess student progress toward the instructional objectives. List the objectives and complete other columns for Assessment Measures and Performance as suggested in this chapter. As evidence of student progress accumulates, write the name of each piece of information in the portfolio and indicate how it reflects progress toward the objectives. Write summary comments to interpret this information at the bottom of the student progress record.

e. Use the portfolio in discussions with each student, in conferences with parents, and in meetings with other teachers as a reflection of the student's progress.

5. Design and use a learning strategies questionnaire.

a. Refer to the learning strategies questionnaires for science (Table 6.5) and those for mathematics, social studies, and literature/composition (Tables 6.6-6.8). Work with a colleague who teaches the same age and proficiency-level students. Revise one or more of the questionnaires so that they reflect your instructional activities and are adjusted to the language level of your students.

b. Try out the revised questionnaire(s) with your students by reading each item to them or having them read on their own.

c. Identify the strategies used by each student. (Refer to the strategy key, Table 6.10).

d. Place the questionnaire(s) in each student's portfolio.

e. After two or three months of strategy instruction, have students complete another questionnaire designed to elicit the same strategies with similar tasks. Record growth/problems with strategy use.

Table 6.7

CALLA LEARNING STRATEGIES QUESTIONNAIRE

Name ______________________________ Date______

MATHEMATICS

You have to read, understand, and solve a word problem in math class.

HOW DO YOU UNDERSTAND AND SOLVE MATH WORD PROBLEMS? CIRCLE THE WORDS THAT TELL WHAT YOU DO. THERE ARE NO RIGHT OR WRONG ANSWERS.

1. When I read the problem, I look for the important information (words and numbers) to solve the problem.

Never Rarely Sometimes Usually Always

2. If I don't understand a word, I stop working on the problem.

Never Rarely Sometimes Usually Always

3. I make a plan of what to do.

Never Rarely Sometimes Usually Always

4. If possible, I work on the problem with other students.

Never Rarely Sometimes Usually Always

5. I remember how I solved other problems like this one.

Never Rarely Sometimes Usually Always

6. I use problem solving steps (such as: Understand the Question, Find the Data, Make a Plan, Find the Answer, and Check Back).

Never Rarely Sometimes Usually Always

7. I draw a picture or chart to help solve the problem.

Never Rarely Sometimes Usually Always

8. I check my answer after I solve the problem.

Never Rarely Sometimes Usually Always

9. What other things do you do to solve word problems in mathematics?

Table 6.8

CALLA LEARNING STRATEGIES QUESTIONNAIRE

Name ____ Date ______________

SOCIAL STUDIES

You have to read some information about the American War for Independence. Tomorrow your teacher is going to ask you questions about this information.

WHAT DO YOU DO TO UNDERSTAND THE INFORMATION THAT YOU READ? CIRCLE THE WORDS THAT TELL WHAT YOU DO. THERE ARE NO RIGHT OR WRONG ANSWERS!

1. Before I read, I look through the pages. I try to get the general idea.

Never Rarely Sometimes Usually Always

2. First I look for words I know, and I skip the words I don't know.

Never Rarely Sometimes Usually Always

3. I ask myself: "What do I already know about the War for Independence?"

Never Rarely Sometimes Usually Always

4. As I read, I look up *every* new word in the dictionary.

Never Rarely Sometimes Usually Always

5. As I read, I try to make good guesses at the meanings of new words.

Never Rarely Sometimes Usually Always

6. As I read, I take notes of the most important ideas.

Never Rarely Sometimes Usually Always

7. I work with a friend and we read and study together.

Never Rarely Sometimes Usually Always

8. After I read, I make a summary of the most important ideas.

Never Rarely Sometimes Usually Always

9. What other things do you do to read and remember information in a social studies book?

Table 6.9
CALLA LEARNING STRATEGIES QUESTIONNAIRE

Name ____ Date ____________

LITERATURE AND COMPOSITION

1. You are reading a story or novel. You have to understand what you read and you have to explain the feelings of the characters.

2. Now you are going to write a story. Your classmates are going to read it.

HOW DO YOU UNDERSTAND WHAT YOU READ? HOW DO YOU WRITE STORIES? CIRCLE THE WORDS THAT TELL WHAT YOU DO. THERE ARE NO RIGHT OR WRONG ANSWERS!

Reading

1. Before I read, I try to think of what I already know about the topic of the story.

Never Rarely Sometimes Usually Always

2. I pay special attention to what the characters in the story do and say.

Never Rarely Sometimes Usually Always

3. As I read, I try to make good guesses at the meanings of new words.

Never Rarely Sometimes Usually Always

4. After reading, I write down the most important ideas.

Never Rarely Sometimes Usually Always

Writing

5. Before I write, I make a plan for the story.

Never Rarely Sometimes Usually Always

6. I try to remember what I already know about story writing or about stories I have read.

Never Rarely Sometimes Usually Always

7. I ask someone else to read my story and make suggestions.

Never Rarely Sometimes Usually Always

8. I check, edit, and revise my story.

Never Rarely Sometimes Usually Always

9. What other things help you to:

Read a story? ____

Write a story? ____

Table 6.10

CALLA LEARNING STRATEGIES QUESTIONNAIRE

KEY

	CONTENT AREA ITEM NUMBER				STRATEGY
STRATEGY	**SCIENCE**	**MATH**	**SOC. ST.**	**LIT./COMP.**	**TOTAL**
Planning	3	3; 6	1	5	5
Sel. Attn.	1	1	2	2	4
Self-Eval.	8	8		8	3
Elaboration		5	3	1; 6	4
Inferencing			5	3	2
Summarizing			8	4	2
Imagery	7	7			2
Resourcing	5				1
Note-taking	4		6		2
Ques./Clarif.	6				1
Cooperation	2	4	7	7	4
Negative Strategies		2	4		2
TOTALS	**8**	**8**	**8**	**8**	**32**

CHAPTER 7

CALLA Program Administration

Overview

Administrators have an essential role in the development, implementation, and evaluation of a CALLA program.

The Administrator's Role

Administrative Planning

Staffing Options
Establishing Communication
Administrative Support

Implementation Guidelines

Student Needs Assessment
Analysis of Grade-Level Program
Establishing CALLA Program Objectives
Curriculum Development and Materials Selection
Meeting Program Objectives

Program Evaluation

Formative Evaluation
Summative Evaluation
Application of Results

CHAPTER 7 CALLA PROGRAM ADMINISTRATION

CALLA PROGRAMS CAN BE IMPLEMENTED MOST EFFECTIVELY when administrators and other school personnel are involved in the design and coordination of instruction. While a single teacher can successfully implement CALLA, administrators can assist program implementation in a number of ways. Administrative support is important for joint planning between CALLA teachers and other teachers of students who are learning English, including other ESL or bilingual teachers and content area teachers. This planning time is necessary for discussing individual students or instructional procedures in which more than one teacher will play a role. Administrative support is also essential when CALLA is implemented in an entire school or school district to guarantee that staff development necessary for full implementation is available. Another important reason for administrative support is to assist in program evaluation and improvement.

The Administrator's Role

Administrators have an essential role in the development, implementation, and evaluation of a CALLA program. These responsibilities include identifying teachers for the CALLA project, establishing communication between ESL and grade-level content teachers, and enlisting continuing support for the program from school principals and district level administrators.

Another key role for the CALLA administrator is in the implementation of the new program. Administrators' activities include an assessment of student needs, including affective, academic, language, and learning strategy needs, and an analysis of the grade-level academic program. Administrative support is also needed in arranging for a team of teachers to develop a CALLA curriculum guide and select and develop appropriate materials.

The administrator is also responsible for identifying a team of ESL and content teachers to develop program objectives, including objectives for student achievement, student attitudes and behaviors, teacher and staff development, and parent involvement. We strongly recommend that teachers play a major role in establishing program objectives and that both student and parent input be sought. When agreement has been reached on major program objectives, the CALLA administrator needs to facilitate the attainment of the objectives through staff development and parent activities. Finally, the program administrator plays a major role in planning and supervising the program evaluation. The administrator suggests ways in which both formative and summative evaluation can be carried out, and manages the components of the evaluation and the staff participating in it.

The CALLA program administrator's most important responsibility is leadership. The program administrator leads by providing guidance to project staff, projecting personal enthusiasm and a vision of outstanding program outcomes, and by seeking and valuing the contributions of all involved in the CALLA project —teachers, students, teacher aides, parents, and support staff.

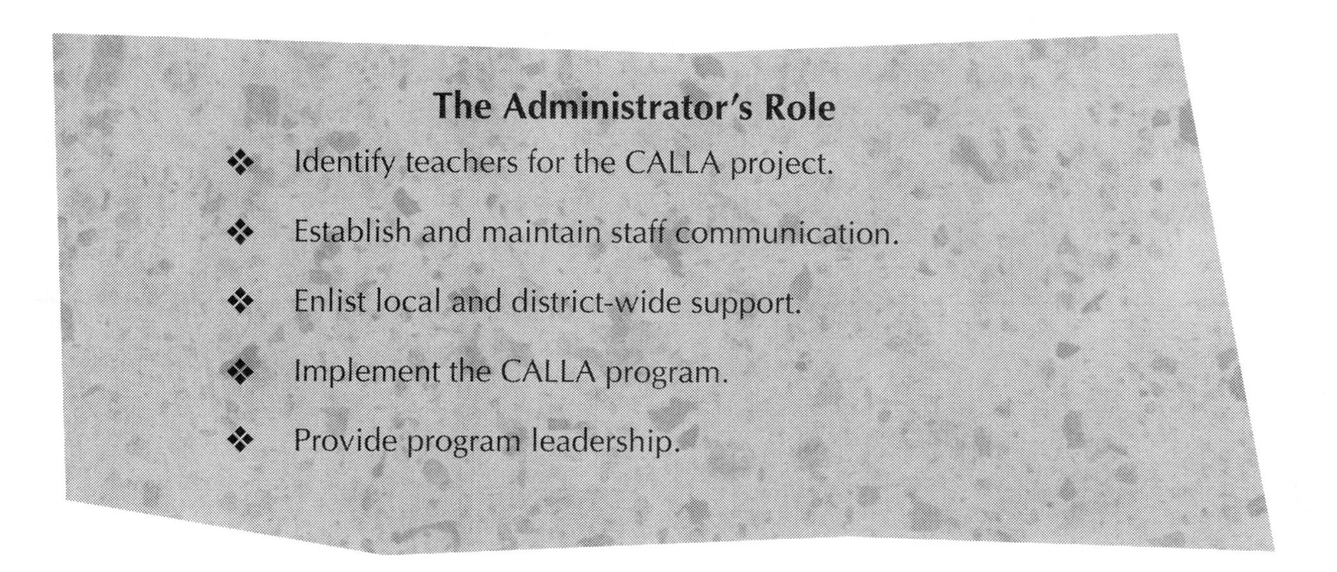

Administrative Planning

Because a CALLA program calls on expertise from different curricular areas, planning and organization by the program administrator are essential.

Decisions Made by Program Administrators

- Who will teach the CALLA curriculum: ESL teachers with content knowledge, content teachers with ESL knowledge, or both?
- What, if any, organizational changes will be required by the CALLA program?
- What types of administrative support are needed to make the CALLA program effective?

STAFFING OPTIONS

The process of selecting teachers to provide CALLA instruction needs careful consideration. The first issue is the interest and willingness of the teacher to experiment with a new approach to instruction. Of nearly equal importance is the teacher's understanding of the language learning process. For example, teachers oriented to a behavioral model of instruction would be uncomfortable with a cognitive approach. Similarly, teachers who believe that students acquire a new language through unconscious processes will find it difficult to accept the overt teaching of learning strategies, which, as we discussed in Chapter 4, is a major feature of CALLA instruction. Another aspect of the teacher's background knowledge that should be considered is the ability to understand and teach the school district's content curriculum. While many ESL teachers are knowledgeable about areas of the curriculum outside of language arts, others may feel uncomfortable with areas of the curriculum such as science and mathematics. This is particularly true at the high school level, where teachers tend to be specialized in one or two content areas. Some school districts have found that providing ESL training to content teachers is more effective than trying to develop content expertise in ESL teachers, while other districts have identified ESL teachers who also have teaching credentials or strong interest in a content subject. Both approaches require staff development, and either could be employed in identifying teachers for a CALLA program.

The context for CALLA instruction may also be important in selecting teachers. At the secondary level, course credit for CALLA content courses may be easier to establish when content teachers certified in the subject provide the instruction. Also, the integration of ESL content courses into the curriculum and the incorporation of CALLA techniques into grade-level instruction may be more readily accomplished when content teachers provide the instruction.

The checklist in Table 7.1 can be used by program administrators in selecting teachers to participate in a CALLA program.

Table 7.1

CHECKLIST FOR IDENTIFYING CALLA TEACHERS

- ❑ 1. Expresses interest in learning a new instructional approach for ESL students.
- ❑ 2. Is willing to teach academic content using modified instructional procedures for ESL students.
- ❑ 3. Understands that cognitive processes are involved in second language acquisition.
- ❑ 4. Wants to get a better understanding of mental processes students use in learning.
- ❑ 5. Possesses classroom management skills that promote student autonomy, such as ability to assign responsibilities to students and expertise in implementing cooperative learning.
- ❑ 6. Has knowledge about or is willing to learn about the school district's academic curriculum for content subjects.
- ❑ 7. Can work collaboratively with grade-level content teachers, or, if a content teacher, with ESL teachers.
- ❑ 8. Is willing to learn about and teach learning strategies.
- ❑ 9. Takes time to plan for instruction.
- ❑ 10. Is willing to evaluate own teaching.

ESTABLISHING COMMUNICATION

A CALLA program operates most effectively in an organizational framework that encourages teamwork and open communication. Lines of communication between ESL and grade-level content teachers need to be established so that ESL teachers feel comfortable in requesting information about curriculum, materials, and instructional approaches from their colleagues. At the same time, grade-level teachers who teach or will be teaching ESL students can learn from their ESL colleagues about different ways of meeting the needs of these students.

Organizing Communication Between ESL and Content Teachers

- Involve both grade-level content teachers and ESL content teachers in all aspects of planning and implementing the CALLA program.

- Ask content specialists to provide subject-specific workshops for ESL teachers.
- Have ESL teachers observe content classes and then meet in small groups to discuss instructional techniques observed, language proficiency required, and specific content presented.
- Invite content teachers to observe their future students in ESL classrooms.
- Set up coaching teams of ESL teachers (or of an ESL and a content teacher) who will observe and assist each other in teaching CALLA lessons.
- Schedule time in which coaching teams can meet for planning and discussion.
- Fund summer curriculum development activities in which both ESL and content teachers can work together to develop or revise the CALLA curriculum.

ADMINISTRATIVE SUPPORT

A new school program needs administrative support from both the district and school level. In a CALLA program this is particularly true because of staff development requirements and the need to establish ongoing communication between ESL and grade-level content teachers. The underlying commitment needed from principals and other district administrators is reflected in the belief that ESL students are everyone's responsibility, rather than the belief that ESL is a remedial program separate from the rest of the academic program.

This commitment and belief is shown in a number of ways. First, ESL teachers are seen as integral members of the school community and are included in all school activities. Second, scheduling is flexible enough to accommodate inter-teacher observation and sufficient planning time to develop and refine CALLA lessons. Third, inter-disciplinary staff development activities are ongoing throughout the school year. Fourth, grade-level curriculum and instructional materials are made available to ESL teachers to adapt for CALLA instruction. Finally, administrators provide for school and district recognition of the achievements of ESL teachers and their students.

This belief in a shared school-wide responsibility for ESL students is all the more important in schools making the shift to school-based decision-making. This response to the educational reform movement places the responsibility for decisions concerning curriculum, staffing, and budget at the building level rather than in the district, where they have traditionally been located. In many of these schools, adoption of CALLA as a school-wide approach for ESL students will require approval of a site-based committee composed of teachers, administrators, other school personnel, and parents and other community members. Those encouraging the adoption will need an understanding of CALLA's requirements for staff development and implementation, as well as an understanding of its characteristics and benefits. The committee will need this type of information as well as information on the impact of adoption on budgetary factors, the selection of materials currently in use, and possible adoption of other instructional materials that are compatible with CALLA.

This institutionalization of the program, or capacity building, places the CALLA program within the overall school administrative and financial structure. What this means in practical terms is that the school principal is not only informed but supportive of CALLA program goals, has set aside funds within the total school budget for CALLA program activities, includes CALLA teachers, students, and parents in all school activities, and is personally committed to achieving and surpassing CALLA program goals. An additional way in which CALLA can be integrated into the total school program is by encouraging grade-level teachers to participate in CALLA staff development activities and to experiment with CALLA in their classrooms with both language minority and native English-speaking students.

Administrative Planning

- Decide who will teach the CALLA curriculum: ESL teacher, content teachers, or both.
- CALLA operates most effectively with teamwork and open communications.
- A CALLA program needs support at both the district and school level.

Implementation Guidelines

To implement CALLA successfully, careful planning and close collaboration between ESL and grade-level content area teachers is essential. The types of professional expertise usually exemplified by second language teachers and by teachers in content areas are quite different, yet both types are needed to plan and carry out a program that can provide content area experiences and develop the academic language skills needed by ESL students for success in the grade-level program. ESL and content teachers therefore need to work in teams to assess student needs, identify the main objectives of the grade-level instructional program, develop curriculum, establish specific objectives for the CALLA program and how they can be met, and participate jointly in program implementation activities such as staff development. As described in the previous section, administrators need to identify such multidisciplinary teams and provide the necessary support for planning, discussion, curriculum and materials development, and ongoing monitoring of the CALLA program. In this section we describe an implementation plan for CALLA that includes these types of activities.

STUDENT NEEDS ASSESSMENT

The academic needs of ESL students should be identified so that the CALLA program can be designed effectively. These needs can be classified as affective needs, academic language needs, content-specific needs, and learning strategy needs.

Insight into students' affective needs can be gained by assessing their attitudes, feelings of self-efficacy, and behavior (classroom participation, attendance, dropout potential).

In identifying students' language needs, proficiency with academic language rather than social language should be assessed. In other words, students' ability to perform context-reduced and cognitively demanding tasks in English, including reading and writing, are tested in order to identify areas of strength and weakness.

Students' knowledge of grade-appropriate content in the different subject areas also needs to be assessed. This type of assessment can best be done through the native language, or, if this is not possible, through a careful analysis of prior school records. Declarative knowledge acquired through the native language can, with appropriate instruction, be transferred to English. However, gaps may exist between a student's L1 content knowledge and equivalent content knowledge of native English speaking peers. These gaps may exist because of differing curriculum structures in the student's native country, or because the student has had an interrupted prior education. In either case, they should be addressed during a transitional ESL

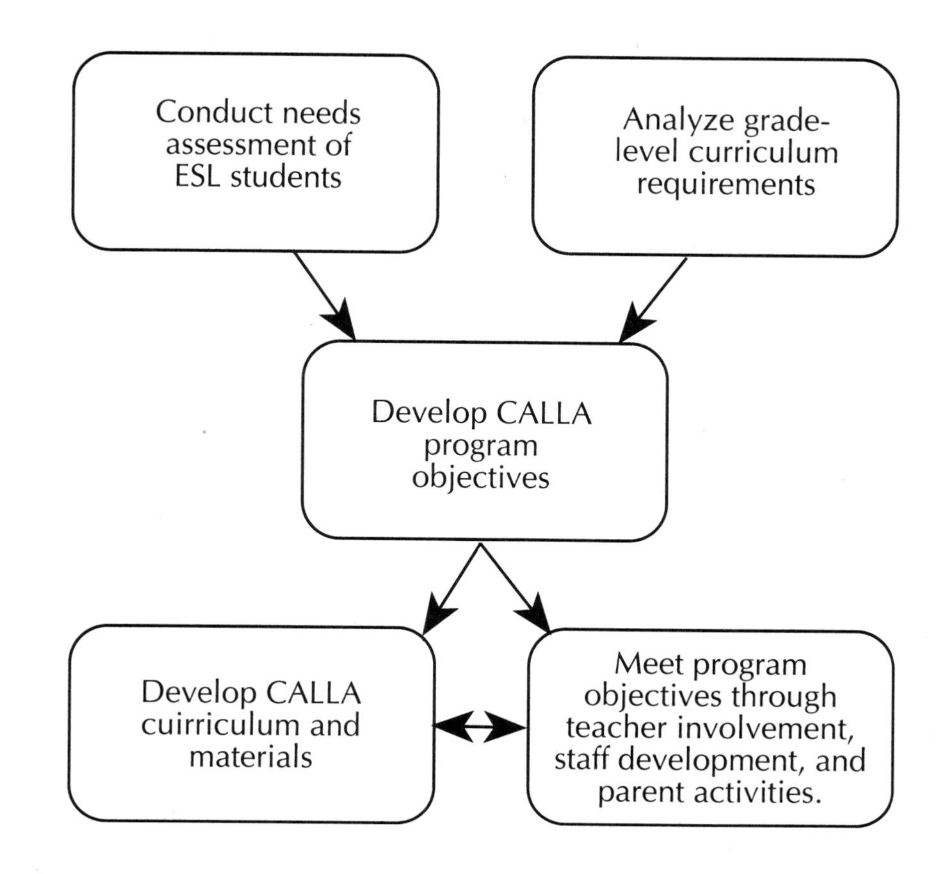

An implementation plan for CALLA

program such as CALLA rather than postponed until the student enters grade-level content classrooms.

Finally, students' current learning strategies need to be identified. Effective strategies developed in the native language can be transferred to English under the CALLA teacher's guidance. However, as we have seen, some types of rote repetition strategies which are effective in one type of educational system may not be productive in CALLA where students are expected to synthesize, question, and evaluate information.

By assessing students' current level of performance in academic English language use and native language competence in subject matter and in learning strategies, CALLA teachers can plan classroom activities that address the identified needs. (See Chapter 6 for examples of assessment measures.) Types of questions to be addressed in a student needs assessment are summarized in Table 7.2.

ANALYSIS OF GRADE-LEVEL PROGRAM

The academic performance level requirements of the grade-level academic instructional program should be identified in order to find out what ESL students need to know before exiting the CALLA program. The types of knowledge required, both declarative and procedural, can be identified through examination of the curriculum, instructional materials, tests, class observations, and discussions with grade-level teachers.

Prerequisite content knowledge will be found in the curriculum for the grades preceding the grade level the ESL student will be entering. Instructional materials for the target grade level will provide information about vocabulary and reading

Table 7.2
STUDENT NEEDS ASSESSMENT

Affective Needs (Conduct in L1 if possible.)

What attitudes do students express towards:

- school in general?
- learning in particular?
- English as a language?
- English-speaking American culture?
- their own self-efficacy as learners?

Curriculum Content Needs (Conduct in L1 if possible.)

For each subject area at the appropriate grade level, what prior knowledge do students have about:

- content subject information?
- content subject procedures and processes?

Academic Language Needs (Conduct in English.)

For each subject area at the appropriate grade level, are students able to:

- understand academic information and explanations presented orally?
- discuss and answer questions on academic topics? describe how an answer was derived? present an oral report?
- read for different purposes in content textbooks, authentic texts, library and trade books, reference materials?
- write short and long answers to questions about content studied? write content-specific text (e.g., narrative, expository, lab notes, problem solutions)?

Learning Strategies Needs (Conduct in L1 if possible.)

- Can students describe their own learning processes?
- Do students plan, monitor, and evaluate their learning activities?
- Do students attribute their academic performance to their own efforts (including learning strategies) rather than to forces outside their own control?
- Are students able to apply appropriate strategies to:
    - a. understanding and remembering new information?
    - b. learning vocabulary?
    - c. engaging in academic oral communication?
    - d. reading for specific purposes?
    - e. producing written texts of different types?
    - f. graphing, mapping, charting?
    - g. solving problems?
    - h. conducting experiments?

level required, and may also reveal assumptions about prior knowledge and cultural background. Some schools may also administer either locally developed or standardized tests in order to place students in special programs or classes. In high school mathematics, for example, such "gate-keeping" tests may be used to place students in either remedial math classes or math classes meeting requirements for college admission. Familiarity with the contents and cut-off scores of such tests can help the CALLA teacher identify information to be included in the CALLA curriculum. However, the CALLA curriculum should not be constrained to match the objectives of these tests, which may be limited or emphasize lower-order cognitive skills.

Classroom observations are particularly important in discovering the types of language demands made on students in different content areas. For example, extensive reading and writing may be required by social studies teachers, while mathematics teachers may ask for little reading or writing but may expect students to be able to make clear oral explanations of the different steps taken to solve a problem. Types of learning strategies and general study skills expected by grade-level content teachers can also be identified through class observation. Thus, both the explicit curriculum as represented by the syllabus and textbook as well as the implicit curriculum as represented by grade-level teachers' language and learning skills expectations need to be analyzed.

Observation of a content classroom can be followed up with an informal discussion about the grade-level teacher's expectations and instructional approach.

Questions to Ask a Content Teacher

- What are the five most important concepts that you expect students to know when they come to your class?
- What procedures related to these concepts should students be able to perform?
- How much and what kind of reading do you expect your students to do?
- What do your students have to write? Can you show me samples?
- How much and what kind of information is delivered orally (by you or students)?
- What kinds of speaking are required? Answering questions? Explaining a procedure? Participating in discussions? Oral reports?
- What kinds of homework assignments do you give? How are they corrected?
- How do you assess your students' progress? Can you show me some of the tests or other assessment measures you use?

ESTABLISHING CALLA PROGRAM OBJECTIVES

At least four types of outcomes should be addressed in a CALLA program: student achievement, student attitudes and behavior, teacher and staff development, and parent involvement. The continued participation of the ESL and content teacher team is essential in developing these objectives.

STUDENT ACHIEVEMENT. Information gathered from the student needs assessment and from the analysis of the grade-level instructional program provide the information needed to set instructional objectives. With the overall goal of preparing students to function successfully in the all-English academic classroom, the team of ESL and content teachers can establish specific objectives for each of CALLA's components. Student achievement outcomes are linked to objectives set for content knowledge and academic language development.

In content areas, objectives for student achievement in both declarative and procedural knowledge need to be stated. For example, in a social studies program students might need to acquire a substantial amount of declarative knowledge about United States history and develop complex procedural skills for reading, discussing, and writing reports. In a science program, the emphasis might be on the acquisition of procedural skills for following the scientific method in conducting experiments, rather than on learning a large number of facts. Content objectives should be planned in collaboration with content teachers so that appropriate emphases and coverage can be established.

Academic language objectives specify the types of language required in different content areas and identify the materials and activities that will be used to develop these academic language functions. Representative language functions include using language to describe, explain, analyze, and justify a position. (See Chapter 3 for a discussion of academic language functions.)

ATTITUDES AND BEHAVIORS. There are two types of attitudinal and behavioral objectives in CALLA: student use of learning strategies and student motivation.

Learning strategy objectives will be based on analysis of the specific content materials selected by the team of ESL and content teachers. The strategies will assist students to learn and use the academic content and language more effectively. The team should focus on selecting learning strategies that are most suitable for the content and for the task students are expected to perform. A mix of strategies would include metacognitive, cognitive, and social/affective strategies, and should strive for metacognitive awareness. Development of student metacognitive awareness and instruction in learning strategies can have a significant impact on students' attitudes and behaviors. For example, when students understand their own learning processes, they can learn how to take internal control of their own learning, rather than relying on external prods or motivational devices. Students who learn to use appropriate learning strategies for school tasks experience academic success, and the experience of success changes both their behavior and their attitudes towards their own self-efficacy and towards school.

Student attitudes toward learning are more positive when they are motivated to engage actively in learning new concepts and skills. CALLA objectives for developing positive student attitudes towards learning include developing an appreciation for the value of academic learning and a feeling of self-efficacy in achieving academic success. Motivation emerges out of valuing the material to be learned (i.e., seeing its application to their own experience), expecting success on the tasks and learning activities, and knowing that the strategies for achieving success are under one's own control.

TEACHER AND STAFF DEVELOPMENT. Objectives for developing the professional expertise of teachers and other staff contributing to a CALLA program are (a) to instill an understanding of the learning principles upon which CALLA is based; (b) to understand the elements of CALLA, including the instructional sequence model and directly teaching learning strategies; and (c) to develop professional expertise in delivering and supporting cognitively-oriented instruction through implementation of CALLA.

PARENT INVOLVEMENT. Parent involvement is an important component of school life. By becoming actively involved with their children's school, parents gain insight into the total school program, develop greater understanding of their children's needs at school, and discover practical ways in which they can assist their children's learning. CALLA program objectives for parents include increasing communication between teachers and parents and developing parents' understanding of CALLA program goals and active assistance in helping their children become academically successful.

CURRICULUM DEVELOPMENT AND MATERIALS SELECTION

By establishing specific CALLA program objectives, a curricular sequence can be planned for the CALLA program so that students are provided with academic experiences to prepare them for grade-level instruction. Information from the student needs assessment and the analysis of the grade-level program can be used to develop a CALLA curriculum and to select appropriate materials for one or more content areas. In planning units of study, the CALLA lesson plan model can be used as a guide for including instruction in content, academic language, and learning strategies. Since four content areas are included in the CALLA program—science, mathematics, social studies, and literature—many opportunities exist for interdisciplinary units and lessons. By integrating mathematics and science or social studies and literature in some lessons, for example, the CALLA program can help students identify common concepts and processes underlying different disciplines. In Appendix A we provide an example of an interdisciplinary CALLA unit.

A team of ESL and content teachers should be assigned to work on developing the curriculum and selecting materials. Depending on the needs and structure of the ESL program, either one curriculum team will develop a curriculum guide and identify materials for integrating several content areas in the ESL period or block of periods, or different curriculum teams will work on separate curriculum guides for each content subject selected for the CALLA program.

These teams of ESL and content teachers serve two important functions that are essential to adoption and implementation of any instructional approach in the schools. Full implementation of CALLA relies heavily on the work performed by these teams. The first function is to provide *substantive* input to the curriculum by specifying the outcomes, instructional methods and materials, and the assessment procedures. The teams use the CALLA model to select content and design lesson plans by ensuring appropriate representation and introduction of content, academic language, and learning strategies. The second function of these teams is to ensure *teacher ownership* of the approach and the design of the curriculum and methods used in instruction. ESL and content teachers must *both* be represented in this process, and work through the difficult decisions of agreeing on student outcomes, materials, lesson plans, and assessment procedures. Other teachers not participating directly in these teams will want to know that the curriculum they are adopting was designed by a team of ESL and content teachers working together, just as they will work together in implementing the approach. Due to the complexity of the task the teams face, they should work during the summer to provide sufficient time for intensive discussions and planning sessions.

The purposes of a summer curriculum and materials project are to develop a draft *curriculum guide* (or guides) and identify *text and non-text materials* that can assist teachers in implementing CALLA instruction. This draft curriculum guide can then be pilot tested by CALLA teachers during the next school year. During the pilot testing it is important to gather comments and suggestions from the teachers using the guide so that revisions can be made during the subsequent summer. In a similar fashion, various combinations of materials can be tried out in a small number of classrooms, teacher reviews of the materials can be gathered, and final decisions about materials to be ordered for the entire program can be made during the spring of the pilot test year.

PLAN A CONTENT SCOPE AND SEQUENCE OUTLINE. This is the first task of the curriculum team in developing the curriculum guide. Team members will need to become thoroughly familiar with the grade-level program and with the findings of

A team of ESL and content teachers should work together to develop curriculum and select materials.

the academic needs assessment of ESL students targeted for the CALLA program. The team should use these two sources to generate a list of possible content topics for one or more subject areas. At this point, the advice of content specialist teachers for narrowing the list to high priority topics is essential. Next, the team can sequence the content topics and decide, based on the student academic needs assessment, what prior knowledge is required for each topic and how to fill any gaps that may exist. The resulting content topic outline forms a content scope and sequence chart for the curriculum guide.

DEVELOP LANGUAGE ACTIVITIES BASED ON THE CONTENT SELECTED. This is the second task of the curriculum team. A useful guideline is to include all language skills within each CALLA lesson. What this means in practice is that listening, reading, speaking, and writing activities become an integral part of every CALLA lesson. We do not advocate separate pre-teaching of vocabulary and grammar structures students will encounter in the text. Rather, we believe that discussing the content of a lesson and allowing students to find real examples of new words in context and grammatical structures as used in a realistic presentation of a content topic leads to situated learning of the language needed in different subjects. Any pre-teaching activities, in our view, should be oriented toward giving students a conceptual understanding of the topic to be presented—as with visuals, films, discussions, etc. —and toward building an understanding of what students already know on the topic.

SPECIFY THE LEARNING STRATEGIES TO BE TAUGHT. This is the third task of the curriculum team. The selection of learning strategies needs to be based on the content and language objectives and activities that have been identified. Metacognitive knowledge (e.g., thinking, talking, and writing about one's own learning processes) and metacognitive strategies (e.g., planning, monitoring, and evaluating) are applicable to all kinds of learning tasks, and should be taught and practiced in all content areas. We believe that social and affective strategies are also useful for all types of learning. Some cognitive learning strategies may be more closely aligned to specific curriculum areas, although strategies like elaboration of prior knowledge and making inferences apply to a wide variety of contexts. Grouping or classification is a particularly useful strategy in mathematics and science, but may also be used in other content subjects. Similarly, summarizing is a strategy usually associated with reading comprehension, yet it can be applied to listening comprehension equally well. What we suggest is that the curriculum team examine the full range of learning strategy possibilities before deciding on the limited number of strategies that will be included in the CALLA instructional program, and that they plan to introduce and practice only a small number of strategies at a time.

INSTRUCTIONAL MATERIALS. Having developed a scope and sequence for one or more content areas, the curriculum team should then investigate the availability of appropriate instructional materials for the CALLA program. Many content materials are available in the different curriculum areas, but few are suitable for ESL students. For example, grade-level textbooks and library reference books are too difficult linguistically for students learning English. Materials from lower grade levels may not provide the conceptual challenge needed by older students, and the language and illustrations in such materials may appear childish to the ESL learner. Table 7.3 summarizes options available and the advantages and disadvantages of each.

Our recommendation is that the curriculum committee select a variety of instructional materials, including print and non-print (audio, visual, graphic, manipulative, concrete) materials, that can be used as resources by teachers. Ultimately, it is teachers who must plan and implement CALLA lessons.

Table 7.3

INSTRUCTIONAL MATERIALS SELECTION

Options	Advantages	Disadvantages
1. Grade-level textbooks	Developmentally appropriate.	Too difficult to read. May require prior knowledge the student lacks.
2. Lower grade-level textbooks	May be easier to read. May supply needed prior knowledge.	May be perceived as childish. May not provide conceptual challenge.
3. Special Education or low-reading/high interest texts	May be easier to read. Illustrations appropriate to age level.	May not provide conceptual challenge or needed prior knowledge. May lack depth and/or breadth.
4. Teacher-prepared materials	Adjusted to conceptual, linguistic, and affective needs of specific students.	Time demands for preparation. May be useful only in one classroom.
5. Published CALLA materials	Adjusted to conceptual, linguistic, and affective needs of ESL students in general.	May not meet needs of specific students. Not yet available in all subjects at all grade levels.

SAMPLE LESSONS. Sample lessons need to be included in the curriculum scope and sequence so that teachers can have an example of how to implement the various components of a CALLA lesson. (See the last sections of each content area chapter for examples of CALLA lessons.) The curriculum development team should collect CALLA lessons that have worked well on a continuing basis so that they can be added to the curriculum guide and used as resources by teachers.

ASSESSMENT INSTRUMENTS. Finally, the curriculum guide needs to include authentic assessment instruments, or at least guidelines for developing curriculum-centered performance assessment. As discussed in Chapter 6, this type of assessment is closely integrated with curriculum objectives and is, from the student's perspective, virtually indistinguishable from regular classroom activities. A CALLA curriculum guide should provide suggestions and examples of items appropriate for assessing students on a continuing (rather than on a final exam) basis.

The CALLA curriculum guide should be tested by teachers for an entire school year, teachers' comments should be gathered, and the curriculum guide should then be revised during the next summer. This field testing and revision process should be ongoing, especially when changes occur in the school district's grade-level curriculum, textbook adoptions, the state curriculum framework, or local or state competency tests.

Table 7.4 is a sample table of contents for a CALLA curriculum guide, containing brief descriptions for each section.

Table 7.4

CALLA CURRICULUM GUIDE CONTENTS

Acknowledgements: Provides names of curriculum development team and other school district personnel, such as program administrator and superintendent.

Introduction: States program objectives, provides rationale for and description of CALLA, and tells how to use the curriculum guide.

Overview: Lists major concepts, language skills, and learning strategies included, perhaps arranged graphically.

Scope and Sequence: Provides a description of content, language, and learning strategy objectives for each unit or strand, including sample activities, suggested materials, and specific book pages.

Lesson Plans: Contains sample lesson plans keyed to representative units or strands. The lesson plans include materials such as worksheets, lists of equipment, and sources for audiovisuals.

Assessment: Includes sample measures to assess content, language, and learning strategies. (See Chapter 6 for models.)

Resources: Lists availability of library, media, equipment, field trip, and community resources, including names of persons to contact.

MEETING PROGRAM OBJECTIVES

In this section we suggest ways in which objectives for student achievement, student behaviors and attitudes, teacher and staff development, and parental involvement can be achieved through implementation of the CALLA program.

PROGRAM PARTICIPATION AND IMPLEMENTATION. The degree to which teachers accept, participate in, and implement the CALLA program will have a major impact on the attainment of objectives for student achievement and attitudes. Teachers need to have expectations of student success in academic tasks, they need to participate in program activities such as staff development, and they should follow guidelines for implementing CALLA as completely as possible.

Participation in the CALLA program by teachers in a school or school district should be on a voluntary basis rather than by administrative fiat. A small number of enthusiastic teachers will get the program off to a good start, and additional participation can be expected to increase as other teachers become convinced that CALLA can benefit their students. Administrators can facilitate this process in a number of ways. Most important is communication about the CALLA program. For example, CALLA teachers can be invited to present "what works" vignettes at faculty meetings, information about CALLA can be included in school newsletters, and school principals can be kept abreast of plans, events, and accomplishments in the CALLA program. Administrators can also make it clear that all teachers, including grade-level teachers, are welcome to participate in the CALLA program. When new teachers express an interest in becoming involved in the program, they should not only be welcomed but also be provided with personal assistance and support as they begin to implement CALLA procedures. Pairing new CALLA teachers with experienced ones in a coaching team is an effective approach to increasing program participation.

STAFF DEVELOPMENT ACTIVITIES. Extensive and ongoing staff development is essential for successful implementation of CALLA. Our own experience as CALLA trainers in a number of school districts has convinced us that one or two days of in-service training are not sufficient for teachers to develop either the knowledge base or procedural skills needed to incorporate CALLA in their classrooms. An ongoing staff development program in which teachers meet on a regular basis to develop additional expertise, try out new procedures, and discuss classroom applications is recommended for CALLA program implementation.

The coaching model[1] provides this type of ongoing staff development and also includes a cooperative learning component in which teachers work in pairs to coach each other in the new techniques that they are learning. Research and experience in staff development for new instructional approaches such as cooperative learning or strategic teaching indicate that a three year staff development plan with intensive in-service days at the beginning of each school year and monthly meetings of participating teachers during the school year is a realistic time frame.[2] A comparable period of time should be allocated for staff development to implement CALLA.

Coaching is an effective way for teachers to work together on developing new instructional techniques.[3] In coaching, pairs of teachers take turns coaching and being coached in the instructional techniques they have chosen to develop. Coaching generally takes place as part of a long-term staff development program which includes these components:[4]

Long-term staff development program, including coaching

- Rationale for the new instructional approach
- Theoretical background of the new approach

- Practice of components of the new approach in a workshop setting, with feedback from workshop leader
- Planning for classroom implementation, often jointly with coaching partner
- Practice of the new approach in the classroom, with observation and discussion with coaching partner
- Regular, usually monthly, meetings with other participants to discuss classroom implementation and to explore additional components of the new approach
- Peer teaching and coaching of new participants, usually during the second year of the staff development program
- Increasing expertise in the new instructional approach leads to the eventual assumption of the role of teacher trainer/model teacher

The coaching model lends itself to CALLA staff development because it provides a plan for long-term staff development rather than occasional unrelated workshops and because it is based on self-directed learning principles in which teachers assume responsibility for their own professional and intellectual growth. Table 7.5 offers suggestions which can help CALLA teachers get started with coaching.

These suggestions illustrate the central philosophical concept of coaching, which is that coaching partners enter into a coaching agreement freely and that each is willing to be both coach and learner as they work towards a common goal of instructional innovation.

PARENT ACTIVITIES. In order to foster parent involvement in the CALLA program, administrators need to plan activities that will encourage parents to get to

Table 7.5

GUIDELINES FOR COACHING WITH CALLA

1. Find a coaching partner who teaches the same ESL level and who wants to try out CALLA.
2. Plan a CALLA lesson together.
3. Decide on the aspect of the planned lesson that each wants the other to focus on. Make a list of the specific instructional techniques that the coach will concentrate on.
4. Observe each other's lessons. If the schedule makes this impossible, arrange to have the lessons videotaped.
5. During the observations, coaching partners take notes only on the aspects of the lesson that have been jointly agreed on.
6. As soon as possible after each observation, coaching partners meet to debrief and comment on each other's lesson. If the lessons have been videotaped, the video can be viewed as part of the debriefing session.
7. Decide jointly on aspects of the lesson/specific techniques that each partner will develop or improve.
8. Begin the cycle again by jointly planning another CALLA lesson.

Provide support through bilingual staff who can communicate with parents in their own language.

know their children's teachers and to participate in furthering their children's academic development. Activities for parents should be designed to make parents feel welcome at school, to provide information about the school program in the parents' native language, to provide support through staff who can communicate with parents in their language, to plan meetings in which parents can communicate their perceptions and desires, and to show parents concrete ways in which they can assist their children in meeting school objectives.

Traditional school activities such as Back to School Night and teacher conferences will attract parents of ESL students if they feel welcome and if language support services are provided. In conducting parent conferences, the teacher needs to be sensitive to cultural differences while at the same time providing information about the student's progress and achievements. A portfolio of student work is an excellent tool for organizing the conference.

Since many parents may feel somewhat uncertain about their role in school activities, it is helpful for bilingual school staff to make direct contact by telephone to explain the purpose of school activities for parents and to assure parents that they are welcome. When parents come to school for conferences or other activities, a translator should be provided to assist in communication. A follow-up telephone call to parents after school meetings can provide an additional link by answering any questions about their experience at school.

Schools can also plan special programs or workshops for parents of ESL students. These meetings should be conducted by bilingual staff members. In addition to providing information about school policies and programs, a parents' workshop can focus on specific things that parents can do to assist their children with school activities. For example, one workshop might provide hands-on practice for reading activities at home, and another workshop could focus on family math activities. Whatever the topic, the main purpose of parent workshops is to show parents how they can participate in enhancing their children's education.

Table 7.6

GUIDELINES FOR PARENT-TEACHER CONFERENCES

1. Focus on what students are learning at school.
2. Use illustrations of student work in an organized portfolio.
3. Show evidence of student progress.
4. Have students participate in selecting work to be shown to parents.
5. Ask parents for their views on the instructional program and their child's progress.

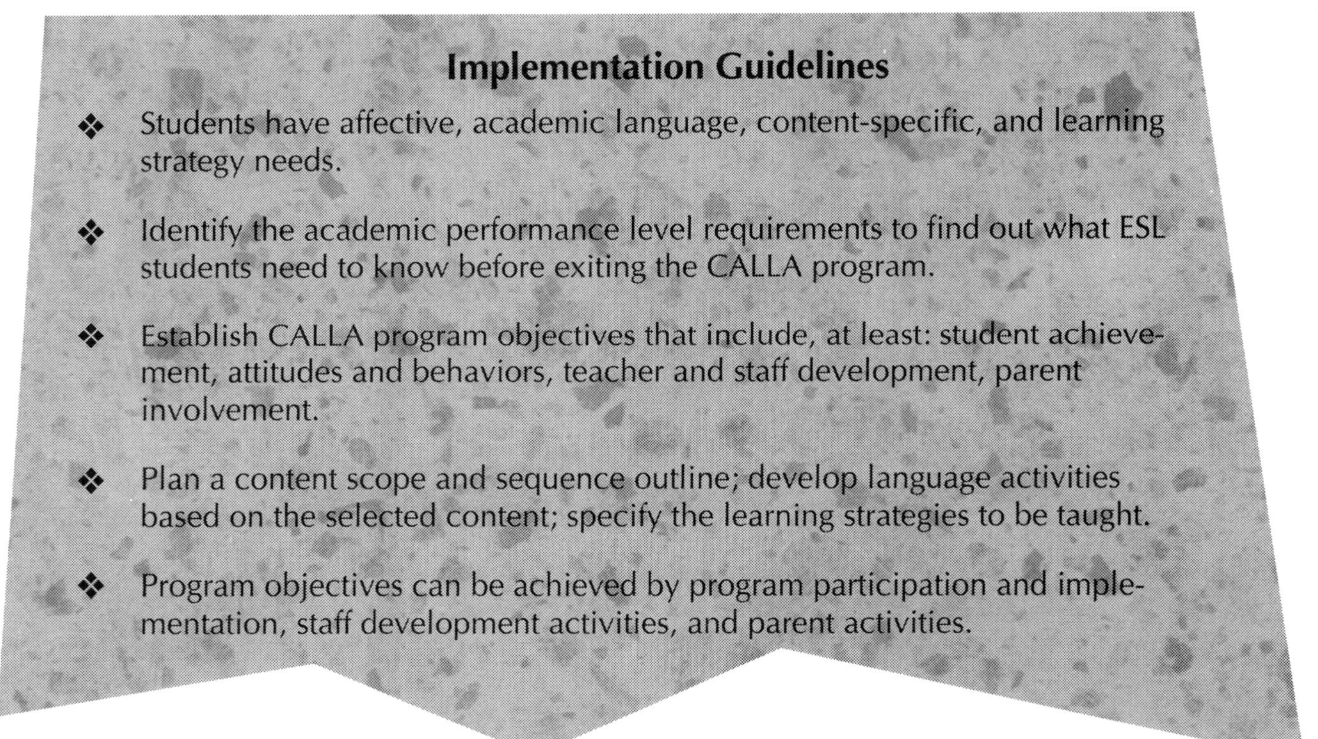

Implementation Guidelines

- Students have affective, academic language, content-specific, and learning strategy needs.
- Identify the academic performance level requirements to find out what ESL students need to know before exiting the CALLA program.
- Establish CALLA program objectives that include, at least: student achievement, attitudes and behaviors, teacher and staff development, parent involvement.
- Plan a content scope and sequence outline; develop language activities based on the selected content; specify the learning strategies to be taught.
- Program objectives can be achieved by program participation and implementation, staff development activities, and parent activities.

Program Evaluation

When a CALLA program is implemented in a school or school district an evaluation plan should be developed and carried out. Both formative and summative evaluations should be included in the plan. The formative evaluation is intended to collect and maintain interim information on the program's implementation and outcomes so that program administrators can adjust staff development or program components as needed throughout the school year. The summative evaluation will provide information on end-of-year effects concerning the major student and other program objectives. While the formative evaluation is intended for all program staff—program planners, staff developers, and teachers—the audience for the summative evaluation should also include administrators, policy makers, and funding agencies. The summative evaluation provides evidence of the program's overall effects and benefits, and is needed to support the allocation of local resources to continue or expand the program.

In this section we provide guidelines for planning and implementing both formative and summative evaluations of a CALLA program, and suggest applications of the evaluation results to program improvement.

FORMATIVE EVALUATION

The focus of the formative evaluation is on program implementation and on interim indicators of student outcomes. Evidence of program implementation ensures that the program design is being carried out. Not all teachers can be expected to implement all of CALLA all of the time. New and continuing teachers will differ in their amount of experience with CALLA and level of exposure to staff development efforts. Information on program implementation can be collected with classroom observations, teacher feedback interviews and questionnaires, and lesson plan records. This information is of critical importance in identifying aspects of the program which need change or improvement, staff development, curriculum revision, and administrative modifications.

The degree to which participating teachers are implementing the program is a major concern in program improvement. For example, a teacher might select one or two components of CALLA to teach, but ignore other aspects of the approach. Administrators need to know how teachers are implementing CALLA so that they can plan staff development activities that provide assistance targeted to those areas in which teachers are encountering difficulties. A teacher might be observed to ascertain how learning strategy instruction is presented. The observer can not only take note of instances of strategy instruction, but also indicate teachable moments during the class in which learning strategies could have been taught and practiced. Sharing this information with teachers can help identify points in a class where learning strategy instruction can be presented or practiced. This type of feedback or coaching can advance the goals of program improvement by helping individual teachers implement the full range of program objectives. Table 7.7 illustrates a checklist which has been used successfully in classroom observations for documenting level of implementation of CALLA objectives.

Another method for collecting information about the level of program implementation is through teacher questionnaires. Questionnaire items should be worded to elicit descriptions of what teachers actually do in the classroom rather than worded in a way that might prompt teachers to claim that they engage in all of the "right" teaching behaviors. In the sample questionnaire in Table 7.8, for example, teachers were asked their opinion about whether learning strategies should be taught explicitly or indirectly, and were given the opportunity to indicate which strategies they taught in each manner. While CALLA workshops had stressed the importance of explicit instruction in learning strategies, teachers were given an option to present a rationale for teaching the strategies indirectly.

The formative evaluation should contain information on interim student outcomes as well as the program implementation data. Indicators of student progress need to be collected with all CALLA objectives for content, academic language, and learning strategies. Because CALLA lesson plans state these objectives explicitly, and because observation procedures are developed during the program design stage, teachers should be able to collect and maintain this type of information effectively. The observation approaches used in CALLA include anecdotal records, checklists, rating scales, analysis of writing samples and oral presentations, reading logs, self-assessment, and other procedures described in Chapter 6 and in the subject area chapters (Chapters 9, 10, 11, and 12). In addition, CALLA teachers can integrate

Table 7.7

CHECKLIST FOR CALLA LESSON OBJECTIVES

- ❑ 1. Objectives stated for content, language, and learning strategies.
- ❑ 2. Content selected is essential for grade level(s) and is aligned with state framework/local curriculum.
- ❑ 3. Activities are included that develop vocabulary, listening, reading, speaking, and writing.
- ❑ 4. One or two learning strategies directly taught and/or practiced.
- ❑ 5. Language somewhat simplified, but not tightly controlled for grammatical structures or vocabulary.
- ❑ 6. Students' prior knowledge elicited in Preparation phase.
- ❑ 7. Context provided through visuals, graphic organizers, manipulatives, realia, hands-on, etc.
- ❑ 8. Cooperative learning activity and active practice with new information presented included in lesson.
- ❑ 9. Self-evaluation activity included in lesson.
- ❑ 10. Higher-level questions posed during lesson.
- ❑ 11. Real-life applications of content addressed through activity and/or discussion.

these records into portfolios that assist in monitoring student progress so that instruction can be adapted and refined as needed. As lesson plans are refined, teachers should note the changes on the lesson plan itself to keep a permanent record of the modifications.

The formative evaluation can also provide useful interim feedback on the staff development and parent outcomes in a CALLA program. Information can be collected from teacher workshop evaluations, from teacher self-ratings of their knowledge of and ability to implement CALLA components highlighted in specific workshops (e.g., see Table 5.1, Teaching Strategies Checklist, and Table 5.2, Teacher Log of Learning Strategy Instruction), from analysis of CALLA lesson plans (see Table 5.3, CALLA Instructional Plan), and from observations of classroom instruction (see Table 5.4, Checklist for Evaluating CALLA Instruction). Through this combination of assessment procedures, a comprehensive image can be derived of the level of implementation of CALLA in each classroom and in the schools overall. Where difficulties in implementation are detected, program planners can assemble focus groups of ESL and content teachers to discuss specific implementation difficulties and develop suggested strategies for overcoming them.

Interim outcomes stated for parents can be assessed using similar self-rating scales combined with questionnaire and interview procedures. Parents are important partners in support of effective instruction for their children and can often be relied on to share oral traditions and stories from the home, ask questions about schoolwork, give recognition for successful completion of work, read to or listen to children read, provide guidance in scheduling homework, and set aside a study area in the home. Questionnaires or interviews can probe which of these practices are used at home. Workshops for parents should convey the essential components of CALLA and elicit their support in engaging in these activities. Parent evaluations of these workshops and recommendations for improving parent activities are important data in the formative evaluation. Parents are also a useful source of information about their child's interests and work habits that can be discussed during parent-teacher conferences. The teacher's anecdotal records of these meetings are important data for the formative evaluation because they can identify ways in which the program can be made more responsive to parent interests and needs as well as ways in which the parent component can be refined.

SUMMATIVE EVALUATION

The summative evaluation of CALLA determines the extent to which major program objectives have been attained for students and also for staff and for parents. The summative evaluation builds on the formative evaluation in using some of the same data but differs in a number of important areas. First, a *comparison group* of non-CALLA students or classrooms should be located which resembles the CALLA students in as many important background characteristics as possible, e.g., level of English language proficiency, language background, age or grade level, and level of education in both English and the native language. Data will be collected on this group of students that enable comparisons to be made with CALLA students on major program outcomes.

Second, in a summative evaluation, information on the *variation in program implementation* from one teacher to the next is used differently than it is in a formative program evaluation. Whereas information on level of implementation would be used for staff development in formative evaluation, in summative evaluation student outcomes in classrooms of low implementation teachers can be contrasted with the outcomes in classrooms where teachers have implemented CALLA successfully.

This leads to the third major difference with the formative evaluation, the use of an *evaluation design* to enable comparisons between CALLA and non-CALLA classrooms to produce the strongest possible conclusions concerning the causal relationship between CALLA and program outcomes. The purpose of the evaluation design is to identify causal connections between CALLA and the program outcomes, which is aided by selecting a design that eliminates as many threats to the causal linkage as is possible. The evaluation design will typically be selected from the standard designs discussed in texts on education evaluation[5] but may also include the gap-reduction design, an evaluation model used in evaluating Title VII programs. In the gap-reduction design, the performance of students in the program is compared to a local or national norm for native English-speaking students on a standardized test or other indicator of performance. The gap evident between program and norm groups at the pretest should be reduced by the posttest. An important limitation of the gap-reduction design is that it does not enable causal conclusions to be drawn between the program and the outcomes. Nevertheless, this design is extremely useful when there are no comparison groups or when comparisons between high and low implementation classrooms are not possible. It is also useful in making comparisons on non-test indicators of student outcomes, such as attendance.

The summative evaluation is performed by following a number of important steps that program administrators should play a key role in managing. These steps include identifying objectives, selecting appropriate outcome measures, and developing an evaluation design that will provide accurate information on areas of strength and weakness in the program.

Table 7.8
CALLA TEACHER QUESTIONNAIRE

Name ______________________________ Date ______________

1. Check the math strands you have covered this year:

- ❑ Whole numbers
- ❑ Geometry
- ❑ Fractions
- ❑ Decimals
- ❑ Time and money
- ❑ Graphs and charts
- ❑ Ratio and percent
- ❑ Statistics and probability
- ❑ Other (Describe) ______________________________

2. Check the average amount of time spent on word problems:

- ❑ Once a week
- ❑ 4-5 times a week
- ❑ 2-3 times a week
- ❑ 1-2 times a month

3. Do you think it is necessary to teach learning strategies directly (e.g., to name the strategy, model it, and tell when to use it?) ❑ YES ❑ NO

Why or why not? ______________________________

____

4. Which learning strategies do you teach explicitly or indirectly ?

Elaborating prior knowledge	❑ Explicitly	❑ Indirectly
Cooperation	❑ Explicitly	❑ Indirectly
Graphic organizers	❑ Explicitly	❑ Indirectly
Classifying/grouping	❑ Explicitly	❑ Indirectly
Making inferences/predicting	❑ Explicitly	❑ Indirectly
Summarizing	❑ Explicitly	❑ Indirectly
Using images/visualizing	❑ Explicitly	❑ Indirectly

5. Do you teach problem-solving strategies? ❑ YES ❑ NO

If yes, check which strategies you teach:

- ❑ Finding needed information
- ❑ Finding patterns
- ❑ Finding extra information
- ❑ Solving simpler problems
- ❑ Guessing and checking
- ❑ Cooperating/working in group
- ❑ Choosing operations
- ❑ Working backward
- ❑ Making organized lists/tables
- ❑ Writing number sentences
- ❑ Drawing pictures/diagrams
- ❑ Using logical reasoning

6. Additional comments:

____

____

____

____

OBJECTIVES. These should include at a minimum the student objectives, but can also include staff development objectives and parent involvement objectives. In the summative evaluation, the objectives are restated as "Evaluation Claims" or hypotheses about the effects of the program.

ASSESSMENT MEASURES. Project staff should determine appropriate measures of student progress towards meeting program goals and objectives, including content knowledge, language outcomes, and student use of learning strategies. Alternative assessment is essential in order to capture the complexities of higher-order thinking skills and academic language that are taught in CALLA. (See Chapter 6 for suggestions.) Some of the suggestions for assessing staff development and parent outcomes in the formative evaluation are useful in the summative evaluation as well.

EVALUATION DESIGN. Students in a CALLA program could be contrasted with comparable students in a non-CALLA program. Alternatively, students in high implementation CALLA classrooms can be contrasted with students in low implementation CALLA classrooms. Students to be evaluated should have participated in the CALLA program for at least 100 days of instruction in the school year in order to ensure that they have had adequate exposure to profit from instruction. Project staff should consult with the school district evaluation specialist to consider appropriate options, given local circumstances such as the availability of a comparison group.

STAFF RESPONSIBILITIES. A plan should be developed which clearly identifies the roles of different staff members and of the project evaluator. Questions to be answered include: Who will be involved in planning the evaluation? Who will select or design the outcome measures? Who will collect the data (e.g., standardized and alternative assessment measures)? Who will analyze the data collected? Who will be involved in drawing conclusions from the data? Who will write the evaluation report (e.g., school district personnel, the evaluator, a collaborative effort)? Who will present and interpret the findings to teachers, local administrators, and parents?

COLLECT OUTCOME DATA. Pretests should be administered to all CALLA students in September or October and should be administered to new students as they enter the program (except for those entering in the spring who will not complete 100 days of instruction). Posttests should be administered in May or June. For standardized tests, use the same instruments that were used in the pretest, but for criterion-referenced tests, the version of the test is used that reflects what students have learned to that point in the school year. Posttests should be administered to all students who have had at least 100 days of CALLA instruction, including those who entered late and those who left early. Students leaving the program early should be tested when they exit the CALLA program, and a record should be maintained of how long they received program services to determine if the minimum 100 days participation has been met.

DOCUMENT PROGRAM IMPLEMENTATION. Throughout the year, project staff should conduct an assessment of the level of program implementation as described in the formative evaluation. The data collection procedures include class observation, learning strategy instruction logs, teachers' observation checklists of student progress (see Chapter 6), and evaluations of staff development and parent involvement activities.

DEVELOP A DATABASE. A database of essential information about each student needs to be maintained in order to track student progress in CALLA and on into grade-level classes. This database should include students' prior education, home language, language proficiency in both languages, standardized and alternative assessment information in both English and the native language (if possible), dates of entry into and exit from CALLA, attendance records, and teacher assessments both in CALLA and in grade-level classes. As described in Chapter 6, multiple measures of student progress are strongly recommended for all ESL students rather than only one measure such as a standardized achievement test. This is particularly important in a CALLA program because students' ability to perform authentic academic tasks successfully provides more useful assessment and diagnostic information than does their performance on a relatively brief paper and pencil test.

ANALYZE DATA. Pretest results can be shared with teachers so that they can use them to identify areas of strength and weakness in their students and make adjustments to the curriculum. Posttest results should be analyzed in time to use them in making placement decisions for the next school year. Program implementation data can be analyzed continuously so that changes and improvements can be made on an ongoing basis. Data analyses of student outcomes should be stratified depending on initial English language proficiency, level of previous schooling, grade level, or other variables that may influence the results. It is also advisable to stratify level of teacher implementation of CALLA.

APPLICATION OF RESULTS

INTERPRET RESULTS. Project staff can work with their school district evaluation specialists to compare and interpret amount of student progress and group gains in meeting CALLA program objectives. It is important to analyze the process measures collected during the year (e.g., checklists, observation notes, workshop evaluations) in order to ascertain the degree to which teachers implemented the CALLA program, the effectiveness of staff development activities, and the value attached by students, teachers, and parents to program activities.

FORMATIVE FEEDBACK. Project staff should provide ongoing feedback to teachers about the results of the formative evaluation as they are collected and analyzed. The formative evaluation results can improve the CALLA program most effectively if teachers can use them in planning and reviewing their instruction.

REPORTING. For the summative evaluation, a formal annual evaluation report should be shared with the school district, CALLA program staff, parents, and the funding agency if appropriate. The yearly evaluation report should be used as a basis for planning changes and improvements in the next year's CALLA program. The evaluation report can also be a source of program information that can be disseminated through presentations, workshops, conferences, newsletters, and articles in professional journals.

Questions in Conducting an Evaluation

- What are the objectives of the CALLA program for the instructional component, for staff development, and for the parent program?
- Which assessment measures or data sources will be used to assess these objectives? Are multiple measures available?
- What evaluation design is being used? Is there a non-project comparison group? Low-implementation comparison group?
- Which staff have a responsibility in the evaluation? What role will they play? What role does the independent evaluator play?
- When will outcome data be collected? Are some data collected on a continuing basis, while other data are collected only in the fall and spring? Which

data will be collected at what points in time? How will student outcome data be used in the formative and summative evaluation?

- How will program implementation be documented? How will this information be used in the formative evaluation and in the summative evaluation?
- What data elements will be used in the database? What background data? Student achievement and behavior?
- When will the data be analyzed and who will be responsible for the analysis?
- Who will report the results to teachers? Parents? Administrators? To the funding agency? What is the time schedule for reporting?

A plan for both formative and summative evaluation of a CALLA program appears in Table 7.9.

Table 7.9
CALLA EVALUATION FRAMEWORK

Claim Type I—Academic Achievement

Objective	Data Source	Time Frame
1.A. CALLA students will show improvements in English language oral proficiency, reading skills, and in writing relative to students not in the CALLA program.	1.A. Formal oral proficiency test, standardized reading test, cloze test, informal reading inventory, reading log, writing samples, checklists or rating scales, teacher observations, course grades.	1.A. Fall-spring pre-posttest, ongoing use of informal measures.
1.B. CALLA students will show improvements in content-area knowledge and skills relative to students not in the CALLA program.	1.B. Standardized test in content area(s), cloze test, reading log, writing samples or reports, checklists or rating scales, teacher observations, course grades.	1.B. Fall-spring pre-posttest, ongoing use of informal measures.

Claim Type II—Teachers' Attitudes and Behaviors

Objective	Data Source	Time Frame
2.A. Teachers who attend CALLA workshops and who receive follow-up staff development will learn and apply CALLA teaching skills (presenting content instruction, language development, and explicit instruction in learning strategies).	2.A. Teacher Needs Assessment, Teacher Implementation Questionnaire, workshop evaluations, classroom observations.	2.A. Needs Assessment and Implementation Questionnaire at end of year; others ongoing.
2.B. Teachers who attend workshops but who receive no followup CALLA inservice will develop fewer new skills than those who receive inservice support.	2.B. Teacher Implementation Questionnaire, Teacher Implementation Observation Checklist, workshop evaluations.	2.B. Implementation Questionnaire at end of year; others ongoing.

Claim Type III—Students' Attitudes and Behaviors

Objectives	Data Sources	Time Frame
3.A. CALLA students will show improvements in the acquisition and use of learning strategies compared to students not in CALLA classrooms.	3.A. Self-report questionnaires of learning strategy use, performance measures of learning strategy use, writing samples, teacher observations.	3.A. Ongoing.
3.B. CALLA students will have improved attitudes about their own ability to learn English language skills and specific academic content.	3.B. Self-report questionnaires of self-efficacy, teacher observations.	3.B. Ongoing.

Claim Type IV—Improvements in Instructional Practice

Objectives	Data Sources	Time Frame
4.A. Improve instruction by developing objectives in content, language, and learning strategies, and designing lessons following the CALLA instructional sequence.	4.A. Teacher lesson plans, observation of teachers.	4.A. Ongoing.
4.B. Improve instruction by teacher participation in staff development, peer-coaching, and other follow-up activities.	4.B. Number of participating teachers.	4.B. Ongoing.
4.C. Teachers implement CALLA model.	4.C. Teacher Implementation Observation Checklist.	4.C. Ongoing.

Claim Type V—Parent Involvement

Objectives	Data Sources	Time Frame
5.A. Parents who attend CALLA workshops will report more frequent practices in the home which support classroom instruction, will learn more about the CALLA approach than parents who do not attend CALLA workshops regularly.	5.A. Interviews, conferences, teacher anecdotal records, parent questionnaires (all in native language).	5.A. Ongoing.

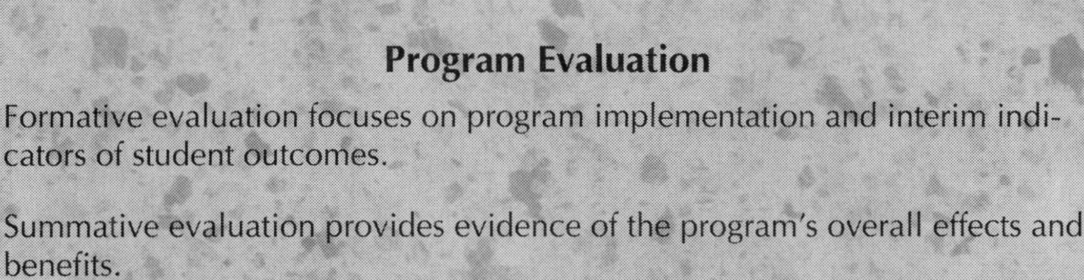

Program Evaluation

- ❖ Formative evaluation focuses on program implementation and interim indicators of student outcomes.
- ❖ Summative evaluation provides evidence of the program's overall effects and benefits.
- ❖ Apply results by comparing and interpreting student progress, providing feedback to teachers, and sharing a formal report with the school district.

Application Activities

The purpose of these activities is to assist administrators in identifying the types of actions needed to plan and implement a CALLA program successfully. These actions include teacher selection, needs assessment, curriculum development, materials selection, planning for program implementation, staff development, and program evaluation.

1. Refer to Table 7.1, the Checklist for Identifying CALLA Teachers. Apply the checklist to a small number of ESL and content teachers. If you do not have sufficient information to answer any of the items listed on the checklist, describe how you would find out this information.
2. Write a brief description of any obstacles that exist in your school or district for implementing the seven suggestions for communication between ESL and content teachers listed on pages 142–143. Brainstorm with one or more colleagues on ways in which each obstacle could be overcome.
3. List the types of information currently available about language minority students in your school or district. Refer to Table 7.2, the Student Needs Assessment. Which questions can be answered using the information already available to you? How could you gather information to answer any questions for which you do not have information already available?
4. Draw up a plan for a summer curriculum and materials project. Identify outcome goals, types of expertise needed on the curriculum development team, resources you should provide, guidance and training for the curriculum development team, and how the project will be monitored and evaluated.
5. Work with a group of colleagues to identify appropriate materials in one or more content areas for ESL students at one level (e.g., upper elementary, middle school, or high school). Resources to use include textbook collections at university or school district libraries, locally adopted materials, locally developed materials, publishers' catalogs, and recommendations from teachers. Analyze the advantages and disadvantages of your choices using the suggestions in Table 7.3, Instructional Materials Selection.

6. Brainstorm with one or more colleagues a list of staff development activities that would be most useful to teachers in your school or district who are currently teaching language minority students. Include both language specialist teachers and content specialist teachers.
7. Refer to Table 7.9, CALLA Evaluation Framework. Adapt to your program, and indicate individuals who would be able to carry out each role identified.

CHAPTER 8

CALLA in Different Contexts

Overview

Identifying the various contexts in which CALLA has been or can be implemented.

- **CALLA at Beginning Proficiency Level**
- **CALLA in Primary Grade Classrooms**
- **CALLA in Bilingual Classrooms**
- **CALLA for Preliterate Upper Elementary and Secondary Students**
- **CALLA in Pull-out ESL Programs**
- **CALLA for 'Sheltered' or Language-sensitive Classes**
- **CALLA in Grade-level Classrooms**
- **CALLA for Compensatory and Remedial Programs**
- **CALLA for Students with Learning Disabilities**
- **CALLA for ESL Students in Community Colleges**
- **CALLA in College and University Intensive English Programs**
- **CALLA in Foreign Language Programs**

CHAPTER 8 CALLA IN DIFFERENT CONTEXTS

CALLA WAS ORIGINALLY DEVELOPED to respond to the needs of intermediate level ESL students in upper elementary and secondary grades. We have seen how CALLA can be adapted for use with ESL students at different grade levels, in different types of programs, and at different levels of language proficiency. The experiences of teachers and program administrators suggest that CALLA principles have even wider applications.

CALLA at Beginning Proficiency Level

Students of any age from kindergarten to adults may be beginners in learning English. In this section we focus on beginning level students in upper elementary and secondary school who are literate and at grade level in their native language. In subsequent sections we discuss younger children and adult ESL students.

Beginning level ESL instruction generally focuses on basic language survival skills and initial literacy in English. Appropriately designed instruction can help beginning students by preparing them for CALLA at the intermediate and advanced ESL levels through what we refer to as a pre-CALLA approach. This approach maintains the basic elements of CALLA but adapts them to the level of student language proficiency.

CONTENT

Beginning level upper elementary and secondary ESL students have not yet developed a language base sufficient for reading the academic language found in grade-level content materials. However, many content appropriate topics can be developed orally and with simple reading and writing tasks. For example, the CALLA teacher can expand the traditional themes taught in beginning level ESL classes (greetings, body parts, numbers, days of the week, food, colors, clothes, etc.) to include content area concepts selected from health science, mathematics, social studies, nutrition, art, and consumer education.

ACADEMIC LANGUAGE

In adding more academic content to beginning level ESL, the CALLA teacher may need to simplify materials or use materials from a lower grade level for reading in content subjects. However, class discussions and activities involving content topics should be geared to the cognitive maturity level of the students. This means that academic language functions requiring higher-level thinking skills can be an integral part of CALLA instruction, even when students' English language proficiency is extremely limited.

LEARNING STRATEGIES

Strategy instruction is also an integral part of a pre-CALLA approach. Beginning level ESL students can learn to use strategies for academic tasks when the strategies are presented in simple and concrete forms. For example, the CALLA teacher can model the use of learning strategies with very simple language. Beginning level teachers should focus on a very small number of strategies, perhaps only two or three. We recommend beginning with *Directed Attention*, in which students focus on the language input they are receiving, consciously ignoring other distractors, and *Elaboration*, in which students use what they know about a content topic or language task to aid their learning.

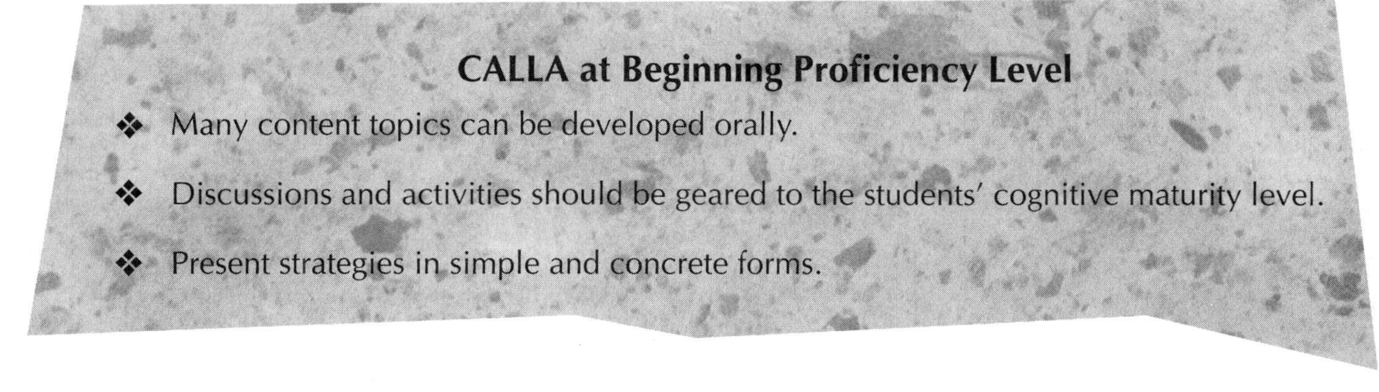

CALLA in Primary Grade Classrooms

Major academic objectives of primary grade (grades K-3) programs are to develop literacy and mathematical concepts and skills that will allow students to read for information as well as appreciation, to communicate in written form, and to use mathematical concepts and computation skills to solve problems. Primary grade children also learn about the world around them through experiences with social studies, science, and the arts.

CONTENT

Much of primary grade subject area content is left to the discretion of the teacher. This level of teacher autonomy is particularly advantageous for developing integrated thematic units that introduce and support important knowledge, skills, and attitudes in a variety of ways. For example, teachers might introduce units on the community which integrate literature about a child's adventures in a city or small town with graphs which show the characteristics of people (numbers, age, sex, occupation, etc.) in a similar community in a particular place. In this example, literature, social studies, and mathematics are combined into a single thematic unit.

In CALLA instruction for primary grade children, we encourage the use of such integrated themes not only because important concepts and skills are introduced and supported in a variety of ways, but also because new information is presented in a context that is rich with meaning. This type of contextualization better enables students to use what they know to learn and to remember by establishing connections with familiar concepts in memory. Integrated content in science and mathematics might include the study of plants and animals (including dinosaurs), measurement of temperature and rainfall, observation with the five senses, and simple word problems based on science topics. Similarly, an integrated thematic approach to social studies and literature could include reading stories about children in other times and places.

ACADEMIC LANGUAGE

Native English-speaking children beginning school in kindergarten or first grade bring with them varying levels of proficiency in communicative social language skills, and in most cases are not proficient in academic language skills. A major task of primary grade teachers is to help students develop the academic language needed to understand, discuss, read, and write about topics in the content areas. In this respect, ESL primary grade students can profit from the same type of language instruction as their native English-speaking peers. However, the teacher should keep in mind that ESL students, unlike native-English speakers, will encounter many words in print which are unfamiliar orally. Teachers should therefore provide extensive language development through techniques such as schematic maps that take advantage of existing concept links that children have developed in their first language.

LEARNING STRATEGIES

Young children are in the process of developing metacognitive awareness of themselves as thinkers and learners. Much of this incipient awareness is tied to children's active learning experiences. For example, when children are working with Cuisenaire rods or other manipulatives, they can be encouraged to talk about what they are doing and thinking. This type of thinking aloud provides practice in developing children's awareness of their own thought processes.

Learning strategies taught to primary grade children should focus on concrete tasks. For example, students might make semantic maps of what they already know about the lesson topic, or predict information they expect to encounter in a content reading selection by looking at the title and illustrations. Teachers can assist, where needed, by drawing the semantic maps on the board or leading a discussion about students' predictions. The teacher can also model some of the questions that children might ask themselves as they are reading or writing, such as, "Does this make sense?"

Learning strategies taught to primary grade children should focus on concrete tasks.

CALLA is appropriate in the non-graded primary classroom where children are grouped by their levels of achievement in different subject areas rather than by chronological age. In non-graded classrooms a six-year-old reading at a higher than first grade level reads with older children at a similar reading level, and an eight-year-old who is not yet able to work in the third grade mathematics program can work with younger children at the appropriate level. This flexibility of grouping and focus on individual progress can be strengthened further through instruction in learning strategies that help children become independent learners.

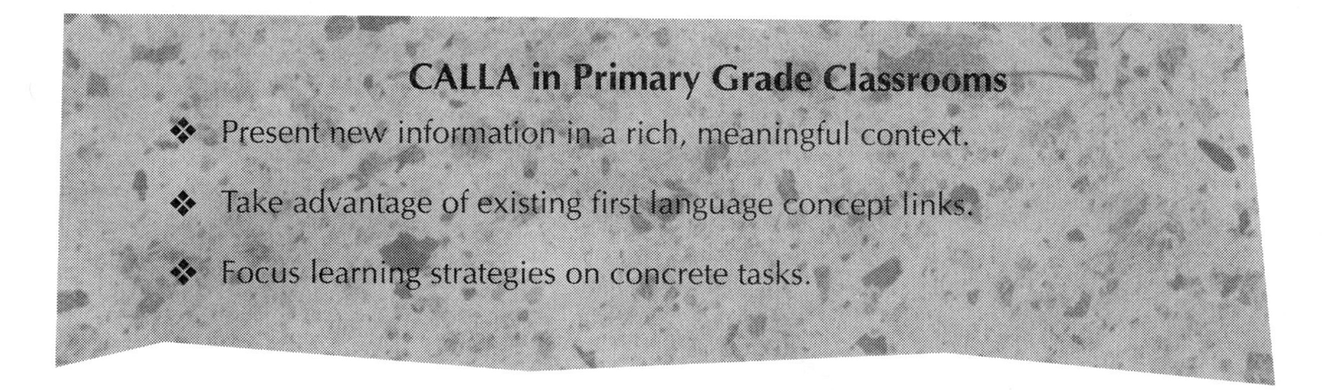

CALLA Bilingual Classrooms

Instruction in a bilingual setting can facilitate many of the objectives that CALLA is designed to achieve. Content, academic language, and learning strategies can be introduced and practiced in the students' native language, thus creating a declarative knowledge base and procedural skills which can be transferred to English.

CONTENT

By teaching the different content areas in a language that students understand, the bilingual CALLA teacher can provide for continuing conceptual development, rather than interrupting development to focus exclusively on learning the new language. The content selected should be aligned to the English curriculum for the appropriate grade level and should also include topics drawn from the students' culture. The types of activities should parallel similar learning activities in all-English classrooms. By including some of the major content of the English instructional program and engaging in similar class activities, the CALLA bilingual program will prepare students to transfer what they learn in their native language to the same kinds of learning experiences in English.

In a CALLA bilingual classroom, the teacher explains to students how the knowledge and skills they are learning in their first language can be applied to the content subjects that they study in English. During English instruction, the teacher asks students to identify knowledge and skills acquired in their first language, and provides specific examples of how such knowledge can be used in English content subjects. Many students need explicit instruction accompanied by scaffolding or gradually decreasing support for ways in which they can transfer information and skills learned in their native language to English.

ACADEMIC LANGUAGE

Academic language can also be developed first in the native language and then transferred to English. Developing reading, writing, and oral academic language skills in students' native language first provides a foundation of academic language functions. For example, if students learn to discuss and write about classifying different types of insects in their native language first, a similar task is greatly facilitated in English because students will have learned both the concept of classification and the fact that certain types of language are needed to describe a classification system. The task in English then becomes one of discovering a different way of expressing familiar concepts and academic language functions.

While students in a bilingual program are developing academic language skills in their first language, they are also beginning to acquire English. They may receive English instruction from their bilingual teacher or from a different ESL teacher. In a CALLA setting, the teacher of English capitalizes on the academic language skills students are learning in their native language by explicitly explaining and providing examples of how parallel skills operate in English. Translation should be avoided. Instead, the CALLA teacher might say:

> *Remember how we wrote some math word problems in Spanish this morning? You had to write a story, include numbers, and ask a question. Now we're going to write some* ***different*** *word problems in English. We're going to organize our problems in exactly the same way that we did in Spanish. Now, let's think about some of the math words we might need to write word problems in English.*

In this way the teacher is teaching for transfer rather than translating, and students are learning to make explicit use of their knowledge of academic language in their first language as they begin to develop academic language skills in English.

LEARNING STRATEGIES

When learning strategies can be taught initially in the native language, students can focus their entire attention on the strategy instruction without encountering difficulties in trying to comprehend the language. Strategies for studying and remembering new content, listening and reading strategies, and strategies for oral and written production can all be practiced with native language materials and activities. The CALLA bilingual teacher models and explains the strategies in the first language, then has students practice and discuss their applications of the strategies. When students become adept at using the strategies with native language content and academic language, the teacher then suggests ways in which they can use the same strategies in ESL and English grade-level classrooms. Scaffolding instruction in learning strategies is particularly important because students cannot be expected to transfer strategies automatically from their first language to English. Scaffolding is provided by gradually reducing the cues and support for specified strategy-task combinations.

BILINGUAL CALLA INSTRUCTIONAL SEQUENCE

The CALLA instructional sequence (described in Chapter 5) lends itself to facilitating transfer of content knowledge from students' first language to English. The Preparation phase, in which students' prior knowledge about the topic is elicited, can be conducted in the first language, thus preparing students to more easily make linkages to the new information presented in English during the Presentation phase of the lesson. When students work in cooperative groups during the Practice phase, the task is presented in English and students are expected to complete the task or produce a product in English. However, they may use their native language to explain, clarify, and interpret the task and language requirements. In the Evaluation phase of bilingual CALLA instruction, students reflect on their own learning by writing in learning logs and journals, and by completing checklists. These self-evaluation activities can all be completed in the native language. Activities conducted during the Expansion phase can also be conducted in either language. For example, the thinking skills discussion questions could be asked in English and discussed in the first language. Family and community interviews could be conducted in the first language and reported on in English. Group projects in class or individual projects at home could be conducted in the native language and then a report or graph of the results could be prepared in English.

In CALLA bilingual instruction the creative use of both languages can support and enhance student learning of both content and language, as well as expand the use of learning strategies and higher-level thinking skills throughout the bilingual curriculum.

CALLA in Bilingual Classrooms

- ❖ Prepare students to transfer what they learn in their native language to the same kind of learning experiences in English.
- ❖ Students learn to use their knowledge of academic language in their first language as they learn these skills in English.
- ❖ Strategies can all be practiced with native language materials and activities.
- ❖ Use of both languages supports and enhances student learning of both content and language.

CALLA for Preliterate Upper Elementary and Secondary Students

Older students who have had limited educational opportunities in their native countries may enter upper elementary or secondary grades without having acquired literacy skills or age-appropriate academic content knowledge in their first language. They will probably need to spend a longer than average period in the ESL or bilingual program in order to develop the academic knowledge and skills needed in the English grade-level classroom. Many CALLA principles can be used successfully with preliterate and other educationally delayed students.

CONTENT

The formal academic content of school may be quite unfamiliar and confusing to students who have focused exclusively on developing successful life survival skills for a number of years before coming to the United States. CALLA techniques for identifying and building on students' prior knowledge can be used successfully with preliterate students, but the teacher should seek to uncover prior experiential knowledge rather than prior academic knowledge. For example, students from rural areas may have had numerous experiences related to farming, such as growth cycles, reproduction, and weather. Urban students who have bought, sold, and bartered goods and services have a great deal of practical knowledge about economics and may have considerable math skills in handling money. Students who have not yet learned to read and write independently may yet possess reserves of knowledge about and appreciation for literature which they have gained through an oral tradition that has been handed down from their parents and grandparents. The CALLA teacher attempts to relate these kinds of experiential knowledge to academic content topics that are part of the school's grade-level curriculum.

ACADEMIC LANGUAGE

In a classroom of preliterate students, the teacher's first concern is to teach initial literacy skills. If at all possible, initial literacy skills should be taught first in students' native language. As discussed above in the section on CALLA for bilingual education programs, learning to read and write is an easier process in one's native language because a highly developed oral language base assists students in making relationships between sounds and written symbols and in comprehending meanings of words encountered in print.

In some cases, however, initial literacy has to be taught in English. Reasons for literacy instruction in English first might include the absence of teachers qualified to teach native language literacy, the presence of multiple native languages in a single class, and the fact that students' native languages may be primarily oral and without a written tradition. In these and similar cases, the teacher must teach students how to read and write in a language which they speak imperfectly.

The Language Experience Approach has proven effective in developing second language initial literacy skills with older students.[1] In this approach, students develop oral narratives, the teacher or aide writes down the student's words, and the resulting text is then read by the student. In this way, the topic of the reading text is familiar to the student and the vocabulary and grammatical structures are confined to what the student already knows orally. As students develop initial writing skills, they begin to write their own stories and read them to classmates and the teacher. Many Language Experience Approach specialists believe that students' sentences should be written down by the teacher exactly as dictated, spelled and punctuated correctly, but not changed to make them more grammatically correct.[2] Similarly, when students begin to write their stories, they should be allowed to use invented spellings and incomplete sentences. Maintaining students' authentic expression is a way of empowering students by demonstrating to them that their own oral language can be written down and then read, thus accomplishing the major goal of written language, communication. Students who learn to read and write their own texts have not only learned literacy processes, but they have also learned literacy functions.

Preliterate older students also need to begin reading texts written by others. Everyday print such as signs, menus, ads, and recipes make good reading materials because students see an immediate use for learning to read them. Students also need experiences with texts with recurring language, referred to as predictable books. Suggestions for specific books can be found in the bibliography of predictable books appropriate for older learners developed by Atwell.[3]

LEARNING STRATEGIES

Students with little formal educational experience may not have a great deal of knowledge about strategies that can assist their school learning. They may need instruction and support in developing an awareness of their own mental processes, in focusing attention on school tasks, and in organizing and remembering information. Instruction in learning strategies for preliterate students needs to be explicit, concrete, and oral. Explicit learning strategy instruction involves naming the strategy and explaining its benefits. Concrete instruction is accomplished through naming the strategy again, modeling it, and calling students' attention to the strategy when it occurs in class. Oral strategy instruction is especially important for students at the early stage of reading, and can be achieved through explanation, discussion, icons that represent a particular strategy, and eliciting from students their descriptions of their individual strategy use.

CALLA for Preliterate Upper Elementary and Secondary Students

- Seek to uncover prior experiential knowledge rather than prior academic knowledge.
- The first concern is to teach initial literacy skills.
- Instruction in learning strategies needs to be explicit, concrete, and oral.

CALLA in Pull-Out ESL Programs

In a typical pull-out ESL program, students spend most of their day in grade-level classrooms, with the ESL teacher taking them from their regular classroom for special English language instruction. This special instruction may range from three times a week to a daily period of 45 to 60 minutes, and in general focuses on social communication skills and grammar.[4] In addition to such time constraints, the pull-out ESL teacher must also manage additional impediments to successful instruction, such as pupil load and the need to move from room to room or even from school to school on a daily basis. Nevertheless, we believe that some CALLA principles can be incorporated into this less-than-ideal model of ESL instruction.

CONTENT

Instructional time limitations make it difficult to incorporate extensive content into an ESL pull-out program. However, the ESL teacher can find out from grade-level content teachers what major content topics are being studied. ESL students can assist in providing this information by sharing accounts of what they are studying in other classes and by showing textbooks and homework assignments to their ESL teacher. The ESL teacher can use this information to plan CALLA units which provide support for content learning and which integrate concepts and skills from as many content areas as possible. (See the Appendix for an example of an integrated thematic CALLA unit.) This type of integration maximizes what may be limited available instructional time.

ACADEMIC LANGUAGE

An important CALLA principle is that content should determine the language syllabus, rather than the reverse. For the pull-out ESL teacher, following this principle may entail a fairly extensive restructuring of the curriculum. Rather than teaching a grammatical sequence, the teacher would derive language activities from the content topics included in integrated thematic units. In general, these language activities should not focus primarily on grammar and vocabulary learning, but should involve practicing academic language for the same functions used in grade-level classes.

LEARNING STRATEGIES

Even if ESL teachers feel that there is simply not enough time to teach their students learning strategies in a pull-out program, we strongly recommend that strategy instruction be made an essential part of the program. By discovering what topics and activities students are exposed to in grade-level classrooms, the pull-out teacher can select a few strategies that can assist students in understanding and learning the content more successfully. Listening and reading strategies will be most helpful in helping ESL students understand what is going on in the grade-level classroom. Students may need extensive support to ensure that strategies practiced in the ESL classroom transfer to the grade-level content classes.

CALLA in Pull-out ESL Programs

- Integrate concepts and skills from as many content areas as possible.
- Derive language activities from the content topics.
- Listening and reading strategies will be most helpful.

CALLA for "Sheltered" or Language-sensitive Classes

"Sheltered language" and "sheltered content" refer to classes in which all students are non-native speakers of English receiving instruction from a content teacher.[5] In this model the language is simplified and additional contextual support is provided to help students understand the content presented.[6] This type of instruction has also been referred to as **language-sensitive** instruction,[7] meaning that the content teacher is sensitive to both the language needs of the students and the language demands of the content subject. As we discussed in Chapter 1, the "sheltered" model shares many features with CALLA, including a focus on content and the provision of visual, auditory, and kinesthetic clues to assist comprehension.

CONTENT

Selecting high-priority content for ESL students should be somewhat easier for content teachers than for ESL teachers to accomplish. However, content teachers who are accustomed to covering an entire textbook or curriculum within a single school year may have difficulty in omitting any of the topics they are accustomed to covering with native English-speaking students. Using the CALLA criteria for selecting content identified in Chapter 2 may be helpful for "sheltered" content teachers as well as ESL teachers.

ACADEMIC LANGUAGE

Content teachers need to include a variety of language activities in classes composed of non-native English speakers. CALLA principles advocate not only reading and writing across the curriculum, but listening and speaking in all content subjects as well. Language activities in "sheltered" content classes should not only include all language skills, but also the academic language functions that promote higher-order thinking skills, such as analyzing, synthesizing, and evaluating.

LEARNING STRATEGIES

Learning strategy instruction can provide non-native English speakers with tools to assist them in comprehending teacher and textbook explanations. Ideally, content teachers of "sheltered" classes modify their language and adapt instructional materials so that they are comprehensible to students. In practice, the widely varying levels of English proficiency found in most classes of non-native English speakers make it difficult to provide comprehensible input to all students on a consistent basis. Students who consciously monitor their own comprehension level and have a repertoire of practical strategies to use when comprehension difficulties are encountered are less dependent on the quality of the input of teachers and instructional materials.

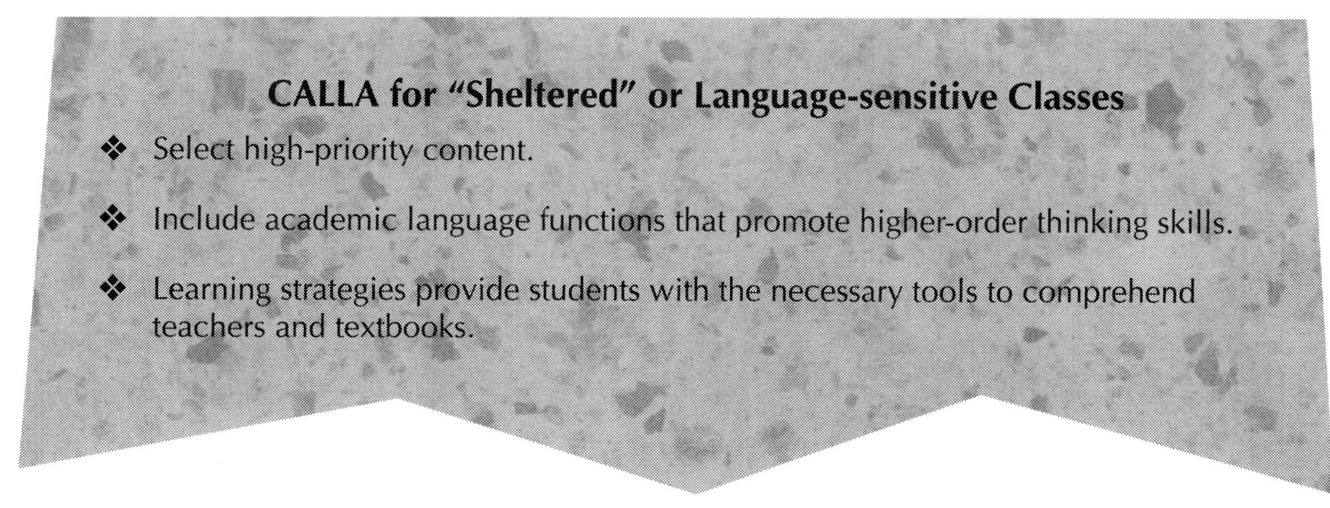

CALLA in Grade-level Classrooms

As explained in Chapter 1, we have followed the suggestion of Enright and McCloskey[8] in using the term **grade-level** to refer to classrooms designed for native English-speaking students. The presence of both native and non-native English-speaking students in a classroom presents a challenge to the grade-level teacher. We believe that an instructional model like CALLA can help both types of students learn more successfully.

CONTENT

Content teachers often complain about the amount of material their students are expected to cover each year. Students may be rushed through a textbook with little opportunity for reflection and integration of new concepts and skills. This process is exacerbated for non-native English speaking students who, because of limited language proficiency, may encounter difficulties in keeping up with the flow of information from teacher and textbook. Using CALLA principles for selecting high-priority content, taking the time to study it in depth, and relating it to students' prior knowledge can make learning more meaningful for both native and non-native English speakers. This "less is more" approach is advocated by curriculum reforms in a number of content areas, including science, mathematics, social studies, and literature.[9]

ACADEMIC LANGUAGE

As discussed earlier in this chapter, a language-across-the curriculum approach is a major feature of the CALLA model. All students, not just non-native English speakers, learn by having many opportunities to communicate about their learning and thinking in their content subjects. Even in mathematics, which traditionally has been believed to be less language-dependent than other subjects, a major goal is for students to communicate about mathematical processes, develop and write problems, and explain their problem solutions.[10]

Cooperative learning is another important feature of the CALLA model which is as useful with native as with non-native English speakers. By working in heterogeneous groups with native English speakers, students learning English are provided with additional models and opportunities to develop academic language functions.[11]

LEARNING STRATEGIES

Much of the research on learning strategy instruction has been conducted with native English-speaking students and has shown positive results.[12] Our own research has indicated that second language learners also profit from learning strategy instruction.[13] We suggest that grade-level teachers could help both their native and non-native English-speaking students achieve greater success and autonomy by incorporating strategy instruction in all curriculum areas.

CALLA in Grade-level Classrooms

- Select high-priority content, study it in depth, and relate it to students' prior knowledge.
- All students learn by communicating about their learning and thinking in their content subjects.
- Research indicates that both first and second language learners profit from learning strategy instruction.

CALLA for Compensatory and Remedial Programs

Special programs that provide supplementary instruction to improve the education of economically disadvantaged and low-achieving students are to be found in most school districts. The largest of these programs is the federally funded Chapter 1 program, which serves one out of every nine children in school.[14] Many of the students in Chapter 1 programs are ESL students. The quality of instruction provided for compensatory and remedial students has been criticized for lack of correlation with regular programs, low teacher expectations of student success, and an emphasis on basic skills and facts over the development of higher-order thinking skills.[15] As a result, most students in Chapter 1 programs remain in compensatory and remedial education throughout their school careers, never attaining the achievement levels needed to exit from the program.[16] We believe that instruction based on the CALLA model could be effective in improving the quality of programs for at-risk students in compensatory and remedial programs.

CONTENT

CALLA procedures for selecting high-priority content aligned to the school district's or state's curriculum can be used to make a better match of the compensatory program's objectives with those of the regular program. By focusing on essential content identified in the adopted curriculum, remedial teachers can be more efficient in accelerating their students' progress. Setting instructional objectives that are in harmony with those of the regular program can also lead teachers to expect more from their disadvantaged students, rather than being satisfied with low-level academic performance.

ACADEMIC LANGUAGE

Academic language is inextricably tied to academic language functions and to higher-order thinking skills. Instruction for students in remedial and compensatory programs relies heavily on individual seat work and completion of low-level worksheets.[17] Students working on their own with drill and practice materials do not have opportunities for communicating about their learning experiences. CALLA's focus on cooperative learning and the development of academic language skills for higher-order thinking skills can make a positive contribution to the progress of remedial students.

LEARNING STRATEGIES

Instruction in effective learning strategies could be the single most powerful tool that remedial teachers can give to their students. By teaching students strategies for understanding, remembering, and expressing information, teachers make it possible for students to become autonomous learners. Autonomous learners are able to take responsibility for their own learning, and their self-esteem and feelings of academic efficacy increase proportionately to their ability to deploy appropriate strategies for different learning tasks.[18]

CALLA for Compensatory and Remedial Programs

- Match the program's content objectives with those of the regular program.
- Focus on cooperative learning and development of academic language skills.
- Learning strategy instruction gives a powerful tool to the students.

CALLA for Students with Learning Disabilities

Special education students learning English as a new language require an instructional program tailored to their unique needs. The environment for such a program should be the least restrictive possible. The instruction should be individualized, focused on content and cognitive development, and provide for both primary language and English language development.[19]

Students with learning disabilities represent the largest category of special education students and are often viewed as being able to profit from learning strategy instruction. CALLA may assist in meeting educational goals for learning disabled students in ESL and bilingual programs in four major ways: content selection and presentation, language development, learning strategy instruction, and lesson plan design.[20] The CALLA lesson plan model lends itself to the development of the Individual Educational Plan (IEP) required in special education because of the delineation of specific objectives and because the model provides the type of structure needed for individual as well as group planning. Each of the five phases of the CALLA instructional sequence provides students with opportunities to accomplish lesson objectives through a variety of language and cognitive modes and to interact with the information strategically rather than passively.[21]

CONTENT

Subject matter content can be made accessible to students with learning disabilities by using a number of CALLA techniques applied to both primary language and English instruction. For example, the teacher selects central content topics from the mainstream curriculum and then contextualizes presentation of the content through graphics, active demonstrations, and audio, visual, and kinesthetic experiences. Students integrate new content into their existing knowledge frameworks through concrete and hands-on activities and through extensive discussion before, during, and after content presentations.

ACADEMIC LANGUAGE

The language skills needed by students with learning disabilities to progress in the mainstream curriculum can be developed through activities which provide for: (a) contextualized practice with academic vocabulary, (b) practice in reading expository texts as preparation for reading for information in textbooks, (c) academic listening and speaking practice, and (d) development of expository writing skills through a process approach.[22]

LEARNING STRATEGIES

Students with learning disabilities may have limitations in metacognitive awareness about themselves as learners, in their ability to manipulate the information to be learned, and in their ability to separate relevant from irrelevant aspects of the learning task.[23] CALLA's focus on learning strategy instruction parallels a similar focus for students in special education, in which limitations in strategic skills are a defining characteristic of learning disability.[24] Explicit instruction in learning strategies for all types of academic tasks in both the first language and English can show students with learning disabilities practical approaches to successfully completing academic tasks that might otherwise appear overwhelming.

CALLA for Students with Learning Disabilities

- Access content through concrete and hands-on activities and extensive discussion.
- Provide activities for contextualized academic skills practice.
- Learning Strategies show students practical approaches to academic tasks.

CALLA for ESL Students in Community Colleges

Community colleges and vocational or technical schools often have ESL programs for students seeking a two-year diploma to either prepare them for employment in technical fields or to fill academic gaps so that they can transfer to a four-year college. Many CALLA principles can be used with ESL students in two-year community college programs.

CONTENT

Content for ESL students enrolled in community colleges should be aligned to the content of the courses they aspire to take. For example, students who are preparing for a technical field should begin to learn about their separate fields in the ESL class, which could incorporate content from courses in automotive repair, welding, health occupations, food occupations, home repairs, graphics and printing, office systems, child care, and other vocational curricula. Similarly, students who are seeking academic preparation for eventual transfer to four-year colleges could be offered content that will familiarize them with basic concepts and skills in science, mathematics, history, geography, economics, and literature and composition.

ACADEMIC LANGUAGE

As with other CALLA applications, the choice of the content determines what academic language functions are appropriate. For example, students might need to read for technical information in courses on automotive and home repairs, but they might have to read for identification of genre or cause and effect relationships when the content is drawn from literature or history content courses. Students in community college ESL classes should be provided with experiences in using language for both lower and higher-order thinking skills.

LEARNING STRATEGIES

ESL students in community colleges can profit from learning strategy instruction that provides know-how and strategic approaches for understanding and learning the curriculum topics and procedures for the content area being studied. For example, students in many vocational programs can profit from strategies for reading and understanding technical manuals and strategies for performing the procedures for carrying out typical tasks required by the particular vocational area. Students pursuing academic courses also need to learn strategies for listening, reading, and writing about different academic content areas.

CALLA for ESL Students in Community Colleges

- Content should be aligned to students' course content.
- Provide experiences in language use for lower and higher-order thinking skills.
- Learning Strategies provide know-how for learning the curriculum topics.

CALLA in College and University Intensive English Programs

Many colleges and universities provide intensive ESL programs designed primarily for foreign students, though non-native English-speaking immigrants may also be included in such programs. In general, foreign students are directed to intensive English programs when their scores on the Test of English as a Foreign Language (TOEFL) fall below the minimum required for university entrance. They may then spend one or more years of intensive study of English before they are admitted to the university. A content-based approach to language instruction (such as CALLA) can provide university students with the background knowledge and skills needed for regular university courses.

CONTENT

Content can be drawn from typical freshman courses such as biology, calculus, government, psychology, and English. The Intensive ESL instructor finds out from colleagues and from students what the major academic objectives are for different disciplines, then includes many of these objectives in the ESL class. A promising instructional approach is the Adjunct Model, in which ESL students enroll in a content course and a complementary ESL course in which the curriculum and assignments are coordinated.[25] In this way ESL instructors can present targeted language activities that provide students with relevant experience in the academic language demands of the content course.

ACADEMIC LANGUAGE

Many students coming from other countries may have had limited experience in participating in a classroom with ideas, questions, and individual viewpoints. These students could gain confidence and skill in classroom participation through practice with the academic language functions identified in CALLA, such as synthesizing, evaluating, and persuading. University writing assignments are most often expository and require extensive reading.[26] The CALLA focus on integrated reading and writing activities in all content areas could be usefully applied in university ESL classes.

LEARNING STRATEGIES

The abundance of study skill centers and "how to learn" courses at the college level testify to the fact that native English-speaking students may lack effective learning strategies for dealing with the academic requirements of their courses. ESL students can profit from explicit learning strategy instruction at all levels of English proficiency. Metacognitive strategies such as planning, selective attention, self-monitoring, and self-evaluation are crucial to successful achievement in college. Cognitive strategies such as elaboration of prior knowledge, making inferences, using resource materials, and summarizing are also important in understanding and remembering new information. Finally, students can learn how to use a social strategy like cooperation to form study groups outside of class that provide mutual assistance in mastering course content.

CALLA in College and University Intensive English Programs

- Draw content from typical freshman courses.
- Students gain confidence practicing academic language functions.
- Students profit from explicit learning strategy instruction.

CALLA in Foreign Language Programs

In foreign language education, the grammatical syllabus and intensive practice of memorized formulas are giving way to a new focus on communicative language teaching and the proficiency-based curriculum.[27] This approach focuses on how language is used, or communicative language functions. That is, the yardstick for foreign language proficiency is the degree to which the learner can engage in communicating meaningfully in the language. Different levels of communication have been specified in proficiency guidelines recommended by the American Council on the Teaching of Foreign Languages (ACTFL),[28] and they range from a novice level of simple language functions (e.g., answering questions related to personal identification) to a more complex level in which students use language for functions such as informing, apologizing, describing, and agreeing or disagreeing. Increasingly, language functions of this nature are taught through authentic texts, or unsimplified listening and reading materials drawn from target language sources. For example, students might have to read a newspaper ad or an article about an election and then state the major points either orally or in writing.

Some foreign language experts are recommending that students go beyond communicative language functions and learn to use the foreign language for academic purposes in a content-based program.[29] In foreign language immersion programs, for example, students gain proficiency by studying content subjects in the foreign language. In less intensive foreign language programs a content-enriched curriculum can be successful in maintaining student interest through the inclusion of more cognitively-demanding tasks than are typically found in the traditional language course.[30] This approach to foreign language education is compatible with CALLA principles and techniques.

CONTENT

Content in the foreign language classroom can focus on cultural topics or can include content from different subject areas as well as cultural content specific to the language being studied. Textbooks from other countries are a useful source of academic content and have the additional advantage of being authentic texts which have not been specially modified for non-native speakers. However, since even elementary textbooks can be quite difficult for beginning level foreign language students, content topics need to be carefully selected and taught through cooperative and hands-on activities. Content topics selected should also be cognitively appropriate to the age of the students. Many topics in science, history, and geography, for example, are appropriate for different age levels and can be adjusted to the proficiency level of the class. Sources for cultural content include selections from literature, newspapers, popular magazines, films and television, interactions with native speakers of the language, and (where possible) actual experiences in the target language community, either in the United States or abroad.

ACADEMIC LANGUAGE

The introduction of curriculum content into the foreign language classroom provides many opportunities to use the target language for academic functions such as seeking information in a text, comparing similarities and differences, explaining a procedure, or writing predictions. Students also develop a varied vocabulary related to different content areas, and learn to read different types of text. Writing exercises can focus on more interesting topics than those found in grammar-oriented classes, and skills can be developed for expository writing as well as personal narratives.

LEARNING STRATEGIES

Learning strategy instruction can help students become better language learners by showing them how to use appropriate strategies for different learning tasks. Our own research with secondary and college foreign language students has found that more effective language learners display more varied and appropriate learning strategies than less effective language learners.[31]

Learning strategy instruction for foreign language students at beginning levels needs to be in English so that students can understand the teacher's explanations, and any instruction in English takes time away from exposure to the target language. We have attempted to resolve this problem in the following ways: (1) teachers explain the strategies in English in brief three to five minute presentations; (2) teachers give the strategy a target language name and thereafter refer to it in the target language; (3) the strategy is illustrated by an icon which is then used to remind students when to use the strategy; (4) vocabulary and structures related to learning strategies are taught in the target language; and (5) directions on student worksheets for strategy practice are initially written in English, but gradually change to the target language.[32]

1. **Ojo**

(Literally, *eye*. Can also mean *pay attention* or *look out!*)

Decide to focus your attention before you start the activity. Resolve not to let yourself get distracted!

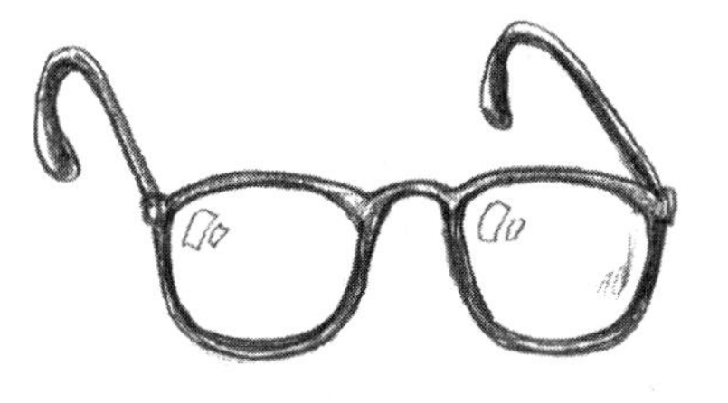

2. **Gafas** (*eyeglasses*)

Decide to pay attention to specific words or types of information before you start to listen or read. What do you need to learn from the upcoming activity?

3. **Cognados** (*cognates*)

Look for similarities between Spanish words and words in English or another language you know—very often they have the same meaning.

4. **La pandilla**

(*a band of friends; a gang*)

Group words, phrases, or things you need to learn in a way that makes sense to you (it doesn't have to make sense to anyone else).

5. **Eco** (*echo*)

Associate the new word or idea to something personally meaningful, so that the new word "echos" something you already know.

6. **La bola de cristal**

(*The Crystal Ball*)

Use your crystal ball to predict what a listening or reading topic is going to be about. What words that you know in Spanish are you likely to encounter? No crystal ball? How about the title, the illustrations, your own prior knowledge about the topic?

Learning Strategy Icons for Spanish[33]

CALLA in Foreign Language Programs

- Teach cultural and academic content topics through cooperative and hands-on activities.
- Many opportunities are provided to use academic language for academic functions.
- Effective language learners show varied and appropriate learning strategies.

Application Activities

The purpose of these activities is for teachers, program administrators, and staff developers to plan ways in which CALLA principles can be applied to various second language instructional contexts.

1. In what types of contexts or programs are students learning a second language in your school or district placed? List the name of the program (e.g., bilingual education, grade-level classroom, special education, "sheltered" instruction, foreign language program). Write a brief description of the features of each context or program.
2. Using the program descriptions above, work with a group of colleagues to identify CALLA principles that are already included in the programs. Then identify one additional CALLA principle that could be added to each program or context described.
3. Work with a colleague to brainstorm ways in which higher-order thinking skills can be elicited in a beginning level ESL class. Share your ideas with the group.
4. Working individually or with a group, develop an activity for a bilingual classroom which provides explicit instruction and practice in transferring content information from students' first language to English. Then develop a second activity that will assist students in transferring a skill learned in their first language to English.
5. Of the different contexts discussed in this chapter, select the one that is most familiar to you and design a CALLA lesson for that context. Refer to Chapter 5, "Planning, Teaching, and Monitoring CALLA," for lesson planning guidelines. If possible, try out the lesson or ask a teacher to do so. Evaluate the results and revise the lesson.
6. List any obstacles to applying CALLA principles to one or more second language contexts in your school or district. Share with the group and brainstorm ways to overcome the obstacles listed. Then make a plan of action for overcoming the obstacles and implementing CALLA principles in the context(s) selected. Table 8.1 provides a suggested outline for such a plan of action.

Table 8.1
PLAN OF ACTION FOR CALLA IN DIFFERENT CONTEXTS

Context: ______________________________

CALLA Principles	Obstacles Anticipated	Actions Needed	When to Take Actions	Who Will Take Actions

PART THREE

Implementing CALLA in the Classroom

CHAPTER 9

CALLA Science

Overview

Science taught as inquiry provides opportunities for the development of academic language and use of learning strategies. Science taught as experiential learning using hands-on activities assists students in understanding the language of science.

CHAPTER 9 CALLA Science

THE SCIENCE CURRICULUM has received a considerable amount of attention in recent years. This attention has resulted in part from an awareness of what our students have been *un*able to do in math and science areas and their poor performance on national and international studies.[1] An inspection of the science teaching in schools revealed that important courses are sometimes unavailable or have limited enrollments, and course content is often based on rote learning designed to prepare students for specific standardized testing programs. This is occurring at the same time that there is a proliferation of scientific knowledge and increasing dependence on scientific information for employment and daily living.

Description of the Science Curriculum

The goals of the science curriculum can be expressed in terms of concepts and generalizations, processes of inquiry and discovery, scientific attitudes, and interest and appreciation.[2] The study of science for concepts and generalizations suggests that students not only gain an understanding of the facts and theories of science but learn the importance of scientific knowledge for solving problems in their environment. Scientific inquiry is the process by which individuals discover new information through the application of scientific procedures. Thus students learn about the applications of data gathering, measuring, classifying, organizing, predicting, and problem solving. Students develop scientific attitudes such as an open-minded approach to data, interest in the experimental approach, and willingness to challenge suspect information. An interest and appreciation of science is important as students unlock the mysteries of the world and expand upon their naive understandings of natural phenomena toward increasing scientific sophistication.

The methods of discovery are inseparably linked to the content of science. School science curricula present students with experiences that familiarize them with both the content and the methods of inquiry, and emphasize methods that will lead to independent discovery of the content. Thus, some science curricula are based on the inquiry teaching approach, or an approach which emphasizes self-discovery of science content through increasing mastery of the methods of science.[3]

COMPONENTS OF SCIENCE

Science study in the K-12 curriculum consists of topics from life sciences, physical sciences, and earth sciences. This curriculum is typically cumulative so that information presented at one level will have been presented with less complexity earlier but, when revisited later, will be presented with increasing detail and sophistication.[4]

LIFE SCIENCES. Study of the life sciences focuses on the characteristics of living things, their structure and functions, and their relationships. This includes the classification and basic structures of living things, the fundamental mechanisms of their heredity and development, the way in which living things consume food and derive energy, the way in which they communicate, and their health. The study of living things extends from simple, one-celled organisms to the study of plants and animals, progresses to the study of human intelligence and group relationships, and includes the evolution of life forms on the earth. Students also study ecosystems, or the study of the interactions between organisms and their natural environment. This can include the study of seasonal change, reproductive systems, migration, population cycles, and the responsibility of humans toward the earth as an ecosystem, as in land use, pollution, energy use, and conservation. Sometimes the health sciences are taught separately, including topics such as human anatomy, exercise, and nutrition.

PHYSICAL SCIENCES. The basic information contained in physical science courses concerns matter and energy. Attention is focused on defining matter, describing its states—solids, liquids, and gases—and determining the properties of matter. The building blocks of matter are described and terms such as atoms, molecules, elements, compounds, and mixtures are introduced to describe matter. A main objective in physical science is the study of different forms of energy, including potential energy (as represented in coal, gasoline, or battteries) and kinetic energy (moving things which do work by exerting force). Included in kinetic energy are electricity, sound, light, radiation, and mass.[5] At an appropriate point in the curriculum, the study of chemical reactions is introduced and students learn that matter can be converted to energy and can be altered through various forces, conditions, and chemical reactions. Students also identify various forces of energy, the characteristics of energy, and study its applications. They may also study ecosystems and how organisms convert substances into energy as part of the food chain or convert one type of energy (light) into another (chemical) in photosynthesis. In studying electricity and magnetism, students become familiar with the terms *attract* and *repel* and may study how electricity is created as well as its uses. Students also study light and sound, their properties and uses, and what happens physiologically when humans respond to light and sound. Many of the instructional objectives in the physical sciences are congruent with objectives in life sciences and earth sciences.

EARTH SCIENCES. Study of the earth sciences often begins with astronomy and the contents and structure of the universe as well as the procedures by which we study objects in the solar system. The earth sciences include geology and natural resources and describe the history of the earth, geologic and geomorphic processes, earthquakes and volcanoes, the formation and classification of rocks and minerals, geographic features of the earth, and the responsibilities of humans toward the earth. Students also study the oceans, the water cycle, and weather and climate as part of the earth sciences.

SCIENTIFIC PROCESSES. The study of science also includes scientific processes or the use of scientific procedures such as observation, classification, description, hypothesis testing, measurement, and data collection. This may include scientific measurements of length, mass, temperature, volume, and time. These processes are typically applied within each of the physical, earth, and life sciences so that students see how scientific processes contribute to the gradual accumulation of information in each area and to the development of evidence supporting theories. Students also study how to communicate the findings of science tradition. In addition, students may study the history of scientific thought, how different kinds of evidence contributed to scientific thinking of the time, and how scientific understandings have changed.

As students progress in their study of science, they often analyze the applications of scientific knowledge in their world in areas such as technology, pollution control, and space exploration.

SCIENCE IN THE CLASSROOM

Science at the elementary level is typically taught by the classroom teacher rather than a science specialist. Teachers often cover a small amount of information in each of the major areas of science—earth, physical, and life sciences—in a single year. Science is probably underrepresented as a content area in the elementary school because relatively few elementary teachers are sufficiently trained in science education to feel comfortable teaching it. The junior high school curriculum typically includes courses such as life science, earth science, and physical science. At the secondary level, science is usually taught by teachers who have specialized in science education, and the curriculum consists largely of the life and physical sciences. Students in the senior high schools typically focus on one area of science each year, such as biology, chemistry, and physics, and in some schools additional offerings such as anatomy, astronomy, zoology and integrated science courses may be available.

TEXTBOOKS

The increasing complexity of the science curriculum across the grades is revealed in a simple comparison of the number of pages devoted to a specific topic such as inherited traits. A representative sixth grade science book devotes eight pages to inherited traits in humans,[6] a junior high life science text has 43 pages on human heredity,[7] and a high school biology text has 91 pages of explanation on the same topic.[8] The type size decreases and illustrations are fewer as the grade level increases, so that the language becomes denser and more decontexutalized.

Description of the Science Curriculum

- Typically cumulative with increasing complexity.
- Includes life, physical, and earth sciences and scientific processes.
- In lower grades all sciences are covered in one year; in the upper grades typically one science is given in a year-long course.
- Textbook language becomes denser and more decontextualized as grade level increases.

What's Difficult in Science for ESL Students?

Students who are acquiring English may face language-related difficulties in science classes at all grade levels due to the introduction of extensive new vocabulary and the complexity of the discourse, grammatical structures, language functions, and study skills required. Furthermore, students are expected not just to listen and understand, but to follow directions and to perform reasonably complex procedures.

Students are faced with an impressive number of technical terms in science. In addition, students must learn that some nontechnical vocabulary has special meanings in science, such as the words *table, work, energy, nerve, sense, compound,* and *mass.* By the time students are in high school, the vocabulary load has become so technical that even native English speakers can be expected to have difficulty. Words of Greek and Latin derivation are often used for scientific terms, and ESL students (especially those from non-Western language backgrounds) may have difficulty in understanding the meanings of roots and affixes derived from these languages. The following example from a high school biology textbook illustrates the vocabulary density that students must contend with:

> The members of the kingdom Monera, the prokaryotes, are identified on the basis of their unique cellular organization and biochemistry. Members of the kingdom Protista are single-celled eukaryotes, both autotrophs and heterotrophs.[9]

DISCOURSE

Expository discourse is used to introduce new concepts in science texts. The texts are often organized into sections that are marked by a heading in dark or large print. Within sections, important words appear in italics or in dark print with definitions accompanying new words as they are introduced. A series of related facts is typically presented, and students must make inferences from these facts to develop hypotheses and conclusions. In written or oral descriptions of experiments, language is organized in a sequence of steps which are to be followed in the order given. This type of discourse structure may be quite different from previous experiences ESL students have had with English narratives or texts requiring comprehension of material that is less cognitively demanding than the complex information often found in scientific texts.

STRUCTURES

Grammatical forms and structures in written science texts become increasingly complex in higher grade levels. Use of the passive voice, multiple embeddings, long noun phrases serving as subjects or objects in a sentence, if...then constructions, and expressions indicating causalities are some of the features of scientific prose that may be difficult for ESL students to comprehend. An example of a difficult structure is the following: "Growing a new plant from a part of another plant is called vegetative propagation."[10] In a sentence such as this, the student must read to the end to discover that the noun phrase which acts as the subject of the sentence is in fact a definition for a new term.

ACADEMIC LANGUAGE SKILLS

All four language skills are required in science classes. In addition to the oral communication skills that accompany the experiential learning in an inquiry approach,

Table 9.1
Language Skills Required by Science

Language Skills	Grades 1-3	Grades 4-6	Grades 7-12
Listening			
1. Understand explanations without concrete referents	L	P	M
2. Understand demonstrations.	M	M	M
3. Follow directions for experiments.	M	M	L
4. Listen for specific information.	L	P	M
5. Work with a partner on an experiment.	P	M	M
Reading			
1. Understand specialized vocabulary.	L	P	M
2. Understand information in textbook.	L	P	M
3. Find information from graphs, charts, and tables.	L	P	M
4. Follow directions for experiments.	L	P	M
5. Find information in reference materials.	L	P	M
Speaking			
1. Answer questions.	M	M	M
2. Ask for clarification.	M	M	M
3. Participate in discussions.	M	M	P
4. Explain and demonstrate a process.	L	P	M
5. Work with a partner on an experiment.	P	M	M
Writing			
1. Write answers to questions.	L	P	M
2. Note observations.	L	L	M
3. Describe experiments.	L	L	M
4. Write reports.	L	L	M

less emphasis	partial emphasis	more emphasis
L	P	M

students must also use receptive language skills to understand information presented orally or by the textbook. They must use productive skills, both oral and written, to participate in activities such as explaining a process, describing observations, classifying into categories, making predictions, and developing hypotheses. Table 9.1 identifies language skills typically required in science instruction. As this table reveals, language skills needed to perform the functions of answering questions, asking for clarification, and participating in discussions are needed at all grade levels. As students move up into higher grade levels, they are expected to learn many important science concepts through listening to the teacher's explanations, which often include many fewer concrete referents than are generally used with younger students. In addition, higher grade levels demand greater literacy skills because students need to be able to read for information and to write, expressing what they have learned.

CONCEPTUAL UNDERSTANDING

In addition to the unique language challenges for students acquiring English, these students share with all students a naive or intuitive understanding of scientific phenomena that may be so thoroughly ingrained as to be unresponsive to new concepts introduced as part of instruction. For example, young children think that sugar ceases to exist when it is dissolved in water,[11] and adolescents frequently use weight to predict that a cube of aluminum will displace less liquid than a steel cube of equal volume.[12] Other examples of misunderstandings of scientific information abound and have been cited elsewhere.[13]

Scientific misunderstandings are remarkably persistent and present difficulties in instruction because they interfere with the acquisition of new information. Such misconceptions are not particularly responsive to information presented in text and persist even when textual information specifically contradicts them.[14] In order to change a student's naive scientific understanding, instruction may have to change the way in which a concept is linked with other information in memory schemata, develop new schemata altogether, or change the concept itself.

A related concern is that students who are less experienced in science tend to organize information poorly and therefore have less information readily available to retrieve during problem solving.[15] The way in which the information is organized plays a role in making the information available for use in solving problems. Students therefore may need ways to link important concepts as much as they need accurate information based on a scientific view of the world. Good problem solvers have been found to possess more domain-specific knowledge than less effective problem solvers, although (as Gagné[16] points out), the question that needs to be addressed is how knowledge influences problem solving.

STUDY SKILLS

Science study skills are similar in many ways to those developed in language arts and social studies. Students need to locate information in textbooks, reference books, and the library. They need to take notes on class presentations and on information in books, and to understand and use non-verbal information such as diagrams, charts, and tables. Students should understand the importance of classification systems in science and use them to recall important information. As in every subject area, students studying science need to develop test-taking strategies and skills.

What's Difficult in Science for ESL Students?

- Discourse structure may be very different from the students' previous English experience.
- Grammatical forms and structures in textbooks become increasingly complex.
- All four academic language skills are required.
- Scientific misunderstandings are remarkably persistent.
- Study skills are similar to those in language arts and social studies.

Teaching Guidelines for CALLA Science

Science is not a set of isolated facts related to specific science areas such as physical or life science, but rather a series of theories which attempt to explain what is observed in the world around us, including observations made possible through instruments which extend our senses. Scientific theories are continually being tested to see how well they explain what can be observed, and theories change or are replaced as new information and new ways of looking at old information are discovered. Thus science "facts" are actually theories which provide the best explanations currently available for observed phenomena. This view of science has important implications for teaching science. For example, science should be taught as a way of systematically inquiring into questions or observations,[17] not just as a body of declarative knowledge to be memorized. By inquiring into science and "doing" science, students develop the ability to think scientifically. Teaching students to think scientifically is an important educational goal because it develops the ability to think critically and to use objectivity in drawing conclusions.

IDENTIFY SCIENCE THEMES

A thematic approach to science teaching in a CALLA program is preferable to the more traditional divisions of life science, physical science, and earth/space science.

UNDERSTAND PRINCIPLES. A theme-based approach helps students understand related science principles and processes, rather than focusing on discrete bodies of knowledge. For example, studying cyclical changes in living things, weather, and land forms helps students understand patterns and processes found in the natural world.[18]

RECOMMENDED BY EDUCATORS. This approach is recommended by scientists and science educators.[19] It is a recommendation of the National Center for Improving Science Education, of the National Science Foundation, and of Project 2061, a project of the American Association for the Advancement of Science which is engaged in a complete reconceptualization of the science curriculum in American schools.

SELECT SCIENCE CONTENT FOR DEPTH. Organizing science instruction around themes assists in the selection of science content for depth rather than breadth of coverage. Because a CALLA curriculum should select high-priority content rather than attempt to duplicate the grade-level curriculum, the selection of a limited number of science themes to be investigated across science areas makes it possible to spend enough time on each theme to ensure that students have an understanding of the principles involved.

RELEVANT CONTENT. A theme-based approach to science facilitates selecting science content that is relevant to students' lives. Students' natural curiosity about the world around them can serve as a springboard to scientific investigation designed to answer questions such as *Where does water come from? What makes things move? Why do people grow and change?*

While the themes selected for CALLA science may vary from one program to another, each should include major science concepts that have parallels across different branches of science. The California Science Framework,[20] for example, identifies six major themes: Energy, Evolution, Patterns of Change, Stability, Systems and Interactions, and Scale and Structure. The draft framework for the Virginia Common Core of Learning[21] identifies five themes which are seen as applicable to all content areas, including science. These themes are Structures/Patterns, Interrelationships/Connections, Balance/Continuity, Transformations/Change, and Variation/Diversity. The themes recommended for science study by the American Association for the Advancement of Science's Project 2061 are Systems, Models, Constancy, Patterns of Change, Evolution, and Scale.

CALLA teachers can be assisted by science teachers in selecting themes for building science units that cross the boundaries of physical, life, and earth sciences to reveal underlying scientific principles and processes.

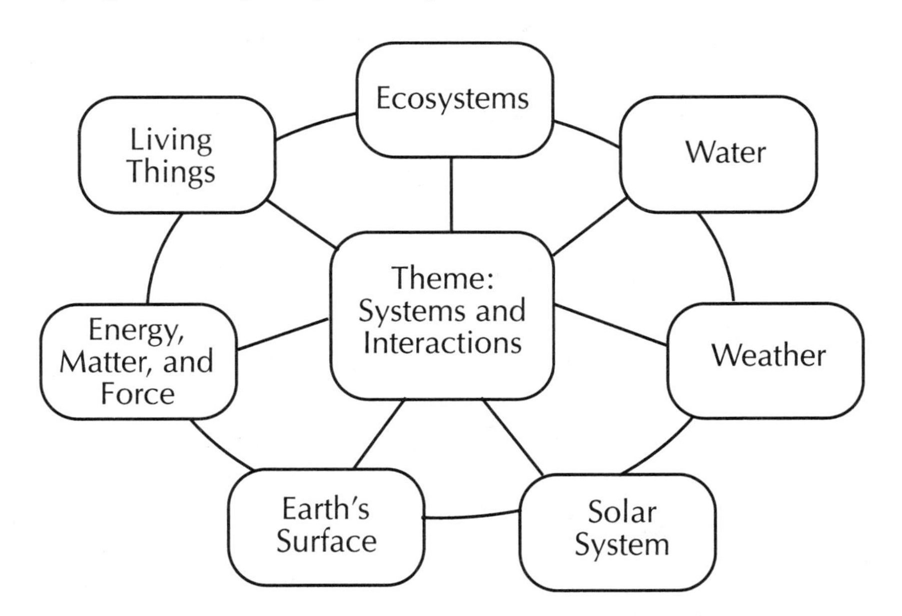

Science units built around themes can help students understand connections and interrelationships in our world.

PRIOR KNOWLEDGE ABOUT SCIENCE

After selecting appropriate themes, CALLA teachers need to gather information about their students' prior knowledge in order to select content for developing science units.

All students have prior knowledge about the world which has been gained through daily living and observation. For example, even young children understand that there is a relationship between dark storm clouds and rain, or that when water is heated it boils and changes into steam. But students' explanations of many scientific phenomena often verge on the magical, because of a naive understanding of scientific principles. For example, they might believe that electricity is "magic" because flipping a switch produces light. In general, students have an incomplete or inaccurate understanding of the scientific phenomena that they have observed in the world around them, and this naive understanding of science can be so strong that it overrides scientific explanations encountered in school.[22] In order to help students restructure naive understandings of science, teachers can have them identify and write down their prior understanding of a scientific phenomenon, then revise what they have written in light of discoveries made by participating in hands-on inquiry.

Activities for eliciting students' prior knowledge about a science concept include brainstorming, making semantic maps, starting K-W-L charts,[23] and making visual representations. Visual representations might include drawing the steps of a process (e.g., readying seeds, planting a crop, watering and cultivating, harvesting, and marketing), or even imagining and then recording an experience related to a science topic (e.g., imagining yourself traveling through the solar system). All of these activities can be organized as whole class, individual, or cooperative group activities. It is important for students to record in words (written, oral, recorded), graphs, or drawings, the understanding of the science topic that they bring to the CALLA classroom.

By having students identify their prior knowledge in science, teachers set the stage for experiences that will challenge students to refine their understanding and reformulate misconceptions about scientific phenomena.

SELECT SCIENCE ACTIVITIES AND MATERIALS

Activities for a CALLA science unit can include demonstrations, observations, structured discussions, exploration of scientific phenomena, gathering and organizing

Practicing scientific processes allows students to act like scientists in systematically investigating a problem or phenomenon.

data, and systematic experimentation. These activities provide practice in the processes of science which are as important in science instruction as the conceptual basis of scientific knowledge. Practicing scientific processes allows students to act like scientists in systematically investigating a problem or phenomena. Observation is the basic process used in conducting scientific inquiry. Other important science processes are classifying, measuring, communicating, predicting, and inferring. More complex processes include controlling variables, interpreting data, making hypotheses, defining operationally, and investigating through experimentation. Science processes require active engagement of students' minds, and many also lend themselves to hands-on activities. We recommend that at least one science process activity be included on a daily basis in the CALLA classroom.

In addition to practicing science processes, students also need hands-on experiences in scientific experimentation, an essential part of the *scientific method.* In planning for science experiments, CALLA teachers should provide students with clear instructions for systematically working through the experiment, recording the data collected, and drawing conclusions. This information should then be included in students' lab reports on the experiment. The steps of the scientific method can be used to prompt students to conduct their experiments and record their observations accurately, as in the example in Table 9.2.

Table 9.2

Science Lab Record

Name of Experiment ______________________________ Date ______________

Student Names

____

____

Please write information for each step of the scientific method as you work through this experiment with your group.

1. The *question/problem* we investigated was: ______________________________

2. The *hypothesis* we made was: ______________________________

3. This is how we *collected data*: ______________________________

____

4. We *recorded* our *data* as follows (chart, graph, table, diagram): ______________________________

5. We *answered the question/solved the problem* as follows: ______________________________

____

In planning science experiments, teachers should always go through the experiment several times on their own to gain facility with manipulating the materials and to make corrections should the experiment fail or produce unexpected results. Teachers also need to be sure that all materials and equipment are available for students on the day of the experiment. Students can work in groups of three or four on science experiments and, as with cooperative groups in other subject areas, each student should be assigned a specific role. For example, one student can be in charge of collecting and putting away the equipment and materials, another can make measurements, and a third could write down the group's observations.

In planning a science unit, teachers should collect a number of different types of materials rather than relying solely on a textbook. Teacher guides are the most valuable component of science textbook materials, because they provide directions for setting up and conducting experiments and demonstrations and explanatory notes on the science concepts illustrated by these activities. A textbook can be a useful resource for students and teacher, but the main part of the CALLA science lesson should involve students in active hands-on experiences designed to develop their ability to think scientifically. For some experiences teachers need materials and equipment typically found in school laboratories. For some lab experiences teachers may need to draw on the resources of their school's science department for advice, technical equipment such as microscopes, and even for organizing and conducting a lab for the ESL class. For many lab experiences, however, simple everyday equipment and materials will suffice. For example, equipment such as a hot plate, measuring cups, a kitchen scale, and an indoor/outdoor thermometer can be used successfully with many science experiments. Similarly, materials such as buttons (for classifying), raisins in a box (for estimating), different coins and an eyedropper with water (for predicting number of drops per coin), and a tennis ball and metric ruler (to collect data on distance bounced) can provide students with experiences in developing science process skills.[24]

In addition to simple equipment and materials, the CALLA science classroom should also have access to a collection of resource materials such as library books, videos, computer programs, photographs, and reference books. These resource materials can be used to stimulate curiosity, to find out additional information, to check conclusions, and to gain an understanding of science and technology in our world. We emphasize, however, that the heart of the CALLA science class is experiencing science through an active hands-on approach.

DEVELOP ACADEMIC LANGUAGE ACTIVITIES

Science activities provide numerous and varied opportunities for language development. The language of science is naturally embedded in science activities, including teacher demonstrations and student experiments. When students are discussing their observations, reasoning through a problem, or stating conclusions, they need to use language that is precise, objective, and scientifically accurate. Students may record their observations and conclusions in lab reports and participate in group projects which involve reading and writing about science. Following are examples of activities which can be used to develop academic language for science:

LISTENING. Listening and taking notes (either graphic or verbal) while the teacher conducts a science demonstration; listening and taking notes on a videotape such as the National Geographic series on animals in the wild; listening to and following directions for carrying out an experiment.

DESCRIBING. Observing and describing observations orally; observing the steps of a procedure, drawing them (or taking notes), then describing them; posing questions and formulating answers; discussing the steps of the scientific method while conducting an experiment; working cooperatively to build a model, then presenting a group report.

READING. Reading graphs and charts; finding information in science textbooks, encyclopedias, and library books; reading and following directions for procedures and experiments; sharing lab reports and other class writing about science.

WRITING. Writing answers to questions posed by the teacher or classmates; writing lab reports on experiments; working with a group to research a science topic and writing a group report about it; writing about personal or imaginative experiences related to science.

In short, almost unlimited opportunities exist for academic language development in the CALLA science class. Encouraging students to talk about their prior knowledge of a science topic, participate in and discuss science lab work, and read and write about science will help them not only develop a scientific outlook, but also learn to use the language of science.

TYPES OF INSTRUCTIONAL APPROACHES

PREDICTIONS. A number of different types of instructional approaches may assist in producing a change in students' persistent misconceptions about science. One is for students to make *predictions* based on their intuitive view of science and then conduct experiments in which the prediction is not supported. However, this does not always work. As one student noted, "You tricked me, you brought magic water,"[25] when presented with an actual demonstration of the displaced volume problem, in which an aluminum and steel cube were shown to displace equal amounts of water.

METAREASONING. Another instructional approach that may aid in dispelling intuitive conceptions of science is to appeal to the *metareasoning* ability of the learner. This refers to the ability to reason about one's own reasoning, i.e., to categorize problems in terms of strategies that lead to their solution, to plan a problem-solving approach, and to assess and revise one's own understanding with experience.[26] In appealing to a student's metareasoning ability, teachers can *explicitly instruct* students to recognize problems as representative of a class with which they have had previous experience and for which they have available solution strategies. Individuals then should be given ample opportunity to test out concepts that are consistent with scientific solutions instead of naive science.

DISCOVERY LEARNING. As an alternative to direct instruction, *discovery learning* can aid students in shifting from naive conceptions to more scientifically accurate concepts and "is potentially the best approach for helping students gain metareasoning skills and deep understanding."[27] Because discovery learning may take considerable time, students can be taught through *directed discovery*, in which students are cued to explore areas that will most readily lead to re-examination of strongly held intuitive notions of science.[28]

DISCUSSION. One additional instructional approach that may aid in dispelling intuitive concepts of science is to encourage students to *discuss* their understandings and to see the contradictions in each other's thoughts.[29] This should probably be accompanied by instruction in metareasoning in order to facilitate discussion and discovery of accurate scientific concepts.

INTEGRATE LEARNING STRATEGY INSTRUCTION

As with academic language development, science is a natural setting for discussion and practice of learning strategies. As in other content areas, teachers should find

Table 9.3

LEARNING STRATEGIES FOR SCIENCE

Metacognitive Strategies:	Students plan, monitor, and evaluate their learning of science concepts and skills.
Advance Organization	What's my purpose for solving this problem or doing this experiment? What is the question? What will I use the information for?
Selective Attention	What is the most important information to pay attention to?
Organizational Planning	What are the steps in the scientific method I will need to follow?
Self-monitoring	Does the plan seem to be working? Am I getting the answer?
Self-assessment	Did I solve the problem/answer the question? How did I solve it? Is it a good solution? If not, what could I do differently?
Cognitive Strategies:	Students interact with the information to be learned, changing or organizing it either mentally or physically.
Elaborating Prior Knowledge	What do I already know about this topic or type of problem? What experiences have I had that are related to this? How does this information relate to other information?
Resourcing	Where can I find additional information about this topic? Encyclopedia? Science book? Library?
Taking Notes	What's the best way to write down a plan to record or to summarize the data? Table? List?
Grouping	How can I classify this information? What is the same and what is different?
Making Inferences	Are there words I don't know that I must understand to solve the problem?
Using Images	What can I draw to help me understand and solve the problem? Can I make a mental picture or visualize this problem?
Social/Affective Strategies:	Students interact with others to assist learning, or use attitudes and feelings to help their learning.
Questioning for Clarification	What help do I need? Who can I ask? How should I ask?
Cooperating	How can I work with others to answer the question or solve the problem?
Self-talk	Yes, I can do this task—what strategies do I need?

APPLYING LEARNING STRATEGIES TO SCIENCE

Science Problem-Solving Steps

Ask a Question

Make a Hypothesis

Collect Data

Record Data

Answer the Question

out what strategies students are already using in science, then build on this strategic base by suggesting additional strategies and new ways of using familiar strategies. New strategies can be introduced most effectively by the teacher modeling how the strategy can be applied. (See Chapter 4 for guidelines on teaching learning strategies.)

As we have seen, the scientific method consists of a number of systematic steps involved in seeking answers to problems or explanations of scientific phenomena. Learning strategies can be taught and practiced in each step of the scientific method.

To conduct an experiment following the steps of the scientific method, students first need to have an understanding of the problem to be solved or question to be answered. This initial understanding is enhanced by *metacognitive awareness* of the type of problem, ways in which similar problems have been solved in the past, and the types of strategies that are helpful at each step. Teachers can assist students in developing their metacognitive awareness by asking them to remember previous problems requiring experimentation, to describe the procedures undertaken, and to identify the learning strategies employed.

Cooperation is a key strategy for all types of science process activities and experimentation. When students work in collaborative groups of three or four, they have more opportunities to discuss the question or problem posed, to share relevant background knowledge, to construct an effective plan for solving the problem, and to monitor their own learning. By working on science experiments cooperatively, students gain experience in taking responsibility for their own learning.

ASK THE QUESTION/IDENTIFY THE PROBLEM. Students use *elaboration* to recall prior knowledge related to the question that is to be answered by experimentation. (See pages 199–200, *Prior Knowledge about Science*, for suggested activities involving elaboration.) As students generate explanations based on their prior knowledge, they should be encouraged to explore additional possibilities and ask *questions for clarification*. Finally, students should *plan* how they will carry out the experiment. The planning could include assignment of responsibilities, writing out the steps to be followed, and allocating a specific time period for accomplishing the tasks involved.

MAKE A HYPOTHESIS. Depending on the amount of prior knowledge group members can bring to the question being investigated, it may be necessary for students to use *resourcing* strategies to find more information before they are able to make a hypothesis. For example, if the question under investigation is *Why does yeast make bread rise?*, they may need to get specific information about bread making and find out exactly what yeast is. Based on the group's information (gained from elaboration and resourcing), students can use *inferencing* to make a logical guess at the answer to the question.

COLLECT DATA. During this stage of the scientific method, students gather data through active experimentation and observation. In addition to *cooperation*, students will probably use learning strategies such as *selective attention* and *grouping* or *classification*. For example, if students are trying to identify the variables that affect plant growth, they will need to make careful observations of plants being grown in different conditions. They will pay *selective attention* to rate of growth, height, number of leaves, and color of each plant. If the experiment involves different kinds of plants, students will need to *group* plants according to characteristics such as amount of water needed and preference for sun or shade. They may need to *classify* the plants scientifically, distinguishing, for example, between flowering plants and conifers.

Careful note-taking is an essential strategy for recording data.

RECORD DATA. This step is often combined with the previous step in which data are collected, and lends itself to *cooperation*. As students collect data through experimentation, they record their observations in an organized and systematic way. Careful *note-taking* is an essential strategy for recording data. Students need to learn how to be concise, accurate, and objective in scientific note-taking. Notes may be amplified by making diagrams, graphs, or other types of graphic organizers to display the information collected. The teacher should make sure that students understand that using *imagery* in this way can assist in helping them understand relationships and organization of the data displayed.

ANSWER THE QUESTION/SOLVE THE PROBLEM. This stage of the scientific method requires students to use a number of learning strategies as they seek to answer the question or solve the problem posed at the beginning of the experiment. Still working in a group, students can prepare an oral or written *summary* of their observations or results of their experimentation. Students should refer to their notes and the graphic organizer developed in the previous step as they write the summary. The summary can help students *make inferences* that explain their findings. It is important for the inferences to be directly linked to what students actually observed during experimentation, rather than to assumptions that they might have as part of prior knowledge. The inferences are used to formulate an answer to the question asked in the first step. A final and essential step in using the scientific method is for students to *evaluate* their understanding of the problem investigated. They should compare the answer based on scientific observation and experimentation with the hypothesis proposed in the second step. The hypothesis may have been influenced by misconceptions and a naive understanding of science phenomena, and students need to recognize differences between what they thought they knew and what they found out through the experiment. In writing the lab report, students should include a self-evaluation paragraph in which they describe how their understanding has changed as a result of their observations and experimentation.

Table 9.4

HOW TO TEACH STRATEGIES FOR THE STEPS OF THE SCIENTIFIC METHOD

ASK THE QUESTION/IDENTIFY THE PROBLEM

1. **Strategy: elaboration.** Students identify their prior knowledge related to topic to be investigated.
2. **Strategy: questioning for clarification.** Students explore areas of uncertainty by questioning the teacher and other authorities.
3. **Strategy: planning.** Students make a written plan for the experiment which includes responsibilities, steps, product, and time allocation.

MAKE A HYPOTHESIS

4. **Strategy: resourcing.** Students build their background knowledge by searching for additional information about the topic.
5. **Strategy: inferring.** Students utilize information from their prior knowledge and the results of resourcing to make a logical inference or hypothesis about the answer to the question.

COLLECT DATA

6. **Strategy: cooperation.** Students work collaboratively to observe and experiment.
7. **Strategy: selective attention.** Students make careful observations of relevant characteristics or variables during experimentation.
8. **Strategy: grouping/classifying.** Students organize data by grouping or classifying according to features or attributes.

RECORD DATA

9. **Strategy: note-taking.** Students write accurate and objective notes on their observations.
10. **Strategy: imagery.** Students supplement notes with diagrams and other graphic organizers.
11. **Strategy: cooperation.** Students continue to work collaboratively to record data.

ANSWER THE QUESTION/SOLVE THE PROBLEM

12. **Strategy: summarizing.** Students prepare oral or written summaries of their observations and experimentation.
13. **Strategy: inferring.** Students use the summary of their observations and experimentation to make logical inferences to answer original question.
14. **Strategy: cooperation.** Students continue to work cooperatively to reach agreement in their group on a scientific answer to the question.
15. **Strategy: self-evaluation.** Students compare the answer derived through observation and experimentation with their original hypothesis, and report on changes in their understanding of the topic investigated.

THE CALLA INSTRUCTIONAL SEQUENCE

The five phases of the CALLA instructional sequence provide a useful framework for teaching science to ESL students. These phases are Preparation, Presentation, Practice, Evaluation, and Expansion. (See Chapter 5 for a discussion of the CALLA instructional sequence.) This approach is compatible with lesson sequences recommended by science educators. Hyde and Bizar,[30] for example, suggest eight phases for science teaching: diagnosing existing schemata, confronting schemata, exploring phenomena, generating opinions, conducting systematic inquiry, debriefing explanations and concepts, debriefing cognitive processes, and broadening schemata. In this section we describe how these phases correspond to the CALLA phases.

PREPARATION. In this phase teacher and students diagnose existing schemata by brainstorming and creating graphic organizers illustrating knowledge (including misconceptions) that students already have about the topic.

PRESENTATION. At this point the teacher can conduct a demonstration that will cause students to confront their existing schemata by observing a phenomenon that appears contrary to their beliefs. For example, the teacher could conduct a simple experiment to illustrate the force of air pressure. In this experiment a small amount of water is heated in a metal soda can. When the water boils and steam emerges from the opening, the can is quickly inverted into a bowl of cold water. Students observe that the can is immediately crushed by an invisible force. Why? Students' interest is engaged because they have observed something that probably runs counter to their prior understanding about air pressure as a force that can crush cans.

PRACTICE. The stage is now set for students to explore the phenomenon by trying out the experiment themselves, using different types of cans, different sizes of openings, different amounts of water, different sources of heat, different heating times, and the like. These explorations provide students with practice in using various science processes, such as observing, classifying, measuring, communicating, predicting, and inferring. By engaging in this type of exploratory inquiry, students begin to discover for themselves causes, effects, characteristics, and variables associated with the experiment.

EVALUATION. During this phase, students generate opinions and explanations for the phenomena they have observed during the Practice phase. Their ideas are written down and will be examined again at the conclusion of the next phase.

EXPANSION. In this phase students conduct systematic inquiry through observation and experimentation, using the steps of the scientific method as a framework for working through their experiment. This experimentation differs from the exploration of phenomena in the Practice phase because it is conducted in a formal and systematic fashion. The science processes used during systematic inquiry include the basic processes used during the exploratory activities conducted in the Practice phase, and may also include more complex processes such as controlling variables, formulating hypotheses, and interpreting data. As discussed in the previous section on teaching the scientific method, students evaluate changes in their own understanding that have come about as a result of scientific observation and experimentation. This self-evaluation may include discussions about students' cognitive processes as well as their conceptual change. Finally, students may broaden their schemata further by searching out additional information about air pressure through both print and non-print materials.

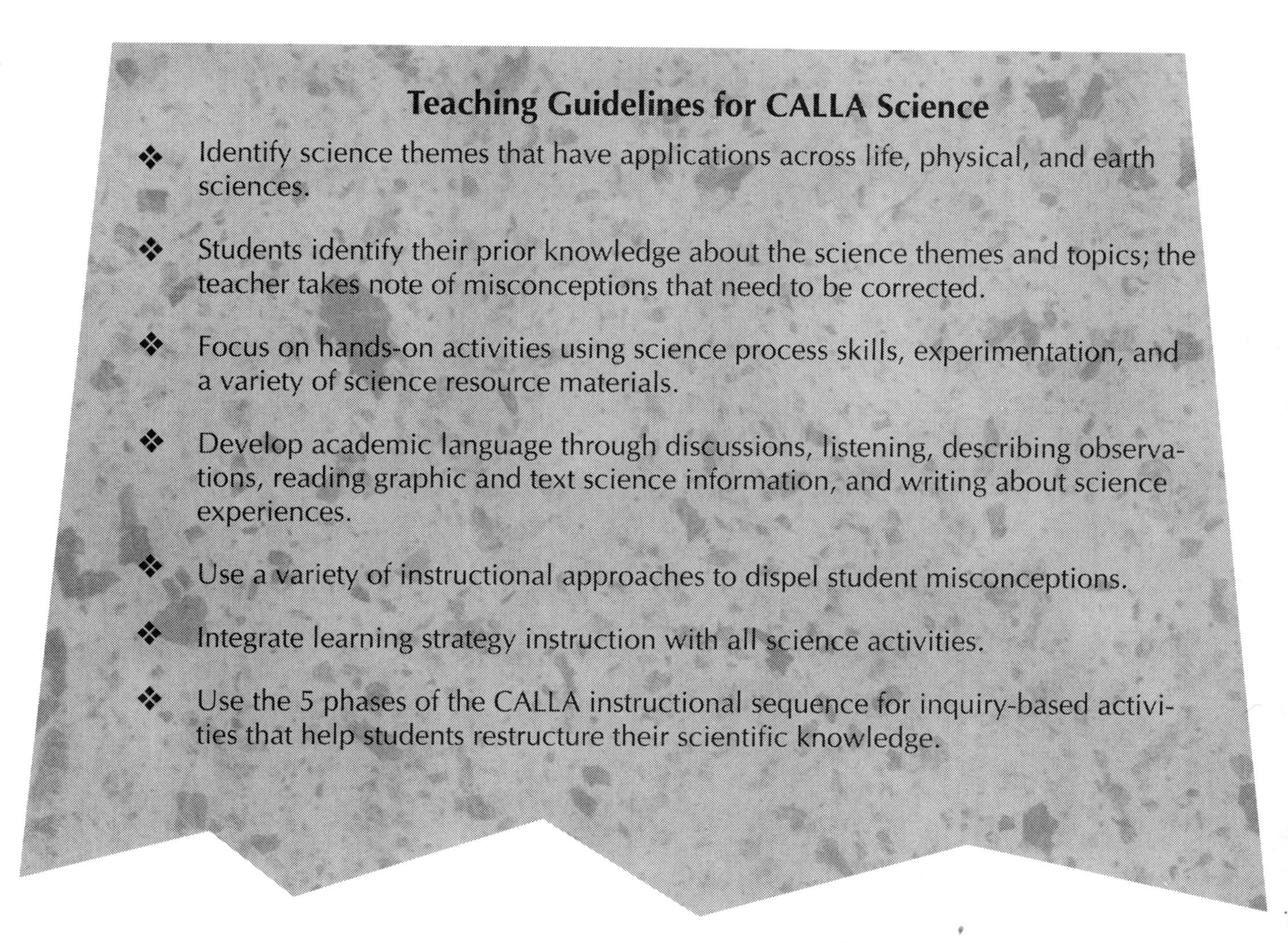

Teaching Guidelines for CALLA Science

- Identify science themes that have applications across life, physical, and earth sciences.
- Students identify their prior knowledge about the science themes and topics; the teacher takes note of misconceptions that need to be corrected.
- Focus on hands-on activities using science process skills, experimentation, and a variety of science resource materials.
- Develop academic language through discussions, listening, describing observations, reading graphic and text science information, and writing about science experiences.
- Use a variety of instructional approaches to dispel student misconceptions.
- Integrate learning strategy instruction with all science activities.
- Use the 5 phases of the CALLA instructional sequence for inquiry-based activities that help students restructure their scientific knowledge.

Model Science Unit

LIFE ON EARTH: STRUCTURES AND FUNCTIONS

Science Content Objectives:

Identify characteristics of all living things. Describe differences in structure and function between plants and animals. Learn about characteristics of simple organisms. Name the five kingdoms of living things and describe characteristics of each.

Science Process Skills:

Compare/contrast different types of living things. Observe the growth of living things in a controlled environment. Develop a hypothesis. Classify a sample of living things into their kingdoms.

Language Objectives:

Discuss and describe prior knowledge about living things. Develop vocabulary related to living things. Read scientific texts about structures and functions of different types of living things. Listen to information about differences between plants and animals. Write answers to questions about living things. Write a hypothesis. Write a lab report.

Learning Strategies:

Elaboration of Prior Knowledge; Selective Attention for Reading and Listening; Observing and Note-taking; Cooperation.

Materials:

Textual information, drawings, and photographs of five kingdoms of living things (plants, animals, and three types of simple organisms: fungi, monerans, protists). Recommended: Microscopes; slides of mushroom, euglena, bacteria. For experiment, each group needs: handful of soil (about 50 ml), small piece of leather, 1 quart-size Ziplock plastic bag, few drops of water, observation chart.

Note. Sample student pages are provided on pages 215–219 for activities marked with an asterisk(*).

PROCEDURES

Preparation 1:* What Do You Know about Living Things?

Students work in pairs to discuss and list 10 living things and their characteristics. Then students discuss and write down their ideas about the characteristics of living things. Teacher gives learning strategy reminder: Think about your *prior knowledge* of the topic to get ready to learn new information.

Presentation 1:* Characteristics of Living Things

Learning strategy instruction: Teacher names, models, and explains usefulness of *Selective Reading* (a type of Selective Attention) for specific information. Students use the strategy to read about characteristics of living things, then correct any inaccurate information on the list they made in Preparation 1.

Practice 1:* Make a Chart About Living Things

Students work in groups to complete a graphic organizer about common structure and functions of living things.

Preparation 2: What Do You Know About Plants and Animals?

Students work in groups to discuss and list differences between plants and animals. Learning strategy reminder: Your *prior knowledge* helps you learn.

Presentation 2: Differences in Living Things

A. Students study drawings of plant and animal cells and label different parts as they listen to a description of each.

B. Learning strategy instruction: Teacher describes and models how to *take notes* on a T-List. Teacher reminds students to *listen selectively* (a type of Selective Attention) so that they can take notes on important information about differences in living things. Then students listen to a brief science talk about different functions of living things (e.g., producers, consumers, and decomposers), taking notes on a T-List.

Different Functions of Living Things

main Ideas	Functions and Examples
1. Producers	make own food. Ex: plants, algae
2. consumers	eat other organisms Ex: animals eat producers and other consumers (humans eat both!)
3. Decomposers	Type of consumers – can break down dead organisms and wastes of living organisms to simple chemicals Ex: bacteria, mushrooms, molds

Sample of student notes on a T-List.

Practice 2: Answer Questions about Plants and Animals

Students work in groups to compare and complete their T-Lists and add to and correct the lists developed in Preparation 2. Each group then lists and illustrates some examples of producers, consumers, and decomposers.

Preparation 3: What Do You Know about the Five Kingdoms?

Students study a blank chart titled "Five Kingdoms of Living Things." Teacher explains that many scientists now classify life on earth into five groups, which are called kingdoms. Teacher challenges students to write the names of the kingdoms they know on the appropriate places on the chart. (Students should know *plants* and *animals*; some students may also know about some simple microscopic organisms such as microbes, bacteria, germs, viruses, fungi).

Students write the names of the kingdoms and examples on the chart.

Presentation 3: Simple Organisms

A. Students observe simple organisms under a microscope, then draw and describe what they see.

B. Students study enlarged photographs of mushroom cells, euglena, and bacteria (if no microscope available). Then students read about the characteristics of each kingdom of simple organisms: *fungi, protists*, and *monerans*. Students write in the correct names of these three kingdoms on their chart in Preparation 3.

Practice 3: Make a Chart Comparing Simple Organisms

Teacher gives learning strategy reminder: When you work *cooperatively* with other classmates, everyone learns more. Students work in groups to complete a compare/contrast chart showing the three types of simple organisms observed in Presentation 3 and indicating which characteristics of each are like plants and which are like animals.

Evaluation:* Complete a Learning Log for Life on Earth

Students complete individual Learning Logs, then discuss what they have learned in pairs, small groups, or as a whole class activity.

Expansion: Find Out More about Living Things

A. Teacher conducts debriefing discussion of what has been learned in the unit. Students are challenged with higher-level questions about life on earth. Examples: *Will people probably see the same plants and animals we see today a hundred years from now? A thousand years from now? A million years? Why or why not? Why do young plants and young animals grow to resemble their parents? Are human beings producers, consumers, or decomposers?* Students do library research to find out more information about these questions.

B. Students work in pairs or groups to conduct a science experiment to discover what living things are present in a sample of soil from their own yards or neighborhoods. Students place soil samples (about 50 ml) in Ziplock bags with a few drops of water and a small piece of leather. Seal bags with air inside and place in sunlight. Students observe bags for two weeks, completing an Observation Chart daily on observations of evidence of living things and their changes. (Possible signs of life include plants sprouting, insects hatching, and mold growing on the leather.) Students write a lab report on experiment, using the following format:

LAB REPORT

Dates of Experiment: ____________________

Place of Experiment: ____________________

Scientists: ____________________

Question: ____________________

Hypothesis: ____________________

Materials: ____________________

Procedures: ____________________

Observations: ____________________

Conclusions: ____________________

____

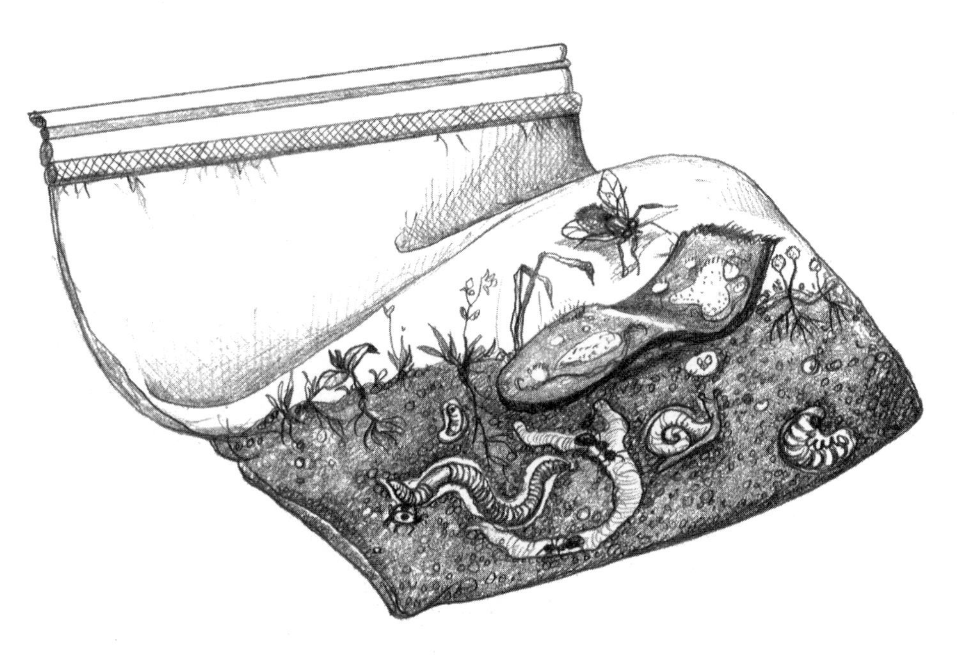

Students observe the growth of living things in a soil sample from their yard or neighborhood.

ASSESSMENT

The following student products can be included in student portfolios and used for informal assessment:

1. Student Learning Logs
2. Observation Charts for Experiment
3. Lab Reports on Experiment
4. Student Assessment Form (sample form below)

STUDENT ASSESSMENT FORM

Record level of student performance for each objective. Scoring: 1 = Performs the objective independently; 2 = Needs assistance in performing the objective; 3 = Not yet able to perform the objective.

Student Names	Identify and describe differences between plants and animals	Read and comprehend science information	Use selective attention to find specific information

LIFE ON EARTH

NAME ______________________________ DATE ______________

Preparation 1: What Do You Know About Living Things?

Work with a partner. Make a list of 10 different living things.

1.____________________ 6.____________________

2.____________________ 7.____________________

3.____________________ 8.____________________

4.____________________ 9.____________________

5.____________________ 10.____________________

What is the difference between something that is alive, like a cat, and something that is not alive, like a rock? What makes the things on your list alive? Discuss your ideas about living things with your partner. Then write your ideas about the characteristics of living things.

1.____

2.____

3.____

4.____

5.____

Presentation 1: Characteristics of Living Things

LEARNING STRATEGY: SELECTIVE READING
When you read selectively, you don't have to read every word.
You look for the important information you need.

Read about the characteristics of living things, then work with your partner to correct (if necessary) your list of the characteristics of living things.

What type of information will you read selectively for?

____

____

____

LIFE ON EARTH (continued)

There are more than five million different kinds of life on earth. Living things, or organisms, may look very different. For example, compare an elephant and a rose!

Elephant

Rose

Even though organisms may look different, they all have a similar structure. A structure is how a thing is built or organized. Every living thing on earth is made of *cells*. All organisms have a structure of cells. A cell is the smallest unit of life. Most cells are so small that you need a microscope to see them.

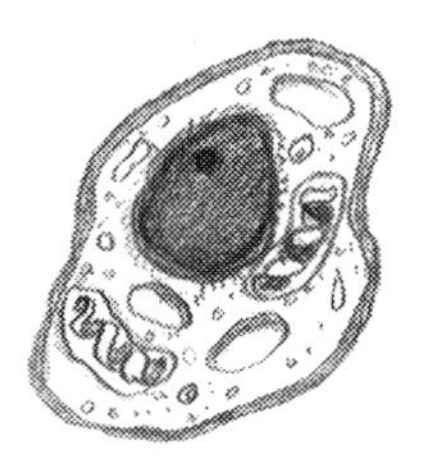

Animal Cell

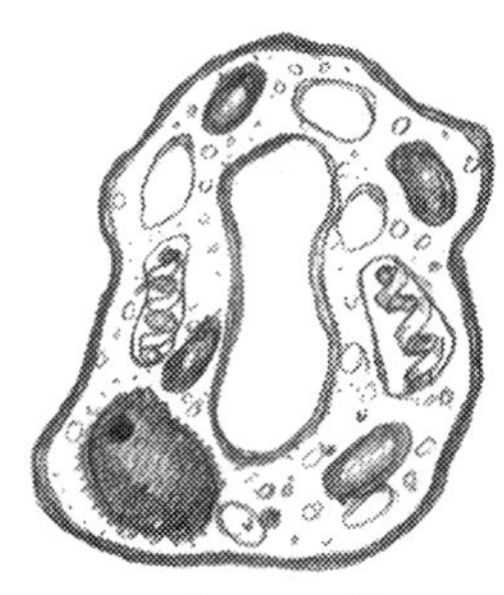

Plant Cell

Other characteristics of living things are their *functions*, or what they do. All organisms have four functions that non-living things do not have. First, all organisms get food and use food to stay alive. Second, organisms control life processes, such as breathing and growing. Third, all organisms respond to their environment, or react to change. Finally, all organisms reproduce, or have offspring.

Practice 1: Make a Chart About Living Things

Work with two or three classmates to complete the chart.

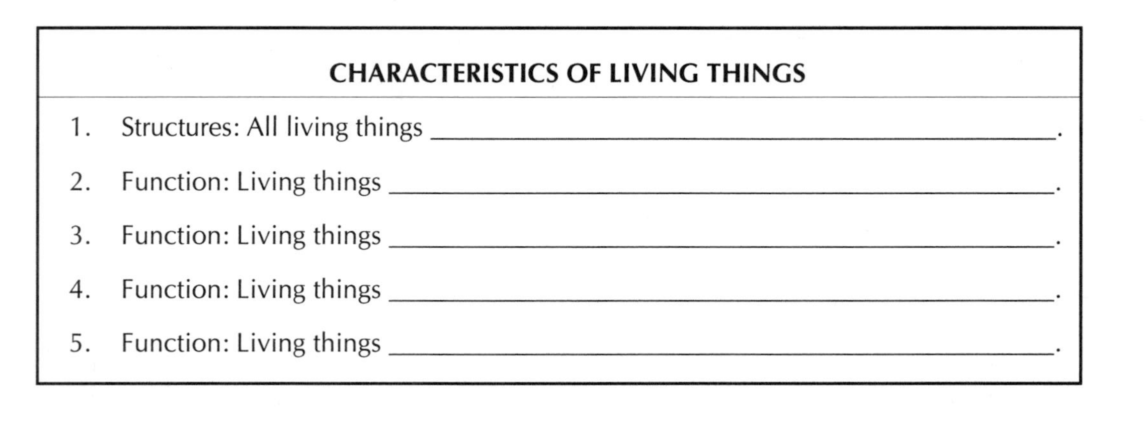

CHARACTERISTICS OF LIVING THINGS
1. Structures: All living things ______________________.
2. Function: Living things ______________________.
3. Function: Living things ______________________.
4. Function: Living things ______________________.
5. Function: Living things ______________________.

Unit Evaluation: Complete a Learning Log about Life on Earth

NAME ______________________________ DATE__________

Complete the Learning Log for the unit LIFE ON EARTH: STRUCTURES AND FUNCTIONS. Check the items that you know or can do, then answer the questions.

LEARNING LOG

VOCABULARY

I can explain the meanings or draw pictures of these words:

- ❑ structure
- ❑ function
- ❑ organism
- ❑ cell
- ❑ reproduce
- ❑ simple organism
- ❑ producer
- ❑ consumer
- ❑ decomposer
- ❑ kingdom
- ❑ plants
- ❑ animals
- ❑ fungi
- ❑ protists
- ❑ monerans
- ❑ mushroom
- ❑ euglena
- ❑ bacteria

SCIENCE KNOWLEDGE AND SKILLS

I can:

- ❑ Identify the characteristics of living things.
- ❑ Describe the differences between plants and animals.
- ❑ Describe the characteristics of simple organisms.
- ❑ Name and describe the five kingdoms of living things.
- ❑ Develop a hypothesis about living things in a soil sample.
- ❑ Make observations about living things that grow in soil.
- ❑ Classify living things observed into their kingdoms.

LANGUAGE

I can:

- ❑ Discuss what I know about plants, animals, and other living things.
- ❑ Read and understand science information about life on earth.
- ❑ Listen to and understand science information about life on earth.
- ❑ Write a lab report of an experiment with living things that grow in soil.

LEARNING STRATEGIES

I can:

- ❑ Use my prior knowledge about living things.
- ❑ Read and listen selectively for new information.
- ❑ Observe carefully and take notes on my observations.
- ❑ Cooperate with classmates to conduct a science experiment.

THINK ABOUT YOUR LEARNING

A. How successful do you feel about learning the different parts of this unit? Circle the place on the line that shows how you feel.

1. Vocabulary

|-------------------------|-------------------------|

Not very successful | Somewhat successful | Very successful

2. Science knowledge and skills

|-------------------------|-------------------------|

Not very successful | Somewhat successful | Very successful

3. Language

|-------------------------|-------------------------|

Not very successful | Somewhat successful | Very successful

4. Learning Strategies

|-------------------------|-------------------------|

Not very successful | Somewhat successful | Very successful

B. Think about your learning and complete the sentences.

1. This is what I learned in this unit:

2. This is what was difficult or confusing:

3. This is how I am going to learn what was difficult:

4. The most interesting thing in this unit was:

CHAPTER 10

CALLA Mathematics

Overview

Mathematics taught as a problem-solving approach focuses on the use of oral and written language to communicate problem-solving procedures and mathematical reasoning. Students learn computation skills in the context of meaningful problem-solving applications.

CHAPTER 10 CALLA MATHEMATICS

NSTRUCTION IN MATHEMATICS HAS GROWN IN SIGNIFICANCE in recent years, in part due to concerns that the United States has not been competing successfully on the international scene relative to the performance of students in other countries. Scores on national tests indicate that many native English-speaking students are unable to handle simple computations and word problems appropriate for students at their age level.[1] As serious as these concerns are, the data probably overestimate the mathematics achievement of U.S. students because students who are learning English are excluded from these testing programs by their school districts. National averages would be even lower if students learning English were tested, in part due to limited proficiency in English but also due to lack of familiarity with math concepts and skills. Concern about the mathematics performance of students nationally is supported by an awareness among mathematics educators that many teachers at all levels have not extended student awareness of mathematics concepts beyond simple computations and limited application of formulas and principles. A call for new standards of student performance and new guidelines for teaching has heavily influenced discussions of the appropriate instructional methods in grade-level mathematics classrooms.[2]

Description of the Mathematics Curriculum

The traditional mathematics curriculum, rather than the curriculum envisioned by professional mathematics educators, is what is being taught in most classrooms today. Information on what is actually taught in mathematics comes from a number of sources, including analyses of curriculum materials, logs maintained by teachers, and observations in classrooms. Studies in which these approaches have been used have concentrated on the topics presented, the material included in lessons, and the instructional methods used.

WHAT IS PRESENTLY BEING TAUGHT

Textbooks on mathematics in the primary grades consist largely of numbers, place value, addition, subtraction, and multiplication with whole numbers.[3] The intent of instruction in these areas is to make the operations conceptually familiar and to make use of the operations automatic and accurate. In the intermediate grades, math consists of multiplication, division, decimals, fractions, ratios, proportions, and percents, with many books containing units on measurement and geometry. Students may also have begun the study of graphing, probability, and statistics, and in most schools will have begun initial acquaintance with automatic calculators. Students will also have had exposure to measurement, time, and money. In the intermediate years and through high school, students may study algebra, trigonometry, geometry, and sometimes calculus.

The mathematics curriculum develops students' capability to *understand concepts* through a variety of problem-solving experiences with manipulative materials or pictorial models prior to working with abstractions. Students develop a foundation in the *basic facts* and skills, as in addition or subtraction, through understanding a concrete model of the mathematical operation. They develop *computational skill* through practicing the procedure or factual knowledge under a variety of circumstances, and applying the factual information to problem-solving situations. Finally, students develop appropriate *problem-solving strategies* by having extensive opportunity to use techniques for solving realistic problems in a wide variety of different settings.

ACTUAL CLASS INSTRUCTION

What does mathematics instruction consist of and what do students actually do in mathematics classes? Analyses of daily logs maintained by middle school teachers revealed that 70 to 75 percent of mathematics instruction was spent teaching in skill areas—how to add, subtract, multiply, and divide, and occasionally how to read a graph.[4] Of the time spent on skills development, about half was spent developing conceptual understanding and the other half teaching problem-solving skills, usually story problems. However, in problem-solving instruction, the procedures necessary to solve a problem were rarely stated explicitly, leaving students essentially without the benefit of an algorithm to solve future story problems. Many of the teachers devoted a small amount of time to a large number of skills, opting for breadth rather than depth. Teachers gave a variety of reasons for preferring broad coverage, including to review work covered in prior grades, to introduce material anticipated in the next grade, and to ensure representation on anticipated assessments. The curriculum across the middle grades was noted to be recursive for these teachers in that there was a high degree of content overlap between grades. The findings are consistent with analyses of the curriculum presented in mathematics textbooks for the middle grades, in which 65 to 80 percent of the exercises were on skill practice, while 10 to 24 percent were on conceptual understanding, and 6 to 13 percent on problem solving.[5]

The format of mathematics instruction in the middle grades is strikingly different from the format used in other content areas such as social studies. In one investigation, almost 41 percent of instructional segments observed in mathematics classrooms consisted of three forms of seatwork: uniform seatwork, in which all students work on the same assignment; diverse seatwork, where students work on a variety of different tasks; and individual seatwork, where students work at their own rate through a sequence of assigned tasks.[6] A segment was defined as an instructional sequence having a beginning and end point and focusing on a particular instructional goal. In contrast to the extensive seatwork in mathematics, only 18 percent of the segments in social studies were devoted to seatwork. In mathematics, less than one percent of the segments were devoted to group work, or face-to-face interaction working on a joint task, while 34 percent of the segments in social studies involved group work. Students in the mathematics classrooms tended to spend their time in recitations, or responding to a teacher inquiry, in the varieties of seatwork, and in contests. Over half the students' time in math classes was spent on a single activity, solving problems at their desks, while student time in social studies was distributed across 14 main activities, such as listening, discuss/listen, question/answer, questions/answers on oral reading, writing, and research. There was also considerably more variety in the instructional topics covered in social studies than in math, with math limited to basic operations followed by fractions, mixed numbers, and decimals. The social studies curriculum covered topics ranging from current events, various countries of interest, geography, history, family relationships, and society.

Students learning mathematics develop attitudes toward the content area that emerge in part from the way in which math is taught, as we have noted earlier. Students taught with a "chalk and talk" method see the instructor as the sole source of information and develop dependency on the teacher for learning. Additionally, students often develop attitudes about their own ability in math. "I'm no good in math," and "I find math easy" are views that students develop over the years of elementary and middle school experience. Because the experiences have continued over a long period of time, the attitudes are hard to dislodge.

Seemingly fixed attitudes in mathematics may be responsive to change as the students gain increasing experience in using learning strategies. One of the reasons for supporting the development of metacognitive knowledge is to ensure that students have a perspective on their own learning and can see the importance of having experience with similar problems in the past and having a repertoire of strategies to deal with them.

CONCLUSIONS ABOUT PRESENT INSTRUCTION

What can we conclude about students exposed to instruction that teaches math concepts and skills through lectures, that focuses on developing automaticity and accuracy with basically lower level skills, where learning is by repetition rather than conceptual analysis, where students have little opportunity for self-direction and autonomy, and where student interaction and discussion of problem-solving approaches is limited? The first conclusion is that students are probably not developing an independent view of their own learning that will lead to autonomy in solving problems in mathematics. When lesson assignments and student evaluation are all external, there is little opportunity for students to expand their awareness of themselves as learners and to develop and apply skills in mathematics independently. A related conclusion is that students will develop dependency on the teacher for assignments and for instructional activities that lead to learning. That is, without the teacher, students will not view learning in math as possible. The total dependence on one source for initial concepts and for learning activities produces a unidirectional view of learning in which other students are not considered as useful resources for information. Another conclusion is that the emphasis in classroom assignments and tests will focus on getting the right answer rather than identifying and applying algorithms that can be extended to similar problems. It seems that what students learn depends on *how* they are taught. If these are legitimate conclusions, and the evidence suggests that they are,[7] we should reconsider the nature of mathematics instruction.

One of the major difficulties in implementing CALLA math with ESL students is that the ESL teachers offering this instruction may find that some grade-level teachers are using a more traditional approach to math instruction. The ESL teachers in CALLA math may teach effective problem-solving procedures, only to find that their problem-solving approach is neither supported nor rewarded when students get to the grade-level classroom. What can the CALLA math teacher do upon finding that a problem-solving approach and cooperative learning are not used in grade-level classrooms? The approach we have tried and succeeded at is to contact the district's curriculum coordinators in math, inform them of the CALLA approach, and request their assistance in assuring that an instructional approach emphasizing problem solving and cooperative learning are incorporated into district-wide workshops on math. The CALLA teacher can then work with the school's math teachers to discuss and coordinate CALLA with these new instructional approaches.

Major advances in the way mathematics education is viewed have been in process since the mid-1980s, despite the fact that classroom instruction appears resistant to change. These advances have developed in the form of theoretical understanding of math problem solving, guidelines for what we expect students to learn, and guidelines for instructional practice.

DECLARATIVE AND PROCEDURAL KNOWLEDGE

A theoretical view of mathematics should address questions about how math knowledge is stored in memory, how it is learned, and how it is retrieved and used. The distinction between declarative and procedural knowledge is a key element in developing a theoretical understanding of mathematics. Declarative knowledge in mathematics consists of math concepts or principles, while procedural knowledge consists of math skills.[8] For example, place value, the meaning of numbers and fractions, and memorized math facts are declarative knowledge and are stored in memory as conceptual frameworks that are connected with related concepts. In contrast, borrowing and carrying in addition, maintaining place value in multiplication, solving math word problems, and following the "rules" of mathematics are procedural skills and are stored in memory in terms of sequences of complex operations. There is an interaction between declarative and procedural knowledge in that procedural knowledge can draw on declarative knowledge as students solve problems. For example, students may solve $8 + 10 = ?$ by generating a procedure in which they combine separate known components of the problem, as with $4 + 4 + 5 + 5 = 18$. Another type of interaction between declarative and procedural knowledge is that declarative knowledge can become procedural through repeated execution, as in repeated application of a math rule with various problems. Connecting math procedures with math concepts will have important benefits since recall and transfer of meaningful information are always easier than with unrelated facts. However, students do not always make these connections. This argues strongly for math instruction in which procedures are learned by establishing links with math concepts rather than through rote memorization.

Recent guidelines for what we expect students to learn go far beyond the emphasis on simple computational skills that seems to dominate classrooms. The National Council of Teachers of Mathematics has established a goal for all students to become mathematically literate, as indicated in the following five goals:[9]

GOALS FOR MATHEMATICAL LITERACY

- ***Learning the value of mathematics:*** to appreciate the role of mathematics in the development of contemporary society and explore relationships and applications of mathematics in the physical and life sciences, the social sciences, and the humanities;
- ***Becoming confident in one's own ability:*** to use one's mathematical understanding to make sense of new problem situations in the world around them;
- ***Becoming a mathematical problem solver:*** to develop abilities to solve problems that take sustained effort and to do so in cooperation with others;
- ***Learning to communicate mathematically:*** learning to use mathematics signs, symbols, and terms to communicate in writing and discussions with others; and
- ***Learning to reason mathematically:*** making predictions, gathering evidence, and building an argument to support one's conclusions.

IMPLICATIONS FOR INSTRUCTION

These changes in the way that mathematics is viewed theoretically and in terms of expectations for students have direct implications for instruction. The instruction should emphasize mathematical literacy and a *communicative approach* to teaching mathematics in which students learn mathematics by talking, writing, and reasoning about mathematics.[9] In this type of instruction, students have opportunities to discuss authentic problems from their personal world that can be solved through mathematics, solve problems that require renewed effort when initial problem-solving attempts do not succeed, solve problems in which cooperative group efforts generate success, and work on problems that require hypothesis-testing, data collection, evaluation, and generation and discussion of alternative conclusions. Thus, mathematics is:

> ...more than a collection of concepts and skills to be mastered; it includes methods of investigating and reasoning, means of communication, and notions of context.[10]

One of the difficulties in implementing a curriculum with these characteristics touches on the breadth versus depth issue raised earlier but also concerns the issue of who provides the instruction. These guidelines call for a major reconceptualization of the way in which mathematics is taught, and should lead to different objectives, curriculum content, and instructional procedures. Mathematics teachers already burdened with meeting local school district guidelines will find it difficult to reprioritize to meet these new emphases. ESL teachers who wish to follow these guidelines may find themselves torn between providing instruction in depth with a process orientation and providing instruction that matches the pace and substance maintained by grade-level teachers in math, which may be more skills directed. There is no simple solution to these problems, but we will address these points later in this chapter.

Description of the Mathematics Curriculum

- What is presently taught—Students develop the capability to understand concepts, basic facts, computational skills, and, to a limited degree, problem-solving strategies.
- How it is taught—Students spend time in recitations, responding to teacher inquiry, and in a variety of seat work activities.
- Conclusions about present instruction—Little opportunity for students to be aware of themselves as learners and to develop mathematical reasoning, problem-solving, and communication skills.
- Instructional Implications—Instruction should emphasize mathematical literacy: a communicative approach involving discussion, application, and analysis of alternative paths to problem solution.

What's Difficult in Math for ESL Students?

Students learning English are often exited from bilingual or ESL programs based on assessment of their general familiarity with English more than their specific knowledge of mathematics or other content areas. The ESL student who is placed in grade-level classrooms may be familiar with general English vocabulary, able to identify objects in English, able to communicate appropriately in social situations, and able to decode simple reading passages at least close to his or her own grade level. The ESL student thus will evidence test performance that is considered adequate for entry into grade-level English language classrooms. ESL students may nevertheless continue to have difficulty mastering content areas because of specialized language requirements that are unique to each subject, and because content area mastery requires that the student be able to use English as a medium of thought.

ESL students encounter difficulties with word problems in mathematics more so than in basic math facts and computation because word problems are highly language dependent. Students who have established separate mastery over reading comprehension and computational skills will not necessarily be able to perform word problems. There is a special difficulty students experience when reading comprehension and computation are combined in a word problem. Findings from the National Assessment of Educational Progress indicate that many 9-, 13-, and 17-year old students cannot choose the correct computational procedures to solve word problems even though they understand the operations required to perform the computations. Teachers also have commented that teaching story problems is one of the most difficult tasks in the elementary school curriculum.[11]

LANGUAGE DEPENDENCE IN MATHEMATICS

ESL students are often placed into grade-level mathematics classes before other subjects because of the mistaken belief that math does not depend on language. In fact, there are many language dependent areas of math. Mathematics skills required in mathematics classes are described in Table 10.1, which indicates that skills in listening, reading, speaking, and writing are typically required in grades 4-6 and may be pervasive in grades 7-12.[12]

One example of the close connection between language and mathematics is illustrated by a teacher's verbal explanation of math concepts and principles. The student must understand explanations often with no more referent than a formula written on the board. Similarly, students are expected to read explanations in the text and to understand written word problems. Students may be called upon in class to verbalize how they solved a problem, and may need to write their own word problems from numeric data.

The language of mathematics creates many difficulties that ESL students may not have the strategies to resolve. In the following discussion, we highlight the language-related reasons linked to vocabulary and grammar why math is difficult for students who are learning English.

VOCABULARY. The language of mathematics is highly specific and lacks the redundancy typically found to assist comprehension with other types of language.[13] ESL students may be easily confused by this specialized vocabulary, which has unique terms such as *addend* and *quotient*, and terms with specialized meanings, such as *altogether, round,* and *table.*[14] To add to the difficulty of understanding this specialized language, the precision with which the language of mathematics is defined (*multiply* in mathematics has an unambiguous meaning) leads to the infrequent use of redundancy or paraphrasing of meanings as is found in other content areas. ESL students therefore have few cues to the meaning of words or phrases apart from the limited and often abstract context that is provided in the words and

Table 10.1
Language Skills Required in Mathematics

Language Skills	Grades 1-3	Grades 4-6	Grades 7-12
Listening			
1. Understand explanations without concrete referents.	L	P	M
2. Understand oral numbers.	M	M	M
3. Understand oral word problems.	M	P	L
Reading			
1. Understand specialized vocabulary	L	P	M
2. Understand explanations in the textbook.	L	P	M
3. Read mathematical explanations.	L	P	M
4. Understand word problems.	P	M	M
Speaking			
1. Answer questions.	M	M	M
2. Ask questions for clarification.	M	M	M
3. Explain problem-solving procedures.	M	M	M
4. Describe applications of math in other content areas	M	P	P
Writing			
1. Write verbal input numerically.	M	P	P
2. Write word problems.	P	P	L
3. Write words for number sentences.	M	P	L

less emphasis	partial emphasis	more emphasis
L	P	M

symbols in the problem statement.[15] There are also combinations or complex strings of words or phrases that have special meanings, such as *square root, multiplication table,* and *least common denominator.*[16]

In some cases, specific words in mathematics signal the use of certain mathematical operations. For example, addition is suggested by the following words:

add	and	plus
sum	total	combine

while subtraction is suggested by these words:

minus	less	less than
difference	decreased by	more than

However, when used in certain ways, some of these words may signal exactly the opposite operation than the one that leads to the correct solution, as in a problem like:

Hilda has 7 records.
She has 5 records less than David.
How many records does David have?

In this problem, the student is required to add rather than subtract, as had been suggested by the term "less than," an easily confusing point for students learning English as well as for other students.

STRUCTURES. The language of mathematics is not often spoken in day-to-day activities, so students have little opportunity to gain experience with this specialized language in other contexts. ESL students may also be confused by the special grammatical constructions in mathematics, where phrases such as *6 is 2 greater than 4* and *five times as high as* are commonplace, but do not appear in other content areas or in beginning level ESL classes. There are at least five syntactic features of math which make the language difficult for students learning English[17] as shown in Table 10.2.

As Spanos et al. note, one of the difficulties of these syntactic features is that they are all likely to appear in textbooks because text writers could easily be inclined to include them for stylistic variation. Grade-level texts are unlikely to be written out of consideration for students learning English, with built-in redundancy and vocabulary support.

Analyses of the various ways in which word problems are commonly stated reveals at least two broad categories of problems and a number of subcategories that vary considerably in semantic complexity and level of difficulty.[18] The two broad categories are defined in terms of the level of action entailed in the problem statement, as in the following:

Action	**Static**
1. Joe has 3 marbles. Tom gave him 5 more marbles. How many does Joe have now?	2. Joe has 3 marbles. Tom has 5 marbles. How many marbles do they have altogether?

The *action* problem entails a shift or exchange of the items being counted, with Tom giving marbles to Joe, while the *static* problem combines the counted items based on the problem wording. Both action and static problems have special features that produce differing levels of complexity based on semantic relationships between

Table 10.2
Syntactic Features of Word Problems

Feature	Structure	Example
1. Comparatives	greater/less than	6 is *greater than* 4
	n times as much as	Mariá earns *six times as much as* Peter.
	as ... as	Lin is *as old as* Roberto
2. Prepositions	divided into	4 (divided) *into* 8
	divided by	10 *divided by* 5
	by	2 multiplied *by* 6 (x)
		vs.
		x exceeds 2 *by* 7 (+)
3. Passive voice		x *is defined* as a number greater than 7
		When 5 *is added* to a number, the result is 7.
4. Reversals		The number *a* is five less than *b*.
		Correct equation: $a = b - 5$ or $b - a = 5$
		Incorrect equation: $a = 5 - b$ or $a - 5 = b$
5. Logical connectors	if ... then	*If* a is positive *then* -a is negative.

words. For example, action problems may consist of either changing or equalizing problems. The action problem above (Problem 1) is an example of a known change with an unknown result because the number of marbles possessed by Joe changes in amounts that are defined by the problem. An example in which the change is unknown is as follows:

3. Joe had 3 marbles.
   Then Tom gave him some more marbles.
   Now Joe has 8 marbles.
   How many marbles did Tom give him?

An equalizing problem calls for the number of marbles possessed by Joe and Tom to be equalized when each person has a known quantity. The importance of these different problem formulations is that, for native English-speaking kindergartners and first graders, action problems with a known change and unknown result (e.g.,

Problem 1) are less difficult than those with a known result but an unknown change (e.g., Problem 3).

There are also two broad categories of static problems defined in terms of the type of process called for in the solution: combine and compare problems. Problem 2 above is a combine problem with an unknown result, whereas a compare problem with an unknown difference is as follows:

4. Joe has 8 marbles.
   Tom has 5 marbles.
   How many more marbles does Joe have than Tom?

Static problems like number 4 are more difficult than static combine problems (e.g., 2 above) or than action problems with an unknown result (1 above) for native English speaking kindergarteners and first graders. These relative orders of difficulty have been confirmed in Spanish with native Spanish-speaking children of approximately the same age.[19]

NON-LINGUISTIC DIFFICULTIES

CONCEPT FORMATION. With word problems ESL students must conceptually process both the language and the mathematical problem before a solution can be reached. The student must be able to use English as a vehicle of thought and to solve the problem in English, a language students may understand imperfectly at this point in their education. Many word problems require formal operations or the ability to think abstractly and to manipulate concepts through language. If the student's thought processes are not automatic in the language in which the problem is expressed, but require deliberation due to confusion over unfamiliar meanings of words or phrases, the student's attempts to solve the problem will be delayed if not interrupted altogether. ESL students in first year algebra courses have been noted to misinterpret problem statements and to require extra linguistic processing time that prevented their completion of timed problem assignments.[20]

CULTURAL BACKGROUND. Other less obvious difficulties in understanding math appear on inspection of the type of mathematics instruction ESL students may have received in their native countries. Two types of differences are typically found: differences in math symbols or in their use, and differences in study or problem-solving procedures.

Differences in the symbols or in their use are likely to confuse students from other countries. In some countries, division problems exchange the position of divisor and dividend, as in the following:

U.S. System	**Selected Spanish-Speaking Countries**
$\begin{array}{r} 8 \\ 4\overline{)\,32} \end{array}$	$\begin{array}{l\|l} 32 & \underline{4} \\ 0 & 8 \end{array}$

Another major difference that could lead to confusion is the use of a period in place of a comma in writing the numerals for multiples of a thousand, and the use of a comma in place of a period for decimals, as in the following examples:

U.S. System	Selected Spanish-Speaking Countries
4,232	4.232
1,258,125	1.258.125
4-1/2 = 4.5	4,5

Another major source of difficulty is math fractions. Students in almost every country outside the United States study the metric system exclusively and thus encounter difficulty not only with the customary units of U.S. measurement (inches, miles, quarts, pounds, etc.) but also the unaccustomed emphasis on fractions in American schools.[21] A measurement system in which every unit has meaning when divided by ten has little use for fractions.

Cultural differences have also been noted in the conceptual strategies students apply to mathematics. The previous mathematics training of recent immigrant Chinese students emphasizes accuracy and speed based on memorization of rules and formulas, in contrast to the American emphasis on more of the analytical and conceptual basis of mathematics.[22] While these difficulties do not affect word problems exclusively, they are important to identify when students appear to understand the meaning of the problem but persist in finding an incorrect solution.

OTHER NON-LANGUAGE FACTORS

The foregoing are unlikely to be the only difficulties ESL students encounter with word problems. Studies with native English-speaking students indicate that reading ability accounts for only a small portion of the errors in word problems.[23] Children with normal reading scores who were able to identify both the setting and the question in word problems were often unable to work the problem or even know where to start. These students experienced procedural, computational, and clerical errors. For these and other students like them, an instructional approach may be required that evokes alternative problem-solving strategies and checks for accuracy.

IMPLICATIONS FOR INSTRUCTION

The numerous difficulties ESL students can expect to experience in math, apart from making simple computational errors, suggests that special procedures are needed that enable students to test hypotheses about language use and other potential problem areas. One such procedure is *cooperative work activities* in which students discuss their interpretation of a problem, identify steps that are necessary to find the solution, test out different aproaches, and check their answers relative to solutions obtained by other students. Quite often the simple act of talking through the problem not only yields a correct solution but, in the long run, gives students critical practice in learning and thinking in the academic language of English. Moreover, as students verbalize alternative solutions to the problem, they have an opportunity to inspect problem-solving approaches advocated by other students relative to the approach developed on their own. Verbalizing problem-solving steps may in fact be the best way to learn them and to ensure that the steps transfer to other problems.

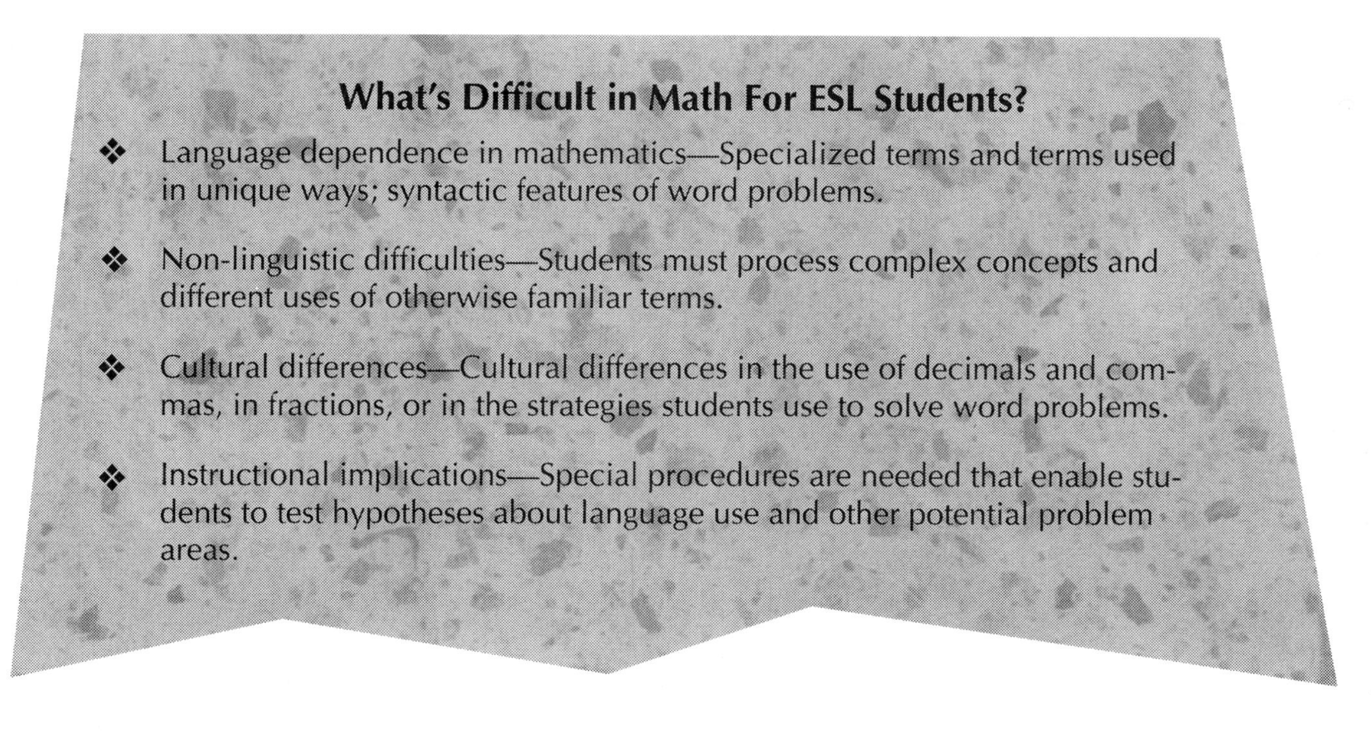

Teaching Guidelines for CALLA Mathematics

One of the major reasons for studying mathematics is to learn how to solve problems. Through the study of mathematics, students are prepared to solve problems they encounter in a natural way in the world around them as well as in the further study of mathematics and sciences. To become effective problem solvers, learners need to understand concepts, know basic facts, use computational skills efficiently, and select and apply appropriate problem-solving strategies.[24]

SELECTING PRIORITY CONTENT

The mathematics curriculum taught in schools today emphasizes breadth of coverage at the expense of depth and contains considerable overlap in content between grades.[25] In CALLA, we suggest that teachers identify high-priority content through discussions with content-area teachers, inspection of grade-appropriate texts, and analysis of math frameworks across the grades. Teachers should look for recurring themes or for specific areas on which ESL students can be expected to have the most serious difficulties and treat these areas in depth. In math, at least two areas stand out in this respect. The first is solving word problems, and the second is fractions. We have decided to concentrate on word problems in our detailed analysis of the CALLA approach in mathematics because of the general applicability of problem-solving procedures across various types of problems. Those interested in strategies for other topics in mathematics will find other resources available.[26]

In our discussion of mathematics instruction for ESL students, we assume the students have some knowledge of elementary mathematical concepts, basic facts, and fundamental computational skills in the four basic operations (addition, subtraction, multiplication, and division). This is simply because we focus on *language* and *problem-solving* skills exclusively and do not describe instructional procedures for introducing basic math skills. However, we do *not* necessarily assume that students will already have acquired accurate and automatic use of basic math facts by the time they begin CALLA math. As Carpenter and his colleagues have indicated, instruction in number facts need not precede instruction in arithmetic problem solving but may be introduced concurrently, and does not detract from but may facilitate acquisition of math facts.[27] What we stress in CALLA is instruction on the *language* required to solve mathematical word problems in English, and the problem-solving *strategies* that will lead to successful solution of word problems.

BASIC APPROACH TO PROBLEM SOLVING

Since many students have difficulty solving word problems, mathematics textbooks often recommend specific problem-solving procedures. These procedures typically take the form of guidelines such as the following five-point checklist:[28]

CHECKLIST FOR NATIVE ENGLISH SPEAKERS

- Understand the problem.
- Find the needed information.
- Choose a plan.
- Solve the problem.
- Check the answer.

Mathematics texts often provide students with experiences using these steps individually and in sequence with word problems, and the better texts provide reminders through a visual cue accompanying each new set of word problems.[29]

While such checklists may be adequate for native English speakers, ESL students continue to have difficulty with such guides to problem solution because of uncertainties with word meanings and their application. How does the student go about understanding the question when the issue of primary concern is determining the meaning of words presented in an abstract context? What information is needed and what is a plan? How does one develop a plan, and what importance does a plan have for solving the problem? What does it mean to check an answer? While useful for many native English-speaking students, these recommendations for problem solution are no substitute for a language-based experiences using techniques for solving mathematics problems.

RATIONALE FOR CALLA INSTRUCTION IN MATHEMATICS

Teaching mathematics to ESL students using CALLA is derived from four key ideas: link word problem language and the path to solution; have mentally active students; verbalize the steps to problem solving; and incorporate learning strategies into problem solving.

LINK LANGUAGE OF WORD PROBLEMS AND SOLUTION. An understanding of the language in a word problem is a minimum condition for solving the problem. While reading at grade level is no guarantee that a student will be able to solve mathematical problems, the student who cannot understand the words or the phrasing in a word problem has little chance of reaching the correct solution. Thus, guidelines must be established that will enable teachers of ESL students to build the necessary language supports for students to be able to understand the language in word problems and begin to use English as a vehicle for communication.

HAVE MENTALLY ACTIVE STUDENTS. The way to do this is to make the steps required for problem solution explicit and provide guided practice or scaffolding in applying the steps. That is, ESL students need explicit instruction in the importance of using these steps in problem solution and in remembering the sequence of steps. They also need to see the link between use of the steps and correct problem solution, perhaps through a teacher's modeling and perhaps through hearing other students talk about their strategy use. Although students in some cases may reach an intuitively corect answer to a word problem without conscious awareness of the steps they undertook in reaching the solution, making the steps in problem solution explicit is especially important for students who encounter word problems for which the correct answer is not immediately apparent. And that probably means most word problems for most students learning English. In CALLA, we give students explicit directions on how to perform these and other steps necessary for solving the problem and guide the students in strategy use on subsequent problems.

VERBALIZE THE STEPS TO PROBLEM SOLVING. When students do this, they derive a higher-order cognitive awareness of the link between the strategies and the correct solution that increases the likelihood that they will use successful strategies again when encountering similar problems. They also provide other students with models of appropriate strategy applications.

INCORPORATE LEARNING STRATEGIES AND PROBLEM SOLUTION STEPS. Learning strategies are useful in assisting students of mathematics perform each of the steps toward problem solution with success. Strategies can be selected from metacognitive, cognitive, and social/affective groupings for this purpose, as identified in Table 10.3. The way in which teachers can use learning strategies with these steps is discussed in the next section. Then, some of these general recommendations will be operationalized as specific lesson plans.

LEARNING STRATEGIES WITH WORD PROBLEMS

Learning strategies can assist students in performing the steps involved in solving word problems. Some learning strategies have more significance with certain problem-solving steps than with others. If specific strategies are linked to individual problem-solving steps, the use of a specific step will cue the strategies that are associated with it. The student will have a varied range of strategies that are suggested by each of the more explicitly defined steps, and can apply these strategies while attempting to solve the problem. Through repeated exercises and scaffolding with these strategies, the student would have a ready repertoire of approaches for understanding the language of mathematics as well as for solving word problems.

Some of the strategies that seem to be linked to the individual problem-solving steps are presented in Table 10.4.

The use of specific strategies with problem solving will be aided by *metacognitive knowledge* or student awareness of the task demands, their personal experience with similar tasks, and the types of strategies that will be most effective with these tasks. This level of understanding of math problems will be easier for middle school and older students who have the mental maturity to manipulate concepts in this way. Teachers can assist students in developing metacognitive awareness during the first problem-solving step, Understand the Problem, by asking leading questions in group discussion, such as *Have we had similar problems before? How did we solve them? Were any strategies particularly useful?*

One of the strategies students should be encouraged to use in all aspects of solving a problem is *cooperation*. Recent studies of problem-solving in small groups indicate that small groups of three or four students may be more effective in ensuring that students have an accurate representation of the problem than students working alone or in pairs.[30] One major function that small groups can serve is to provide

Table 10.3

LEARNING STRATEGIES FOR MATHEMATICS

Metacognitive Strategies:	Students plan, monitor, and evaluate their learning of mathematics concepts and skills.
Advance Organization	What's my purpose for solving this problem? What is the question? What will I use the information for?
Selective Attention	What words or ideas cue the operation?
	Where are the data needed to solve the problem?
Organizational Planning	What plan will help solve the problem? Is it a multiple-step plan?
Self-monitoring	Does the plan seem to be working? Am I getting the answer?
Self-Assessment	Did I solve the problem/answer the question? How did I solve it? Is it a good solution? If not, what could I do differently?
Cognitive Strategies:	Students interact with the information to be learned, changing or organizing it either mentally or physically.
Elaborating Prior Knowledge	What do I already know about this topic or type of problem? What experiences have I had that are related to this? How does this information relate to other information?
Taking Notes	What's the best way to write down a plan to solve the problem? Table? Chart? List? Diagram?
Grouping	How can I classify this information? What is the same and what is different?
Making Inferences	Are there words I don't know that I must understand to solve the problem?
Using Images	What can I draw to help me understand and solve the problem? Can I make a mental picture or visualize this problem?
Social/Affective Strategies:	Students interact with others to assist learning, or use attitudes and feelings to help their learning.
Questioning for Clarification	What help do I need? Who can I ask? How should I ask?
Cooperating	How can I work with others to answer the question or solve the problem?
Self-talk	Yes, I can do this task—what strategies do I need?

APPLYING LEARNING STRATEGIES TO MATHEMATICS

Mathematics Problem-Solving Steps

Understand the Question

Find the Needed Information

Choose a Plan

Solve the Problem

Check the Answer

Table 10.4
Learning Strategies for Math Problem-Solving Steps

Problem-Solving Step	Learning Strategy
1. Understand the Problem	Elaboration
	Imagery
	Inferencing
	Summarizing
	Cooperation
2. Find the Needed Information	Selective Attention
3. Choose a Plan	Prediction
	Imagery
4. Solve the Problem	Cooperation
5. Check the Answer	Self-evaluation
	Cooperation

feedback on preliminary attempts to represent the problem. Students will be led to examine their own information and strategies based on group challenges, disbelief, or affirmation. A second major function of small groups is to supply background information that individual students may not possess. A strategy such as "select only the numbers that are needed to solve the problem" may have little meaning if the student does not possess enough information to identify the relevant numbers. Lack of adequate background information is one of the major obstacles to successful problem solution among native English-speaking students,[31] and should be an even more important obstacle to students from other cultures. A third major function served by small groups is that effective problem solvers who verbalize their own problem-solving processes are modeling the avenues to problem solution for less effective problem solvers. The students can profit from observing each other's thought processes as they are verbalized. These externalized verbalizations of problem solving processes are more likely to occur in small groups of three or four than in pairs.[32] A fourth significant benefit from working in small groups is that students who verbalize problem-solving steps and the strategies associated with them are more likely to transfer problem-solving procedures to subsequent problems. As a final benefit, students who work in small groups independent of the teacher's immediate control are taking responsibility for their own learning and rehearsing independent working skills. Basically, a student does not have to work alone to become an independent learner. Teachers of ESL students can capitalize on the effectiveness of small groups in mathematics by encouraging cooperation in reaching problem solutions.

Teachers using cooperative learning with math problem solving can capitalize on the problem-solving steps outlined below by asking students to focus on the specific steps rather than on the correct answer. Cooperative learning groups in mathematics too often progress to sharing the correct answer without discussing the steps used in obtaining the correct solution. By asking students to verbalize these steps and their application to any word problem, teachers will have an effective means of assigning meaningful work to small groups.

Teaching Guidelines for CALLA Mathematics

- Identify high-priority content through discussion with teachers, inspection of texts, and analysis of math frameworks.
- Teach problem solving steps: Understand the question, find the needed information, choose a plan, solve the problem, check back.
- Introduce problem-solving steps concurrent with math facts.
- Assist students in developing the vocabulary and structures used in word problems; in becoming mentally active; and in verbalizing problem-solving steps and incorporating learning strategies into their problem solving.
- Help students develop a repertoire of learning strategies for understanding and solving word problems.

How to Teach Problem-solving Steps

In the following discussion, we identify implications for instructional practice in mathematics that derive from CALLA. We have merged recommendations based on language approaches with those based on an analysis of learning strategies used in problem solving. The principal objectives of these activities are to provide students with the language skills and the conceptual strategies necessary to solve mathematical word problems. The organizing framework for our discussion is the discrete steps that students follow in solving word problems.

UNDERSTAND THE PROBLEM

TEACH ELABORATION. The first step in a student's attempt to solve word problems is to understand the question, which requires comprehension of the words and phrases used in the problem statement. Teachers can assist students in understanding the question by teaching them to use the learning strategy *elaboration*. In using elaboration, students discuss what they know about the topic of the problem and what previous experiences they have had related to the type of problem presented. Teachers should identify the strategy by name and remind students to use elaboration on successive word problems. Teachers can also teach elaboration by asking questions and by fostering group discussions. Topics for the discussion can be words or phrases that seem unclear, experiences students have had with similar problems, experiences students have had with the specific subject matter treated in the word problem, and the student's mental representation of the problem.

TEACH STUDENTS IMAGERY. The mental representation is a mental image of the elements of the problem. Teachers can encourage students to form mental images of word problems by asking students to draw a diagram or picture of the problem or otherwise represent the problem through drawing. The mental representation in some cases can be used throughout the problem solution to guide the direction of the problem-solving steps. Students can use *imagery* in developing an internal or external representation of the problem. Images reported by effective problem solvers are often visual rather than verbal and may consist of a pattern or an arrangement of objects.[33] Suppose, for example, that students are presented with the following problem:

> Juan is 8 years younger than Mariá.
> Juan is 12.
> How old is Mariá?

An internal visual representation of this word problem might take the form of a boy who is the younger brother of an older sister, or a boy who is shorter (and younger) than a girl. A solution to the word problem that results in a number which is greater than 12 would be consistent with this image.

Encourage students to form mental images of word problems.

REWRITE THE QUESTION AS A STATEMENT. Teachers can ask students to demonstrate their understanding of the question by rewriting the question as a statement in which they leave a blank for the correct answer. Teachers can also ask students to paraphrase the question in a way that makes sense to them. Exercises in which students rewrite the question provide them with experience in thinking through the meaning of the question. For example, if the question is "How many apples are in each bowl?" students write "There are _____ apples in each bowl."

Teachers can develop student familiarity with the meaning of individual words and phrases in word problems in a number of ways. Students can be taught new words in context using manipulatives or demonstrations and to place words in context as they learn them by writing them in sentences or drawing the object they represent (e.g., square, triangle). The ability to use these words as part of their own vocabulary can be fostered by having the students write alternative questions to the same word problem[34] or write their own word problems and share these with their peers in small groups. The dialogue in small groups that follows from sharing their own word problems adds further experiences in using the language of mathematics.

In understanding the question, ESL students use *inferencing* to guess at the meanings of some of the terms, which may be suggested by the context in which the words are used. Students use *summarizing* in rewriting a question as a statement in that they must reformulate the wording of the question. *Cooperation* is useful when students share with each other their interpretation of the problem, describe their image or representation of the problem, or collaborate on identifying the meaning of unfamiliar words.

Teachers can take an active role in assisting their students to identify strategies that are useful for understanding the problem by asking them to think aloud as they work out the solution to a problem. Students can be given mathematical problems of various kinds, seated in small groups, and asked to describe their thoughts as they solve a problem. They can also be asked how they performed different steps in the sequence from Understanding the Problem to Check Back. Our experience has been that students who are intermediate in English proficiency are generally quite capable and interested in expressing the kinds of strategies they use in understanding English. We would expect this same willingness to apply in expressing the strategies they use in solving mathematics word problems.

FIND THE NEEDED INFORMATION

Data in word problems may be stated directly in the problem, may be in a table, or could be in other sources outside the problem. For example, students might be required to use their own knowledge to supply some of the data, as in multiplying by 60 to convert minutes to seconds when the multiplier is not provided as part of the problem.

SELECTIVE ATTENTION. Word problems often contain irrelevant distractor numbers that are not necessary to solve the problem, as in:

> Wanda completed the 100 meter race in 13.4 seconds.
> Wanda was 2.5 seconds faster than Rita.
> In how many seconds did Rita finish the race?

If the student has established an accurate representation of the problem, the information necessary to solve the problem can be more easily identified. Teachers can assist students in gaining an accurate understanding of the problem by using *selective attention* to focus only on the numbers that are needed in the problem solution. Teachers can have students circle required numbers and cross out distractors to assist students in finding the needed information.

CHOOSE A PLAN

IDENTIFY THE OPERATION AND WHAT THE PROBLEM CALLS FOR. To choose a plan often means to choose an operation or operations but may also mean to identify if the problem is a single- or multiple-step problem. Students can be instructed to *selectively attend* to vocabulary in the word problems so they will be able to determine the correct operation called for by the problem. Exercises that require the student to circle key words that cue the operation to be used may be important for ESL students. However, as we noted earlier, focusing on one key word alone can sometimes lead the student astray without a broader understanding of what the problem calls for.

Most current math texts and workbooks acknowledge the difficulty of selecting the operation or operations based on selected individual words and emphasize obtaining a broad understanding of what the problem calls for. In one such text,[35] students in the middle grades are encouraged to choose the operation by thinking about what they want to know or what the problem calls for, as suggested in Table 10.5.

Table 10.5

Requirements and Operations in Word Problems

Operation	What the Problem Calls for
Addition	Finding the total after putting parts together
Subtraction	Taking away
	Comparing how many more in one set than another
	Finding how many are left
	Finding how many more are needed
Multiplication	Finding the total for a number of same-size sets
Division	Finding the number of same-size sets
	Finding the number in each same-size set

To teach this type of information, teachers can start by teaching the addition and subtraction part of the table separately from multiplication and division. Review the meaning of each operation, providing examples of each. Then ask students to discuss in small groups specific word problems and describe what is called for in terms of the second column and which operation is appropriate.

Based upon the mathematical operation the student has identified, and his or her understanding of the question, the student should choose a plan for solving the problem. The plan can consist of writing a number sentence (e.g., 25 + 37 = ?), using a formula (e.g., perimeter = 2L + 2W, distance = rate x time), or separating the problem into component parts if it is a multiple-step problem and working on each part individually. These separate parts may entail using different operations, as in a problem on averages where the student must first obtain a total and then divide by the number of cases.

Students may be able to solve some problems in their head. Students who are able to solve the problem in their head should be encouraged to do so without further delay. If they can solve the problem by writing it down on paper, they should also be encouraged to proceed. The plan in either of these cases is implicitly obvious to the student and may not need to be expressed.

Students who have difficulty selecting a plan that results in an acceptable answer should review problem-solving steps 1 and 2 to ensure that a simple rereading of the problem will not produce an appropriate plan. Students should have an option to select plans that are appropriate for working alone or plans that are involve working with other students. Whether students work alone or in small groups, brainstorming is necessary in order for them to identify alternative plans and test them out against their understanding of the problem.

WORKING ALONE. Students who work alone may use a variety of approaches to develop a plan. The following may be helpful:

- Draw a picture illustrating the internal representation of the problem.
- Make a table entering the key numbers or showing important relationships.
- Make a list of items in the problem and indicate the important number associated with each.
- Find a pattern or look for a relationship between numbers in an ordered series, such as 1, 4, 7, ...
- Solve a simpler problem in which either the number of steps or the size of the numbers is smaller.
- Guess at the answer by substituting different values to see if they make sense.

WORKING IN A SMALL GROUP. Students who work in small groups of three or four students may wish to use some of these approaches to develop a plan:

- Read the problem aloud to friends. Sometimes simply reading the problem aloud is sufficient to give the student a new awareness of the problem.
- Paraphrase or explain one's understanding of the problem. Obtain feedback from friends on the accuracy of one's understanding of the question and selection of key words and numbers.
- Ask friends to explain their understanding of the problem. Have them focus on their understanding of the question and selection of key words and numbers. Then have them focus on how they selected a plan. Do *not* ask them to focus on the answer.

In choosing a plan, students identify the appropriate mathematical operation to use by *selective attention* to key words used in the problem statement. As we have noted earlier, because some mathematical vocabulary may be used in different ways in some problems, students should check their selection of the operation against whatever else they know about the problem. For example, the mathematical operation selected by the student can be verified against the visual representation discussed above. A student who subtracts 8 from 12 in the word problem on p. 239 and concludes that the sister is 4 while the brother is 12 will produce an answer that is inconsistent with his or her representation of the problem in which the sister is taller than the brother.

SOLVE THE PROBLEM

In this step the students perform the calculations required to solve the problem. Students solve different steps of the problem separately, as required. Students may cooperate with other students to obtain the answer, verbalizing each of the foregoing steps and describing the problem-solving process.

With multi-step plans involving more than one operation, students can write out the steps. If they encounter difficulties, they can use cooperation, in which they review with other students the approach they used in the first three problem-solving steps.

CHECK THE ANSWER

USE IMAGERY. Students should check the entire process of problem understanding and solution, not merely the calculations performed in getting the answer. The students will check their understanding of the question and verify that the answer they have obtained makes sense in terms of their original representation of the problem.[36] In the problem on p. 239, the student could subtract 8 from 12 correctly and obtain the incorrect but mathematically accurate answer of 4.

USE OTHER APPROACHES. Students will also check to determine that they have used the key numbers and key words consistent with the plan that was formulated. Students may estimate the correct answer to determine if their solution matches the estimate, use a calculator to check on their calculation, or use a different problem-solving approach altogether to check for accuracy. Teachers can caution their students to check the answer with respect to their original understanding of the problem in addition to checking the accuracy of the computation.

How to Teach Problem-solving Steps

- Understand the question—Teach students to understand the problem through elaboration and imagery.
- Find the needed information—Help students use selective attention to find needed information.
- Make a plan—Have students identify the operation and what the problem calls for, then choose a plan (e.g., write a number sentence, identify parts of the problem, work with a peer, make a table, make a list).
- Solve the problem—Students write out the steps of the problem and solve it, using cooperation to review the steps they have taken.
- Check the answer—Students use a variety of approaches to verify that their answer makes sense.

Model Mathematics Unit

SOLVING ADDITION PROBLEMS

Mathematics Content Objectives:

Find the sum of whole numbers in problem situations. Apply knowledge of addition in writing problems. Find perimeter.

Mathematics Problem-solving Strategies:

Use the five-point problem-solving procedure to: (1) State the question in a problem in own words; (2) Find the data needed to solve a problem; (3) Formulate a plan and an appropriate solution strategy; (4) Implement a solution strategy; and (5) Evaluate the reasonableness of an answer.

Language Objectives:

Describe own problem-solving procedures; read word problems; write word problems; listen and follow directions for drawing diagrams.

Learning Strategies:

Elaboration of prior knowledge; selective attention; imagery; organizational planning; cooperation; self-evaluation.

Materials:

Classroom objects such as desks, books, pencils, etc. Examples of squares, rectangles, and triangles, including classroom objects, cut-out shapes, pictures, and household objects.

Note: Sample student pages are provided on pages 249–252 for activities marked with an asterisk(*).

PROCEDURES

Preparation 1: What Do You Know About Problem Solving?

Students work in pairs or small groups to count objects in the classroom and use the information to develop addition problems. Teacher calls on individual students to write one of their addition problems on the board.

Teacher leads discussion of what students have written, identifying the structure of addition problems by pointing out the numbers to be added (the addends) and the sum. Teacher then writes a simple word problem on the board and asks students to solve it and to describe how they solved it. Examples of problems to use:

- **a.** In our classroom, there are 12 boys and 13 girls. What is the total number of students?
- **b.** There are 5 chairs at the first table, 7 chairs at the second table, and 6 chairs at the third table. How many chairs are there at these three tables?

Teacher discusses student problem-solving procedures, identifying steps used to solve problems, and writes them on the board grouped into the following five-point checklist:

QUESTION—Understand the question.

DATA—Find the data needed to solve the problem.

PLAN—Develop a plan to solve the problem.

ANSWER—Solve the problem by following the plan.

CHECK—Check back to see if the answer was correct.

(To review the five-point checklist, refer to the section on "How to Teach Problem-Solving Steps" on pages 238–243.)

Teacher gives learning strategy reminder: Thinking about your *prior knowledge* will help you solve problems. Teacher discusses what students already know about addition, about the language used in addition, and about problem-solving steps; teacher stresses that it is important to use your *prior knowledge* about addition and about problem solving.

Presentation 1: Using the Five-Point Checklist to Solve Problems

Teacher reminds students that after *understanding the question* and *finding the data* in a word problem, they need to *make a plan.* Teacher explains that one type of plan is *making a picture in your mind* or actually drawing a picture.

Teacher writes a word problem with a strong visual component on the board. Example:

Greg can reach 50 inches with his arms stretched out.

María can reach 10 inches more than that.

How many inches can María reach?

Teacher calls on individual students to come to the board and (1) underline the question, and (2) rewrite the question as a statement, leaving a blank for the answer. Teacher asks all students to form in their minds a picture of Greg and María with their arms outstretched. Two students then act out stretching out their arms while a third student measures the length of each person's reach with a yardstick. Teacher has students draw what they see and label with correct measurements.

Learning strategy instruction: Using the word problem on the board, teacher names, models, and explains usefulness of using *imagery* or making a picture to solve word problems.

Teacher calls on a student to complete the solution of the problem on the board by going through the remaining parts of the five-point checklist (*solve the problem* and *check back*), then asks the student to describe the entire problem-solving procedure.

Practice 1:* Plan What to Do: Draw a Picture

Students complete word problems by first rewriting the question, then planning what to do by drawing a picture to represent the problem. After working on the problems individually, students work in small groups to share drawings and discuss how they used *imagery* to solve their problems.

Preparation 2: What Do You Know About Writing Problems?

Teacher leads discussion about how word problems are structured, eliciting from students and writing on board the main parts: story or situation, data, question. Students brainstorm ideas for word problems, and teacher notes their ideas on the board.

Presentation 2: Planning a Word Problem

Learning strategy instruction: Using some of the ideas written on the board, the teacher names, models, and explains usefulness of *organizational planning* as preparation for writing. Teacher explains how to use this strategy to develop and write word problems, challenging students to create problems that are neither too easy nor too difficult for their classmates to solve. (Teacher may suggest adding extra information or data to the problems to increase their difficulty.)

Practice 2:* Write Your Own Problems

Students use *organizational planning* to develop word problems involving addition. Then students work in small groups, taking turns to read their word problems aloud while other group members write down information needed to solve each problem and solve the problems.

Preparation 3: What Do You Know About Perimeter?

Teacher asks students how they would find out the distance around the sides of the classroom, the school cafeteria, the playground, the parking lot, and other familiar locations. Students can work in teams to actually measure the sides of the classroom or other school locations. Teacher reviews names and provides example of these shapes: *square, rectangle, triangle.*

Presentation 3: Shapes and Sizes of Objects

Teacher defines *perimeter* as the distance around the outside of an object, provides examples, asks students for additional examples, and writes them on the board. Teacher elicits from students the rule for calculating perimeter (add the lengths of the sides of the object).

Teacher gives learning strategy reminder: *I'm going to describe a shape or object and give its measurements. Use* selective attention *to listen for the important information, then use* imagery *to draw a diagram of the shape or object. Then find the perimeter for each shape or object.*

Practice 3:* Finding the Perimeter

Teacher dictates the following listening text, and students draw diagrams, write measurements, and find the perimeter for each object:

1. Draw a square with one side equal to 27 inches. Find the perimeter.
2. Draw a rectangle with a length of 38 inches and a width of 13 inches. Find the perimeter.
3. Draw a triangle with all 3 sides the same length. The length of one side is 956 inches. What is the perimeter?

Evaluation: Complete a Learning Log on Solving Addition Problems

Students complete a Learning Log identifying what they have learned in the unit, including concepts, vocabulary, problem-solving procedures, language, and learning strategies. (See Science Unit pages 217–219 for a sample Learning Log.) Teacher leads a class discussion of Learning Logs, asking students to describe verbally their problem-solving strategies and encouraging students to share different ways of solving problems.

Expansion: Find Out More About Addition Problems

Teacher conducts debriefing discussion of what has been learned in unit. Students work beyond the immediate problem to apply what they have learned to a new situation. For example, students can bring addition problems to class that they experience in other content classrooms or in their home. Another way to expand on the students' knowledge is to use scaffolding, in which some of the cues for the problem-solving steps are removed. For example, students could solve problems using the five problem-solving steps by writing them on a blank piece of paper, rather than being provided with a paper that has QUESTION, DATA, etc. on it.

ASSESSMENT

The following types of student products and teacher assessment can be included in student portfolios for informal assessment:

1. Work sheets with sample problems.
2. Assignments to explain problem-solving procedures verbally or in writing.
3. Assignments to write their own problems.
4. Performance measures in which students construct a product in which mathematics has been used.
5. Student Learning Logs completed during Evaluation phase.
6. Other types of self-evaluation of their successes and difficulties in learning mathematics. The following suggested activities are based on the notion that student writing in all content areas is useful for gaining a better understanding and control over concepts and processes. The approach here is adapted from Kennedy.[37]
   a. Students write a daily letter to the teacher in which they note what they are learning in the math classroom. In their letters, students respond to three questions: (1) What did you understand (with examples) about the work in class today? (2) What don't you understand (with examples)? (3) What questions would you like to ask? Information in the letters can be used to address items not understood and questions students would like to ask. Students should be encouraged to verbalize questions identified in their letters to gain practice with asking questions in class. The teacher may also write comments on students' letters, as in a Dialogue Journal.
   b. Students keep Learning Logs in which they maintain a record of their learning on a weekly basis or at the end of each unit. This type of Learning Log is less structured than the sample Learning Log provided in the Science Unit, and provides an opportunity for the students to write summaries of what they are learning in class. The Log can address three types of questions that are linked to CALLA objectives: (1) What new math concepts did you learn? (2) What strategies did you learn for solv-

ing problems? What strategies worked best? With which kind of problem did they work? (3) What new vocabulary or language in math did you learn? The Learning Log can also include interpretive notes or comments by students on their attitudes about learning mathematics.

c. Once a week, the teacher can have students write a Process Report to indicate the problem-solving process they used to solve a specific problem. Students use the five-point problem-solving checklist to guide their description. The Process Reports can be rated on the following 4-1 scale:

4 = Student can explain the process used to solve the problem and got the correct answer;

3 = Student can explain the process used to solve the problem but made a computation error;

2 = Student is unable to explain the problem-solving process but got the correct answer;

1 = Student approached the problem but was unable to get the answer correct or explain the problem-solving process;

0 = No obvious strategy to solve the problem and did not get the correct answer.

STUDENT PAGES

Practice 1

Plan What to Do: Draw a Picture

A. Sometimes drawing a picture makes it easier to know what to do. This is part of planning. You can make the picture any way you want.

Look at the sample problem. The question is underlined and rewritten, with space for the answer. Finish the problem and write the answer. Then do the four problems below.

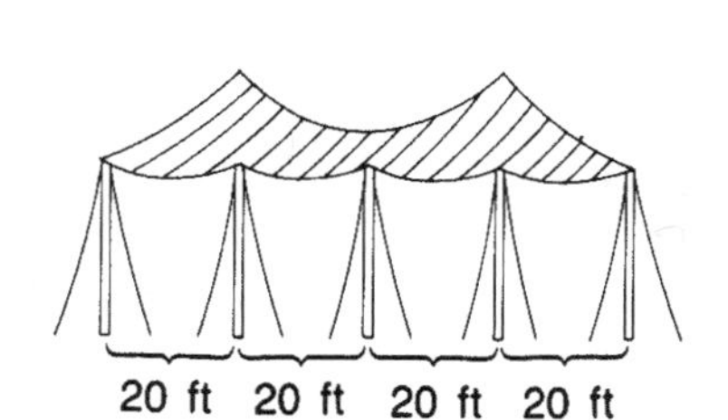

(Draw your picture here.)

Sample problem: A large circus tent has 5 poles from one end to the other end. The poles are 20 feet apart. **How long is the tent?**

Rewrite the question: The tent is _____ long.

B. Do these problems. Work by yourself.

1. Juan has a model train set with one engine, 3 passenger cars, and a caboose. How many cars are on the train altogether?

   Rewrite the question: ____________________

2. Nu Trinh is 56 inches tall. Her mother is 4 inches taller. How tall is Nu Trinh's mother?

   Rewrite the question: ____________________

3. María had 3 posters. On her birthday, each of her four friends gave her a poster. How many posters did she have altogether?

   Rewrite the question: ____________________

4. Tran was reading a book called *The Planet Earth.* He learned that there are 2 planets that are closer to the sun than the Earth is. Six planets are farther from the sun than the Earth is. How many planets are in the solar system altogether?

   Rewrite the question: ____________________

C. Share your drawings with a small group of friends. Did they have the same kinds of drawings as you? Did your pictures help you understand the problems? How?

Practice 2

Write Your Own Problems

Now it is your turn to write your own addition word problems. Follow these steps:

1. Organize your ideas.
2. Write a word problem.
3. Read your problem to two friends. Solve each other's problems.
4. Check your answers with your friends.

A. Organize your ideas. First choose an addition equation.

Examples: 33 + 82 = 115   264 + 367 = 631

Then think of a story to go with the equation.

Examples: My brother has 33 records and my dad has 82.
José had 264 stamps in his stamp collection. His uncle gave him 367 more stamps.

B. Write a word problem. First write the story you thought about. Then write a question to go with the story. Remember to use words that tell what math operation to use.

Examples: How many records do they have altogether?
How many stamps does José have in all?

C. Now try writing other addition word problems.

Problem 1

Addition equation: ______________________________

Story: ______________________________

____

Question: ______________________________

Problem 2

Addition equation: ______________________________

Story: ______________________________

____

Question: ______________________________

Practice 2 (continued)

Problem 3

Addition equation: ______________________________

Story: ______________________________

____

Question: ______________________________

Problem 4

Addition equation: ______________________________

Story: ______________________________

____

Question: ______________________________

D. Sit with two friends. Take turns reading your problems and solving them. Read your problems aloud. As you read, your friends will write down the important numbers. Then they will solve your problems. When it is your turn to solve their problems, remember to use the 5-Point Checklist.

Use this space to solve your friends' problems.

E. Now work with your two friends to check your work. (You may use a calculator.) How many correct answers did you

have? ________ Which problems were easy? ________

Difficult? ________ Look again at the problems that were difficult. Decide why they were difficult. Is the math too hard? Are the words too hard? Write a sentence that tells what was difficult.

____

Practice 3

A. The distance around the outside of an object is called the **perimeter.** The object can be a picture, a bulletin board, a park, a baseball field, or anything that has sides. It can also be a figure such as a square, a triangle, or a rectangle. We use measurements of length and distance to find the perimeter.

Rule: To find the perimeter of an object or figure, add the lengths of its sides together.

Example: José ran around the outside of a field. How far did he run?

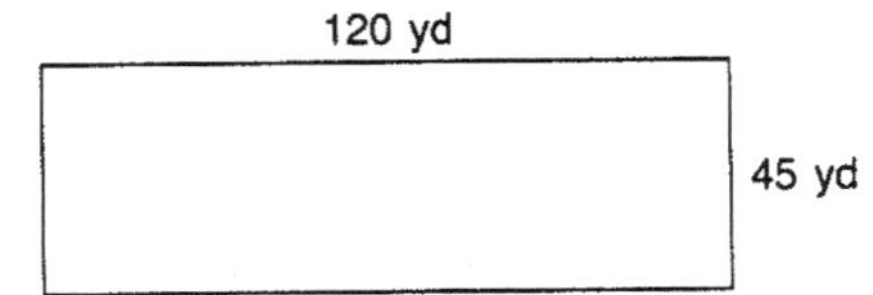

We add the lengths of the four sides to get the total distance around the field:

$$\begin{array}{r} 120 \\ 45 \\ 120 \\ +\ 45 \\ \hline 330 \end{array}$$

José ran 330 yards.

B. Now your teacher will read some perimeter problems. Draw a picture of the object or figure. Write down the numbers that tell the lengths of the sides. Then solve the problem.

1. Draw a picture and write the numbers:

   Write the answer: ____________

2. Draw a picture and write the numbers:

   Write the answer: ____________

3. Draw a picture and write the numbers:

CHAPTER 11
CALLA Social Studies

Overview

The academic language and prior knowledge background needed makes this a difficult subject for ESL students.

Description of the Social Studies Curriculum

- Curriculum Objectives
- Knowledge About History, Geography, and Culture
- Democratic and Civic Values
- Study Skills, Social Skills, and Thinking Skills
- Scope and Sequence

What's Difficult in Social Studies for ESL Students?

- Conceptual Understanding
- Vocabulary
- Language Functions and Discourse
- Structures
- Academic Language Skills
- Study Skills and Learning Strategies

Teaching Guidelines for CALLA Social Studies

- Students' Prior Knowledge
- Identify Content Objectives
- Develop Academic Language Activities
- Integrate Learning Strategy Instruction
- Instructional Sequence

Model Social Studies Unit

CHAPTER 11 CALLA SOCIAL STUDIES

CONTENT AREA OF MAJOR IMPORTANCE in the curriculum is social studies, referred to by some educators as social science. The study of history, geography, government, and civics falls within the curricular area of social studies. While social studies is an area of intrinsic interest for many ESL teachers, the academic language and prior knowledge background needed for learning about social studies in the middle and upper grades make this a difficult subject for many ESL students.

Description of the Social Studies Curriculum

An understanding of the objectives, scope, and sequence of the social studies curriculum is essential for planning social studies topics to include in a CALLA program. Since the CALLA teacher cannot duplicate the entire grade-level social studies curriculum, the selection of major topics needs to be based on an understanding of the complete curriculum. (See Chapter 2 for guidelines for selecting content.)

The social studies curriculum seeks to help students understand themselves and others by learning how people live now, how they have lived in the past, how society has developed in different regions of the world, how geography has affected people's lives, and how both change and continuity are constants in the human story. An important outcome of social studies in American schools is to develop in students an understanding of democratic values, of the need for responsible citizenship, and of how they themselves can become responsible citizens as adults. To accomplish these goals, the social studies curriculum seeks to impart both historical and geographical knowledge and an understanding of the ethics and values inherent in a democratic society. Another objective of the social studies curriculum is to teach various procedural skills that will assist students in acquiring and using the knowledge and values studied. These procedural skills include both study skills and social skills.

While curriculum writers and teachers may include procedural skills as an important component of social studies, the amount of factual information included in textbooks can make students view social studies as consisting of declarative knowledge that must be "learned." A recent study conducted interviews with upper elementary students about their experiences in math and social studies, and found considerable differences in student's descriptions of types of activities in the subject areas and in their attitudes towards each of them.[1] This study confirmed previous descriptions of instructional practices in these two subject areas. Social studies classrooms tend to be more varied than math classrooms in both goals and activities. Objectives may include mastery of factual information, comprehension of text, research procedures, problem solving, and the development of attitudes and social skills. Activities in social studies classes can include reading the textbook, listening to information presented orally by the teacher, working in groups, and doing projects and simulations. This contrasts with typical math classrooms in which the teacher explains a mathematical procedure to the whole class and then students practice the procedure individually, using worksheets or the textbook. In spite of the variety of activities in social studies classes, however, students had generally negative attitudes towards this subject; positive attitudes were expressed only when the content was personally interesting to students. This attitude contrasted with students' concerns in mathematics for the level of difficulty of the material and their own success with it. In math the questions were, "How difficult is it?" and "Did I get it right?" In social studies the question was, "Was it fun or was it boring?" Math was viewed as important and relevant, whereas social studies was judged on its entertainment value.

This study clearly points to the need for social studies curriculum content that students perceive as important, and to an instructional approach that is relevant as well as intrinsically interesting. In this section we describe a curriculum designed to help students understand why social studies is important and how it relates to their own lives and interests. We have selected the *California History-Social Science Framework*[2] as exemplary of the objectives and content that are meaningful not only to native English-speaking students but also to students learning English in a CALLA program.

CURRICULUM OBJECTIVES

The California History-Social Science Framework includes three major types of goals: (1) knowledge and cultural understanding; (2) democratic understanding and civic values; and (3) skills attainment and social participation. The concepts and skills identified in other representative social studies curricula can also be classified within these three major goals. In this section we identify types of curricular content which are designed to accomplish these goals.

KNOWLEDGE ABOUT HISTORY, GEOGRAPHY, AND CULTURE

The emphasis in social studies content is on the history and geography of different peoples and places. Some aspects of political science, economics, sociology, psychology, and anthropology are often integrated into the social studies curriculum in the middle and upper grades. Content from the humanities may also be included in order to highlight the importance of the cultural achievements in different human eras.

The traditional approach to teaching social studies has stressed the importance of acquiring basic factual knowledge about historical events and geographical features. More recent social studies approaches seek to teach not only historical and geographical literacy, but also to develop concepts with universal applications, such as concern for ethics and human rights, the nature of culture and its relationship to history, the interaction between people and the environment, the interdependence of peoples and nations, and comparisons of different political and economic systems. Such concepts are not learned as simple declarative knowledge, but rather as complex schemata which are developed over a period of years. This type of conceptual development in social studies requires active and thoughtful participation by students, which can be facilitated through activities involving the use of learning strategies and academic language skills. Current approaches to social studies instruction recognize the importance of students' background knowledge and focus on strategic teaching and learning.[3]

DEMOCRATIC AND CIVIC VALUES

A second major goal of the social studies curriculum is to develop students' understanding of democracy both as a political system and as a system of human values. Students need to understand that the United States is a multicultural society, a nation of immigrants. Appreciating common beliefs in values such as equality and political freedom is as important as appreciating the diversity of Americans. Students also need to comprehend that even though these common values have not always been practiced, they nevertheless continue to symbolize our identity as a nation.

In order to understand democracy, students must learn how the Constitution came to be, its historical antecedents, its provisions, and how it has been amended to safeguard the rights of all citizens. In addition to gaining a clear concept of the principles of democracy, students also need to understand how democracy works on an everyday level. This practical understanding of democracy can best be achieved by engaging in democratic processes in the school and classroom, including debates, cooperation, respect for differing opinions, representation, voting, and elections of representatives. These personal experiences with democratic processes need to be related to both historical and current events in the local community, the nation, and the world.

Thus, the goal of developing democratic and civic values is achieved through a combination of conceptual understanding and hands-on practice, in both of which learning strategies and academic language play important roles.

An understanding of the Consititution is key to understanding democracy.

STUDY SKILLS, SOCIAL SKILLS, AND THINKING SKILLS

In addition to developing knowledge and understanding of historical, geographical, cultural, and democratic concepts, the social studies curriculum is also designed to teach procedural knowledge essential to the discipline. This procedural knowledge includes both traditional study skills and the social skills needed for participation in cooperative and democratic activities. Study skills include: social studies reading and listening skills; academic communication skills; map, graph, globe, table, picture, and chart skills; information-locating skills for both print and non-print resources; and report writing skills.

Social skills include group discussion skills, the ability to argue a point of view, the ability to work cooperatively with classmates, and skill in participating in classroom and school democratic processes such as elections and debates.

Many social studies curricula also include the development of thinking skills through activities in which students discuss and define problems, seek alternative solutions, and justify the problem solution chosen. Other critical thinking skills might involve students in identifying bias and propaganda, or judging the truth value of information encountered.

The procedural skills included in the social studies curriculum should not be neglected, for students can apply these skills to other academic areas and to their lives outside of school. Study skills, social participation skills, and critical thinking skills help students become lifelong learners.

SCOPE AND SEQUENCE

The content of social studies and the sequence in which it is presented is similar in most curriculum guides and state frameworks. Young children begin by learning about their immediate environment of family, school, and neighborhood. The scope expands in middle grades to include their city, state, and nation, and they begin to learn about life in other parts of the world and in other periods of history. United States history is typically taught at three levels: fifth grade, eighth grade, and eleventh grade. World regions, ancient civilizations, world history, political geography, and government (citizenship) are other content areas generally found in the social studies curriculum.

The California framework has modified this traditional sequence in order to allow for depth rather than breadth of coverage.[4] This is accomplished by identifying topics and themes which merit in-depth and extended study, and by eliminating a great deal of the repetition of topics typically re-taught at different grade levels. For example, instead of presenting an overview of American history in fifth, eighth, and eleventh grades, American history is presented *chronologically*. The fifth grade curriculum focuses on early inhabitants and settlers in North America and the development of a new nation, with a preview of later events in U.S. history. In the eighth grade, students briefly review early American history, then continue their study by learning about the Constitution and the development of the country to 1850, and conclude with a preview of modern U.S. history. This sequence of brief review of earlier periods followed by concentrated study of the next chronological period is continued in eleventh grade, where the focus is on U.S. history in the twentieth century. A similar chronological approach to world history is recommended, beginning in sixth grade with ancient civilizations in different areas of the world, and continuing in seventh grade with medieval societies in Europe, Africa, Asia, and America. In seventh grade, students also learn about early modern Europe and the age of exploration, which leads them to their study of the birth and early development of the United States in eighth grade. World history is continued in the tenth grade with an in-depth study of events and ideas of the modern world.

Another innovation in the California framework is the introduction of history at the primary grade-level through stories, folk tales, and legends. The objective is to engage young children's interest in history through children's literature about other times and places, thus preparing students for a formal introduction to history with the fourth grade curriculum focus on state history.

For CALLA teachers it is important to understand both the scope and the sequence of their local social studies curriculum so that they select the history and geography content that will best prepare their students for grade-level study of this subject. This is especially true in a chronological curriculum such as the one outlined above, where students will be expected to have knowledge about historical periods prior to the one under study.

Description of the Social Studies Curriculum

- Promotes knowledge and cultural understanding, democratic and civic values, and skills attainment and social participation.
- Stresses historical and geographical literacy, important concepts about human society, approaches to solving problems.
- Teaches democracy's development, values, and current practice in the U.S.A.
- Designed to teach procedural knowledge (study skills and social skills) needed for participation in cooperative and democratic activities.
- Scope and Sequence align to school district's curriculum by grade level; presents historical events chronologically.

What's Difficult in Social Studies for ESL Students?

Because the social studies curriculum requires a high level of literacy and because the concepts developed often deal with abstract ideas rooted in philosophy, anthropology, political science, and economics, we suggest that this content area be introduced to ESL students after they have had some experience with science and mathematics lessons in the CALLA program.

Since social studies depends so heavily on language, ESL students encounter many difficulties in understanding information presented by the teacher. Even more difficult to understand is the generally decontextualized language that needs to be read in social studies textbooks. Information in social studies texts is often presented without the level of explanation needed for students to identify causes and make connections between different events.[5] In addition to understanding the language used to discuss social studies topics, students must also be able to discuss the concepts being developed, and acquire competence in the skills taught. In this section we identify some typical difficulties related to conceptual understanding, language, and learning strategies that ESL students may encounter in social studies classes.

CONCEPTUAL UNDERSTANDING

As discussed in the preceding section on the scope and sequence of the social studies curriculum, the topics studied in social studies begin to move away from the student's personal experience by third or fourth grade. In order to travel backward in time and outward to distant areas of the world, students need to develop concepts of time, chronology, distance, and differing ways of life. While some ESL students may come with a rich understanding of the history, geography, and culture of their native country, others may have only a superficial familiarity with their country's story and physical setting. And in some cases, students may harbor misconceptions or lack of a knowledge foundation due to limited educational opportunities in their native country. Many ESL students have never studied world history and geography, and most have little knowledge about the history, institutions, geography, and culture of the United States. CALLA teachers need to be concerned about these types of gaps in their students' prior knowledge and seek ways to provide the background knowledge framework that students will need in grade-level classrooms. Social studies can be an important tool assisting the acculturation process of ESL students by providing both explicit and implicit information about everyday American culture and values.[6]

VOCABULARY

As in other disciplines, a specialized vocabulary exists for social studies which students need to learn in order to discuss and report on the ideas presented. As an example of the vocabulary required for just one area of social studies, the state of Maryland lists 94 technical terms which students are expected to learn as preparation for a competency exam in citizenship required for high school graduation. As students move up through the grades, the social studies vocabulary becomes increasingly difficult because of the complexity of the concepts it represents. Words like *democracy* and *representation*, for example, are more than simple vocabulary items because they stand for a complex set of ideas developed from a philosophy of government which may be unfamiliar to an ESL student. The following paragraph from a study guide for high school students, while written fairly simply from the grammatical point of view, illustrates the density of words which stand for important concepts.[7]

> Federalism means the division of governmental powers between the national and state governments. Both levels of government may act directly on citizens through their own officials and laws. Both levels of government derive their power to act from our Constitution. Each level of government has certain subjects over which its powers are supreme. Both levels of government must agree to changes in the Constitution.

LANGUAGE FUNCTIONS AND DISCOURSE

As with other academic subjects, the language functions in social studies include both lower and higher-order thinking skills. Functions such as informing, describing, and explaining are central to social studies instruction, but students are also asked to analyze, compare, contrast, and make judgments about social studies information.

Expository discourse is used to present facts and concepts in social studies. The usual pattern is to begin with a series of chronological events, as in history, or clusters of related facts, as in geography. This initial presentation is frequently followed by or integrated with a discussion of the causes, effects, and evolution of the events or facts described. Students are encouraged to make inferences about meanings, relationships, and unifying concepts. This type of discourse is substantially different both in organization and in content from the narrative discourse found in ESL textbooks and readers which may constitute a ESL student's total previous experience with extended text in English.

STRUCTURES

In social studies textbooks, long sentences with multiple embedded clauses are found even at the elementary level, and difficult sentences increase at upper grade levels. Cause and effect statements are frequent, and a common stylistic variant is to begin sentences with the *because* phrase. While this may be chronologically logical, it is grammatically difficult because ESL students may be accustomed to finding the subject of a sentence close to its beginning, rather than in its second clause. The following examples from third and fourth grade textbooks illustrate this point:

> Because there will be more people in the world in the future, we will need more land on which to build towns and cities.[8]
>
> Because wheat is so often used to make bread, Kansas is called the Breadbasket of America.[9]

Social studies texts also use various tense forms and markings in historical narrative to describe temporal relationships to the period being studied. Examples from sixth grade textbooks (with verb and verb phrase underlining added) illustrate the variety of tense forms found in historical texts:

"I <u>found</u> Rome a city of bricks and <u>left</u> it a city of marble." Augustus <u>is supposed to have spoken</u> these words as he <u>lay dying</u>. He <u>was</u> Rome's first emperor, and <u>started</u> the first of its great building programs. He <u>claimed</u> that he <u>had had</u> over 80 temples rebuilt.[10]

> Ivan III <u>decided</u> that Moscow <u>need</u> no longer <u>fear</u> the Mongols. He <u>knew</u> that Moscow <u>had grown</u> stronger and the Mongols <u>had grown</u> weaker. They <u>had given up</u> the ways of Batu. They no longer <u>dwelled</u> in tents on the steppes, but in their own city at Kazan.[11]

In the first passage, the verb forms used clarify the sequence of past events, but the variety of forms and use of complex structures such as is *supposed to have spoken* and *had had* could make comprehension difficult for an ESL student. Likewise in the second passage, simple past tense, subjunctive (*need...fear*), and past perfect need to be understood in order to make sense of the text.

Another structural feature used frequently in social studies textbooks is the use of pronouns such as *it* or *they* as referents to previously cited people, events, facts, or conclusions. When a sentence starts with *it*, the less proficient English reader may have difficulty in identifying what it refers to without going back to the previous sentence or even to a previous paragraph.

ACADEMIC LANGUAGE SKILLS

Emphasis on particular language skills in social studies may vary with the grade level and the teacher, but in general students must be able to learn primarily through listening and reading, and to express understanding of the facts and concepts presented through participation in class discussions and through written communication. Language input is often decontextualized, dealing with abstract ideas and information removed in space and time from students' own experiences. Table 11.1 describes the use of the four language skills in the social studies classroom at different grade levels. As this table demonstrates, some classroom language activities such as understanding explanations, answering questions, and asking for clarification are important at all grade levels. The more cognitively demanding tasks of the higher grade levels require a high degree of literacy, because in these grades students must be able to read to learn and to write to express learning. This table can be used by the teacher preparing CALLA lessons to identify types of academic language activities to include at different grade levels.

STUDY SKILLS AND LEARNING STRATEGIES

As described in the previous section, study skills, thinking skills, and social skills are important components of the social studies curriculum. ESL students may not have developed the learning strategies that underlie these skills, and thus may encounter difficulties when asked to read a map or chart, or to present information by constructing a graph. Library location skills need to be learned when students have previously not had access to a library. Strategies for listening, reading, recalling, and writing are essential in coping with the extensive information presented in grade-level social studies classrooms.

The preceding discussion has provided an indication of the range of experiential and language-related difficulties that ESL students may encounter in the area of social studies. In the next section of this chapter, we suggest ways in which CALLA teachers can help students profit from social studies instruction in various ways.

Dealing with abstract and unfamiliar information and concepts can be difficult for ESL students.

Table 11.1
Language Skills Required by Social Studies

Language Skills	Grades 1-3	Grades 4-6	Grades 7-12
Listening			
1. Understand explanations without concrete referents.	M	M	M
2. Listen for specific information.	L	P	M
Reading			
1. Understand specialized vocabulary.	L	P	M
2. Understand information in textbook.	L	P	M
3. Find information from graphs, charts, tables, and maps.	L	P	M
5. Find information in reference materials.	L	P	M
6. Adjust reading rate for different purposes (e.g., skim, scan, re-read).	L	P	M
Speaking			
1. Answer questions.	M	M	M
2. Ask questions for clarification.	M	M	M
3. Participate in group and class discussions.	M	P	P
4. Present oral reports.	L	P	P
Writing			
1. Write answers to questions.	L	M	M
2. Label maps, graphs, and charts.	M	P	L
3. Contribute to group reports.	P	P	P
4. Write research reports.	L	P	M

less emphasis	partial emphasis	more emphasis
L	P	M

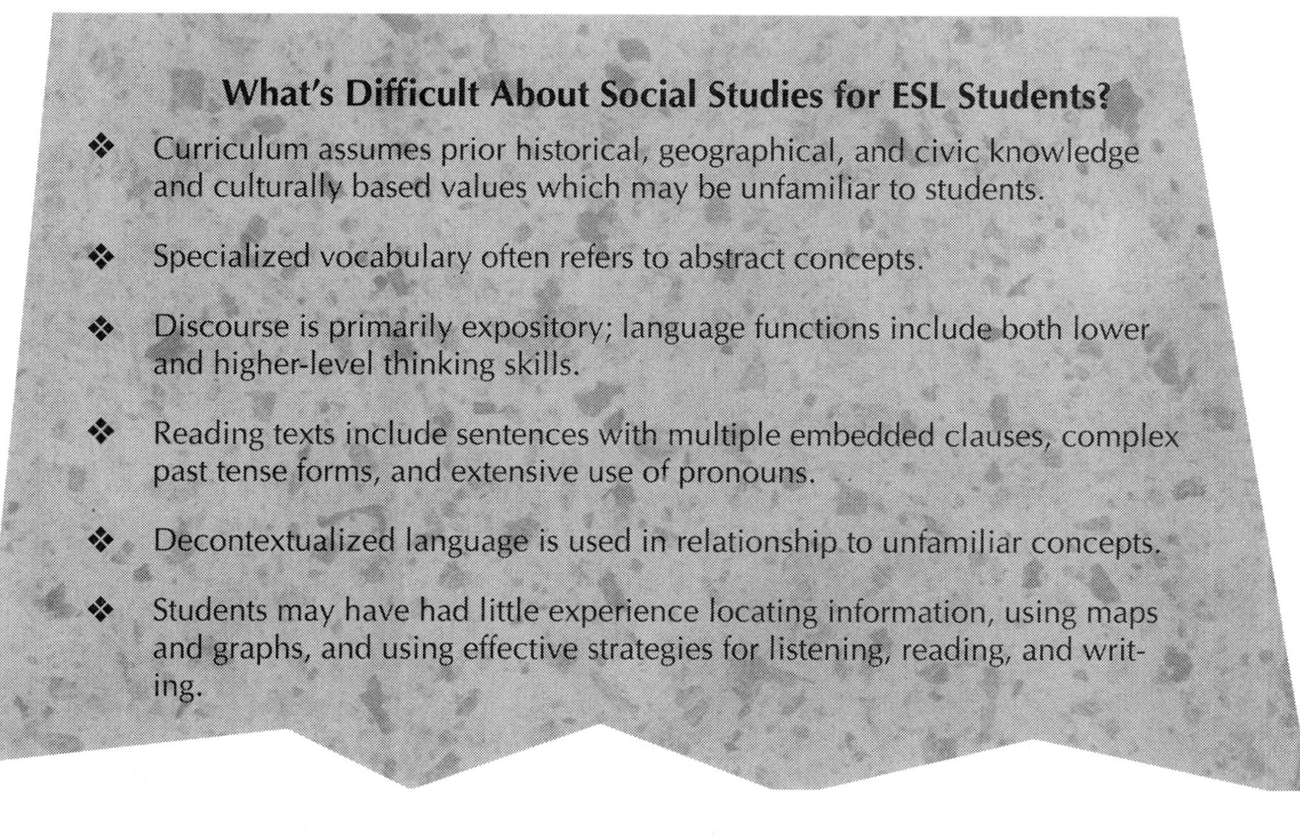

What's Difficult About Social Studies for ESL Students?

- ❖ Curriculum assumes prior historical, geographical, and civic knowledge and culturally based values which may be unfamiliar to students.
- ❖ Specialized vocabulary often refers to abstract concepts.
- ❖ Discourse is primarily expository; language functions include both lower and higher-level thinking skills.
- ❖ Reading texts include sentences with multiple embedded clauses, complex past tense forms, and extensive use of pronouns.
- ❖ Decontextualized language is used in relationship to unfamiliar concepts.
- ❖ Students may have had little experience locating information, using maps and graphs, and using effective strategies for listening, reading, and writing.

Teaching Guidelines for CALLA Social Studies

CALLA social studies lessons should be designed to prepare students for grade-level classrooms by providing experiences with content and academic language appropriate to their prior knowledge and developmental level. History, geography, and civics are also curricular areas in which students can learn and practice important learning strategies and study skills. Rather than learning merely names and dates in social studies, students should gain an understanding of the social and geographical context in which events occurred and the causal relationships between context and events.

STUDENTS' PRIOR KNOWLEDGE

As we have indicated in earlier chapters, discovering students' background knowledge about a topic is an essential first step in CALLA instruction. In the case of geography, for example, teachers need to find out what map skills students have and the amount of knowledge they have about the geography of their native countries and of the current home area. In history, teachers need to explore students' concept of time and their knowledge of historical events in their own and other countries. The following types of activities can be used to elicit and build on students' prior knowledge of geography and history:

ACTIVITY: WHAT DO WE KNOW ABOUT GEOGRAPHY?

Display a large world map. Use a different color pushpin and matching yarn for each country represented in your class. Have students mark their city or town of origin with a pushpin, then use the matching yarn to trace their trip to their current home. Intermediate stops should be marked with additional pushpins. Students may need to interview family members for details of their journeys to the United States. Have students contribute geographical information about their countries, such as climate, cities, land forms, products, way of life. Provide reference materials (atlas and encyclopedia) and show students how to find additional information. Discuss with students how geography affected their lives in their native countries, and how geography affects their lives where they are presently living. Develop with students the concept that geography is the study of the interaction between people and the environment in which they live. Explain to students that thinking about what they already know about geography will help them learn new geographical information and skills; using prior knowledge, or *elaboration,* is an important learning strategy.

ACTIVITY: WHAT DO WE KNOW ABOUT HISTORY?

Discuss with students their own family histories, and have them make timelines showing the important events in their own family's story. Have them interview family members to get as much information as possible about the lives of their parents and grandparents (and great grandparents, if possible). Show students how to count backwards with dates, how to find a person's birth date by subtracting their age from the current date, how to estimate dates in their family story where precise dates are not available. Have students discuss their family timelines and find similarities in their family stories. Then ask students to contribute information about historical events in their native countries. Make a class timeline that incorporates all of the historical events (and as many family events as applicable) and discuss which events happened at about the same time, earlier, or later in the different countries. Develop with students the concept that history is the study of how people lived in different times and places—and that history includes not only the lives of famous people but also the lives of ordinary people. Explain to students that thinking about what they already know about history will help them learn new historical information and skills; using prior knowledge, or *elaboration*, is an important learning strategy.

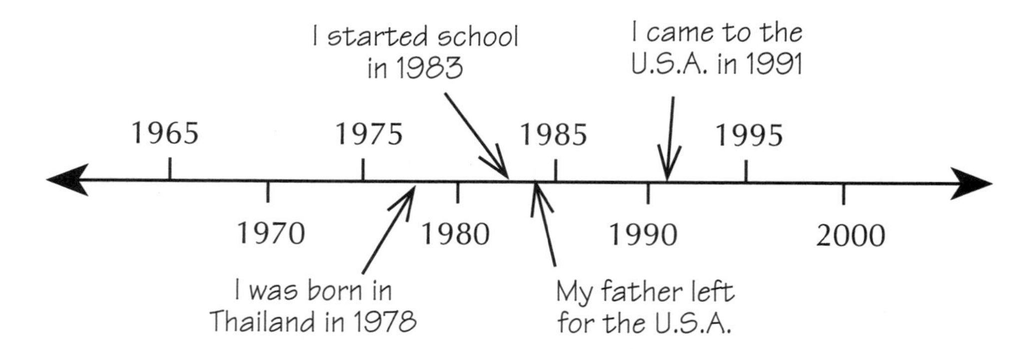

Have students make time lines showing the important events in their own family's story.

IDENTIFY CONTENT OBJECTIVES

Social studies content objectives are drawn from the school district or state curriculum framework. (See Chapter 2 for suggestions on selecting high priority content from the adopted curriculum.) Objectives selected for CALLA lessons should include both declarative and procedural knowledge. That is, students should not only acquire social science concepts, but should also practice "how to" or application skills used by social scientists. In addition, social studies content objectives should encompass both lower and higher-order thinking skills. Examples of content objectives are as follows:

- Use a map of North America to answer questions about geographical land forms.
- Construct a timeline that shows major events/developments between 300 B.C. and A.D. 500 in a western and non-western civilization.
- Explain why early civilizations developed near rivers.
- Draw a semantic map that illustrates causes and effects of the Civil War.
- Describe the powers exercised by each branch of the United States government.
- Identify major inventions of the following civilizations: Sumer; Ancient Egypt; Maya; Ghana; Han Dynasty; Ancient Rome.
- Observe a set of ancient artifacts (facsimiles or photographs) and deduce their functions.
- Conduct a class opinion survey about an environmental issue.

DEVELOP ACADEMIC LANGUAGE ACTIVITIES

Content topics selected for CALLA social studies lessons should determine the types of language activities which need to be included. (See Chapter 3 for guidelines on selecting and teaching academic language.) As with other content subjects, language activities for social studies should further the development of concepts and skills that are specifically related to the topics studied. Because social studies topics tend to deal with abstract ideas and events removed from students' own experiences, care should be taken to provide contextual support in language activities. Illustrations, posters, maps, globes, timelines, and models are essential materials in social studies classrooms. The school library and social studies department can further enrich the CALLA social studies classroom with photographs, reproductions of historical paintings, films and videos, facsimiles of original documents, and recordings of speeches, songs, and narratives. Following are examples of activities which can assist in developing academic language for social studies:

- Reading and listening to historical narratives, geographical descriptions, and newspaper articles about current and past events; reading and listening to stories about historical personages, biographies, letters, and diaries; reading facsimiles of historical documents; reading reference and library books on social studies topics; identifying, explaining, and using social studies vocabulary and terminology.
- Discussing current and past events; making individual and group presentations about historical or geographical topics; playing games to learn and practice recall of social studies information; role playing important historical events; debating political and economic issues; inventing "what if" stories (e.g., What if Columbus had never reached America?).
- Writing study questions; taking notes; writing outlines; developing summaries; writing opinions about current and past events; researching and writing reports; keeping journals and learning logs about social studies topics; writing geographical descriptions; writing persuasive texts, scripts, ads, puzzles, and riddles; writing stories about people in other times and places.

INTEGRATE LEARNING STRATEGY INSTRUCTION

Students need to learn a variety of strategies if they are to understand and remember social studies content and skills. (See Chapter 4 for guidelines on selecting and teaching learning strategies.) Learning strategies taught as part of the CALLA social studies program should build on strategic strengths students bring to the class and introduce additional strategies that students will be able to use later in grade level classrooms. Often teachers need to identify strategies students are already using and call students' attention to them. To teach new strategies, teachers should name them and provide a rationale for their usefulness. As described in Chapter 4, the teacher's modeling of strategies is a highly effective way of demonstrating learning strategies in action. In practicing previously introduced strategies, the teacher can scaffold instruction by reminding students of the strategy's name and asking them to identify the strategy they are using. Table 11.2 identifies major learning strategies that are useful in social studies, and provides samples of questions that students can ask themselves to prompt strategy use.

The activities suggested below demonstrate how learning strategies can be practiced in social studies.

PRACTICING READING STRATEGIES IN SOCIAL STUDIES

1. Start by eliciting students' prior knowledge (*elaboration*) about the topic to be read. This might include brainstorming, developing a graphic organizer such as a semantic map, and/or previewing important vocabulary.
2. Have students preview the text (*advance organization*) by looking through a chapter or unit before reading it in order to get a general idea of the topics covered and how they are interrelated. Have students look at photographs and their captions, section headings, maps, graphs, and discussion questions in the text or in margins. Ask students to identify some of the main ideas they will encounter in the text. Remind students of the name of the learning strategy they have just used (*previewing* or *advance organization*).
3. Have students scan the text (*selective attention*) for specific information and identify main ideas, such as people and dates in a history text or geographical features and resources in a geography text. Encourage students to use *imagery* to visualize events and places. Ask students to identify the name of the strategy they have just used (*scanning, reading selectively*, or *selective attention; visualizing* or *making mental pictures*) and to explain how it helps them understand a text.
4. Identify or have students identify new words in the text and have them use context clues to guess at their meanings (*inferencing*). Discuss the use of this strategy.
5. *Note-taking* and *summarizing* are two additional strategies that can assist in the recall of material read. Students can use these strategies to retell the information in a text in oral or written form. Other ways to reformulate historical or geographical information include making semantic maps (such as spider maps or T-Lists) that identify major points to be remembered.

LEARNING SOCIAL STUDIES VOCABULARY

1. Have students classify new words according to functions or semantic categories (*grouping*). This strategy can be combined with *imagery*, in which students make a mental or actual picture of the word or concept to be remembered. Have students discuss their use of these strategies.

Table 11.2

LEARNING STRATEGIES FOR SOCIAL STUDIES

Metacognitive Strategies:	Students plan, monitor, and evaluate their learning of social studies concepts and skills.
Advance Organization	Can the title and section headings help me understand this text?
Selective Attention	What is the most important information to pay attention to?
Organizational Planning	What's my purpose for reading, listening, speaking or writing? How should I organize my report or presentation? How do I begin and end? What's the best sequence of ideas?
Self-monitoring	Am I understanding this? Does it make sense? Am I achieving my purpose? How is this task going? Do I need to make any changes right now?
Self-assessment	Did I understand this information? What was the main point I got from reading or listening? What revisions are necessary? Do I need more information? Should I re-read?
Cognitive Strategies:	Students interact with social studies concepts and skills, changing or organizing the material to understand and learn it.
Resourcing	Where can I find additional information about this topic? Atlas? Encyclopedia? History book? Library?
Elaborating Prior Knowledge	What do I already know about this country or period? What experiences have I had that are related to this? How does this information relate to other things I know about history, geography, or government?
Taking Notes	What's the best way to write down this information? Outline? Chart? List? Diagram? Geographical map? Timeline?
Grouping	How can I classify this information? Can I organize this information graphically?
Making Inferences	What does this word or phrase probably mean? What clues can I use? What predictions can I make?
Summarizing	What's the most important information to remember about this topic? Should my summary be oral, written, or mental?
Using Imagery	What can I learn from the illustrations, diagrams, and maps in the text? Can I draw something to help me understand this information? Can I make a mental picture or visualize this event or place?
Linguistic Transfer	Are there any geographical terms or historical names that I recognize because of their similarity to my native language?
Social/Affective Strategies:	Students interact with peers, teachers, and other adults to assist learning, or use attitudes or feelings to assist learning.
Questioning for Clarification	Who should I ask for additional explanation or correction or suggestions? How should I ask?
Cooperating	How can I work with friends or classmates to understand this or complete this task or improve what I have written or presented orally?
Self-talk	Yes, I can do this—I just need the right strategies!

2. *Cooperation* is a useful strategy for vocabulary learning because students can work together to brainstorm possible word meanings, analyze the meanings of new words, look up definitions in dictionaries, quiz each other, or work together on crossword puzzles. Again, remind students of the reasons why *cooperation* is a good learning strategy.

LISTENING TO SOCIAL STUDIES INFORMATION

1. Start by having students discuss what they already know about the topic to be presented (*elaboration*). This prior knowledge can be recorded on a K-W-L chart.[12] (See Chapter 2 for suggestions.) Remind them of the importance of this strategy (*using what you know, using background knowledge*, or *elaboration*). K-W-L charts can also be used when students read a social studies text.
2. Remind students to listen selectively (*selective attention*) for the most important facts, such as causes of an event, important dates, names, or products. They will also use selective attention when they attend to the language markers that give clues to the type of information the teacher is about to present.
3. Two other important strategies that can assist listening comprehension are *note-taking* and *summarizing*. Social studies information lends itself to the T-List system of note-taking. (See Chapter 4 for a description.) Oral or written summaries can be developed from the information noted on the T-List.
4. After listening to the teacher's presentation, have students work in small groups to reconstruct as much of the information as possible by pooling what each recalls (*cooperation*). This strategy can be used in conjunction with note-taking (students compare notes) and summarizing (students prepare group summaries). Remember to discuss strategy applications as well as the content of students' notes and summaries.

DEVELOPING ORAL OR WRITTEN REPORTS

1. An essential strategy for developing a social studies report is *organizational planning*. Have students plan the organization of the presentation or report and then check to identify the language that will be needed. Planning includes discussion of both content and structure of the report, identification of what is already known (*elaboration*), jotting down key ideas (*note-taking*), and deciding where to find additional information (*resourcing*). This strategy needs extensive teacher guidance and modeling.
2. After the initial planning stage students can begin preparing their reports through the use of additional strategies such as *resourcing* and *cooperation*. Finding information from reference materials is greatly facilitated through group rather than individual work.
3. For oral reports, students should prepare notes on their talk (*note-taking*) and practice their presentation. (See Chapter 4 for suggestions for *rehearsal*.) In making their oral presentations, students' anxiety can be reduced through positive *self-talk* (as well as careful preparation and practice).
4. For written reports, students should prepare initial drafts that focus on content, then check their drafts for organization, completeness, and coherence (*self-evaluation*). Students should also consult with the teacher and/or classmates on the draft report and gather their suggestions for revision. The second draft should continue to focus on content and organization; only for the final draft do students need to check mechanics such as spelling, grammar, and punctuation.

5. A chart or poster listing the sequence of strategies to use in developing a report can be used as a reminder for students. For example, Harris and Graham[13] used a chart with the mnemonic TREE (note down the Topic sentence and the Reasons, Examine the reasons, and note down the Ending) as a way to help students during the planning stage of writing an essay.

INSTRUCTIONAL SEQUENCE

The CALLA five-phase instructional sequence is a useful framework for developing social studies lessons and units that build on students' prior knowledge and provide them with opportunities to make personal and practical applications of the abstract concepts and numerous skills that characterize this discipline. (See Chapter 5 for guidelines on planning the CALLA instructional sequence.)

PREPARATION. Instruction begins with activities in which students identify and reflect on their prior knowledge about the social studies topic to be studied. Activities such as "What Do We Know about Geography?" (page 263) and "What Do We Know about History?" (page 264) are examples of ways in which students can begin to link their own personal knowledge and experience to topics in geography and history. Viewing a video about the unit topic and having students discuss and free-write about their personal associations is another way to help activate students' prior knowledge.

PRESENTATION. The teacher presents new information in varied ways and provides extensive contextual supports which can include maps, globes, artifacts, facsimiles of original documents, photos, art reproductions, products and resources of the area studied (e.g., bag of rice, fruits and vegetables, examples of minerals, manufactured goods). History can be made more vivid through videos of re-enactments of historical events.

PRACTICE. In this phase students actively practice the new information and skills, usually in cooperative groups. In social studies students can make maps and timelines and read cooperatively using strategies for identifying specific information and clarifying difficult ideas or vocabulary. They can develop graphic organizers after reading that can be used later as study aids, or write group summaries of the information presented.

EVALUATION. After active practice with the new social studies information, students check and reflect on their own learning in order to develop their metacognitive awareness of their own learning processes. Activities can include checklists, discussions, learning logs, and journal entries. Teachers can also ask students to reflect on and analyze their own performance assessments, then select for their individual portfolios the ones that represent their best work.

EXPANSION. In this concluding phase of the social studies unit, students engage in activities that call for higher-order thinking skills to illustrate applications of what they have learned. Activities and assignments involving their families can help students see relationships between topics in social studies and their own personal lives and cultural backgrounds. For example, students might compare historical events studied to events in their own countries or to events happening today in their own communities. Group projects could include making posters comparing ancient and modern political systems, or the impact of geography on people in other times and on their own lives.

Teaching Guidelines for Social Studies

- Assess students' prior knowledge about social studies topics.
- Select high priority content objectives from the school's grade-level curriculum; include both lower and higher-order thinking skills.
- Provide academic language activities in which students read, listen to, discuss, make presentations on, and write about social studies content.
- Teach and have students practice learning strategies with all social studies activities.
- Follow the five phases of CALLA instructional sequence.

Model Social Studies Unit

EUROPEAN COLONIES IN NORTH AMERICA[14]

Social Studies Content Objectives:

Learn about purposes, characteristics, and way of life of Spanish, English, French, and Dutch colonists in North America. Learn about interaction between colonists and Native Americans.

Social Studies Process Skills:

Use map skills to locate areas of North America colonized by Europeans. Make a timeline of major events in North America during the colonial period and of events in other parts of the world during the same period. Develop a research report on colonies in other areas of the world.

Language Objectives:

Discuss prior knowledge about European colonies in North America. Develop vocabulary related to the establishment and government of the colonies. Read and listen to information about events and way of life in colonial America. Answer questions and write summaries of information read or listened to. Describe photographs of re-creation of colonial life in Plymouth orally and in writing. Write and present a report on colonies in other areas of the world.

Learning Strategies:

Elaboration of prior knowledge, selective attention (scanning for reading), note-taking, summarizing, cooperation.

Materials:

Classroom map of United States, Canada, and Mexico. Student outline maps of United States, Canada, and Mexico showing borders, state names, major rivers. Photographs of scenes from Plimoth Plantation ("living museum" in Massachusetts). Glossary of major vocabulary, and/or dictionary. Reference books, library books about colonial life, encyclopedia, atlas.

Note Sample student pages are provided for on pages 275–279 activities marked with an asterisk(*).

PROCEDURES

Preparation 1: What Do You Know About Colonies in North America?

A. Teacher gives learning strategy reminder: Thinking about your *prior knowledge* helps you get ready to learn new information.

Students work in groups with outline maps of United States, Canada, and Mexico to brainstorm and share their prior knowledge about areas where European countries established colonies. Students make color key for map to indicate areas settled by Spanish, English, French, and Dutch.

B.* Learning strategy instruction: Teacher names, models, and explains usefulness of *previewing* a text by looking at the title and section headings to get a general idea of the topic as a preparation for reading. Students study questions about text (Presentation 1) and indicate the section heading where they expect to find answers.

Presentation 1:* Spanish Colonies

Students work in groups to read text about Spanish colonies. Reciprocal Teaching techniques may be used. (See Chapter 5 for directions for Reciprocal Teaching.)

Practice 1:* Understanding What You Read

Still working in groups, students read comprehension statements about Spanish colonies, indicating which are true and correcting false statements to make them true. Teacher gives learning strategy reminder: Scanning is using *selective attention* to find specific information in a text. Students scan the text (Presentation 1) to identify four states where the Spanish established missions or colonies, then color them appropriately on map studied in Preparation 1.

Preparation 2:* England in the New World—Before You Read

Teacher gives learning strategy reminder: When you *cooperate* with classmates, everyone learns more. Students work in groups to share prior knowledge related to English colonies by working cooperatively on a vocabulary crossword puzzle. Words and concepts not known by anyone in the group are looked up in glossary or dictionary.

Presentation 2: The First English Colonies

Students read text about English colonies (Jamestown and Plymouth). Reciprocal Teaching may be used.

Practice 2: Understanding What You Read

A.* Teacher gives learning strategy reminder: *Scanning,* or *selective attention,* is a good way to quickly find specific pieces of information. Students scan the text in Presentation 2 and take notes on a graphic organizer. Students work in groups to compare and contrast Jamestown and Plymouth colonies and present oral summaries to the rest of the class.

B.* Students identify states where Jamestown and Plymouth colonies were located, and color them appropriately on outline map.

C. Students study and describe photographs of a modern re-creation of life in Plymouth colony, then work in groups to write descriptions and make class presentations.

Preparation 3: What Do You Know About Native Americans?

Teacher leads brainstorming discussion to elicit students' prior knowledge about Native Americans, including their way of life and interactions with European explorers and colonists. Information is recorded on a semantic map or other graphic organizer.

Presentation 3: Massasoit

Teacher gives learning strategy reminder: Use *selective attention* to listen for important ideas. To demonstrate note-taking, teacher writes one paragraph from listening text on board or overhead transparency, and asks students which words can be erased or abbreviated while still retaining meaning. Teacher proceeds to erase important words, and students eventually reconstruct text from remaining "notes." Then students listen to text about Massasoit's relations with the colonists in Plymouth.

Practice 3:* Listening and Taking Notes

As students listen, they complete a T-List about Massasoit. After listening, students work in groups to compare and complete their notes, then use the completed T-List as a guide to write summaries of the information.

Evaluation: Complete a Learning Log for European Colonies in North America

Students complete a Learning Log identifying what they have learned in the unit, including concepts, vocabulary, language, and learning strategies. (See Science Unit, page 217–219 for a sample Learning Log.) Teacher leads a class discussion of Learning Logs and what students have learned in the unit.

Expansion: Find Out More about Colonies Around the World

A. Teacher conducts debriefing discussion of what has been learned in unit. Students are challenged with higher-level questions about colonization. Examples: *How were Spanish and English colonists similar? How were they different? Why were there conflicts between Europeans and Native Americans? How could these conflicts have been solved peacefully? What would North America be like today if Europeans had not established colonies here? In what other areas of the world did Europeans establish colonies? Have any other nations or groups established colonies? Who, when, and where?*

B. Students research colonization in their native countries, using resources such as parents and community members, library, and books in their native language(s). Students develop a class timeline about events in North America and in their native countries during colonization periods, then write individual or group reports about the characteristics and results of colonization in their native countries.

ASSESSMENT

Include the following student products and teacher assessment in student portfolios to use for informal assessment:

1. Student Learning Logs
2. Graphic Organizers comparing/contrasting Jamestown and Plymouth colonies
3. Student summaries of presentation on Massasoit
4. Student Assessment Form (two sample forms follow)

Sample Form 1:

STUDENT ASSESSMENT FORM

Record level of student performance for each objective. Scoring: 1 = Performs the objective independently; 2 = Needs assistance in performing the objective; 3 = Not yet able to perform the objective.

Student Names	Make a timeline of events during colonial period.	Discuss interaction of Native Americans and colonists.	Listen and take notes on a T-List.

Sample Form 2:

America: The Early Years

CHECKLIST OF LANGUAGE, CONTENT, AND LEARNING STRATEGY OBJECTIVES

Student name ______________________ Date ______________

Key: Level of Mastery
Yes = ☒ With Help = ⧅ Not yet = ☐

Content Objectives

Expresses understanding of main ideas related to these topics:

Unit 1: The First Americans

- Origins and migrations of first Americans. ☐
- Representative North and South American Indian cultures. ☐
- Geographical characteristics of Polar Regions. ☐
- Map and graph skills introduced in unit. ☐

Unit 2: Exploration of the New World

- Early explorers of America: the Vikings and Columbus. ☐
- Major European explorers in North America. ☐
- Geographical characteristics of Wet Tropical Regions and of Northern Forest Regions. ☐
- Map and graph skills introduced in unit. ☐

Unit 3: Colonies in the New World

- Early colonies in New World. ☐
- Origin of Thanksgiving. Importance of Massasoit. ☐
- Beginnings of democratic governments. Issue of religious freedom. ☐
- Geographical characteristics of Mid-latitude Forest Regions. ☐
- Thirteen English colonies. ☐
- French and Indian War. ☐
- Map and graph skills introduced in unit. ☐

Unit 4: A New Nation

- Causes of War for Independence. ☐
- Declaration of Independence and major events of the American Revolution. ☐
- Importance of George Washington, Benjamin Franklin and other heroes of War for Independence. ☐
- Major ideas embodied in Constitution, (emphasis on Bill of Rights) and operation of the three branches of government. ☐

Language Objectives

Produces the following language and practices the following skills:

- Understands and recalls main ideas of a reading selection. ☐
- Understands mini-lectures presented by teachers and peers. ☐
- Prepares and presents brief oral reports. ☐
- Discusses ideas and supports opinions. ☐
- Takes notes (listening and reading). ☐
- Makes summaries (oral and written). ☐
- Organizes and writes simple reports. ☐

Learning Strategy Objectives

Applies the following learning strategies independently:

- Guesses at meanings of new words from context. ☐
- Makes inferences and generalizations in listening and reading. ☐
- Recognizes cause and effect; predicts outcomes. ☐
- Skims a reading text for an overview of the major information presented. ☐
- Scans a reading text to find specific information. ☐
- Relates previous knowledge to new information. ☐
- Relates new information to own conceptual framework; synthesizes and elaborates. ☐
- Evaluates degree to which new information has been understood. ☐

Teacher's Comments: ______________________

____
____
____
____
____
____

STUDENT PAGES

Preparation 1B

Spain in the New World

BEFORE YOU READ: Using Section Headings

There are four section headings in the reading, "Spanish Colonies."

A. Spanish Territories in the New World
B. Colonies and Missions in North America
C. Slaves are Brought to the Colonies
D. U.S. Cities with Spanish History

Under which heading would you look to find the answers to the following questions? Write the letter of the section heading on the line.

1. What is a mission? ______
2. What land did Spain own in the New World? ______
3. Was the city of Santa Fe, New Mexico, a Spanish colony? ______
4. Why did Spanish colonists start to use slaves? ______

Presentation 1

Spanish Colonies

Spanish Territories in the New World

Spain claimed large areas of America, and named these lands New Spain. New Spain covered much of South America and all of Central America and Mexico. New Spain also included large parts of what became the southern and western United States.

The Spanish found gold and silver in Mexico and Peru. They looked for gold in parts of what is now the United States but they never found very much.

Colonies and Missions in North America

The Spanish established colonies in various parts of what is now the United States. In these colonies, the Spanish way of life, the Spanish language, and the Christian religion became very important.

Spanish priests taught the Native Americans about the Christian religion. In many places they set up missions. A mission was a church and the houses around it.

When Indians (Native Americans) came to live at the Spanish missions, they learned to speak, read, and write Spanish. They also learned about the Christian religion. The Indians worked hard at the missions. The Spanish would not allow the Indian workers to leave.

Slaves Are Brought to the Colonies

The Spanish needed more people in their colonies to build their cities and work on their farms. The Indians worked very hard, but the Spanish often treated them badly. Many of the Indians got sick and died. The Spanish decided to bring slaves from Africa to work for them at the missions and in the colonies of New Spain.

U.S. Cities with Spanish History

Many cities in the United States have Spanish names because they used to be Spanish colonies or missions. For example, San Juan, Puerto Rico, was founded and settled by the Spanish in 1521. It is the oldest city in the United States. In 1565, the Spanish founded St. Augustine, Florida. In 1610, they established another colony in Santa Fe, New Mexico.

The Spanish also settled in Texas. In 1682, a mission was established in El Paso. Another mission was set up in San Antonio, Texas, in 1720.

The Spanish set up colonies in California last. The first Spanish mission was established at San Diego, in 1769. Later, Spanish priests and settlers established many other missions in California.

Practice 1

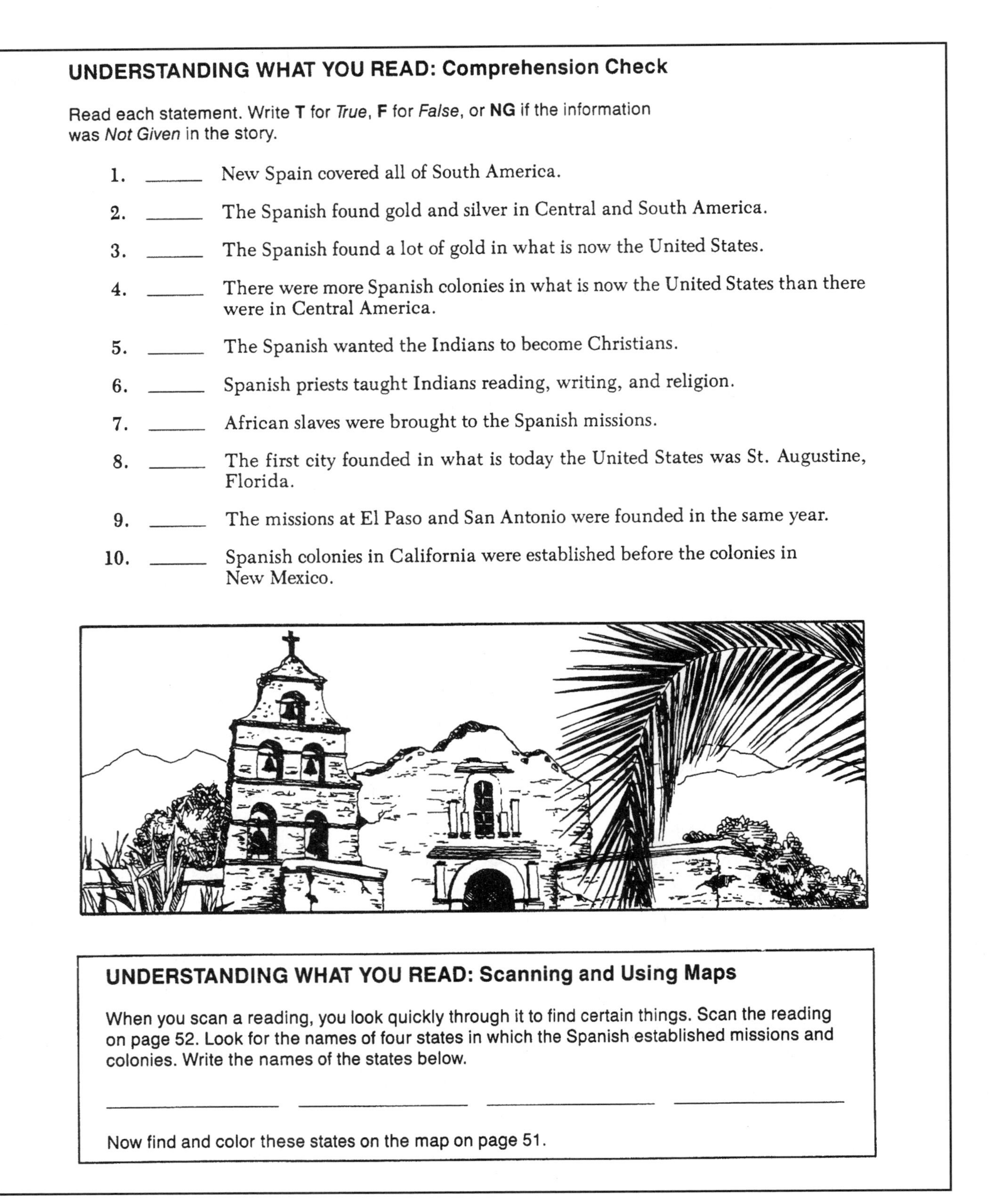

UNDERSTANDING WHAT YOU READ: Comprehension Check

Read each statement. Write **T** for *True*, **F** for *False*, or **NG** if the information was *Not Given* in the story.

1. ______ New Spain covered all of South America.
2. ______ The Spanish found gold and silver in Central and South America.
3. ______ The Spanish found a lot of gold in what is now the United States.
4. ______ There were more Spanish colonies in what is now the United States than there were in Central America.
5. ______ The Spanish wanted the Indians to become Christians.
6. ______ Spanish priests taught Indians reading, writing, and religion.
7. ______ African slaves were brought to the Spanish missions.
8. ______ The first city founded in what is today the United States was St. Augustine, Florida.
9. ______ The missions at El Paso and San Antonio were founded in the same year.
10. ______ Spanish colonies in California were established before the colonies in New Mexico.

UNDERSTANDING WHAT YOU READ: Scanning and Using Maps

When you scan a reading, you look quickly through it to find certain things. Scan the reading on page 52. Look for the names of four states in which the Spanish established missions and colonies. Write the names of the states below.

________________ ________________ ________________ ________________

Now find and color these states on the map on page 51.

Preparation 2

England in the New World

BEFORE YOU READ: Vocabulary

You will need to understand the words in this crossword puzzle as you read about the English colonies. The vocabulary words are listed in the Word Box at the bottom of this page. Fill in the crossword puzzle. Use a dictionary or the glossary if you need help.

ACROSS

3. Lasting forever (or a very long time).
4. To build homes and live in a new area.
5. To think the same thing.
8. A big meal with special food.
9. To pick or gather crops when they are ready to eat.
11. Government by the people.
13. People smoke the leaves of this plant in cigarettes and pipes.
15. The part of the year after winter and before summer.

DOWN

1. Rules set by the government that people must follow.
2. Chose.
6. The people or the system that rule a country, city, etc.
7. More than half the total number of people.
8. Human rights; the opposite of slavery.
10. Having the same rights.
12. A group of people who help govern, make laws, etc.
14. Plants grown for food or money.

WORD BOX			
agree	equal	harvest	selected
council	feast	laws	settle
crop	freedom	majority	spring
democracy	government	permanent	tobacco

Practice 2A

UNDERSTANDING WHAT YOU READ: Scanning and Taking Notes

Scan the paragraphs about Jamestown and Plymouth to find the missing information for the chart on this page. Remember that when you scan, you read quickly to find certain facts or other pieces of information. Use the chart to take notes on what you find. You do not need to write complete sentences. Just write the important words.

	JAMESTOWN	PLYMOUTH
1. Year established		
2. The first winter: problems		
3. Farming: solving the problems, main crops		
4. The Indians and the colonists		
5. Type of government		
6. Importance of colony		

Practice 2B

UNDERSTANDING WHAT YOU READ: Using Maps

In what state was the Jamestown colony? In what state was the Plymouth colony? People of what country established these two colonies? Find the two states on the map on page 51 and color them with the color for that country.

Practice 3

Massasoit

LISTENING AND TAKING NOTES

You are going to listen to some information about Massasoit, the Native American chief who helped the Pilgrims. As you listen, take notes on the information using the T-List below. Remember, the *main ideas* are written on the left. You have to complete the *details* on the right.

MAIN IDEAS	DETAILS AND EXAMPLES
A. Who Massasoit was; what he did for Pilgrims	**1.** ______________ of Wampanoag ______________ .
	2. Peace treaty with ______________ in ________ .
B. First Thanksgiving	**1.** ______________ friendly, helpful.
	2. Pilgrims invited ______________ to ______________ .
C. Massasoit and Pilgrims helped each other	**1.** When Massasoit ______________ Pilgrims helped him get well.
	2. Massasoit ______________ Pilgrims about ______________ .
D. Problems after Massasoit's death	**1.** Son Metacomet (______________ Philip) attacked ______________ .
	2. War for ______________ years.
	3. Many ______________, both sides.
E. Conclusion: Importance of Massasoit	**1.** Signed treaty with ______________ .
	2. Believed in ______________ .

CHAPTER 12
CALLA Literature and Composition

Overview

Language arts should be experienced and practiced as a whole rather than separated into sub-skills or component parts.

Description of the Literature and Composition Curriculum

- Curriculum Objectives
- Traditional Reading and Writing Instruction
- Current Approaches to Reading and Writing
- Integrated Learning Instruction

What's Difficult in Literature and Composition for ESL Students?

- Culture and Concepts
- Vocabulary
- Language Functions and Structures
- Reading and Writing Strategies

Teaching Guidelines for CALLA Literature and Composition

- Build on Background Knowledge and Student Interests
- Identify Academic Language Activities
- Incorporate Learning Strategy Instruction
- Instructional Sequence

Model Literature and Composition Unit

CHAPTER 12 CALLA LITERATURE AND COMPOSITION

LITERATURE AND COMPOSITION ARE LINKED TOGETHER because of the contribution that each makes to the development of the other. Students learn to be better writers through extensive reading and to be better readers through frequent writing. Oral language also plays a major role in developing students' reading and writing ability. Listening to a poem, retelling a story, and discussing the motivations of characters in a novel are oral activities that enhance students' understanding and appreciation of literature. Similarly in composition, students' ability to communicate in written form grows when they explore their ideas through discussion, verbalize their writing plans, and read their compositions to others. For these reasons, we believe that language arts should be experienced and practiced as a whole rather than separated into subskills or component parts.

Description of the Literature and Composition Curriculum

In the elementary school, Reading and Language Arts (which include writing, grammar, and often spelling) are frequently scheduled as separate classes, while secondary schools tend to have a single class labeled English which includes the study of literature, grammar, and the development of writing skills. In this section we discuss the overall curriculum for native English language instruction, with particular emphasis on upper elementary and secondary programs.

CURRICULUM OBJECTIVES

The school curriculum includes both procedural (the *how*) and declarative (the *what*) objectives for reading and writing. The major procedural objective of the school reading curriculum is to develop in students the ability to comprehend, interpret, and acquire information from different types of written text. To this end, considerable instructional time is devoted to instruction in the reading process throughout the elementary school, and even into the secondary school in cases where students continue to experience difficulties in reading comprehension. Procedural skills are also important in the writing/composition curriculum. From young children's first painstaking efforts to produce a written message to the high school student's no less effortful attempts to produce a meaningful piece of writing that conforms to a particular style of discourse, the process of writing communicatively is a major emphasis of the English–Language Arts curriculum.

Objectives for declarative knowledge for reading and writing specify the content of what is taught. For example, elementary school students might read stories in basal readers written especially for students at a specified reading level, or read children's literature that is not controlled for reading level. At the secondary level, students' reading focuses on literary works, including both contemporary and classical authors. In writing, elementary students are encouraged to express their own ideas and to write mainly about their own experiences. Secondary students continue to use personal knowledge to write creatively, but also need to write expository texts about factual information that they gain from studying different content areas at school.

TRADITIONAL READING AND WRITING INSTRUCTION

A familiar model for reading instruction for elementary schools starts with reading readiness activities in which children are made aware of print, and continues with beginning reading activities such as experience charts, in which children discuss a group or individual experience, the teacher writes it in simple sentences on a large sheet of paper that the whole group can see, and then uses the words and sentences contributed by the children for reading practice. A basal reading is generally introduced next, in which children are guided through stories of graded difficulty and complete exercises which develop a variety of discrete skills, such as phonics, structural analysis, and vocabulary development.

Once decoding has been fairly well established and students can attach appropriate sounds to written words, the focus shifts to comprehension of meaning. Reading comprehension instruction begins with literal comprehension and moves on to making inferences, reading critically, reading for aesthetic appreciation, varying reading rates, and reading for information in the content areas. As the focus of the reading program turns from decoding to comprehension, oral reading is in large part replaced by silent reading. At the upper elementary and secondary level, students use previously developed reading skills for a variety of texts, including stories, novels, poetry, drama, essays, and content area topics in science, mathematics, and social studies. Some programs provide special instruction in study skills such as dictionary skills, library skills, note-taking and outlining, skimming and scanning, and using graphic information to assist comprehension.

Beginning writers in the primary grades traditionally learn to write through a bottom-up process similar to the way in which reading is taught. The mechanics of handwriting are developed first, followed by copying of words and sentences, exercises for punctuation and spelling, and finally the development of paragraphs or longer compositions on assigned or free topics. These separate writing skills are analogous to the various reading skills presented in most basal reading series. This traditional approach to reading and writing emphasizes a mainly bottom-up approach in which the building blocks of the reading and writing processes are mastered separately. The assumption underlying this approach is that students will eventually be able to integrate all the separate skills and thus will be able to read for comprehension and write to express meaning.

Code-based reading instruction seeks to help beginning readers recognize the structure of words and the relationship of that structure to their phonological sound. A recent review of research evidence on approaches to reading instruction finds that approaches which include code-based instruction lead to levels of comprehension equivalent to other approaches and to superior ability to spell and recognize words.[1]

CURRENT APPROACHES TO READING AND WRITING

In newer approaches to reading and language arts instruction, the meaning of what is read and written is considered to be more important than the separate skills underlying reading and writing.

Recent research on reading has focused on the process of comprehension and has identified three main factors which account for successful comprehension: prior knowledge, text structure, and the reader's text processing strategies.[2] Reading is understood as an interactive process in which the reader interacts with the text by using what he or she already knows to assist comprehension. This reading comprehension model involves both top-down processing in which the reader uses knowledge of the world to interpret a text, and bottom-up processing in which the reader uses decoding skills to repair comprehension difficulties.

SCHEMATA. As we saw in Chapter 1, prior knowledge is organized into schemata, or frameworks of ideas and events. For example, one can have a schema about the attributes and characteristics of whales, and one can also have a schema about the sequence of steps involved in applying for a job. These schemata, which represent one's knowledge of how things work in the world of one's own experience, are called upon to assist both listening and reading comprehension. When reading a story, for example, the reader compares the events in the story with his or her own relevant experiences in order to assist in comprehension. When unfamiliar aspects of a reading text are encountered, the reader can assist comprehension by making inferences based on existing schemata. Readers who have a greater degree of prior knowledge on a topic are able to comprehend a more difficult reading passage on that topic much more easily than readers whose knowledge of the topic is limited or non-existent.

TEXT STRUCTURE. A second factor which influences the degree to which a reader is able to comprehend a text is the way in which the text is structured. Texts—whether literary, expository, or utilitarian—have an organizational structure. The most extensively researched text structure has been that of simple stories, whose structure is organized around a series of events in a certain order, linked by cause-effect relationships.[3] For example, a typical story has characters who live in a particular setting. One or more characters may encounter a problem that needs a solution. A series of events comprise the plot of the story, and the story ends with a resolution of the problem. This "story structure" or "story grammar" allows a reader to anticipate what is likely to happen in a typical story. Other types of written texts have different structures, which may be persuasive, referential, literary, or expressive in nature. When a reader encounters new information, it is mapped onto an existing schema in order to further the goal of comprehension. An assumption in the reading curriculum for native English speakers is that students have at least a partial schematic understanding of many of the different types of texts they encounter in school.

LEARNING PROCESSES. The ways in which a reader is able to process different types of texts is the third factor contributing to reading comprehension. Readers who understand their own learning processes and who can exercise control over their own actions while reading comprehend text better than those who believe that reading consists of decoding words.[4] Successful readers are able to monitor their own comprehension and seek remedies when comprehension breaks down. Good readers use metacognitive strategies as well as cognitive strategies to assist comprehension.[5] For example, good readers monitor their level of comprehension as they are reading (a metacognitive strategy), and when they realize that they are not understanding something in the text, they select cognitive strategies such as elaboration and inferencing to resolve their comprehension difficulties.

The cognitively-oriented approach to the process of reading described above can be applied to all types of content, including stories written especially for basal readers and authentic texts found in literary works and everyday print.

Some current approaches to reading instruction also provide specific guidance on what students should read. In these approaches, students read authentic literary texts rather than basal readers. Some curricula may specify which works of literature should be studied at different grade levels, while others recommend more generally that students at all grade levels should read books of high literary quality, with specific selections left to the judgment of the school, the teacher, and the individual student.

Recent elementary reading series reflect current approaches by including a variety of authentic texts, literature-based reading experiences, and integration of language skills. For example, the Heath Reading[6] program features selections from children's literature, folk tales, myths, science fiction, poems, and other authentic texts, including songs, biography, general informational articles, and content-specific texts. Selections are clustered within a common theme, such as *Help!, New Beginnings, A Spider's Web,* and *What Are Friends For?*. Language skills are integrated through listening to and discussing literature and through process writing. This type of reading program represents a significant change from basal series that focus on sequential skills in which students apply a number of decoding skills to texts that are specially written or simplified.

Research in writing and composition has also contributed to a re-evaluation of how writing should be taught in schools. Studies of how writers actually go about the task of producing written text and of the differences between novice and expert writers have resulted in a process-oriented approach to writing instruction which emphasizes the communication of meaning through writing and de-emphasizes the importance of correct form until the final editing process. One of the advantages of this approach is that students begin to use writing functionally; that is, they write as a means to accomplish a communicative purpose. They learn to write to a specific audience, and if the intended audience does not fully comprehend the intended message, the novice writer adjusts the message accordingly. Meaning is attended to before correcting form, which is seen as part of the editing process, not as part of the composing process.

A number of important educational principles derive from current recommendations for writing for meaning. For beginning writers the focus on communication of personal meaning leads to an abundance of writing, much of which may lack formal correctness. Inexperienced writers who are trying to communicate meaning through written forms often make mistakes in spelling, punctuation, grammar, and lexical choice. Invented spellings, stream-of-speech writing, and lack of formal structure attest to the beginning writer's desire to say something of importance rather than to say something that is merely correct.

The current emphasis on writing as a process allows the writer to move back and forth between the three phases of planning, composing, and revising in an effort to think through the meaning to be communicated, to fashion the most effective means of communicating the meaning to a particular audience, and to revise the product so that it communicates more effectively. Because communication of meaning is the major writing objective, students discover for themselves how effectively they are communicating their ideas by sharing what they write with classmates, teachers, parents, and others in the school community.

MAJOR PRINCIPLES AND PRACTICES OF CURRENT APPROACHES

- Reader's prior knowledge assists comprehension.
- Text structure affects level of comprehension.
- Learning strategies assist comprehension.
- Students read literature and other authentic texts.
- Writing involves three recursive phases of planning, composing, and revising.
- Students write to communicate their own ideas.
- Students share their writing with others.

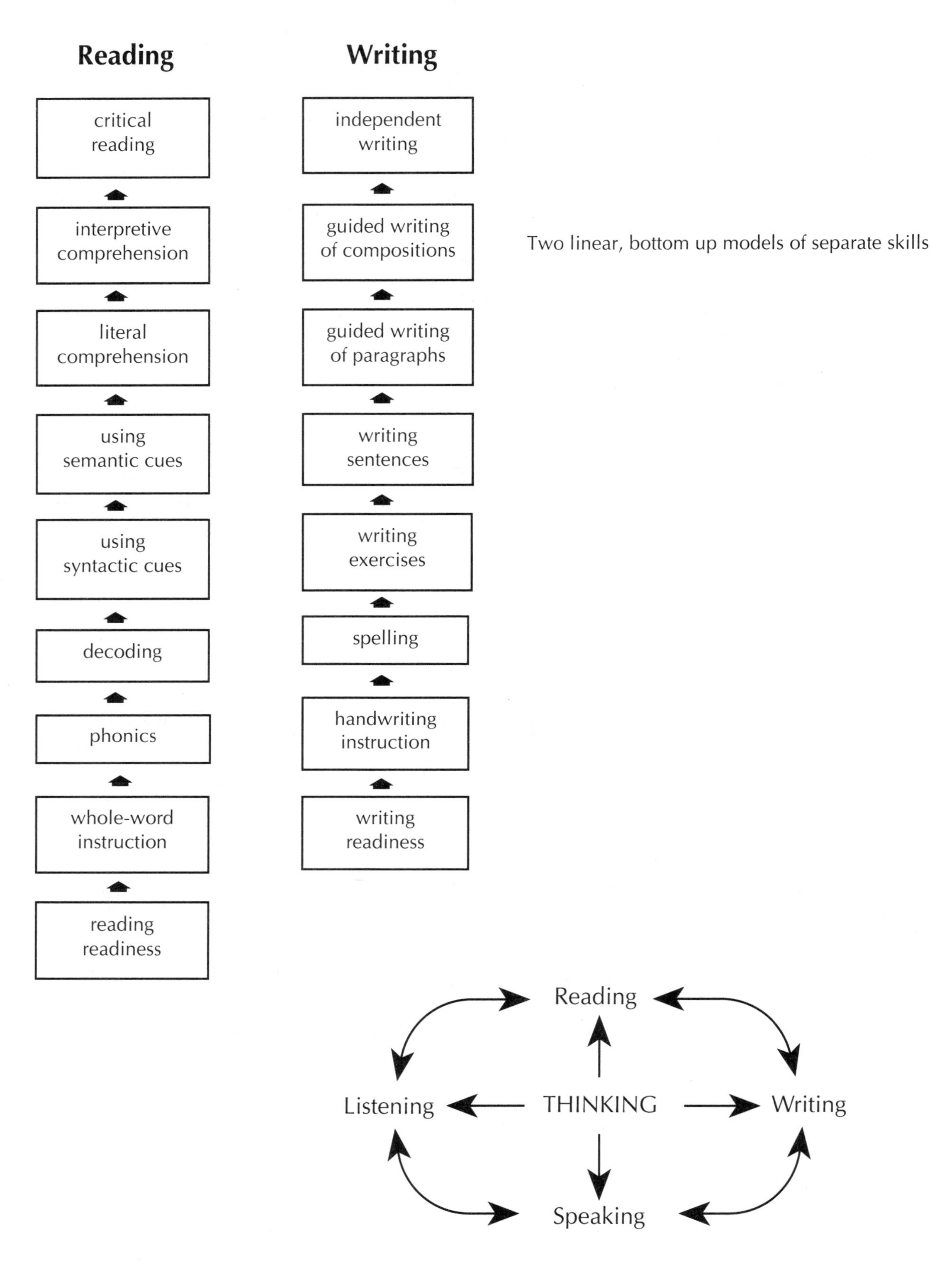

Two linear, bottom up models of separate skills

An integrated language model

INTEGRATED LEARNING INSTRUCTION

An important contribution of recent theories on reading and writing processes is the principle that language should be experienced and taught as a whole, rather than divided into a study of its component parts.[7] One implication of this principle is that listening, reading, speaking, and writing should be taught and practiced concurrently rather than in sequence. This integration of language skills is frequently accompanied by the use of authentic texts for listening and reading. In writing, the focus is on communicating ideas of personal importance to an audience larger than the teacher alone. Students read books and stories written as literature rather than specially written stories designed to develop particular reading skills. Similarly, students write about topics of genuine interest to them and share their writing with an audience wider than a single teacher.

In integrated language instruction, a theme is identified which unifies a variety of language activities. These might include reading, listening to, discussing, and writing stories, poems, songs, and informational articles related to the theme. A thematic approach can also be expanded to include additional information and insights drawn from other areas of the curriculum, such as science and social studies. Themes might include major concepts such as interdependence, communication, cycles, and change.

Description of the Literature and Composition Curriculum

- Students should develop the ability to comprehend, appreciate, and learn from different types of text; develop the ability to communicate ideas and express own insights in written form.
- Traditional instruction includes graded basal readers and drills for phonics, spelling, and grammar.
- Current approaches stress an interactive process; authentic texts, process writing, and integration of language skills predominate.
- Integrated language instruction is organized around themes which can be explored through a variety of types of text, including content area subjects.

What's Difficult in Literature and Composition for ESL Students?

In some ESL programs students may never encounter authentic literary texts, they may be encouraged to focus on the mechanics of writing, spelling, punctuation, and grammar, and they may have little practice in planning, developing, and revising narrative or expository texts at the discourse level. This type of program almost guarantees that ESL students will be ill-prepared for success in grade-level classrooms.

In this section we discuss the various types of difficulties that ESL students frequently encounter in grade-level English and language arts classes and identify areas in which CALLA teachers should focus their attention. Cultural and conceptual knowledge, the language of literature and composition, and reading and writing strategies are all potential areas of difficulty for ESL students.

CULTURE AND CONCEPTS

No area of the school curriculum is more closely linked to culture than literature. Novels, stories, and poems reflect and illuminate social settings, people, values, and traditions of a cultural milieu. The degree to which readers share the same cultural background affects the degree to which they can comprehend the text. Readers who have grown up with similar kinds of stories are more likely to know what to expect from a new story, while readers who have grown up with stories from a different cultural setting may find the whole premise of the new story incomprehensible. In addition to specific cultural details and assumptions in a story, the way in which a story is organized may also reflect a particular culture. For example, stories written from a Western European perspective tend to follow a particular structure or story grammar, and characters cast as heroes or villains tend to display certain personality types. A leading character is likely to have an assertive and goal-oriented approach to life, and the successful overcoming of obstacles leads to a reward that is often material—such as a pot of gold or the hand of a prince or princess. This type of story grammar is quite different from a traditional Japanese story grammar in which the main character's adventures are brought about through chance or fate rather than through active pursuit of a tangible goal, and rewards result from the protagonist's kindness and goodness, rather than through personal desires or goals.[8] The respect of others is more important than any material advantage. Differences in story grammar type may thus reflect cultural values and belief systems.

Other forms of written discourse are also organized in culturally specific ways. Native English-speaking students develop an understanding of different types of discourse structure as they read and learn to write. ESL students may have conflicting discourse models which not only make English story grammar difficult to understand, but also lead them to write narrative and expository text which may not communicate clearly to English speakers.

CALLA teachers need to be sensitive to the impact of culture on their students' ability to comprehend literature and to express their ideas comprehensibly. They can ask students to share stories from their own cultures, analyze their structure, and make comparisons with the structure of stories read in English. Direct teaching of story grammar can also increase students' comprehension of stories. Students can be prompted to answer a series of questions about the structure of a story, or they can complete a story map which identifies the story's main features and sequence of events. In either approach, the teacher models and explains the rationale and procedures for analyzing a story's grammar.[9]

VOCABULARY

The diversity and richness of vocabulary in literature can contribute positively to ESL students' English development as long as they know how to use appropriate strategies to address the potentially overwhelming array of unfamiliar vocabulary found in literature and other authentic texts. Virtually any page chosen at random from such texts reveals words that are unusual or poetic, words used in a new way, words used colloquially, words with specific cultural and literary referents, words used metaphorically, and words which have fallen into disuse in contemporary English. Native English speakers may encounter difficulty with these types of words; for ESL students the difficulties may be overwhelming. The following words drawn randomly from a reading series, children's literature, and classical and contemporary literature illustrate the wide range of vocabulary that students encounter in literature.

1. "My dad.......He's an <u>entomologist</u>, remember?"..."Dad says they only bite you if you bother them, or if you're <u>squashing</u> them."[10]

Name: Lucia Ramos Date: May 20

Title of Story: The Baboon and the Tortoise

CHARACTERS	TIME AND PLACE
1. Baboon 2. Tortoise	Story doesn't say time. Place is Africa - first Baboon's house in tree - then Tortoise's house near river.

PROBLEM: Baboon won't let Tortoise eat any food at his party.

EVENTS

Baboon invites Tortoise to party at his house in big tree.
Baboon says: you got to be polite - sit to eat.
Tortoise try to sit, but he fall down many times. So he can't eat.
another day, Tortoise invites Baboon to party at his house.
Tortoise burns grass around his house. When Baboon arrives, his hands dirty from burned grass.
Tortoise says: You got to be polite - wash your hands to eat.
Baboon wash hands in river, then come back - but hands dirty again (baboons have to walk on hands and feet).
Every time Baboon can't eat because hands dirty - So, no food for Baboon.

PROBLEM SOLUTION: Tortoise pay back Baboon - don't let him eat any food at *his* party.

MORAL: Be nice to your friends - or they won't be nice to you.

Completing a story map can help increase students' comprehension of a story.

2. In his head he drew the shadowy castle with the tortured prince pacing the parapets.[11]
3. The abhorrence in which I held the man, the dread I had of him, the repugnance with which I shrank from him, could not have been exceeded if he had been some terrible beast.[12]
4. "No, he was just moseyin' along, so slow you can't hardly tell it. He's comin' this way."[13]
5. Tilting and horsemanship had two afternoons a week, because they were easily the most important branches of a gentleman's education in those days.[14]

While some of the underlined words in the five examples above can be defined simply (*entomologist, abhorrence*), others assume specific kinds of background knowledge on the part of the reader (*parapets, tilting*).

Lack of an extensive vocabulary may also impede ESL students from expressing their ideas in writing as fully as they might wish. Finding *the* right word presents difficulties for all writers; for an ESL writer, finding *a* right word is the major challenge.

Since ESL students are developing oral language skills simultaneously with reading, they encounter many words that are unfamiliar in both print and oral form. CALLA teachers need to be aware of the vocabulary demands of all kinds of authentic text and show their students how to comprehend and enjoy what they read by using strategies such as inferencing to develop their own vocabularies.

LANGUAGE FUNCTIONS AND STRUCTURES

Understanding and making use of language functions and structures in literature and composition is a formidable task for non-native as well as for many native speakers of English. The functions of literary text are more varied than for any other content area, and may include (in addition to describing and narrating) persuading, entertaining, and teaching values. Functions, structures, vocabulary, and cultural concepts are interwoven in literary texts to form a complete message in which the author speaks in a highly personal way, and the reader comprehends in an equally personal way. The excerpt below from Katherine Paterson's *Bridge to Terabithia*[15] illustrates some of the complexities found in literary texts.

This novel tells the story of an unlikely friendship between a boy in a poor rural area and a girl from a sophisticated and intellectual background. She shows him how to use his imagination as they create an imaginary kingdom they call Terabithia. The girl, Leslie, is killed in an accident, and the boy's grief takes the form of anger and rejection. The understanding shown by his father and by his and Leslie's teacher finally allows him to come to terms with the tragedy:

> He thought about it all day, how before Leslie came, he had been a nothing—a stupid, weird little kid who drew funny pictures and chased around a cow field trying to act big—trying to hide a whole mob of foolish little fears running riot inside his gut.
>
> It was Leslie who had taken him from the cow pasture into Terabithia and turned him into a king. He had thought that was it. Wasn't king the best you could be? Now it occurred to him that perhaps Terabithia was like a castle where you came to be knighted. After you stayed for a while and grew strong you had to move on. For hadn't Leslie, even in Terabithia, tried to push back the walls of his mind and make him see beyond to the shining world—huge and terrible and beautiful and very fragile? (Handle with care—everything—even the predators.)
>
> Now it was time for him to move out. She wasn't there, so he must go for both of them. It was up to him to pay back to the world in beauty and caring what Leslie had loaned him in vision and strength.

> As for the terrors ahead—for he did not fool himself that they were all behind him—well, you just have to stand up to your fear and not let it squeeze you white. Right, Leslie?
>
> Right.

This excerpt reveals the powerful way in which literature can communicate emotions, insights, and values. An ESL student, however, may encounter obstacles which impede this communication. For example, some background knowledge about European medieval life and the code of chivalry is needed to understand the allusion to coming to a castle to be knighted. New words, special uses of familiar words ("he had been a nothing"), and complex sentences and grammatical structures, can all act to make comprehension difficult.

Since literature and other authentic text can present so many difficulties for ESL students, should teachers provide them with simplified texts? While some ESL teachers may find it necessary to use simplified texts at the beginning ESL level, by the intermediate level (the level recommended for CALLA), teachers should be introducing authentic texts. The CALLA teacher helps students understand what they read by providing necessary background knowledge and by showing them how to use learning strategies that assist comprehension. CALLA teachers also vary the task requirements according to their students' knowledge and English proficiency. Some students might listen to a story, while others might read it cooperatively. Some students might write a group summary of a story, while others might retell it to the teacher, aide, or other students.

In composition, ESL students frequently encounter similar difficulties as they write for different purposes. English conventions of narrative, expressive, expository, and persuasive discourse may not be immediately apparent to a student whose native language has differing discourse styles. ESL students may avoid or make inaccurate use of complex sentences and grammatical structures that communicate subtleties and nuances in written English. The CALLA teacher needs to be aware of such difficulties when they occur, and provide students with information about discourse styles and strategies for using English to communicate exactly what they want to say.

READING AND WRITING STRATEGIES

ESL students may not have been taught reading and writing strategies in their previous schooling, or they may not be aware that strategies useful in first language reading and writing can be transferred to English. Second language readers, for example, may rely on bottom-up or word-by-word proecessing strategies exclusively and may not take advantage of top-down strategies such as using background information about the topic (*elaborating prior knowledge*) or *making inferences* as unfamiliar words and phrases are encountered. Similarly in writing, ESL students may not know how to plan and sequence their ideas before writing (*organizational planning*) or conduct memory searches which include knowledge and experience gained through their first language (*elaborating prior knowledge*). Lack of effective reading and writing strategies can limit students' ability to construct meaning from text and to communicate their ideas in written form.

While the literature and composition curriculum can present many difficulties for ESL students, it can also provide unique insights and experiences that develop students' cultural, linguistic, and aesthetic understanding. ESL students can achieve more success with literature and composition when learning strategy instruction is incorporated into classroom activities and when the focus is on depth rather than on breadth of coverage.

What's Difficult in Literature and Composition for ESL Students?

- Literature reflects cultural values, shared knowledge, and discourse organization which may be different from that of students' native cultures.
- The rich variety of vocabulary in literature may make the text difficult to understand; in composition, finding appropriate words to express intended meaning may not be easy.
- The full range of language functions and structures in literature and other authentic texts can lead to comprehension and expression difficulties.
- Students may lack learning strategies to assist comprehension and to develop writing ability.

Teaching Guidelines for CALLA Literature and Composition

CALLA literature and composition lessons should provide students with varied knowledge and experiences that reflect many of the objectives and types of activities that they can expect to encounter later in grade-level classrooms. Students also need to learn reading and writing strategies that can be used in all areas of the curriculum. We believe that spending time investigating many facets of a small number of novels and stories is more valuable to ESL students than trying to read through a large collection of selections. When students have an opportunity to explore a few works in depth they have time to think through meanings, inferences, and cultural allusions, building a deeper understanding of a piece of literature. This deeper processing of a reduced number of literary selections is more valuable than superficial processing of a larger number of selections because it provides students with the opportunity of engaging higher-level thinking skills with literature.

Similarly in composition, ESL students need to experience higher-level thinking skills as they find their own voices to express their ideas through building, extending, revising, and editing their written production. Taking the time to craft and polish a single piece of writing teaches ESL students how to use linguistic forms and devices to create a written message that communicates the author's thoughts clearly.

An important reason for emphasizing depth rather than breadth in literature and composition is that it allows students the time needed for developing strategies to comprehend text and to write communicatively. When the CALLA teacher models and provides instruction in learning strategies for a limited amount of reading and writing, students can focus their attention on using the strategies to comprehend and appreciate different aspects of a work of literature and for planning, composing, and revising a piece of writing.

In this section we suggest guidelines and activities for CALLA literature and composition lessons, including identifying content related to student interest and background knowledge, setting academic language objectives, teaching learning strategies for reading and writing, and organizing instruction into the five phases of the CALLA instructional sequence.

BUILD ON BACKGROUND KNOWLEDGE AND STUDENT INTERESTS

Before suggesting what students are to read and write about, the teacher needs to determine their background, interests, concerns, and prior experience. Most important is to determine students' level of literacy in their native language, because students' prior knowledge and skills can be applied to reading and writing in English. Teacher observation, discussion, and shared experiences should be used to identify possible themes that are meaningful to students and that lend themselves to developing a literature and composition unit. Many themes are broad enough to encompass different interests and a variety of texts to read and write, and these are preferred to themes which might be of interest to only some of the students in the class. In the ESL program in Arlington Public Schools in Virginia, for example, a unifying theme each quarter allows students to explore language and communication through different types of reading, listening, speaking, and writing activities centered on a single major conceptual theme. These themes are: *Self, Relationships, Responsibilities,* and *Discovery.*[16]

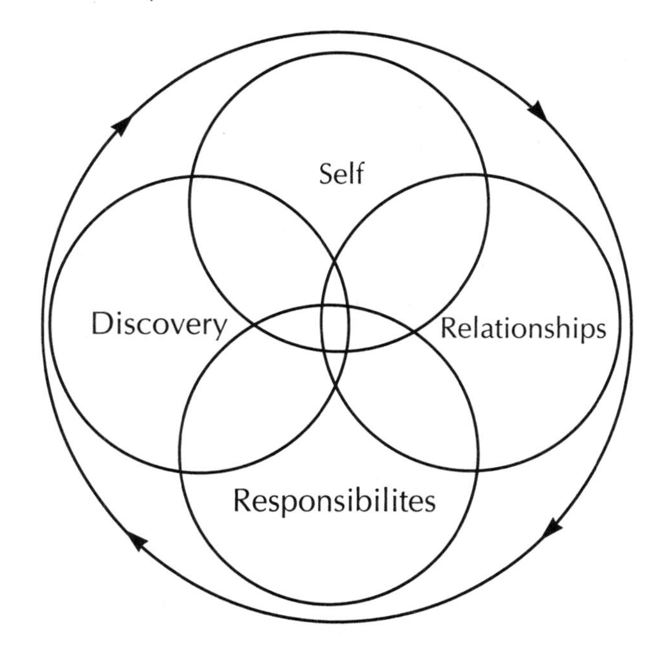

Arlington's Integrated Model

Each theme allows for reading a variety of fiction and non-fiction texts and for writing paragraphs, character sketches, reports, journals, stories, and plays. More importantly, each theme provides students with opportunities for discussion and thinking about their own individuality, their relationships with family, friends, and the new culture, their responsibilities to themselves and to others, and their discoveries about the world and their own aspirations.

Reading materials from students' cultural background, such as folk tales, legends, and other familiar stories retold in English, provide familiar themes which can enhance the relevancy and comprehensibility of what students read.[17] When students do read culturally unfamiliar material, however, the teacher should take care to build background knowledge as a pre-reading activity. Videos and films, for example, can be used to provide students with information about a historical period or unfamiliar locale that they will later encounter in a story or novel.

Novels should be included in the CALLA literature curriculum because they provide an opportunity for students to become more deeply involved with the plot and characters than they can with short stories. An effective approach to teaching novels to ESL students is to pre-teach the first two or three chapters. This is accomplished by discussing the characters, plot, and setting with students, and eliciting and developing their prior knowledge through discussions, illustrative art work, writing activities, and viewing films or videos.[18] As students read each chapter, they can work individually or in groups to reread and take notes on details of characters, setting, plot, and the development of the novel's theme. As a culminating activity, students can work in groups on different chapters to develop a class presentation on their understanding and interpretation of their chapter.[19]

SELECTION CRITERIA FOR READING AND WRITING MATERIALS AND ACTIVITIES

- Choose well written, high-quality stories and novels.
- Select authentic rather than rewritten texts.
- Find different genres so that fables, folk tales, stories, poems, novels, non-fiction, and drama are included.
- Include selections representing students' own cultures as well as unfamiliar cultures.
- Group selections within themes that reflect student interests and concerns.
- Provide a real purpose and a real audience that students can write for.
- Allow students to experiment with different types of writing, including journals, poems, narratives, observations, self-analysis, letters, stories, and plays.
- Use the themes selected for grouping literature as springboards to writing.
- Plan for the sharing of writing with classmates, the school community, and the family.

IDENTIFY ACADEMIC LANGUAGE ACTIVITIES

While content and academic language objectives in literature and composition are closely intertwined and form part of an integrated language experience for students, objectives can nevertheless be identified for academic language development. The primary purposes of literature and composition are to help students understand themselves and others, and also to develop their ability to comprehend authentic texts and to express their ideas in writing.

CALLA literature and composition objectives identify what is to be read, written, and discussed, and *how* these activities will proceed. Oral language development can be linked to literature and composition objectives.

WAYS TO LINK ORAL LANGUAGE AND LITERATURE OBJECTIVES

- Provide ample time for discussing students' own experiences and ideas about the themes selected.
- Ask and encourage students to ask questions requiring higher-order thinking skills.
- Read aloud to students every day.
- Have students read what they have written to a friend.
- Have students work cooperatively to develop and present oral reports on their reading.

INCORPORATE LEARNING STRATEGY INSTRUCTION

CALLA teachers have many opportunities for providing direct instruction in learning strategies in all aspects of teaching literature and composition. Helping students become aware of their own mental processes while reading and writing enables them to reflect on themselves as active rather than as passive readers and writers. This metacognitive awareness helps students understand and evaluate the strategies they are already using for reading and writing. The CALLA teacher (and classmates) can explain and model additional strategies for students to practice. (See Chapter 4 for guidelines on selecting and teaching learning strategies.) Discussions of literature read can also include comments about the reading strategies used to understand and enjoy the text. Similarly, as students apply new strategies to the writing process, post-writing discussions can center around how they used writing strategies to communicate their ideas. Table 12.1 identifies major learning strategies that are effective with literature and composition, and provides examples of questions that students can ask themselves to prompt strategy use.

Research on native language reading comprehension and instruction supports the teaching of five major reading strategies.[20] The first strategy recommended is teaching students how to determine what is important in the text. Dole et al.[21] indicate that what helps students determine importance is their knowledge about the structure of the text and about the author's purposes, and their use of their own prior knowledge of the world. The remaining four strategies recommended are summarizing information, drawing inferences, generating questions, and monitoring comprehension. The last strategy involves identifying a comprehension problem when it occurs and then using appropriate strategies to repair it. The authors go on to say that a strategy should be taught by modeling accompanied by practice with the whole text to be comprehended. Strategies should not be taught by breaking them down into component skills. The authors emphasize that strategies are flexible and can be applied in a variety of ways, and that there is no single "correct" strategy for a given reading task. The strategies identified by Dole et al.,[22] and their recommendations for teaching them are familiar to CALLA teachers. Instruction in these reading strategies should be an important component in the CALLA literature classroom.

Strategy instruction can similarly help students write more effectively. Research on writing in native language contexts indicates that effective instruction develops student's metacognitive awareness and ability to independently select appropriate strategies to solve writing problems.[23] A recent study investigated the effects of three aspects of good writing strategy instruction on the expository writing of native English-speaking learning-disabled and non-learning disabled fourth and fifth grade students.[24] The three aspects of instruction are an emphasis on inner and collaborative dialogue while writing, scaffolded instruction which provides assistance in writing strategies as needed, and developing a writing community in which writers and readers have regular conferences and dialogues with each other. The combination of these components was named Cognitive Strategy Instruction in Writing (CSIW). Materials were developed to assist students in thinking about and using learning strategies to assist their writing. For example, students had a "think-sheet" for each stage of the writing process. By writing down and talking about their writing strategies, the strategies were made visible. The results of this study indicated that students taught to use and talk about writing strategies improved the overall quality of their writing, that they were able to transfer the strategies to new tasks, and that their sensitivity to the audience they were writing to increased.

The results of studies on learning strategy instruction for reading comprehension and writing that have been conducted with native English-speaking students suggest that the same strategies can probably be taught to ESL students with equally positive results.

Table 12.1

LEARNING STRATEGIES FOR LITERATURE AND COMPOSITION

Metacognitive Strategies:	Students plan, monitor, and evaluate their understanding of literature and development of writing skills.
Advance Organization	Can the title and chapter headings help me get a general idea of what this story is about?
Selective Attention	What are the most important parts of the story to pay attention to?
Organizational Planning	What's my purpose for reading, listening, speaking or writing? How should I organize my story, book report, or presentation? How do I begin and end? What's the best sequence of ideas or events? How can I describe and present the characters?
Self-monitoring	Am I understanding this? Does it make sense? Am I achieving my purpose? How is this task going? Do I need to make any changes right now?
Self-assessment	Did I understand this story or poem? What was the main point I got from reading or listening? How do I feel about the story and characters? What revisions are necessary in my writing? Do I need more information? Should I re-read?
Cognitive Strategies:	Students interact with literature and composition experiences, relating it to what they know and personalizing or organizing the material to understand and appreciate it.
Elaborating Prior Knowledge	What do I already know about this type of literature or writing? What experiences have I had that are related to this? How does this information relate to other things I know about literature or writing?
Taking Notes	What's the best way to write down what I need to remember? Outline? Chart? List? Diagram? Story map? Drawing?
Grouping	How can I classify the characters or events in this story? Can I organize this information graphically?
Making Inferences	What does this word or phrase probably mean? What clues can I use? What predictions can I make?
Summarizing	What's the most important information to remember about this story? Should my summary be oral, written, or mental?
Using Imagery	What can I learn from the illustrations, diagrams, and pictures in the text? Can I draw something to help me understand this story? Can I make a mental picture or visualize this event or place or character?
Linguistic Transfer	Are there any words, prefixes, or suffixes that I recognize because of their similarity to my native language?
Social/Affective Strategies:	Students interact with peers, teachers, and other adults to assist learning, or use attitudes or feelings to assist learning.
Questioning for Clarification	Who should I ask for additional explanation or correction or suggestions? How should I ask?
Cooperating	How can I work with friends or classmates to understand this or complete this task or improve what I have written or presented orally?
Self-talk	Yes, I can do this—I just need the right strategies!

Plan "Think-Sheet"

Name:______________________________ Date__________

Topic:______________________________

WHO: Who am I writing for?

____

____

WHY: Why am I writing this?

____

____

____

____

____

WHAT: What do I know? (Brainstorm)

1.______________________________
2.______________________________
3.______________________________
4.______________________________
5.______________________________
6.______________________________
7.______________________________
8.______________________________

HOW: How can I group my ideas?

How will I organize my ideas?

❑ Comparison/Contrast ❑ Explanation ❑ Problem/Solution ❑ Other:__________

The activities suggested below illustrate some of the many ways that learning strategy instruction can be integrated into the literature and composition curriculum.

WAYS TO INTEGRATE LEARNING STRATEGY INSTRUCTION INTO LITERATURE AND COMPOSITION CURRICULUM

Reading a Short Story or Novel

1. Conduct pre-reading activities in which students identify their prior knowledge about the topic or theme and tell students that this strategy is called elaboration and that it will help them understand the text to be read. Present two or three important ideas from the text to be read and ask students to use elaboration by describing their own knowledge and experiences related to the ideas. Semantic mapping, drawing pictures illustrating their knowledge, free writing about the topic, and pair or group discussions about personal experiences are techniques that help students recall their prior knowledge. Tell students that elaboration is a good reading strategy because it helps you understand the story better.

2. Have students preview the story (*planning*) by looking at the title, illustrations, and headings, or by skimming through the story to get the gist. Ask students to predict (*inferencing*) what the story is about. Write their ideas on the board. Ask students why it is important to use reading strategies like *previewing* and *predicting* before reading a story. Have them write their ideas in their journals.

3. Discuss with students their purposes for reading the story. Remind them that setting a purpose for reading is a *planning* strategy that will help them read with more understanding. Ask them to express their personal purposes as questions, and have them write the questions on the board or have students write their questions in journals.

4. Students can experience a story in different ways. For example, the teacher can read the story to all or part of the class. In this case, ask students to practice listening strategies such as *selective attention*, during which they will be listening for the answers to the questions they identified when setting their purpose for reading. Selective attention can also be practiced as students read the story and look for the answers to their questions.

5. An effective way for students to understand and enjoy a story is through *Reciprocal Teaching*.[26] This technique incorporates a related set of learning strategies that assist students in building comprehension of the text. Students work in small groups (cooperation) to read and discuss a story or other type of text. After reading a section, students take turns leading a discussion. The leader first gives a short summary of the section read (*summarizing*), then poses questions to the other group members. Through teacher modeling, students are shown how to move from literal questions to inferential and critical questions that call for higher-order thinking skills. Next, the leader identifies any difficulties encountered in the text (*comprehension monitoring*) and the group attempts to resolve the difficulties (*cooperation*). Finally, the leader makes a prediction about what will happen next in the story (*predicting, making inferences*), and the group continues to read and then discuss, following the same procedures. When giving directions for Reciprocal Teaching, remember to name the different strategies and model how to use them.

6. Post-reading activities offer another good opportunity to teach and practice learning strategies. *Self-evaluation* can take a number of forms. Students can look back to the purposes that they had for reading the story (see paragraph 3 above) and determine whether they have met those purposes. Students can record their reactions to the story and can describe the strategies they used to understand it. Students can also develop their own questions about the text which can be answered by other students. Or they can use a checklist or rating scale to record different aspects of comprehension. A rating scale might include vocabulary development, identification of language functions, literal comprehension, and higher-order thinking skills such as inferential comprehension, application to new contexts, and evaluation. Another suggestion is for students to re-read all or part of the story aloud and record it, then listen and evaluate themselves. This is most effective when repeated at regular intervals so that students can hear for themselves how their oral reading has improved over time. With all post-reading self-evaluation activities, teachers need to remind students of the value of this learning strategy.

WRITING A STORY OR ESSAY

1. Process writing lends itself to learning strategy instruction. As students plan, compose, revise, share, and edit, teach them strategies for each writing stage. Model the entire writing process by thinking aloud and writing on an overhead transparency while you plan, compose, and revise a story or essay.

2. *Elaboration* and *organizational planning* are the major strategies used in the pre-writing or planning stage. Brainstorming and semantic mapping are familiar techniques for eliciting students' prior knowledge of a topic, and are also useful ways to convince students that they do have more knowledge than they may at first realize, since much of it has been obtained in their native language. After identifying what they already know on a topic, students need to select and organize the ideas they will use in their story. Some students may prefer to jump into writing with little planning, then plan and reorganize after they have produced a partial text. A planning graphic organizer can help students retrieve and organize their prior knowledge. Remember to name the strategies and model them if necessary.

3. During the composing stage, probably the most useful strategy is *self-management.* This strategy involves metacognitive awareness of the circumstances that foster one's ability to write, and the conscious decision to express ideas directly in English rather than through translation from the native language or constant recourse to a bilingual dictionary. *Self-monitoring* at this point should focus on monitoring of the writing process rather than of the writing product. These strategies can be demonstrated effectively through teacher modeling.

4. The revising stage of writing calls mainly for *self-evaluation,* although other strategies such as *elaboration* (of knowledge about form and discourse organization) and *resourcing* (using reference materials) may also be helpful. Students can be assisted in their efforts to evaluate and revise what they have written by teacher suggestions or checklists which identify organizational features that students can use to check the content/comprehensibility of their story. Note that this is not the same as editing, the final stage of process writing. Be sure to name the strategies used for revising and ask students to explain why they are useful.

5. For ESL students a sharing stage of writing can be particularly beneficial. In this stage students share their stories or essays with one or more classmates, either by reading aloud or by providing a copy for the other(s) to read. The learning strategies for this stage are mainly *cooperation* and *questioning for clarification*. Teachers need to remind students that these strategies will prove helpful in improving their ability to communicate ideas in written form.
6. Editing is the final writing stage, and involves checking the mechanics of grammar, spelling, punctuation, and capitalization. The learning strategy used is *self-evaluation* at a lower order thinking skills level. *Deduction* may be helpful as students check grammar; access to a spelling checker in a word processing program can eliminate obvious misspellings; other mechanical errors may need to be checked with reference materials or the teacher (*resourcing* and *questioning for clarification*).

INSTRUCTIONAL SEQUENCE

A theme-based integrated language approach to literature and composition lends itself particularly well to the CALLA instructional sequence of Preparation, Presentation, Practice, Evaluation, and Expansion.

PREPARATION. The Preparation phase calls for elicitation and illumination of students' prior knowledge about the theme of the story or novel. Students can work in pairs or groups to discuss their opinions and knowledge about the theme, then share their ideas with the rest of the class. Teachers can provide context and help develop background knowledge through visuals, realia, audiotapes, videos, and dramatic readings. Recalling prior knowledge is an important component of both reading and writing. The teacher may preview some essential vocabulary, but leave some unfamiliar vocabulary for students to encounter in context when they read the text.

PRESENTATION. In the Presentation phase students interact with an authentic text which may be presented orally by the teacher or as a reading. The text can be a story, a novel, an article or newspaper column, a folk tale, a poem, a play, or a text written by a classmate. The interaction may involve reading silently, reading aloud to others, listening to the text, or viewing a video. Cooperative reading techniques also enhance text comprehension. Instruction in reading strategies during the Presentation phase is important because using the strategies will make authentic texts more easily understood. CALLA teachers should provide explanations and modeling of learning strategies for reading comprehension and writing expression during this phase of the lesson.

PRACTICE. In the Practice phase students discuss, investigate, and reflect on the text they have read, listened to, or viewed. Or they may begin to write about an idea or theme suggested by the text or in classroom discussion. In order to develop metacognitive awareness of their own reading and writing processes, students might be asked to tape record themselves as they think aloud while composing or during pauses in reading, thus making visible their thought processes. Another Practice phase activity is sustained silent reading, in which the whole class and the teacher (including perhaps the entire school) set aside a daily time period in which each individual can quietly enjoy reading something of personal interest. In this phase students are active and conscious participants in literacy experiences.

EVALUATION. In the Evaluation phase students reflect on their own comprehension, revise their compositions, and evaluate their progress in reading comprehension and writing. In this phase it is important to teach students how to evaluate and improve their ability to read and write. An activity which can help students achieve these goals is dialogue journal writing. Students write personal comments and reflections on reading and writing assignments in a private journal which is shared only with the teacher. In reading students' journals, teachers respond to ideas rather than the correctness of student entries, and they write in the journals comments about the content of student entries. This approach demonstrates to students that the communication of their own ideas to an audience is central to the development of their reading comprehension and writing expression. Another self-evaluation technique is to have students develop their higher-order thinking skills by generating their own evaluative and critical questions on a specific aspect of the text read and answer them either verbally or in writing.

An effective self-evaluation activity is a checklist of reading and writing objectives which students complete by checking a statement that describes their perceived level of achievement, such as the following:

___ I can do this without any problems.
___ I had some problems with this.
___ I couldn't do this—it was too difficult.

The self-assessment checklist can also include a place for students to indicate their plan for learning the objectives which were difficult. Self-evaluation activities such as these can be collected and included in student portfolios.

EXPANSION. In the Expansion phase students apply the ideas, reflections, and skills introduced earlier to new contexts. For example, students might read a favorite story or passages from a novel to a younger sibling, and they could also agree to set aside a specific amount of time for reading at home. Or students might write stories for younger ESL students to read. Another activity would be for students to ask their parents to tell them folk tales and ghost stories from their native cultures which they can then write down and share with classmates. During the thinking skills discussions in the Expansion phase students should be encouraged to think critically about what they have read, to understand the author's point of view, and to evaluate the meaningfulness of the text as it applies to their own lives. In this phase there are no right or wrong answers, but rather an opportunity for students to relate their lessons in CALLA literature and composition to their own personal experiences.

Have students read to a younger sibling or write stories for younger ESL students to read.

Teaching Guidelines for CALLA Literature and Composition

- Before selecting unit themes, determine students' background, interests, concerns, prior experience, and level of literacy in their native language.
- After selecting a theme, identify content and language objectives that integrate literature, composition, and oral language experiences.
- Teach learning strategies that assist students in comprehending text and in expressing their ideas in written form; model, teach, and have students practice and discuss strategies for each stage of reading and writing.
- Follow the five phases of CALLA instructional sequence.

Model Literature and Composition Unit

A FOLK TALE FROM JAPAN

Literature Objectives:

Enjoy and appreciate a Japanese folk tale, *Ooka and the Stolen Smell.*[27] Analyze the characteristics of the "Trickster-Hero" or "Clever Person" type of folk tale. Compare the structure of *Ooka and the Stolen Smell* to a similar folktale from a different country.

Language Objectives:

Discuss and share trickster-hero folk tales already known. Listen to and read a Japanese folk tale. Develop vocabulary related to folk tales studied. Retell orally or summarize in writing the Japanese folk tale. Write a new (or retell a familiar) folk tale. Share with peers, revise, edit, make a class presentation or play.

Learning Strategies:

Elaboration of prior knowledge; reciprocal teaching strategies (summarizing, questioning, self- monitoring, predicting); cooperation; self-evaluation.

Materials:

For Japanese folk tale: Map of Japan showing location of Tokyo; pictures of traditional Japanese dress, houses, gardens, etc.; Japanese art objects such as fans, carvings, paintings, wood *blocks*, screens, etc.; overhead of illustration and text for *Ooka and the Stolen Smell.* For folk tales from other countries: library books and illustrations of folk tales from around the world. (See Suggested Sources at the end of this chapter.)

Pronunciation Guide:

Yedo, or Edo (eh'do); Ooka (oh-oh-ka'); Tadasuke (ta-da-sue'keh); Echizen-no-Kami (eh-chi-zehn'-noh-ka'mee); tempura (tehm-poo'-ra); mon (mohn).

Note: Sample student pages are provided on pages 307–314 for activities marked with an asterisk(*).

PROCEDURES

Preparation 1: What Do You Know About Japan?

Make a Japanese exhibit in the classroom by bringing in and having students bring in traditional Japanese pictures, illustrations, and objects. Brainstorm with students to find out what they already know about Japan. Write their ideas on the board. Learning strategy reminder: Think about your *prior knowledge* about Japan— this will help you understand and enjoy reading a Japanese folk tale. Have students work in groups of three or four to make a semantic map of what they already know about Japan.

Introduce *Ooka and the Stolen Smell* by explaining that they will be listening to and reading a Japanese folk tale about a judge who was famous for making very clever decisions to solve disputes between people. This judge was named Ooka (oh-oh-ka'), and he is supposed to have lived more than a hundred years ago in the capital city of Japan, Yedo (eh'doh), which is today called Tokyo. (Note: Edo is the more usual spelling of the old capital.) Show students the map of Japan and point out the location of Tokyo. Pre-teach or review vocabulary in the listening text by providing examples and pictures of: *case, court, judge, evidence, shopkeeper, rage.*

Presentation 1:* Listen to the First Part of a Japanese Folk Tale

Learning Strategy Instruction: Show the overhead of the title and illustration of *Ooka and the Stolen Smell.* Say: *Before you read a story, think about the title and look at the pictures. Predict, or Make Inferences about the story. Predicting helps you understand the story.*

Have students predict what they think the story of *Ooka and the Stolen Smell* will be about. Write their predictions on the board.

Read aloud to students the first part of *Ooka and the Stolen Smell.* Remind students that they can enjoy the story even if they do not understand every word—they can still get the main ideas.

Practice 1:* Complete a Comprehension Check

Have students work in groups to complete the comprehension check.

Preparation 2: Predict What Happens Next in the Story

Discuss students' predictions about the verdict of the trial and have them give reasons for their predictions.

Presentation 2: Learn Four Reading Strategies

Model Reciprocal Teaching;[27] with a group of three students. Write on the board (or overhead): *Summarize. Ask Questions. Identify Difficulties. Predict.* Sit in a circle in front of the class. Explain that each person in the group (including you, the teacher) will read the first part of the *Ooka* story section by section, and take turns "teaching" a section by *summarizing, asking questions about the section, identifying any difficult words or ideas,* and *predicting what will happen next.* Ask the class to focus on the learning strategies the group will model, since they already are familiar with the first part of the *Ooka* story. Provide each student in the class with a copy of the listening text so that they can follow along as the group models; the text should be arranged in four sections. The group reads the text silently, one section at a time. After reading the first section, the teacher models the four strategies. Then the group reads the second section, and a student is asked to summarize briefly, ask one or two questions (which the other students answer), identify difficulties and discuss with other students, and predict what will happen in the next section.

Practice 2: Read *Ooka and the Stolen Smell,* Part 2

A.* Have students sit in groups of four and use the Reciprocal Teaching technique to read the rest of the story.

B. Have each group select three new words in the story that they would like to learn the meanings of. Write each group's words on the board or an overhead, and ask students to use the story's context to make inferences about the meanings of the words listed.

C.* Remind students of different parts of a story included in a Story Map: characters, place and time, problem(s), events, problem solution, moral or main point. Still working in groups, have students complete the Story Map. Learning strategy reminder: Making a Story Map helps you understand and remember the story better.

Preparation 3: What Other Folk Tales Do You Know?

Ask students to think of stories they know in which a very clever or wise person or animal solved a problem or got the better of a bad person. If necessary, prompt students with reminders about stories they may be familiar with, such as fairy tales or folk tales from their countries. Write the names of the stories and what students remember about them on the board.

Presentation 3: Talk About "Trickster-Hero" Stories

Explain to students that stories about very clever people or animals are sometimes called "Trickster Hero" or "Clever Person" stories, and that they have been told for thousands of years in all different parts of the world. Briefly introduce some of the additional folk tales you have collected for the class library, such as Aesop's fables, the Brer Rabbit stories, the Anansi the Spider tales. (See Suggested Sources.) Point out similarities and differences in the main characters of the stories.

Practice 3: Read More Folk Tales

Have students select one or more additional folk tales to read and enjoy. Have students develop Story Maps for the folk tales they read, then use the Story Maps to retell the stories to their classmates.

Evaluation:* Complete a Unit Learning Log

Have students complete the Learning Log individually, then discuss as a class.

Expansion: Write a Folk Tale

A. Conduct a discussion of what has been learned in the unit. Challenge students with questions such as: *Is it true that it is the smell that makes food taste good? How could you find out? Do you agree that a smell can be stolen? Why or why not? Can you think of a different ending for the story ? Could Judge Ooka punish the student in a different way? What do you think happened afterwards to the shopkeeper and the student?*

B. Have students interview family members about a favorite folk tale from their countries and take notes, or, have students conduct library research on folk tales from their native countries. Assist students through individual conferences and group sharing to plan, compose, revise, and edit their folk tales. Folk tales can be shared with the class, other members of the school community, and families through reading aloud, making and illustrating books, contributing to school publications, and dramatic presentations.

ASSESSMENT

Include the following student products in portfolios for informal assessment:

1. Student Learning Logs
2. Story Maps of additional folk tales read
3. Folk tales written by students
4. Student Assessment Form (sample form below)

STUDENT ASSESSMENT FORM

Record level of student performance for each objective. Scoring: 1 = Performs the objective independently; 2 = Needs assistance in performing the objective; 3 = Not yet able to perform the objective

Student Names	Make Story Map of folk tale	Write a familiar folk tale	Use Reciprocal Teaching technique for reading

SUGGESTED FOLK TALE SOURCES

Cole, J. 1982. *Best-loved Folk Tales of the World.* Garden City, NY: Anchor Press/Doubleday.

Deutsch, B., and Yarmolinsky, A. 1952. *Tales of Faraway Folk.* New York: Harper & Row.

Hamilton, V. 1985. *The People Could Fly: American Black Folk Tales.* New York: Alfred A. Knopf.

Jacobs, J. 1964. The Fables of Aesop. New York: Macmillan.

Lester, J. 1988. More Tales of Uncle Remus. New York: Dial Books.

Smallwood, B.A. 1991. *The Literature Connection: A Read-aloud Guide for Multicultural Classrooms.* Reading, MA: Addison-Wesley.

Yolen, J., ed. 1986. *Favorite Folk Tales From Around the World.* New York: Random House.

STUDENT PAGES

Presentation 1

Presentation 1: Listening Text

Ooka and the Stolen Smell, Part 1

Now it so happened in the days of old Yedo, as Tokyo was once called, that the storytellers told marvelous tales of the wit and wisdom of His Honorable Honor, Ooka Tadasuke, Echizen-no-Kami.

This famous judge never refused to hear a complaint, even if it seemed strange or unreasonable. People sometimes came to his court with the most unusual cases, but Ooka always agreed to listen. And the strangest case of all was the famous Case of the Stolen Smell.

It all began when a poor student rented a room over a tempura shop—a shop were fried food could be bought. The student was a most likable young man, but the shopkeeper was a miser who suspected everyone of trying to get the better of him. One day he heard the student talking with one of his friends.

"It is sad to be so poor that one can only afford to eat plain rice," the friend complained.

"Oh," said the student, "I have found a very satisfactory answer to the problem. I eat my rice each day while the shopkeeper downstairs fries his fish. The smell comes up, and my humble rice seems to have much more flavor. It is really the smell, you know, that makes things taste so good."

The shopkeeper was furious. To think that someone was enjoying the smell of his fish for nothing! "Thief!" he shouted. "I demand that you pay me for the smells you have stolen."

"A smell is a smell," The young man replied. "Anyone can smell what he wants to. I will pay you nothing!"

Scarlet with rage, the shopkeeper rushed to Ooka's court and charged the student with theft. Of course, everyone laughed at him, for how could anyone steal a smell? Ooka would surely send the man about his business. But to everyone's astonishment, the judge agreed to hear the case.

"Every man is entitled to his hour in court," he explained. "If this man feels strongly enough about his smells to make a complaint, it is only right that I, as city magistrate, should hear the case." He frowned at the amused spectators.

Gravely Ooka sat on the dais and heard the evidence. Then he delivered his verdict.

from: *Ooka the Wise: Tales of Old Japan.*

Practice 1: Complete a Comprehension Check

Ooka and the Stolen Smell

NAME ______________________________ DATE ____________

Work with two or three classmates and answer the questions about the first part of the story.

A. Information in the Story

1. The characters in this story are: ______________________________

____

2. The setting of this story is: ______________________________

3. Tell what happened in the first part of the story:

____

____

____

B. Thinking about the Story

1. How do you know that the student is poor?

____

2. Was the shopkeeper right to be furious? Why or why not?

____

3. What do you predict will happen next in the story?

____

____

C. Vocabulary in Context

Read the sentence and discuss the underlined word. Write your group's ideas about the meaning.

1. The shopkeeper was a <u>miser</u> who suspected everyone of trying to get the better of him. **Miser** probably means:

____

2. <u>Scarlet</u> with rage, the shopkeeper rushed to Ooka's court. **Scarlet** probably means:

____

3. The shopkeeper <u>charged</u> the student with theft. **Charged** in this sentence probably means:

____

4. Ooka heard the evidence. Then he delivered his <u>verdict</u>. **Verdict** probably means:

____

Practice 2A: *Ooka and the Stolen Smell,* Part 2

Names of people in our group:____

____

Directions: Read silently. Stop reading at the stop sign. One person summarizes, asks questions, identifies difficulties, and predicts what will come next. Do the same with the other two parts of the story, taking turns to use the four strategies.

"The student is obviously guilty," he said severely. "Taking another person's property is theft, and I cannot see that a smell is different from any other property."

The shopkeeper was delighted, but the student was horrified. He was very poor, and he owed the shopkeeper for three month's smelling. He would surely be thrown into prison.

"How much money have you ?" Ooka asked him.

"Only five mon, Honorable Honor," the boy replied. "I need that to pay my rent or I will be thrown out into the street."

SUMMARIZE
ASK QUESTIONS
IDENTIFY DIFFICULTIES
PREDICT

"Let me see the money," said the judge.

The young man held out his hand. Ooka nodded and told him to drop the coins from one hand to the other.

The judge listened to the pleasant clink of the money and said to the shopkeeper, "You have now been paid. If you have any other complaints in the future, please bring them to the court. It is our wish that all injustices be punished and all virtue rewarded."

SUMMARIZE
ASK QUESTIONS
IDENTIFY DIFFICULTIES
PREDICT

"But, Honorable Honor," the shopkeeper protested. "I did not get the money! The thief dropped it from one hand to the other. See! I have nothing." He held up his empty hands to show the judge.

Ooka stared at him gravely. "It is the court's judgment that the punishment should fit the crime. I have decided that the price of the smell of food shall be the sound of money. Justice has prevailed as usual in my court."

SUMMARIZE
ASK QUESTIONS
IDENTIFY DIFFICULTIES
PREDICT

Practice 2C

Name:______________________________ Date:__________

Title of Story______________________________

CHARACTERS	TIME AND PLACE

PROBLEM:

EVENTS

PROBLEM SOLUTION:

MORAL:

Unit Evaluation: Complete a Learning Log About Folk Tales

NAME ______________________________ DATE ______________

Complete the Learning Log for this unit. Check the items that you know or can do, then answer the questions.

LEARNING LOG

VOCABULARY

I can explain the meanings of these words:

- ☐ case
- ☐ charged
- ☐ court
- ☐ evidence
- ☐ injustice
- ☐ judge
- ☐ judgment
- ☐ verdict
- ☐ clink
- ☐ gravely
- ☐ miser
- ☐ prevailed
- ☐ rage
- ☐ scarlet
- ☐ shopkeeper
- ☐ virtue

KNOWLEDGE ABOUT FOLK TALES

I can:

- ☐ enjoy folk tales from different countries.
- ☐ answer questions about a folk tale.
- ☐ describe the characteristics of a "Trickster-Hero" story.
- ☐ make a Story Map of different folk tales.
- ☐ retell a folk tale.

LANGUAGE

I can:

- ☐ discuss and share folk tales I know.
- ☐ listen to and read folk tales.
- ☐ write and share a folk tale.

LEARNING STRATEGIES

I can:

- ☐ Use my prior knowledge about Japan and about folk tales.
- ☐ Predict what may happen in a story.
- ☐ Summarize, ask questions, identify difficulties, and predict while I read.
- ☐ Use a Story Map to understand a story better.
- ☐ Work cooperatively with my classmates.

THINK ABOUT YOUR LEARNING

A. How successful do you feel about learning the different parts of this unit? Circle the place on the line that shows how you feel.

1. Vocabulary

Not very successful	Somewhat successful	Very successful

2. Knowledge about Folk Tales:

Not very successful	Somewhat successful	Very successful

3. Language

Not very successful	Somewhat successful	Very successful

4. Learning Strategies

Not very successful	Somewhat Successful	Very successful

B. Think about your learning and complete the sentences:

1.This is what I learned in this unit:

2.This is what was difficult or confusing:

3.This is how I am going to learn what was difficult:

4.The most interesting thing in this unit was:

Outline for an Integrated CALLA Unit

Overview

Science, mathematics, social studies, literature and composition, and other subject areas are integrated in a single thematic unit to illustrate the use of CALLA across the curriculum.

Living Rivers

Major Concepts
Content Objectives
Language Objectives
Learning Strategies

Overview of Unit Topics

Part 1: Rivers and Life
Part 2: The Life of a River
Part 3: People and Rivers in History
Part 4: People and Rivers in Literature
Part 5: Rivers in Our lives

OUTLINE FOR AN INTEGRATED CALLA UNIT

In Chapters 9-12 we outlined sample CALLA units for science, mathematics, social studies, and literature to illustrate how CALLA principles can be translated into lesson plans for different subject areas. We also mentioned that integrating different content areas into thematic units is an effective way of organizing a CALLA curriculum, and is particularly appropriate in classrooms where a single teacher is responsible for several content areas. The most important benefit of integrated units is that studying meaningful cross-curriculum themes helps students understand the links and relationships between the subjects studied in school as well as the unique approach to knowledge of each discipline.

This appendix provides an outline of a sample CALLA integrated unit on the theme of rivers. The unit incorporates topics in life science, earth science, geography and history, literature, and environmental studies, with mathematics problem-solving activities based on the content topics. Additional areas of the curriculum such as art and music can further enrich this type of integrated unit.

Living Rivers

MAJOR CONCEPTS

(1) Rivers are, and have always been, important in people's lives.

(2) Rivers need to be protected and kept clean.

CONTENT OBJECTIVES

Identify and classify life forms in and near rivers. Describe the characteristics and history of a river, and the effects of water erosion. Use data about rivers to construct graphs and write word problems. Locate important rivers of the world. Explain why early civilizations began near rivers. Identify the importance of rivers in science and social studies texts and in stories, novels, and poems. Use knowledge about rivers to write reports, stories, and poems. Identify major causes and dangers of pollution in rivers and describe how they can be prevented.

LANGUAGE OBJECTIVES

Listen to/view information about rivers. Describe diagrams of river life. Discuss ways to keep rivers clean. Make oral reports on river topics in science, social studies, and literature. Read stories, poems, and factual information about rivers. Write word problems using data about rivers. Write about river topics in science, social studies, and literature.

LEARNING STRATEGIES

Elaboration of prior knowledge, selective attention, self-evaluation, resourcing, note-taking, cooperation; organizational planning; Reciprocal Teaching strategies (summarizing, questioning for clarification, self-evaluation, predicting).

Overview of Unit Topics

PART 1: RIVERS AND LIFE

PREPARATION. The teacher identifies students' prior knowledge about rivers and life in/on rivers through activities such as brainstorming, sharing information about rivers in their native countries, and making semantic maps of prior knowledge.

PRESENTATION. The teacher takes students on a field trip to a nearby river (or stream) to observe, take notes, and sketch life in and near the river. Learning strategy instruction on *elaboration of prior knowledge* is modeled by the teacher.

PRACTICE. Students work in groups to make reports about their observations on life in/on the river they visited. The teacher shows students how to use data from the group reports to classify living things observed as producers (plants), consumers (animals), and decomposers (most fungi and some other simple organisms). The teacher models the strategy *selective attention* as a way to focus on specific information when reading or listening. Students extend their knowledge through reading and viewing information about life in and near rivers.

EVALUATION. The teacher provides a learning strategy reminder, telling students that *self-evaluation* can help them think about what they have learned and what they still need to work on. Students then complete a self-evaluation checklist or write in a learning log.

EXPANSION. The teacher leads a discussion that focuses on higher-order thinking skills. Sample questions: *Is there one plant or animal or protist in the river environment that should be destroyed? Why? What would happen if this living thing were destroyed? Choose a river plant or animal and explain how it helps people. What would happen in the world if there were no more rivers?* As a home activity, students can find out more information about plants and animals that live in or near rivers in their native countries.

PART 2: THE LIFE OF A RIVER

PREPARATION. The teacher explores students' concepts of a life span, introducing examples such as people, animals, and plants. Students develop a chart showing comparative life spans, and use the data to develop and solve mathematics problems. The teacher provides a learning strategy reminder: using (or elaborating) *prior knowledge* helps people connect new information to old information. The teacher leads a discussion on whether a river also has a life span, writing student ideas on the board.

PRESENTATION. The teacher provides learning strategy instruction on *resourcing,* or how to make use of reference materials. Students are provided with various sources of information about the formation and development of rivers, including the effects of running water on land. Suggested sources: textbooks and library books at various reading levels, videos, photographs, magazines, encyclopedias.

PRACTICE. Students work in groups to develop graphic organizers visually depicting the life of a river. Each group presents their information to the rest of the class and classmates answer comprehension questions.

EVALUATION. The teacher reminds students of the strategy of *self-evaluation,* and each group completes a checklist on their degree of effectiveness in communicating their information to the rest of the class.

EXPANSION. Students make maps of the school grounds, indicating areas of erosion from water runoff. After a rain storm, students check their maps for evidence of additional erosion and record their observations on the maps. The teacher leads a discussion of their findings with questions such as: *Where does the water that runs off the school grounds go? What does it take with it? How could erosion on the school grounds be stopped?*

PART 3: PEOPLE AND RIVERS IN HISTORY

PREPARATION. The teacher leads a brainstorming session in which students identify the names and locations of important rivers they know about, and asks them to identify the strategy they are using (*elaboration* to activate their prior knowledge).

PRESENTATION. The teacher helps students locate the rivers they have mentioned on a world map, adding to their list of rivers the names and locations of other major rivers (e.g., the Nile, the Congo, the Tigris, the Euphrates, the Ganges, the Yangtze, the Amazon, the Mississippi, the Rhine, the Rhone, etc.). The teacher gives strategy instruction on *selective attention* (reading or listening for specific information) and *note-taking*. Then students listen to brief summaries of early people near three or four major rivers, taking notes on T-Lists.

PRACTICE. The teacher reminds students that *cooperation* is a strategy that helps everyone learn more. Students work in groups, with each group selecting one major river to find out more information about the history of people living in that area. The teacher provides resource materials, and students write group reports on the history connected with the river each group has chosen.

EVALUATION. The teacher provides questions on the group reports. Students answer the questions and reflect on what they have learned in their learning logs.

EXPANSION. The teacher leads a discussion which focuses on higher-order thinking skills, asking questions such as: *Why did early people settle near rivers? Why was Ancient Egypt called "the gift of the Nile?" Is it important today for cities to be located on rivers? Why or why not? How would you define the most important river in the world (length, amount of water, importance to life, human settlements, other)?* As an additional expansion activity, students can graph information about major rivers of the world, write and solve mathematics word problems about rivers, and investigate early settlements near a local river.

PART 4: PEOPLE AND RIVERS IN LITERATURE

PREPARATION. Students are asked to name stories they know in which rivers are important. The teacher records the story name, country of origin, brief character description and/or plot outline, and reason(s) why the river was important in the story. The teacher reminds students that *elaborating their prior knowledge* in this way will help them understand new stories on the same river theme.

PRESENTATION. The teacher reads to students a short story or poem on a river theme (suggested literature is listed at the end of this part of the Living Rivers unit outline), modeling Reciprocal Teaching strategies as follows: *summarizing, questioning for clarification, self-evaluation,* and *predicting.* The teacher asks students to describe the strategies he/she has just used and suggest why they were used, then writes students' suggestions on the board. The teacher explains that students can use the same strategies to understand a story, and that these strategies can be used in conjunction with *cooperation.*

PRACTICE. Students read in groups of four a story with a river theme (see suggested literature sources at the end of this part), using the Reciprocal Teaching strategies modeled and explained by the teacher.

EVALUATION. The teacher leads a debriefing discussion in which students are asked to describe how the Reciprocal Teaching strategies worked (or did not work) for them and why. Then students retell the story orally or in writing as a comprehension check.

EXPANSION. The teacher leads a discussion about the motives, strengths, and weaknesses of the characters in the story, and students develop a graphic organizer that describes the personalities of the characters. The teacher then asks students to describe people they know or characters in stories from their native countries that are similar to the characters in the story they have read. Students develop and compose individual stories or poems with a river theme, share them with classmates and the teacher, revise and edit, and have their stories and poems published as part of a class anthology of river stories. Students may also translate their stories and poems into their native language(s) to share with family members.

SUGGESTED LITERATURE RESOURCES

Cherry, Lynne. 1992. *A River Ran Wild.* San Diego: Harcourt Brace Jovanovich. The story of a New Hampshire river is told from the time early Native Americans settled there, through colonial settlements, the Industrial Revolution, the pollution of the river, and its rescue through the efforts of two young people who carry out a campaign to clean up the river.

Child, Lydia Maria. 1987. *Over the River and Through the Woods.* New York: Scholastic. The complete song of the same title is illustrated and presents an account of a traditional Thanksgiving.

Dickinson, Emily. 1890. "My river runs to thee." In S. Bradley, R.C. Beatty, and E.H. Long, eds., *The American Tradition in Literature,* Third Edition, Volume 2, p. 180. New York: Grosset and Dunlap.

Frost, Robert. 1928. "West-running Brook." In S. Bradley, R.C. Beatty, and E.H. Long, eds., *The American Tradition in Literature,* Third Edition, Volume 2, p. 1093-1095. New York: Grosset and Dunlap.

Grahame, Kenneth. 1966. *The Wind in the Willows.* New York: Grosset & Dunlap. This classic story of humanized river animals recounts the adventures of Mole, Rat, Badger and especially Toad, whose stubborn desire for adventure leads to all kinds of problems.

Michl, Reinhart. 1985. *A Day on the River.* Woodbury, NY: Barron's Educational Service. Translated from German, this is the story of the adventures of three boys who skip school and spend a day exploring a nearby river.

Paterson, Katherine. 1977. *Bridge to Terabithia.* New York: Harper & Row. In this story a river is the dividing line between ordinary life and the magical kingdom of Terabithia, where two friends share the power of imagination. (See Chapter 12 for additional information about this novel.)

Twain, Mark (Samuel L. Clemens). 1883. *Life on the Mississippi.* Selected from chapters such as "Frescoes from the past", "The Boys' Ambition", and "A Mississippi Cub-pilot." In S. Bradley, R.C. Beatty, and E.H. Long, eds., *The American Tradition in Literature,* Third Edition, Volume 2, pp. 200-223. New York: Grosset and Dunlap.

Williams, Vera B. 1981. *Three Days on a River in a Red Canoe.* New York: Greenwillow Books. This is a story about a camping trip on a river which includes useful factual "how-to" information about logistics.

PART 5: RIVERS IN OUR LIVES

PREPARATION. The teacher leads a discussion about what students know about the effect of rivers in their lives. Then students work in groups to develop K-W-L charts by listing on a three-columned sheet of paper the following information: KNOW (What We Already Know About Rivers in Our Lives), WANT (What We Want to Find Out About Rivers in Our Lives), LEARNED (What We Have Learned About Rivers in Our Lives) which will be filled in during the Evaluation phase of the lesson. The teacher reminds students that they have just used *elaboration* to recall their prior knowledge and *organizational planning* to develop a plan for learning.

PRESENTATION. The teacher discusses the information students have recorded on their K-W-L charts and consolidates the information onto a class chart. Using this information, the teacher reviews major facts that students already know about water in their lives (e.g., living things need water to live; water goes through a cycle which includes evaporation, condensation, precipitation, and storage; water exists in three physical states: solid [ice], liquid [water], and gas [water vapor]). Students view or listen to information about the ways in which water can be polluted (sewage, animal wastes, chemicals, and heat) and the results of such pollution (contaminated drinking water, poisoning of plants and animals, and upsetting of ecological balance, as when water becomes so clogged with algae that all other water life dies).

PRACTICE. Students work in pairs to observe and record how organisms in river water are affected by fertilizers. Materials needed for each pair: water from a slow-moving river or pond in three baby food jars; diluted and undiluted fertilizer; rubber gloves; dropper. Students add a dropper full of undiluted fertilizer to one jar, of diluted fertilizer to the second jar, and nothing to the third jar. Jars are covered and placed in sunlight. Students observe and record changes in jars for two weeks, then write a lab report on the observed differences in algae growth in each jar.

EVALUATION. The teacher provides a learning strategy reminder about the value of *self-evaluation.* Students work in groups to write summaries of what they have learned about water in their lives (the L section of the K-W-L chart).

EXPANSION. The teacher leads a discussion that focuses on higher-order thinking skills. Sample questions: *What would our life be like if our water became so polluted that we could not use it for drinking? For washing?* As an expansion activity, students can find out what anti-pollution regulations exist in their community. Students can work in groups to draw up action plans of how they can personally help keep water and the rest of their environment free from pollution.

References

PREFACE

1. Thomas, W.P. 1992. *County of Arlington VA ESEA Title VII program: The Cognitive Academic Language Learning Approach CALLA Project for Mathematics, 1991-1992.* Unpublished manuscript.

CHAPTER 1: WHAT IS CALLA?

1. Chamot, A.U., and O'Malley, J.M. 1986. *A Cognitive Academic Language Learning Approach: An ESL Content-based Curriculum.* Washington, DC: National Clearinghouse for Bilingual Education.

2. Enright, D.S., and McCloskey, M.L. 1988. *Integrating English: Developing English Language and Literacy in the Multilingual Classroom.* Reading, MA: Addison-Wesley.

3. Brown, A.L., and Palincsar, A.S. 1982. Inducing strategies learning from texts by means of informed, self-control training. *Topics in Learning and Learning Disabilities, 2* (1), 1-17.

Dansereau, D.F. 1978. The development of a learning strategies curriculum. In H.F. O'Neil, Jr., ed. *Learning Strategies,* pp. 1-29. New York: Academic Press.

O'Neil, H.F., Jr., ed. 1978. *Learning Strategies.* New York: Academic Press.

Weinstein, C.E., and Mayer, R.E. 1986. The Teaching of Learning Strategies. In M.R. Wittrock, ed., *Handbook of Research on Teaching,* 3rd ed. pp. 315-27. New York: Macmillan.

Wittrock, M.C. 1974. Learning as a generative process. *Educational Psychologist, 11,* 87-95.

4. Bialystok, E. 1981. The role of conscious strategies in second language proficiency. *Modern Language Journal, 65,* 24-35.

Cohen, A.D., and Aphek, E. 1981. Easifying second language learning. *Studies in Second Language Learning, 3*:221-36.

Hosenfeld, C., Arnold, V., Kirchofer, J., Laciura, J., and Wilson, L. 1981. Second language reading: A curricular sequence for teaching reading strategies. *Foreign Language Annals, 14* (5), 415-422.

Naiman, N., Frohlich, M., Stern, H.H., and Tedesco, A. 1978. *The Good Language Learner.* Toronto: Ontario Institute for Studies in Education.

Rubin, J. 1975. What the "good language learner" can teach us. *TESOL Quarterly,* 9:41-51.

Rubin, J. 1981. Study of cognitive processes in second language learning. *Applied Linguistics* 11:117-31.

Rubin, J., and Thompson, I. 1982. *How to Be a More Successful Language Learner.* Boston, MA: Heinle and Heinle.

5. O'Malley, J.M., Chamot, A.U., Stewner-Manzanares, G., Russo, R.P., and Küpper, L. 1985a. Learning strategies used by beginning and intermediate ESL students. *Language Learning, 35,* 21-46.

6. O'Malley, J.M., Chamot, A.U., Stewner-Manzanares, G., Russo, R.P., and Küpper, L. 1985b. Learning strategy applications with students of English as a second language. *TESOL Quarterly, 19,* 285-296.

7. O'Malley, J.M., Chamot, A.U., and Küpper, L. 1989. Listening comprehension strategies in second language acquisition. *Applied Linguistics, 10* (4).

8. Oxford, R. 1990. *Language Learning Strategies: What Every Teacher Should Know.* New York: Newbury House.

Wenden, A., and Rubin, J. 1987. *Learner Strategies in Language Learning.* Englewood Cliffs, NJ: Prentice-Hall.

9. Cummins, J. 1980. The construct of proficiency in bilingual education. In J.E. Alatis, ed., *Georgetown University Round Table on Languages and Linguistics, 1980.* Washington, DC: Georgetown University Press.

Cummins, J. 1981. Age on arrival and immigrant second language learning in Canada: A reassessment. *Applied Linguistics,* 2, 132-49.

10. Cummins, J. 1984. *Bilingualism and Special Education: Issues in Assessment and Pedagogy.* San Diego, CA: College-Hill Press.

11. Collier, V.P. 1987. Age and rate of acquisition of second language for academic purposes. *TESOL Quarterly,* 21:617-641.

Collier, V.P. 1989. How long? A synthesis of research on academic achievement in a second language. *TESOL Quarterly,* 23:509-531.

12. Mohan, B.A. 1979. Relating language teaching and content teaching. *TESOL Quarterly,* 13:171-182.

13. De Avila, E.A., and Duncan, S.E.. 1984. *Finding Out/Descubrimiento. Training Manual.* San Rafael, CA: Linguametrics Group.

14. Cohen, E.G., DeAvila, E., and Intili, J.A. 1981. Executive summary: Multicultural improvement of cognitive ability. Report to State of California Department of Education.

15. Chamot, A.U., and O'Malley, J.M. 1986. *A Cognitive Academic Language Learning Approach: An ESL Content-based Curriculum.* Washington, DC: National Clearinghouse for Bilingual Education.

16. Center for Applied Linguistics. 1989. *Communicative Math and Science Teaching: A Video and Teachers' Guide.* Washington, DC: Center for Applied Linguistics.

Center for Language Education and Research. 1986. *Strategies for Integrating Language and Content Instruction.* Washington, DC: Center for Applied Linguistics.

Crandall, J.A., ed. 1987. *ESL Through Content-area Instruction: Mathematics, Science, Social Studies.* Englewood Cliffs, NJ: Prentice Hall-Regents.

Crandall, J.A., Dale, T.C., Rhodes, N.C., and Spanos, G. 1989. *English Skills for Algebra: Math-language Activities for Algebra Students. Book I: Tutor Book and Resource Materials. Book 2: Student Workbook.* Englewood Cliffs, NJ: Prentice Hall-Regents.

Short, D.J., Crandall, J.A., and Christian, D. 1989. *How to Integrate Language and Content Instruction: A Training Manual.* Los Angeles: Center for Language Education and Research, UCLA. [ERIC ED305824.]

17. National Clearinghouse for Bilingual Education and the Georgetown University Bilingual Education Service Center. 1985. *Issues in English Language Development.* McLean, VA: Inter-America Research Associates, Inc.

18. Mohan, B.A. 1986. *Language and Content.* Reading, MA: Addison-Wesley.

19. Cantoni-Harvey, G. 1987. *Content-area Language Instruction: Approaches and Strategies.* Reading, MA: Addison-Wesley.

20. Enright, D.S., and McCloskey, M.L. 1988. *Integrating English: Developing English Language and Literacy in the Multilingual Classroom.* Reading, MA: Addison-Wesley.

21. Snow, M.A., Met, M., and Genesee, F. 1989. A Conceptual framework for the integration of language and content in second/foreign language instruction. *TESOL Quarterly.* 23:201-217.

22. Spanos, G. 1990. On the integration of language and content instruction. *Annual Review of Applied Linguistics,* 10:227-240.

23. Pressley, M. and Associates 1990. *Cognitive Strategy Instruction That Really Improves Children's Academic Performance.* Cambridge, MA: Brookline Books.

Pressley, M., and Harris, K. 1990. What we really know about strategy instruction. *Educational Leadership, 48* (1), 31-34.

24. Derry, S.J. 1990. Learning strategies for acquiring useful knowledge. In B.F. Jones and L. Idol, eds., *Dimensions of Thinking and Cognitive Instruction,* pp. 347-379. Hillsdale, NJ: Lawrence Erlbaum.

Garner, R. 1987. *Metacognition and Reading Comprehension.* Norwood, NJ: Heinemann.

Gagné, E.D. 1985. *The Cognitive Pyschology of School Learning.* Boston: Little, Brown.

Harris, K.R., and Graham, S. 1992. *Helping Young Writers Master the Craft: Strategy Instruction and Self-Regulation in the Writing Process.* Cambridge, MA: Brookline Books.

Jones, B.F., Palincsar, A.S., Ogle, D.S., and Carr, E.G. 1987. *Strategic Teaching and Learning: Cognitive Instruction in the Content Areas.* Alexandria, VA: Association for Supervision and Curriculum Development.

Palincsar, A.S., and Brown, A.L. 1984. Reciprocal teaching of comprehension-fostering and comprehension-monitoring activities. *Cognition and Instruction,* 1:117-175.

Peterson, P.L., Fennema, E., and Carpenter, T. 1989. Using knowledge of how students think about mathematics. *Educational Leadership, 46* (4), 42-46.

Weinstein, C.E., and Mayer, R.E. 1986. The teaching of learning strategies. In M.R. Wittrock, ed., *Handbook of Research on Teaching,* pp. 315-27. 3rd ed. New York: Macmillan.

25. Anderson, J.R. 1976. *Language, Memory, and Thought.* Hillsdale, NJ: Erlbaum.

Anderson, J.R. 1980. *Cognitive Psychology and Its Implications.* San Francisco: Freeman.

Anderson, J.R. 1983. *The Architecture of Cognition.* Cambridge, MA: Harvard University Press.

26. O'Malley, J.M., Chamot, A.U., and Walker, C. 1987. Some applications of cognitive theory to second language acquisition. *Studies in Second Language Acquisition, 9,* 287-306.

27. O'Malley, J.M., and Chamot, A.U. 1990. *Learning Strategies in Second Language Acquisition.* New York: Cambridge University Press.

28. Gagné, E.D. 1985. *The Cognitive Psychology of School Learning.* Boston: Little, Brown.
29. Shuell, T.J. 1986. Cognitive conceptions of learning. *Review of Educational Research, 56,* 411-436.

30. Weinstein, C.E., and Mayer, R.E. 1986. The teaching of learning strategies. In M.R. Wittrock, ed., *Handbook of Research on Teaching,* pp. 315-27. 3rd ed. New York: Macmillan.

31. Zimmerman, B.J., and Pons, M.M. 1986. Development of a structured interview for assessing student use of self-regulated learning strategies. *American Educational Research Journal, 23,* 614-628.

32. Chamot, A.U., and O'Malley, J.M. 1986. *A Cognitive Academic Language Learning Approach: An ESL Content-based Curriculum.* Washington, DC: National Clearinghouse for Bilingual Education.

33. Ibid.

O'Malley, J.M., and Chamot, A.U. 1990. *Learning Strategies in Second Language Acquisition.* New York: Cambridge University Press.

34. Brown, A.L., Bransford, J.D., Ferrara, R.A., and Campione, J.C. 1983. Learning, remembering, and understanding. In J.H. Flavell and M. Markman, eds., *Carmichael's Manual of Child Psychology,* Vol. 3, 77-166. New York: Wiley.

35. Weinstein, C.E., and Mayer, R.E. 1986. The teaching of learning strategies. In M.R. Wittrock, ed., *Handbook of Research on Teaching.* 3rd ed. pp. 315-27. New York: Macmillan.

36. O'Malley, J.M., and Chamot, A.U. 1990. *Learning Strategies in Second Language Acquisition.* New York: Cambridge University Press.

37. O'Malley, J.M., Chamot, A.U., Stewner-Manzanares, G., Russo, R.P., and Küpper, L. 1985a. Learning strategies used by beginning and intermediate ESL students. *Language Learning, 35,* 21-46.

38. Gagné, E.D. 1985. *The Cognitive Psychology of School Learning.* Boston: Little, Brown.

Shuell, T.J. 1986. Cognitive conceptions of learning. *Review of Educational Research, 56,* 411-436.

39. Anderson, J.R. 1985. *Cognitive Psychology and Its Implications.* 2nd ed. New York: Freeman.

Lachman, R., Lachman, J.L., and Butterfield, E.C. 1979. *Cognitive Psychology and Information Processing.* Hillsdale, NJ: Erlbaum.

Shuell, T.J. 1986. Cognitive conceptions of learning. *Review of Educational Research, 56,* 411-436.

40. Anderson, J.R. 1980. *Cognitive Psychology and Its Implications.* San Francisco: Freeman.

Anderson, J.R. 1983. *The Architecture of Cognition.* Cambridge, MA: Harvard University Press.

41. Canale, M. and Swain, M. 1980. Theoretical bases of communicative approaches to second language teaching and testing. *Applied Linguistics, 1,* 1-47.

42. O'Malley, J.M., Chamot, A.U., and Walker, C. 1987. Some applications of cognitive theory to second language acquisition. *Studies in Second Language Acquisition, 9,* 287-306.

43. Chamot, A.U., Dale, M., O'Malley, J.M., and Spanos, G.A. 1993. Learning and problem-solving strategies of ESL students. *Bilingual Research Journal,* 16 (3+4), 1–38.

44. Polya, G. 1957. *How to Solve It.* 2nd ed. New York: Doubleday.

Polya, G. 1973. *Induction and Analogy in Mathematics.* Princeton, NJ: Princeton University Press.

45. Anderson, J.R. 1980. *Cognitive Psychology and Its Implications.* San Francisco: Freeman.

46. Gagné, E.D. 1985. *The Cognitive Psychology of School Learning.* Boston: Little, Brown.

47. Perkins, D.N. March, 1989. Teaching metacognitive strategies. Paper presented at the American Educational Research Association Annual Meeting, San Francisco.

48. Marland, M. 1977. *Language Across the Curriculum: The Implementation of the Bullock Report in the Secondary School.* London: Heinemann.

49. Van Allen, R., and Allen, C. 1976. *Language Experience Activities.* Boston: Houghton Mifflin.

50. Edelsky, C., Draper, K., and Smith, K. 1983. Hookin' 'em in at the start of school in a "whole language" classroom. *Anthropology and Education Quarterly, 14* (4), 257-281.

Enright, D.S., and McCloskey, M.L. 1988. *Integrating English: Developing English Language and Literacy in the Multilingual Classroom.* Reading, MA: Addison-Wesley.

Goodman, K. 1986. *What's Whole in Whole Language?* Portsmouth, NH: Heinemann.

51. Pearson, P.D., and Raphael, T.E. 1990. Reading Comprehension as a Dimension of Thinking. In Jones, B.F., and Idol, L., eds., *Dimensions of Thinking and Cognitive Instruction,* pp. 209-240. Hillsdale, NJ: Lawrence Erlbaum.

Pressley, M. and Associates 1990. *Cognitive Strategy Instruction That Really Improves Children's Academic Performance.* Cambridge, MA: Brookline Books.

52. Harris, K.R., and Graham, S. 1992. *Helping Young Writers Master the Craft: Strategy Instruction and Self-regulation in the Writing Process.* Cambridge, MA: Brookline Books.

53. Kagan, S. 1986. Cooperative learning and sociocultural factors in schooling. In California State Department of Education, *Beyond Language: Social and Cultural Factors in Schooling Language Minority Students,* pp. 231-298. Los Angeles: Evaluation, Dissemination, and Assessment Center, California State University.

54. Johnson, D.W., Johnson, R.T., Holubec, E.J., and Roy, P. 1984. *Circles of Learning: Cooperation in the Classroom.* Alexandria, VA: Association for Supervision and Curriculum Development.

Slavin, R.E. 1987. Cooperative learning and the cooperative school. *Educational Leadership, 45* (3), 7-13.

55. Chamot, A.U., and O'Malley, J.M. 1989. The cognitive academic language learning approach. In P. Rigg and V.G. Allen, eds., *When They Don't All Speak English: Integrating the ESL Student Into the Regular Classroom,* pp. 108-125. Urbana, IL: National Council of Teachers of English.

McGroarty, M. 1992. Cooperative learning: The benefits for content-area teaching. In P.A. Richard-Amato and M.A. Snow eds., *The Multicultural Classroom: Readings for Content-area Teachers,* pp. 58-69. White Plains, NY: Longman.

56. Jones, B.F., and Idol, L. 1990 Introduction. In B.F. Jones and L. Idol, eds., *Dimensions of Thinking and Cognitive Instruction,* pp. 1-13. Hillsdale, NJ: Lawrence Erlbaum.

57. Leinhardt, G. 1992. What research on learning tells us about teaching. *Educational Leadership, 49* (7), 20-25.

58. Onosko, J.J. 1992. Exploring the thinking of thoughtful teachers. *Educational Leadership, 49* (7), 40-43.

59. Jones, B.F., Palincsar, A.S., Ogle, D.S., and Carr, E.G. 1987. *Strategic Teaching and Learning: Cognitive Instruction in the Content Areas.* Alexandria, VA: Association for Supervision and Curriculum Development.

60. Enright, D.S., and McCloskey, M.L. 1988. *Integrating English: Developing English Language and Literacy in the Multilingual Classroom.* Reading, MA: Addison-Wesley.

61. Cummins, J. 1984. *Bilingualism and Special Education: Issues in Assessment and Pedagogy.* San Diego, CA: College-Hill Press.

62. Ibid.

CHAPTER 2: THE CONTENT-BASED CURRICULUM IN CALLA

1. Leydon, M., Johnson, G., and Barr, B. Introduction to Physical Science. P. 133. Menlo Park, CA: Addison-Wesley Publishing Company.

2. Barman, C., et al. 1989. Addison-Wesley Science, Grade 4. P.179. Menlo Park, CA: Addision-Wesley Publishing Company.

3. Hewitt, Paul G. 1992. *Conceptual Physics: The High School Physics Program,* Second Edition. Pp. 28, 29, 30. Menlo Park, CA: Addison-Wesley Publishing Company.

4. Prawat, R.S. 1992. From individual differences to learning communities—our changing focus. *Educational Leadership, 49* (7), 9-13.

5. Ogle, D. 1986. K-W-L group instruction strategy. In A.S. Palincsar, D.S. Ogle, B.F. Jones, and E.G. Carr, eds., *Teaching Reading as Thinking.* Alexandria, VA: Association for Supervision and Curriculum Development.

6. Jones, B.F., Pierce, J., and Hunter, B. 1988/1989. Teaching students to construct graphic representations. *Educational Leadership, 46* (4), 20-25.

CHAPTER 3: ACADEMIC LANGUAGE DEVELOPMENT IN CALLA

1. Cummins, J. 1984. *Bilingualism and Special Education: Issues in Assessment and Pedagogy.* San Diego, CA: College-Hill.

2. Bloom, B., and Krathwohl, D. 1977. *Taxonomy of Educational Objectives: Handbook I: Cognitive Domain.* White Plains, NY: Longman.

3. Marzano, R.J., Brandt, R.S., Hughes, C.S., Jones, B.F., Presseisen, B.Z., Rankin, S.C., and Suhor, C. 1988. *Dimensions of Thinking: A Framework for Curriculum and Instruction.* Alexandria, VA: Association for Supervision and Curriculum Development.

CHAPTER 4: LEARNING STRATEGY INSTRUCTION IN CALLA

1. Gagné, E.D. 1985. *The Cognitive Psychology of School Learning.* Boston: Little, Brown.

Shuell, T.J. 1986. Cognitive conceptions of learning. *Review of Educational Research, 56,* 411-36.

2. O'Malley, J.M., and Chamot, A.U. 1990. *Learning Strategies in Second Language Acquisition.* New York: Cambridge University Press.

O'Malley, J.M., Chamot, A.U., Stewner-Manzanares, G., Küpper, L., and Russo, R. 1985a. Learning strategies used by beginning and intermediate ESL students. *Language Learning, 35,* 21-46.

3. Wenden, A., and Rubin, J., eds., 1987. *Learner Strategies in Language Learning.* Englewood Cliffs, NJ: Prentice Hall.

4. Weinstein, C.E., and Mayer, R.E. 1986. The teaching of learning strategies. In M.C. Wittrock, ed., *Handbook of Research on Teaching.* 3rd ed. pp. 315-27. New York: Macmillan.

5. O'Malley, J.M., and Chamot, A.U. 1990. *Learning Strategies in Second Language Acquisition.* New York: Cambridge University Press.

6. Derry, S.J., and Murphy, D.A. 1986. Designing systems that train learning ability: From theory to practice. *Review of Educational Research, 56,* 1-39.

7. Chamot, A.U., Dale, M., O'Malley, and Spanos, G. 1993. Learning and problem-solving strategies of ESL students. *Bilingual Research Journal,* 16 (3+4) 1–38.

8. Paris, S.G., and Winograd, P. 1990. How metacognition can promote academic learning and instruction. In B.F. Jones and L. Idol, eds., *Dimensions of Thinking and Cognitive Instruction,* pp. 15-51. Hillsdale, NJ: Lawrence Erlbaum.

9. O'Malley, J.M., Chamot, A.U., Stewner-Manzanares, G., Küpper, L., and Russo, R. 1985a. Learning strategies used by beginning and intermediate ESL students. *Language Learning, 35,* 21-46.

10. O'Malley, J.M., Chamot, A.U., Stewner-Manzanares, G., Russo, R., and Küpper, L. 1985b. Learning strategy applications with students of English as a second language. *TESOL Quarterly, 19,* 285-296.

11. Weinstein, C.E., and Mayer, R.E. 1986. The teaching of learning strategies. In M.C. Wittrock, ed., *Handbook of Research on Teaching.* 3rd ed. pp. 315-27. New York: Macmillan.

12. Brown, A.L., Bransford, J.D., Ferrara, R.A., and Campione, J.C. 1983. Learning, remembering, and understanding. In J.H. Flavell and M. Markman, eds., *Carmichael's Manual of Child Psychology.* Vol. 3. pp. 77-166. New York: Wiley.

Brown, A.L., and Palincsar, A.S. 1982. Inducing strategies learning from texts by means of informed, self-control training. *Topics in Learning and Learning Disabilities, 2* (1), 1-17.

13. O'Malley, J.M., and Chamot, A.U. 1990. *Learning Strategies in Second Language Acquisition.* New York: Cambridge University Press.

14. Brown, A.L., Bransford, J.D., Ferrara, R.A., and Campione, J.C. 1983. Learning, remembering, and understanding. In J.H. Flavell and M. Markman, eds., *Carmichael's Manual of Child Psychology.* Vol. 3. pp. 77-166. New York: Wiley.

Paris, S.G., and Winograd, P. 1990. How metacognition can promote academic learning and instruction. In B.F. Jones and L. Idol, eds., *Dimensions of Thinking and Cognitive Instruction,* pp. 15-51. Hillsdale, NJ: Lawrence Erlbaum.

15. Weinstein, C.E., and Mayer, R.E. 1986. The teaching of learning strategies. In M.C. Wittrock, ed., *Handbook of Research on Teaching.* 3rd ed. pp. 315-27. New York: Macmillan.

16. Krashen, S.D. 1982. *Principles and Practice in Second Language Acquisition.* Oxford: Pergamon Press.

17. Pressley, M., Goodchild, F., Fleet, J., and Zajchowski, R. 1988. The challenges of classroom strategy instruction. *Elementary School Journal, 89,* 301-342.

18. O'Malley, J.M., Chamot, A.U., Stewner-Manzanares, G., Russo, R., and Küpper, L. 1985b. Learning strategy applications with students of English as a second language. *TESOL Quarterly, 19,* 285-296.

19. Pressley, M. and Associates 1990. *Cognitive Strategy Instruction That Really Improves Children's Academic Performance.* Cambridge, MA: Brookline Books.

20. Pressley, M., Goodchild, F., Fleet, J., and Zajchewski, R. 1988. The challenges of classroom strategy instruction. *Elementary School Journal, 89,* 301-342.

21. Pressley, M. and Associates 1990. *Cognitive Strategy Instruction That Really Improves Children's Academic Performance.* Cambridge, MA: Brookline Books.

22. Adapted from El-Dinary, P., and Brown, R. (1992), from:

Bergman, J.L. 1992. SAIL—A way to success and independence for low-achieving readers. *The Reading Teacher, 45,* 598-602.

Chamot, A.U. and O'Malley, J.M. 1989. The Cognitive Academic Language Learning Approach. In P. Rigg and V.G. Allen, eds., *When They Don't Speak English: Integrating the ESL Student Into the Regular Classroom,* p. 108–125. Urbana, Il: National Council of Teachers of English.

Pearson, P.D., and Gallagher, M.C. 1983. The instruction of reading comprehension. *Contemporary Educational Psychology, 8,* 317-344.

23. O'Malley, J.M., Chamot, A.U., Stewner-Manzanares, G., Küpper, L., and Russo, R. 1985a. Learning strategies used by beginning and intermediate ESL students. *Language Learning, 35,* 21-46.

24. Bruner, J.S. 1976. Early social interactions and language acquisition. Cited in J.V. Wertsch, ed., *Culture, Communication, and Cognition.* Cambridge, England: Cambridge University Press.

Wood, D., Bruner, J.S., and Ross, G. 1976. The role of tutoring in problem solving. *Journal of Child Psychology and Psychiatry, 66,* 181-91.

25. Chamot, A.U. 1987. *Language Development Through Content: America: The Early Years.* P. 20. Reading, MA: Addison-Wesley Publishing Company.

26. Zimmerman, B.J. 1990. Self-regulated learning and academic achievement: An overview. *Educational Psychologist, 25* (1), 3-17.

27. Paris, S.G., and Oka, E.R. 1986. Children's reading strategies, metacognition, and motivation. *Developmental Review, 6,* 25-56.

CHAPTER 5: PLANNING, TEACHING, AND MONITORING CALLA

1. Prawat, R.S. 1992. From individual differences to learning communities—our changing focus. *Educational Leadership, 49* (7), 9-13.

2. Johnson, D.W., Johnson, R.T., Holubec, E.J., and Roy, P. 1984. *Circles of Learning: Cooperation in the Classroom.* Alexandria, VA: Association of Supervision and Curriculum Development.

Slavin, R.E. 1987. Cooperative learning and the cooperative school. *Educational Leadership, 45* (3), 7-13.

3. Kagan, S. 1986. Cooperative learning and sociocultural factors in schooling. In California State Department of Education, *Beyond Language: Social and Cultural Factors in Schooling Language Minority Students*, pp. 231-298. Los Angeles: Evaluation, Dissemination and Assessment Center, California State University.

McGroarty, M. 1992. Cooperative learning: The benefits for content-area teaching. In P.A. Richard-Amato and M.A. Snow, eds., *The Multicultural Classroom: Readings for Content-area Teachers*, pp. 58-69. White Plains, NY: Longman.

4. Palincsar, A.S., and Brown, A.L. 1984. Reciprocal teaching of comprehension-fostering and comprehension-monitoring activities. *Cognition and Instruction*, 1:117-175.

Palincsar, A.S., and Brown, A.L. 1986. Interactive teaching to promote independent learning from text. *The Reading Teacher, 39* (8): 771-777.

5. Joyce, B., and Showers, B. 1988. *Student Achievement Through Staff Development*. White Plains, NY: Longman.

6. Ogle, D. 1986. The K-W-L: A teaching model that develops active reading of expository text. *The Reading Teacher, 39*, 564-70.

CHAPTER 6: ASSESSING STUDENT PROGRESS IN CALLA

1. DeGeorge, G.P. 1988. Assessment and placement of language minority students: Procedures for mainstreaming. Silver Spring, MD: National Clearinghouse for Bilingual Education.

O'Malley, J.M. 1989. Language proficiency testing with limited English proficient students. In J.E. Alatis, ed., *Georgetown University Roundtable on Languages and Linguistics*, pp. 235-44. Washington, DC: Georgetown University.

2. Herman, J.L. 1992. What research tells us about good assessment. *Educational Leadership, 49* (8), 74-78.

O'Malley, J.M. 1989. Language proficiency testing with limited English proficient students. In J.E. Alatis, ed., *Georgetown University Roundtable on Languages and Linguistics*, pp. 235-44. Washington, DC: Georgetown University.

3. Baker, E. 1991. Workshop on performance assessment. Presented at the American Educational Research Association Annual Meeting, Chicago.

4. Haney, W., and Madaus, G. 1989. Searching for alternatives to standardized test: Whys, whats, and whithers. *Phi Delta Kappan, 70*, 683-87.

Mitchell, R. 1992. *Testing for Learning: How New Approaches to Evaluation Can Improve American Schools*. New York: The Free Press.

Wiggins, G. 1989a. A true test: Toward more authentic and equitable assessment. *Phi Delta Kappan, 70*, 703-13.

5. Pierce, L.V., and O'Malley, J.M. 1992. *Performance and Portfolio Assessment for Language Minority Students*. Washington, DC: National Clearinghouse for Bilingual Education.

6. Roeber, E.D. 1990. *Performance Assessment: A National Perspective*. Oak Brook, IL: North Central Regional Educational Laboratory.

Stiggins, R.J. 1987. Design and development of performance assessments. *Educational Measurement: Issues and Practices, 6* (1), 33-42.

7. Stiggins, R.J. 1990. *The Foundation of Performance Assessment: A Strong Training Program*. Oak Brook, IL: North Central Regional Educational Laboratory.

8. California Department of Education. 1990. *California: The State of Assessment*. Sacramento, CA: California Department of Education.

9. Ibid.

10. Ibid.

11. Ibid.

12. Stenmark, J.K. 1989. *Assessment Alternatives in Mathematics*. Berkeley, CA: Lawrence Hall of Science.

13. Ibid.

14. California Assessment Program. 1988-89. *Sample Items*. Sacramento, CA: California Department of Education.

15. Ibid.

16. Ibid.

17. Stenmark, J.K. 1989. *Assessment Alternatives in Mathematics*. Berkeley, CA: Lawrence Hall of Science.

18. Wiggins, G. 1989b. Teaching to the authentic test. *Educational Leadership, 46* (7), 41-47.

19. Hamayan, E.V., Kwiat, J.A., and Perlman, R. 1985. *The Identification and Assessment of Language Minority Students: A Handbook for Educators*. Arlington Heights, IL: Illinois Resource Center.

Oller, J.W. 1979. *Language Tests at School*. London: Longman.

20. Cooper, K.S. 1986. Europe, Africa, Asia and Australia. P. 266. Morristown, NJ: Silver Burdett Company.

21. Hamayan, E.V., Kwiat, J.A., and Perlman, R. 1985. *The Identification and Assessment of Language Minority Students: A Handbook for Educators*. Arlington Heights, IL: Illinois Resource Center.

22. Ibid.

23. Nunan, D. 1988. *The Learner-Centered Curriculum.* Cambridge, England: Cambridge University Press.

24. Maryland State Department of Education. (n.d.). *Questions for Quality Thinking.* Baltimore, MD: Author.

25. Mitchell, R. 1992. *Testing for Learning: How New Approaches to Evaluation Can Improve American Schools.* New York: The Free Press.

Moya, S.S., and O'Malley, J.M. (in press). A portfolio assessment model for ESL. *Journal of Educational Issues of Language Minority Students.*

Valencia, S.W. 1990. Alternative assessment: Separating the wheat from the chaff. *The Reading Teacher, 43,* 60-61.

Tierney, R.J., Carter, M.A., and Desai, L.E. 1991. *Portfolio Assessment in the Reading-Writing Classroom.* Norwood, MA: Christopher Gordon Publishers.

26. Moya, S.S., and O'Malley, J.M. 1993. A portfolio assessment model for ESL. *Journal of Educational Issues of Language Minority Students.*

Pierce, L.V., and O'Malley, J.M. 1993. *Performance and Portfolio Assessment for Language Minority Students.* Washington, DC: National Clearinghouse for Bilingual Education.

27. Moya, S.S., and O'Malley, J.M. 1993. A portfolio assessment model for ESL. *Journal of Educational Issues of Language Minority Students.*

Pierce, L.V., and O'Malley, J.M. 1992. *Performance and Portfolio Assessment for Language Minority Students.* Washington, DC: National Clearinghouse for Bilingual Education.

CHAPTER 7: CALLA PROGRAM ADMINISTRATION

1. Joyce, B., and Showers, B. 1988. *Student Achievement Through Staff Development.* White Plains, NY: Longman.

2. Ibid.

Ogle, D.M. 1988-1989. Implementing strategic teaching. *Educational Leadership, 46* (4), 47-60.

3. Joyce, B., and Showers, B. 1988. *Student Achievement Through Staff Development.* White Plains, NY: Longman.

4. Ibid.

5. Cook, T.D., and Campbell, D.T. 1979. *Quasi Experimentation.* Boston: Houghton-Mifflin.

CHAPTER 8: CALLA IN DIFFERENT CONTEXTS

1. Rigg, P. 1989. Language experience approach: Reading naturally. In R. Rigg and V.G. Allen,eds., *When They Don't All Speak English: Integrating the ESL Student Into the Regular Classroom.* Urbana, IL: National Council of Teachers of English.

2. Cantoni-Harvey, G. 1987. *Content-area Language Instruction: Approaches and Strategies.* Reading, MA: Addison-Wesley.

Rigg, P. 1989. Language experience approach: Reading naturally. In R. Rigg and V.G. Allen, eds., *When They Don't All Speak English: Integrating the ESL Student Into the Regular Classroom.* Urbana, IL: National Council of Teachers of English.

3. Atwell, M. 1985. Predictable books for adolescent readers. *Journal of Reading, 34* (2): 18-22.

4. Chamot, A.U., and Stewner-Manzanares, G. 1985. *A Summary of Current Literature on English as a Second Language.* Washington, DC: National Clearinghouse for Bilingual Education.

5. Brinton, D., Sasser, L., and Winningham, B. 1992. Language minority students in multicultural classrooms. In P.A. Richard-Amato and M.A., Snow, eds., *The Multicultural Classroom: Readings for Content-area Teachers.* White Plains, NY: Longman.

6. McGroarty, M. 1992. Cooperative learning: The benefits for content-area teaching. In P.A. Richard-Amato and M.A., Snow, eds., *The Multicultural Classroom: Readings for Content-area Teachers.* White Plains, NY: Longman.

7. Spanos, G.A. 1990. On the integration of language and content instruction. *Annual Review of Applied Linguistics, 10,* 227-240.

8. Enright, D.S., and McCloskey, M.L. 1989. *Integrating English: Developing English Language and Literacy in the Multilingual Classroom.* Reading, MA: Addison-Wesley.

9. Bragaw, D.H., and Hartoonian, H. M. 1988. Social studies: The study of people in society. In R.S.. Brandt, ed., *Content of the Curriculum: 1988 ASCD Yearbook.* Alexandria, VA: Association for Supervision and Curriculum Development.

California Department of Education 1987. *History-social science framework.* Sacramento, CA: California State Department of Education.

California Department of Education 1990. *Science Framework for California Public Schools.* Sacramento, CA: California State Department of Education.

Campbell, P.E., and Fey, J.T. 1988. New goals for school mathematics. In Brandt, R.S., ed., *Content of the Curriculum: 1988 ASCD Yearbook.* Alexandria, VA: Association for Supervision and Curriculum Development.

10. National Council of Teachers of Mathematics 1989. *Curriculum and Evaluation Standards for School Mathematics*. Reston, VA: National Council of Teachers of Mathematics.

11. McGroarty, M. 1992. Cooperative learning: The benefits for content-area teaching. In P.A. Richard-Amato and M.A., Snow, eds., *The Multicultural Classroom: Readings for Content-area Teachers*. White Plains, NY: Longman.

12. Gagné, E.D. 1985. *The Cognitive Psychology of School Learning*. Boston: Little, Brown.

Garner, R. 1987. *Metacognition and Reading Comprehension*. Norwood, NJ: Heinemann.

Jones, B.F., Palincsar, A.S., Ogle, D.S., and Carr, E.G. 1987. *Strategic Teaching and Learning: Cognitive Instruction in the Content Areas*. Alexandria, VA: Association for Supervision and Content Development.

Palincsar, A.S., and Brown, A.L. 1984. Reciprocal teaching of comprehension-fostering and comprehension-monitoring activities. *Cognition and Instruction*, 117-175.

Pressley, M., and Harris, K. R. 1990. What we really know about strategy instruction. *Educational Leadership, 48* (1), 31-34.

13. Chamot, A.U., Dale, M., O'Malley, J.M., and Spanos, G.A. 1993. Learning and problem-solving strategies of ESL students. *Bilingual Research Journal*, 16 (3+4) 1–38.

O'Malley, J.M., and Chamot, A.U. 1990. *Learning Strategies in Second Language Acquisition*. Cambridge, England: Cambridge University Press.

14. Office of Educational Research and Improvement 1987. *The Current Operation of the Chapter 1 Program*. Washington, DC: Office of Educational Research and Improvement.

15. Anderson, L.W., and Pellicer, L.O. 1990. Synthesis of research on compensatory and remedial education. *Educational Leadership, 48* (1), 10-16.

Pogrow, S. 1990. Challenging at-risk students: Findings from the HOTS program. *Phi Delta Kappan, 71:* 389-397.

16. Anderson, L.W., and Pellicer, L.O. 1990. Synthesis of research on compensatory and remedial education. *Educational Leadership, 48* (1), 10-16.

Pogrow, S. 1990. Challenging at-risk students: Findings from the HOTS program. *Phi Delta Kappan, 71:* 389-397.

17. Anderson, L.W., and Pellicer, L.O. 1990. Synthesis of research on compensatory and remedial education. *Educational Leadership, 48* (1), 10-16.

18. Zimmerman, B.J. 1990. Self-regulated learning and academic achievement: An overview. *Educational Psychologist, 25* (1), 3-17.

19. Carrasquillo, A. L., and Baecher, R.E. 1990. *Teaching the Bilingual Special Education Student*. Norwood, NJ: Ablex.

20. Chamot, A.U., and O'Malley, J.M. 1990. Adaptations of the Cognitive Academic language Learning Approach CALLA to special education. In A.L. Carrasquillo and R.E. Baecher, eds., *Teaching the Bilingual Special Education Student,* pp. 218-223. Norwood, NJ: Ablex.

21. Ibid.

22. Ibid.

Harris, K., and Graham, S. 1992. Self-regulated strategy development: A part of the writing process. In *Promoting Academic Competence and Literacy in Schools,* pp. 277-309. New York: Academic Press.

23. Loper, A.B. 1980. Metacognitive development: Implications for cognitive training. *Exceptional Education Quarterly, 1,* 1-8.

24. Deshler, D.D., and Schumaker, J.B. 1986. Learning strategies: An instructional alternative for low-achieving adolescents. *Exceptional Children, 52,* 583-590.

Rabinowitz, M., and Chi, M.T. 1987. An interactive model of strategic processing. In S.J. Ceci, ed., *Handbook of Cognitive, Social, and Neuropsychological Aspects of Learning Disabilities,* 83-102. Hillsdale, NJ: Lawrence Erlbaum.

25. Snow, M.A., and Brinton, D.M. 1988. Content-based language instruction: Investigating the effectiveness of the Adjunct Model. *TESOL Quarterly, 22* (4): 553-574.

26. Ibid.

27. Met, M. 1988. Tomorrow's emphasis in foreign language: Proficiency. In R.S. Brandt, ed., *Content of the Curriculum: 1988 ASCD Yearbook*. Alexandria, VA: Association for Supervision and Curriculum Development.

Omaggio, A.C. 1986. *Teaching Language in Context: Proficiency-oriented Instruction*. Boston: Heinle and Heinle.

28. American Council on the Teaching of Foreign Languages. 1986. *ACTFL Proficiency Guidelines*. Hastings-on-Hudson, NY: American Council on the Teaching of Foreign Languages.

29. Curtain, H.A. and Pesola, C.A. 1988. *Languages and Children—Making the Match*. Reading, MA: Addison-Wesley.

Met, M. 1988. Tomorrow's emphasis in foreign language: Proficiency. In R.S. Brandt, ed., *Content of the Curriculum: 1988 ASCD Yearbook*. Alexandria, VA: Association for Supervision and Curriculum Development.

Snow, M.A., Met, M., and Genesee, F. 1989. A conceptual framework for the integration of language and content instruction. *TESOL Quarterly, 23,* pp. 201-217.

30. Curtain, H.A. and Pesola, C.A. 1988. *Languages and Children—Making the Match.* Reading, MA: Addison-Wesley.

Snow, M.A., Met, M., and Genesee, F. 1989. A conceptual framework for the integration of language and content instruction. *TESOL Quarterly, 23,* pp. 201-217.

31. Chamot, A.U., and Küpper, L. 1989. Learning strategies in foreign language instruction. *Foreign Language Annals, 22* (1), 13-24.

O'Malley, J.M., and Chamot, A.U. 1990. *Learning Strategies in Second Language Acquisition.* Cambridge, England: Cambridge University Press.

32. Chamot, A.U. (in press). Learning strategy instruction in the foreign language classroom. *Foreign Language Annals.*

Chamot, A.U., O'Malley, J.M., Barnhardt, S., and Nishimura, M. 1991. Teaching learning strategies in the foreign language classroom. Paper presented at the American Council on Teaching Foreign Languages Annual Meeting, Washington, DC.

33. Georgetown University Language Research Projects, 1992. "Learning Strategy Icons for Spanish."

CHAPTER 9: CALLA SCIENCE

1. Carnegie Commission on Science, Technology, and the Government. 1991. *In the National Interest: The Federal Government in the Reform of K-12 Math and Science Education.* New York: Author.

Linn, M.C. 1986. Science. In R.F. Dillon and R.J. Sternberg, eds., *Cognition and Instruction,* pp. 155-204. Orlando, FL: Academic Press.

2. Blough, G.O., and Schwartz, J. 1990. *Elementary School Science and How to Teach It.* Chicago: Holt, Rinehart and Winston.

3. Duckworth, E., Easley, J., Hawkins, D., and Henriques, A. 1990. *Science Education: A Minds-on Approach for the Elementary Years.* Hillsdale, NJ: Lawrence Erlbaum.

Loucks-Horsley, S., Kapitan, R., Carlson, M.D., Kuerbis, P.J., Clark, R.C., Melle, G.M., Sachse, T.P., and Walton, E. 1990. *Elementary School Science for the '90s.* Alexandria, VA: Association for Supervision and Curriculum Development.

4. California State Department of Education. 1990. *Science Framework for California Public Schools.* Sacramento, CA: California State Board of Education.

5. Hazen, R.M. and Trefil, J. 1991. Science Matters: Achieving Scientific Literacy. New York: Doubleday.

6. Barman, C., Di Spezio, M., Guthrie, V., Leyden, M.B., Mercier, S., Ostlund, K., and Armbruster, B. 1989. *Addison-Wesley Science.* Menlo Park, CA: Addison-Wesley.

7. Heimler, C.H., and Lockard, J.D. 1981. *Focus on Life Science.* Columbus, OH: Merrill.

8. Curtis, H., and Barnes, N.E. 1985. *Invitation to Biology.* 4th ed. New York: Worth.

9. Ibid.

10. Heimler, C.H., and Lockard, J.D. 1981. *Focus on Life Science.* Columbus, OH: Merrill.

11. Carey, S. 1990. Cognitive science and science education. In C. Hedley, J. Houtz, and A. Baratta, eds., *Cognition, Curriculum, and Literacy,* pp. 149-166. Norwood, NJ: Ablex.

12. Linn, M.C. 1983. Content, context, and process in adolescent reasoning. *Journal of Early Adolescence, 3,* 63-82.

13. Bat-Sheva, E., and Linn, M.C. 1988. Learning and instruction: An examination of four research perspectives in science education. *Review of Educational Research, 58,* 251-301.

Carey, S. 1990. Cognitive science and science education. In C. Hedley, J. Houtz, and A. Baratta, eds., *Cognition, Curriculum, and Literacy,* pp. 149-166. Norwood, NJ: Ablex.

Linn, M.C. 1986. Science. In R.F. Dillon and R.J. Sternberg, eds., *Cognition and Instruction,* pp. 155-204. Orlando, FL: Academic Press.

14. Ibid.

15. Linn, M.C. 1983. Content, context, and process in adolescent reasoning. *Journal of Early Adolescence, 3,* 63-82.

16. Gagné, E.D. 1985. *The Cognitive Psychology of School Learning.* Boston: Little, Brown.

17. Hyde, A.A., and Bizar, M. 1989. *Thinking in Context: Teaching Cognitive Processes Across the Elementary School Curriculum.* White Plains, NY: Longman.

18. California State Department of Education. 1990. *Science Framework for California Public Schools.* Sacramento, CA: California State Board of Education.

19. Ibid.

Carmichael, H., and Rezba, C. 1991. *A Framework for Developing the Virginia Common Core of Learning.* Richmond, VA: Virginia Department of Education.

Sachse, T.P. 1989. Making science happen. *Educational Leadership, 47,* 3: 18-21.

Rutherford, F.J., and Ahlgren, A. 1988. Rethinking the science curriculum. In R.S. Brandt, ed., *Content of the Curriculum: 1988 ASCD Yearbook.* Alexandria, VA: Association for Supervision and Curriculum Development.

20.California State Department of Education. 1990. *Science Framework for California Public Schools.* Sacramento, CA: California State Board of Education.

21. Carmichael, H., and Rezba, C. 1991. *A Framework for Developing the Virginia Common Core of Learning.* Richmond, VA: Virginia Department of Education.

Rutherford, F.J., *et al.* 1989. *Science for All Americans.* Washington, DC: American Association for the Advancement of Science.

22. Anderson, C.W. 1987. Strategic teaching in science. In B.F. Jones, A.S. Palincsar, D.S. Ogle, and E.G. Carr, eds., *Strategic Teaching and Learning: Cognitive Instruction in the Content Areas.* Alexandria, VA: Association for Supervision and Curriculum Development.

Minstrell, J.A. 1989. Teaching science for understanding. In L.B. Resnick and L.E. Klopfer, eds., *Toward the Thinking Curriculum: Current Cognitive Research. 1989 ASCD Yearbook.* Alexandria, VA: Association for Supervision and Curriculum Development.

Roth, K.J. 1990. Developing meaningful conceptual understanding in science. In B.F. Jones and L. Idol, eds. *Dimensions of Thinking and Cognitive Instruction.* Hillsdale, NJ: Lawrence Erlbaum.

23. Ogle, D.S. 1986. K-W-L group instruction strategy. In A.S. Palincsar, D.S. Ogle, B.E. Jones, and E.G. Carr, eds., *Teaching Reading as Thinking.* Alexandria, VA: Association for Supervision and Curriculum Development.

24. Ostlund, K.L. 1992. *Science Process Skills: Assessing Hands-on Student Performance.* Menlo Park, CA: Addison-Wesley.

25. Linn, M.C. 1986. Science. In R.F. Dillon and R.J. Sternberr, eds., *Cognition and Instruction,* pp. 155-204. Orlando, FL: Academic Press.

26. Ibid.

27. Ibid.

28. Ibid.

29. Ibid.

CHAPTER 10: CALLA MATHEMATICS

1. Carnegie Commission 1991. *In the National Interest: The Federal Government in the Reform of K-12 Math and Science Education.* New York: Author.

2. Driscoll, M. 1988. Transforming the "underachieving" math curriculum. *ASCD Curriculum Update,* January 1988.

West, P. 1991. Math groups urge changes in teacher preparation. *Education Week,* 5, March 13, 1991.

3. Stodolsky, S.S. 1988. *The Subject Matters: Classroom Activity in Math and Social Studies.* Chicago: University of Chicago Press.

4. Porter, A. 1989. A curriculum out of balance: The case of elementary school mathematics. *Educational Researcher, 18* (5), 9-15.

5. Freeman, D.J., and Porter, A.C. 1989. Do textbooks dictate the content of mathematics instruction in elementary schools? *American Educational Research Journal, 26* (3), 403-421.

6. Stodolsky, S.S. 1988. *The Subject Matters: Classroom Activity in Math and Social Studies.* Chicago: University of Chicago Press.

7. Ibid.

Stodolsky, S.S., Salk, S., and Glaessner, B. 1991. Student views about learning math and science. *American Educational Research Journal, 28* (1), 89-116.

8. Silver, E.A., and Marshall, S.P. 1990. Mathematical and scientific problem solving: Findings, issues, and instructional implications. In B.F. Jones and L. Idol, eds., *Dimensions of Thinking and Cognitive Instruction.* Hillsdale, NJ: Lawrence Erlbaum.

9. Santiago, F., and Spanos, G. 1993. Meeting the NCTM communication standards for all students. In G. Cuevas and M. Driscoll, eds., *Reaching All Students with Mathematics,* p. 133–145. Reston, VA: National Council of Teachers of Mathematics.

10. National Council of Teachers of Mathematics NCTM 1989. *Curriculum and Evaluation Standards for School Mathematics.* Reston, VA: Author.

11. Blankenship, C.S., and Lovitt, T.C. 1976. Story problems: Merely confusing or downright befuddling? *Journal of Research in Mathematics Education, 7,* 290-298.

12. Chamot, A.U., and O'Malley, J.M. 1986. *A Cognitive Academic Language Learning Approach: An ESL Content-based curriculum.* Washington, DC: National Clearinghouse for Bilingual Education.

13. Chamot, A.U. 1985. English language development through a content-based approach. In *Issues in English Language Development.* Rosslyn, VA: National Clearinghouse for Bilingual Education.

Chamot, A.U., and O'Malley, J.M. 1985. Mathematics learning strategies for limited English proficient students. Paper presented at the Washington Area Teachers of English to Speakers of Other Languages Annual Conference. College Park, MD.

Secada, W. 1983. The educational background of limited English proficient students: Implications for the arithmetic classroom. Mimeograph. Arlington Heights, IL: Bilingual Education Service Center, Northwest Educational Cooperative.

Secada, W. 1985. Literacy for mathematics. *Linguathon, 1* (4), 3.

14. Cuevas, G.J. 1984. Mathematics learning in English as a second language. *Journal of Research in Mathematics Education, 15* (2), 134-144.

Dale, T.C. and Cuevas, G.J. 1992. Integrating mathematics and language learning. In P.A. Richard-Amato and M.A. Snow, eds., *The Multicultural Classroom: Readings for Content-area Teachers,* pp. 330-348. White Plains, NY: Longman.

15. Dawe, L. 1983. Bilingualism and mathematical reasoning in English as a second language. *Educational Studies in Mathematics, 14,* 325-353.

Dawe, L. 1984. A theoretical framework for the study of the effects of bilingualism on mathematics teaching and learning. Paper presented at the Fifth International Congress on Mathematical Education, Adelaide, Australia.

16. Spanos, G., Rhodes, N.C., Dale, T.C., and Crandall, J. 1988. Linguistic features of mathematical problem solving: Insights and applications. In R.R. Cocking and J.P. Mestre, eds., *Linguistic and Cultural Influences on Mathematics,* pp. 221-240. Hillsdale, NJ: Lawrence Erlbaum.

17. Ibid.

18. Riley, M.S., Greeno, J.G., and Heller, J.J. 1983. Development of children's problem-solving ability in arithmetic. In H.P. Ginsburg, ed., *The Development of Mathematical Thinking,* pp. 153-196. New York: Academic Press.

19. Secada, W. 1988. The mathematical education of Hispanic students: Towards a research-based vision of the possible. Paper presented at the Symposium on Equity Issues in Mathematics and Science Achievement, Culver City, CA.

20. Mestre, J.P. 1984. The problem with problems: Hispanic students and math. *Bilingual Journal,* Fall, 15-32.

21. Chamot, A.U. 1985. English language development through a content-based approach. In *Issues in English Language Development.* Rosslyn, VA: National Clearinghouse for Bilingual Education.

22. Tsang, S.L. 1983. Mathematics learning styles of Chinese. Final Report. Rosslyn, VA: National Clearinghouse for Bilingual Education.

23. Knifong, J.D., and Holtan, B. 1976. A search for reading difficulties among erred word problems. *Journal for Research in Mathematics Education, 8,* 227-230.

24. Eicholz, R.E., O'Daffer, P.G., and Fleener, C.R. 1985. *Addison Wesley Mathematics: Teacher's Edition Book 5.* Menlo Park, CA: Addison Wesley.

25. Porter, A. 1989. A curriculum out of balance: The case of elementary school mathematics. *Educational Researcher, 18* (5), 9-15.

26. Lindquist, M.M. 1987. Strategic teaching in mathematics. In B.F. Jones, A.S. Palincsar, D.S. Ogle, and E.G. Carr, eds, *Strategic Teaching and Learning: Cognitive Instruction in the Content Areas,* pp. 111-134. Alexandria, VA: Association for Supervision in Curriculum Development.

Pressley, M. *et al.* 1990. *Cognitive Strategy Instruction That Really Improves Children's Academic Performance.* Cambridge, MA: Brookline Books.

Romberg, T.A., and Carpenter, T.P. 1986. Research on teaching and learning mathematics: Two disciplines of scientific inquiry. In M.R. Wittrock, ed., *Handbook of Research on Teaching,* pp. 850-873. New York: Macmillan.

27. Carpenter, T.P. 1985. Learning to add and subtract: An exercise in problem solving. In E.A. Silver, ed., *Teaching and Learning Mathematical Problem Solving: Multiple Research Perspectives,* pp. 17-40. Hillsdale, NJ: Lawrence Erlbaum.

Carpenter, T.P., Fennema, E., Peterson, P.L., Chiang, C., and Loef, M. 1985. Using knowledge of children's mathematical thinking in classroom teaching: An experimental study. Paper presented at the American Educational Research Association Annual Meeting, New Orleans, LA.

28. Eicholz, R.E., O'Daffer, P.G., and Fleener, C.R. 1985. *Addison Wesley Mathematics: Teacher's Edition Book 5.* Menlo Park, CA: Addison Wesley.

29. Ibid.

30. Noddings, N., Gilbert-MacMillan, K., and Leitz, S. 1983. What do individuals gain in small group mathematical problem solving? Paper presented at the American Educational Research Association Annual Meeting, Montreal.

31. Hart, L.C. 1985. Factors impeding the formation of a useful representation in mathematical problem solving. Paper presented at the American Educational Research Association Annual Meeting, Chicago.

32. Noddings, N., Gilbert-MacMillan, K., and Leitz, S. April, 1983. What do individuals gain in small group mathematical problem solving? Paper presented at the annual meetings of the American Educational Research Association, Montreal.

33. Yackel, E., and Wheatley, G.H. 1985. Characteristics of problem representation indicative of understanding in mathematics problem solving. Paper presented at the American Educational Research Association Annual Meeting, Chicago.

34. Santiago, F., and Spanos, G. 1991. Meeting the NCTM communication standards for all students. In G. Cuevas and M. Driscoll, eds., *Reaching all Students with Mathemlatics,* p. 133–145. Reston, VA: National Council of Teachers of Mathematics.

35. Eicholz, R.E., O'Daffer, P.G., and Fleener, C.R. 1985. *Addison Wesley Mathematics: Teacher's Edition Book 5.* Menlo Park, CA: Addison Wesley.

36. Noddings, N., Gilbert-MacMillan, K., and Leitz, S. 1983. What do individuals gain in small group mathematical problem solving? Paper presented at the American Educational Research Association Annual Meeting, Montreal.

37. Kennedy, B. 1985. Writing letters to learn math. *Learning, 13* (6), 59-60.

38. Chamot, A.U., and O'Malley, J.M. 1988. *Mathematics Book A: Learning Strategies for Problem Solving.* Reading, MA: Addison-Wesley.

39. Ibid.

40. Ibid.

41. Ibid.

CHAPTER 11: CALLA SOCIAL STUDIES

1. Stodolsky, S.S., Salk, S., and Glaessner, B. 1991. Student views about learning math and social studies. *American Educational Research Journal, 28* (1), 89-116.

2. California State Department of Education. 1987. *History-Social Science Framework for California Public Schools.* Sacramento, CA: California State Department of Education.

3. Alvermann, D. 1987. Strategic teaching in social studies. In B.F. Jones, A.S. Palincsar, D.S. Ogle, and E.G. Carr, eds., *Strategic Teaching and Learning: Cognitive Instruction in the Content Areas,* pp. 92-110. Alexandria, VA: Association for Supervision and Curriculum Development.

4. California State Department of Education. 1987. *History-Social Science Framework for California Public Schools.* Sacramento, CA: California State Department of Education.

5. Beck, I.L., and Dole, J.A. 1992. Reading and thinking with history and science text. In C. Collins and J.N. Mangieri, eds., *Teaching Thinking: An Agenda for the 21st Century,* pp. 3-21. Hillsdale, NJ: Lawrence Erlbaum.

6. King, M., Fagan, B., Bratt, T., and Baer, R. 1992. Social studies instruction. In P.A. Richard-Amato and M.A. Snow, eds., *The Multicultural Classroom: Readings for Content-area Teachers,* pp. 287-299. White Plains, NY: Longman.

7. Maryland State Department of Education. 1985. *Instructional Content Domains, Maryland Test of Citizenship Skills.* Baltimore, MD: Maryland State Department of Education.

8. Buggey, J. 1983. *Our Communities,* p. 233. Chicago: Follett.

9. Cangemi, J. 1986. *Holt Social Studies: Regions,* p. 168. New York: Holt, Rinehart, and Winston.

10. Marvin, M., Marvin, S., and Cappelluti, F.J. 1976. *The Human Adventure.* Menlo Park, CA: Addison-Wesley.

11. Cooper, K.S. 1986. *Europe, Africa, Asia and Australia.* Morristown, NJ: Silver Burdett.

12. Ogle, D.M. 1986. K-W-L group instruction strategy. In A.S. Palincsar, B.F. Jones, and E.G. Carr, eds., *Teaching Reading as Thinking.* Alexandria, VA: Association for Supervision and Curriculum Development.

13. Harris, K.R., and Graham, S. 1992. *Helping Young Writers Master the Craft: Strategy Instruction and Self-regulation in the Writing Process.* Cambridge, MA: Brookline Books.

14. Chamot, A.U. 1987. *Language Development Through Content: America: The Early Years,* pp. 52-54, 57, 64. Reading, MA: Addison-Wesley.

15. Chamot, A. U. 1987. *Teacher's Guide—America: The Early Years and America: After Independence,* p. 57. Reading, MA: Addison-Wesley.

CHAPTER 12: CALLA LITERATURE AND COMPOSITION

1. Adams, M.J. 1990. *Beginning to Read: Thinking and Learning About Print.* Cambridge, MA: Bradford Books/MIT Press.

2. Orasanu, J., and Penney, M. 1986. Introduction: Comprehension theory and how it grew. In J. Orasanu, ed., *Reading Comprehension: From Research to Practice.* Hillsdale, NJ: Lawrence Erlbaum.

Pearson, P.D., and Rapahel, T.E. 1990. Reading comprehension as a dimension of thinking. In B.F. Jones and L. Idol, eds., *Dimensions of Thinking and Cognitive Instruction,* pp. 209-240. Hillsdale, NJ: Lawrence Erlbaum.

3. Wilson, P.T., and Anderson, R.C. 1986. What they don't know will hurt them: The role of prior knowledge in comprehension. In J. Orasanu, ed., *Reading Comprehension: From Research to Practice.* Hillsdale, NJ: Lawrence Erlbaum.

4. Brown, A.L., Armbruster, B.B., and Baker, L. 1986. The role of metacognition in reading and studying. In J. Orasanu, ed., *Reading Comprehension: From Research to Practice.* Hillsdale, NJ: Lawrence Erlbaum.

Pearson, P.D., and Rapahel, T.E. 1990. Reading comprehension as a dimension of thinking. In B.F. Jones and L. Idol, eds., *Dimensions of Thinking and Cognitive Instruction,* pp. 209-240. Hillsdale, NJ: Lawrence Erlbaum.

5. Garner, R. 1987. *Metacognition and Reading Comprehension.* Norwood, NJ: Ablex.

6. Alvermann, D., Bridge, C.A., Schmidt, B.A., Searfoss, L.W., Winograd, P., Bruce, B., Paris, S.G., Priestley, M., Priestley-Romero, M., and Santeusanio, R.P. 1989. *Heath Reading.* Lexington, MA: D.C. Heath.

7. Enright, D.S., and McCloskey, M.L. 1988. *Integrating English: Developing English Language and Literacy in the Multilingual Classroom.* Reading, MA: Addison-Wesley.

Goodman, K. 1987. *What's Whole in Whole Language?* Portsmouth, NH: Heinemann.

Pearson, P.D., and Rapahel, T.E. 1990. Reading comprehension as a dimension of thinking. In B.F. Jones and L. Idol, eds., *Dimensions of Thinking and Cognitive Instruction,* pp. 209-240. Hillsdale, NJ: Lawrence Erlbaum.

8. Matsuyama, U.K. 1983. Can story grammar speak Japanese? *The Reading Teacher,* March, 1983: 666-669.

9. Pressley, M., and Associates 1990. *Cognitive Strategy Instruction That Really Improves Children's Academic Performance.* Cambridge, MA: Brookline Books.

10. Jukes, M. 1991. Like Jake and me. In *Rare as Hens' Teeth, Heath Reading, Grade 5.* Lexington, MA: D.C. Heath.

11. Paterson, K. 1977, 1987. *Bridge to Terabithia.* New York: Harper & Row, 1987.

12. Dickens, C. 1861; Washington Square Press edition, 1973. *Great Expectations.* New York: Washington Square Press.

13. Lee, H. 1960; Warner edition, 1982. *To Kill a Mockingbird.* New York: Warner Books.

14. White, T.H. 1939; Dell edition 1963. *The Sword in the Stone.* New York: Dell.

15. Paterson, K. 1977, 1987. *Bridge to Terabithia.* New York: Harper & Row, 1987.

16. Arlington Public Schools 1989. *HILT/HILTEX Language Arts Curriculum Guide: An Integrated Model.* Arlington, VA: Arlington Public Schools, ESOL/HILT.

17. Hudelson, S. 1984. Kan yu ret an rayt en Ingles: Children become literate in English as a second language. *TESOL Quarterly, 18:* 221-238.

18. Smith, L. 1992. Personal communication.

19. Ibid.

20. Dole, J.A., Duffy, G.G., Roehler, L.R., and Pearson, P.D. 1991. Moving from the old to the new: Research on reading comprehension instruction. *Review of Educational Research, 61* 2: 239-264.

21. Ibid.

22. Ibid.

23. Harris, K.R., and Graham, S. 1992. *Helping Young Writers Master the Craft: Strategy Instruction and Self-regulation in the Writing Process.* Cambridge, MA: Brookline Books.

Paris, S.G., Lipson, M.Y., and Wixson, K.K. 1983. Becoming a strategic reader. *Contemporary Educational Psychology, 8,* 293-316.

24. Englert, C.S., Raphael, T.E., Anderson, L.M., Anthony, H.M., and Stevens, D.D. 1991. Making strategies and self-talk visible: Writing instruction in regular and special education classrooms. *American Educational Research Journal, 28* (2), 337-372.

25. Pressley, M. and Associates 1990. *Cognitive Strategy Instruction That Really Improves Children's Academic Performance.* Cambridge, MA: Brookline Books.

26. Palincsar, A.S., and Brown, A.L. 1984. Reciprocal teaching of comprehension-fostering and comprehension-monitoring activities. *Cognition and Instruction,* 1:117-175.

27. Edmonds, I.G. 1961. *Ooka the Wise: Tales of Old Japan.* Indianapolis: The Bobbs-Merrill Company.

28. Palincsar, A.S., and Brown, W.L. 1986. Interactive teaching to promote independent learning from text. *The Reading Teacher, 39* (8): 771-777.

Palincsar, A.S., and Klenk, L. 1992. Examining and influencing contexts for intentional literacy learning. In C. Collins and J.N. Mangieri, eds., *Teaching Thinking: An Agenda for the 21st Century,* pp. 297-315. Hillsdale, NJ: Lawrence Erlbaum.

Index